Shem + Paul
Christmas 1997

THE
NEW
TEXAS
CUISINE

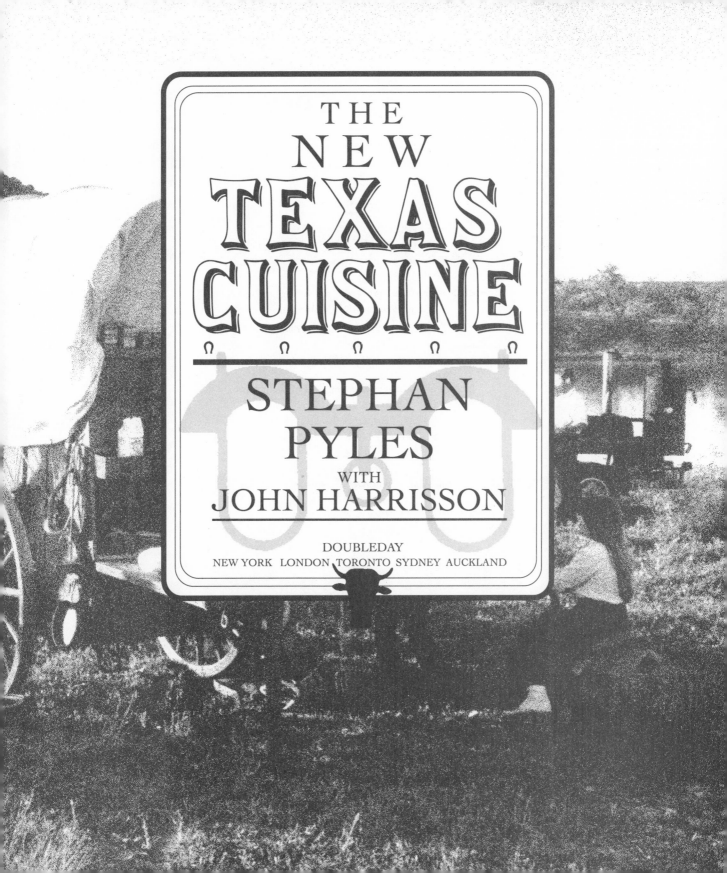

THE NEW TEXAS CUISINE

STEPHAN PYLES

WITH
JOHN HARRISSON

DOUBLEDAY
NEW YORK LONDON TORONTO SYDNEY AUCKLAND

PUBLISHED BY DOUBLEDAY
a division of Bantam Doubleday Dell Publishing Group, Inc.
1540 Broadway, New York, New York 10036

DOUBLEDAY and the portrayal of an anchor with a dolphin
are trademarks of Doubleday,
a division of Bantam Doubleday Dell Publishing Group, Inc.

Library of Congress Cataloging-in-Publication Data

Pyles, Stephan.
The new Texas cuisine / by Stephan Pyles with John Harrisson.
p.   cm.
Includes index.
1. Cookery, American — Southwestern style.   2. Cookery — Texas.
I. Harrisson, John.   II. Title.
TX715 .2.S69P94   1993
641.5976 — dc20   92-31496
                                                               CIP

ISBN 0-385-42336-5

BOOK DESIGN AND ORNAMENTATION BY SIGNET M DESIGN, INC.
PHOTOGRAPHY BY MATTHEW SAVINS

For
Eulene
and
Austin

ACKNOWLEDGMENTS

I owe a great deal of thanks to many people who not only have helped me bring forth this book but also have put their faith in me and supported me over the years.

Those who have been important catalysts for my career are Michael James and Billy Cross. Through them I was introduced to a host of outstanding individuals that have influenced me profoundly: Robert Mondavi, Margaret Biever, Jean and Pierre Troisgros, Georges Blanc, Michel Guerard, Gaston Lenôtre, Alain Chapel, Simone Beck, and especially Julia Child. Working with Julia and becoming her friend has been a real career highlight.

Thanks also:

To Sharron Smith for her undying support.

To Madeleine Kamman, France's great gift to America, who taught me why the French are French.

To my incredibly patient agent, writer, and editor, John ("I was gonna say") Harrisson, who now knows more about Texas than any other Brit in the world.

To my talented and sometimes wild photographer, Matthew Savins, for sharing my vision.

To Judy Kern, my editor at Doubleday, for believing in this project as much as I do.

To the key players at the "Great Schleps of Chance"—Axel Fabre, Gary Jennaneyan, Catherine Brandel, and Michael Thorburn.

To Alice Waters for setting the standard by which our industry is now judged.

To Wolfgang Puck for bringing star quality to the field.

To Mark Miller for being the culinary world's devil's advocate.

To Larry Forgione for standing up to the French and forever dispelling the myth that American cooking is inferior.

To Michael Bauer, Phyllis Richman, and Marion Burros for believing in me from the beginning.

To Wayne Kostroski for being the fireball of Minneapolis and for believing in the issue of hunger as much as I do.

To Rick O'Connell, with whom I have eaten and laughed enough for two lifetimes, for providing my safe haven in San Francisco.

To Paula Lambert for just being Paula (and making outstanding cheeses).

To Susy Davidson for being supportive of me since day one, and to Linda Waterman for introducing us.

To Sheila Lukins for her impeccable taste and quiet strength.

To Becky Murphy for Cristal by the pool and outrageous Christmas parties.

To Renie Steves for keeping my Januaries occupied.

To Zarela Martinez for showing me the beauty of San Cristobal de las Casas and the spirit of Mexico as well as New York.

To Susan and Ed Auler for picnics at the Falls and bringing Hill Country chic to the Texas wine industry.

To Bobby and Jennifer Cox and Don Brady for proving that my West Texas is capable of producing something other than cotton, oil, cactus, and tumbleweeds.

To Patricia Quintana for bringing elegance to Mexican cuisine in America.

To Pat Miller and Noel Cunningham for making me feel so at home in Denver.

To Al Morris for his gracious hospitality in Tyler and to his lovely wife, Frances, in memoriam.

To Anne Lindsey Greer for energizing the Southwestern cuisine movement long before most people knew what to call it.

To Robert Del Grande and Dean Fearing for being my comrades in that movement.

To my Big Spring set designers and trail cooks: Cinda and Dicky Stanley, Paula and Guy Talbot, Sue and Stan Partee, and Glynna and Drew Mouton.

To Tommy Birdwell, Ben Hutchison, Kirk Parks, and Katie Taylor for their diligent recipe testing. And to Jeffrey Dunham for keeping them (and me) organized.

To Tim Anderson, Mark Haugen, and Kevin Rathbun for their dedication and zeal.

To Melinda James for eternal cheerfulness and making me meet my deadlines.

To Erwin Felix for helping me balance my obsession with food and the necessity to exercise.

To all my staff, past and present.

And especially to Brenda, Jo, Alena, Greg, Mary, Janice, Andrew, Meg, Routhie, and Sebastian, who are always there no matter what.

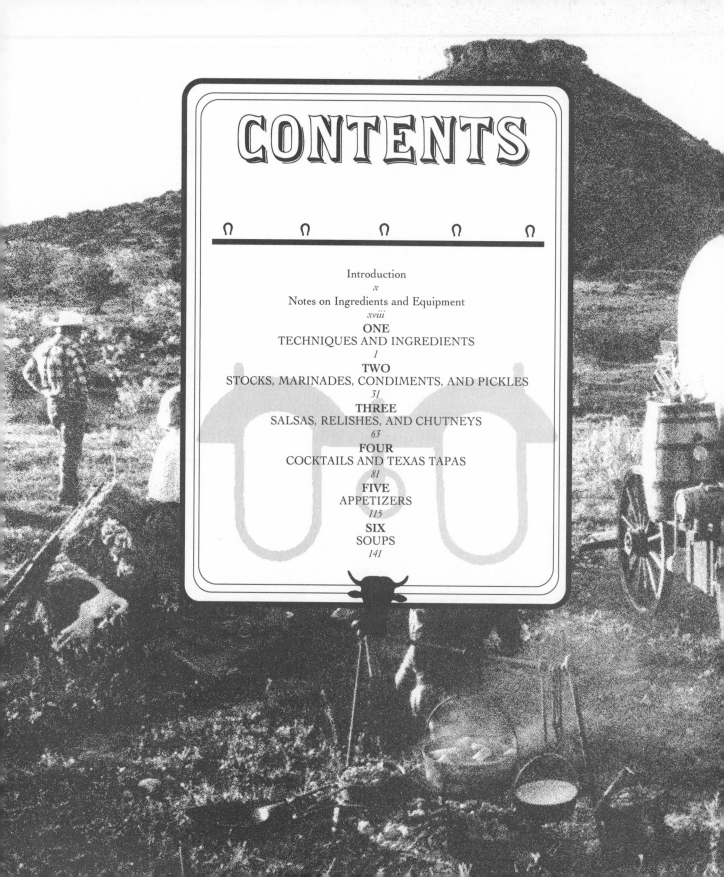

CONTENTS

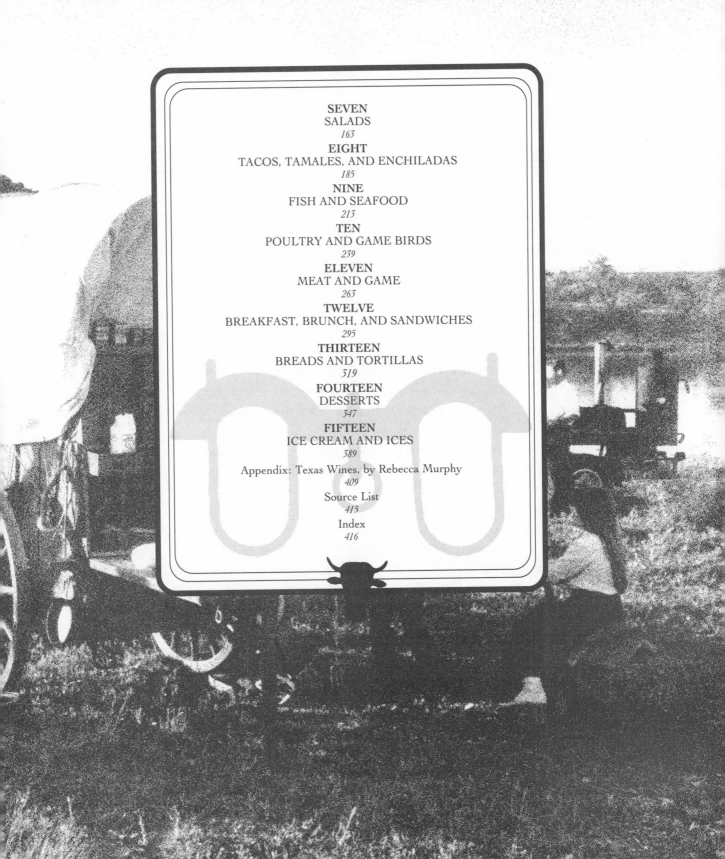

INTRODUCTION

Ask any Texan from Dalhart to Brownsville to describe Texan food, and you'll get as many answers as there are miles (or armadillos) between the two cities.

Ask the same question of a Yankee or Californian, and the reply will almost always be "barbecue, Tex-Mex, and chili." This response, while accurate as far as it goes, does scant justice to the depth, range, and complexity of Texas cookery, which is as rooted in the state's complex and epic history as is its fierce, independent pride. At least twenty-five different national and ethnic influences, reflecting the diversity of the region's settlers over the centuries, have molded Texas cuisine as we know it. But the foods of Texas reflect the state's tremendous diversity in many other respects as well. Texas is huge: at more than 267,000 square miles, it is the largest of the lower forty-eight states, and is larger than France. Its scale also leads to great variations in climate, topography, socio-economic and cultural demographics.

Texas contains five of the seven physiographic regions that exist in the United States. The different landscapes within the state include the high plains of the Panhandle in the northwest; the dry rangelands and limestone mesas of West Texas, dotted with sage, mesquite, and prickly pear; the rugged, mountainous Big Bend National Park basin and arid border region in the southwest; the fertile valley and coastal plain in the south; the golden beaches of the Gulf Coast; the extensive farming areas of central and northeast Texas; the piney woods of East Texas; and the Spanish moss and bayou country of the southeast.

Just as the regions within Texas yield great geographical variations, so the main influences on the food are widely diversified. Southern cooking, with its strong African heritage, predominates in the eastern part of the state, while the Mexican influence is especially prevalent in the southern border region. "Cowboy" cooking and barbecue, in turn influenced by the Sonoran "Norte" style of northern Mexico, are associated with West Texas, while the French Cajun and Creole styles are foremost in the Gulf Coastal region. The result of this "ethnic layering," over the centuries, is a cuisine that reflects a unique blend of its components, which, nevertheless, have each retained their individual personalities. It is an evolution that mirrors the pride Texas and its people have always taken in their independence and their own individual way of doing things.

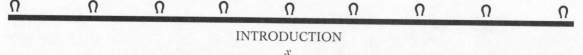

Growing up in Big Spring, Texas, about three hundred miles west of Dallas, I was exposed to these styles of cooking at an early age. There's a saying in Big Spring: "No, this isn't the end of the earth, but you can see it from here." About the most exciting thing to happen there was the Rattlesnake Roundup every March. Back then, in the '50s and '60s, the town's population was about 40,000 and our family ran a truck-stop restaurant on Highway 80, as well as three other cafés.

My mother, who grew up in West Texas, was a great Southern cook, and she made the desserts for our restaurants. At home, she'd cook us fried chicken, catfish, and pot roast with mashed potatoes. We grew all kinds of vegetables in our garden — okra, black-eyed peas, squash, collard and turnip greens — and I remember with fondness the fresh-picked vegetables we had at every meal. And, of course, my mother would make us peach cobbler, chocolate or coconut cream pie, and devil's food chocolate cake.

Since the early 1800s, Texas has been strongly influenced by the South; the first Anglo-American settlers in East Texas moved there from the Southern states, attracted by the rich farmland. The genteel way of life they had known on the plantations of the South became a part of the rich heritage they brought to Texas. The state has always been a magnet for those seeking religious or political freedom, and it is no coincidence that the food of Texas reflects this spontaneity of style.

What most of us think of as Southern cooking was developed by black Africans in the South. The history of Africans in America does not follow the usual pattern of settlers who left their native countries to seek better economic opportunity or freedom of expression. Instead, they were a people uprooted from their homeland and brought to the New World as slaves. Once slavery was firmly established, black women often cooked in white homes. When cooking for themselves, they often ate what their masters did not want. Even after emancipation in 1865, most blacks couldn't afford choice cuts of meat, so hog jowls, pigs' feet and internal organs were frequently used instead. These meats were supplemented with okra, black-eyed peas, turnip and collard greens, and even small game such as possum, rabbit, and squirrel. The diet was rounded out with sweet potatoes, grits, and breads made from corn. Because Southern food has been strongly influenced by African (and especially West African) cooking, certain ingredients, such as peanuts and chiles, and certain types of dishes (stews for example) are common to both.

Examples of the Southern influence in my cooking are dishes such as Arugula-Fried Okra Salad with Roast Corn Vinaigrette, Jalapeño–Blue Cornmeal Hush Puppies, Black Bottom–Pecan Pie, Honey-Fried Chicken with Spicy Whipped Sweet Potatoes and Buttermilk Biscuits, as well as Whole Fried Catfish with Ancho Tartar Sauce.

Sometimes other influences would creep into my mother's cooking: tamales, enchiladas, or pickled jalapeños. Every Sunday, after church, we ate out, and we'd always argue over whether we wanted Mexican food (it was really Tex-Mex), or barbecue. There were several Mexican restaurants on the north side of Big Spring, which was predominantly Mexican and black, but my favorite was La Posada; I just loved the pervasive aroma of fried corn tortillas. Many of the ingredients I use today in my restaurants I learned about from these trips to eat Tex-Mex food.

Southwestern cuisine, which uses ingredients indigenous to the Southwest in innovative ways, is certainly the most significant style of cookery in Texas today. I like to call it "the haute cuisine of the Southwest." It has captured national attention, and its heritage is rooted primarily in the rich Mexican culture that is a product of Spanish and Native American influences. Again, history is instructive in understanding the cuisine.

The territory that is now Texas came under Spanish influence in the sixteenth century, when the first European explorers led expeditions from Mexico. The Spanish were drawn to the region by trade, ranching, and missionary opportunities, and intermittently made settlements there. The Spanish ruled Texas from Mexico until 1821 and the conclusion of the Mexican War of Independence, following which Texas came directly under Mexican rule. However, in 1836, following General Sam Houston's military defeat of Mexican forces at San Jacinto, the Anglo-American colonists established the independent Republic of Texas. (Texas subsequently joined the United States as the twenty-eighth state in 1845.)

Although Mexico's rule of Texas lasted only fifteen years, the preceding three hundred years of Spanish influence had a profound impact on our art, food, and culture. The obvious culinary contributions of the Spanish and Mexicans are a myriad of chiles; herbs and spices such as oregano and cumin; fruits and vegetables such as tomatillos, black beans, jicama, and avocados; and beef production through cattle ranching.

Tex-Mex, as most Texans know it — the familiar fajitas, burritos, chili, tacos, and nachos — is a cuisine that crossed the border from the neighboring Mexican states of Sonora, Monterrey, and Chihuahua, and after years of gradual change, evolved its own style. The mix of cultures and the evolution of cuisines is perhaps best typified by the use of corn (or masa), the basic starch of both Mexican and Tex-Mex food. Sixteenth-century Spanish missionaries discovered several tribes of Indians growing corn throughout what is now East Texas, where the vegetable was served as a form of tamale. Archaeological evidence now indicates that corn had been grown in the region since at least the first century A.D., and possibly for several centuries before that. Although the spices used by these tribes were different, it seems likely that tamales were also an indigenous food item,

and not necessarily introduced from Mexico. (Incidentally, it seems fitting that the name of the state is derived from the Hasinai Indian word *tejas*, which means "friend," as Texas and Texans have always enjoyed a reputation for warmth and friendliness).

Examples of both Mexican and Tex-Mex influences on the food at Star Canyon are the Smoked Rabbit–Black Bean Tostadas, Duck Confit Empanadas, and our Lobster-Papaya Quesadillas with Mango Cream. We occasionally offer a wild game tamale such as Venison Tamales with Cranberries and Pecans.

Barbecue was another style of cooking with which I grew up. On those Sundays when we did not choose Tex-Mex, we'd get really good barbecue from Odell's, a tiny shack only about ten feet square, with a pit bigger than the storefront. I vividly remember the gallon jars of pickled peppers sitting on the counter and the walls that were black with smoke and grease. I craved the unique, smoky, vinegary smell inside; in fact, just thinking about it now makes me hungry! We'd take the barbecue home and eat it with baked beans and coleslaw.

There are many theories as to the origin of barbecue. The period 1840 to 1860 saw a great influx of European immigrants to Texas, especially from Germany and central Europe; they were drawn by economic opportunity and the unstable political, social, and economic situations at home. By 1860, the Germans had established themselves as an influential ethnic group in Texas, and they even outnumbered those of Mexican origin. Cities in central Texas such as Fredericksburg and New Braunfels still bear the indelible imprint of their founders' origins. The German tradition of sausage-making and curing meats in smokehouses is most likely to have been the forerunner of barbecue. However, the word itself is derived from a Veracruz Indian dialect: *barbacoa* referred to a means of slow cooking in stone-lined pits in the ground.

There are many recipes for Texas barbecue sauce, offering endless permutations of heat, texture, and flavor; some of the most pungent I've tried come from South Texas, close to the Mexican border. Almost all share common ingredients—tomatoes, sugar, vinegar, and smoke. While Texas barbecue is close kin to Kansas City barbecue, the other best-known variety, which originates in North Carolina, is quite different, being mustard-based and usually lacking tomatoes. From social back-yard gatherings to political fundraisers, the barbecue is an event closely associated with Texas, having reached its zenith nationally during the Johnson administration, when White House barbecues were all the rage. At Star Canyon, this heritage has been adapted to create Veal Chops with Barbecued Corn Sauce and Buttermilk-Cayenne Onion Rings; or Barbecued Brisket of Beef with Ranch-style Beans and Assorted Vegetable Pickles.

Barbecue is one aspect of what I call Cowboy Cooking, the style most folks in the rest of the country think of as Texan. From the days of the Spanish settlers and early Anglo-American pioneers, Texans have been cattlemen and ranchers. By the 1880s, the major cattle drives had become part of the lore of the state, and with the invention of barbed wire, large enclosed ranches transformed both the cattle industry and the topography of Texas. So it comes as no surprise that the state's most famous dishes are derived from beef. No Texan town is too small for a little barbecue shack like Odell's. Chicken fried steak, which is almost as commonplace as barbecue, was probably invented when some trail cook sliced off a piece of beef from the hindquarter, tenderized it by pounding, seasoned it with salt, floured it, and then pan-fried it in hot oil over an open fire. The cowhands he cooked for obviously demanded something new, and so the inventive cook developed a pan gravy made with milk to top the steak.

Perhaps the most famous — or infamous — Texas dish is chili, that fiery "bowl of red" about whose origins there are several theories. I ate my first bowl of chili at my uncle's. I was so young I hardly remember it, but I do recall it was burning hot. My uncle would invite all his relatives over once a month for a big chili cookout. Chili was his specialty, just as my dad's was barbecue and tacos, and another uncle's was fried catfish. I gradually got used to eating my uncle's chili, and another vivid childhood memory is the wonderful aroma of onions and garlic that arose as the stew would slowly cook. I remember it would simmer as we played outside, all of us sensing that it was something that couldn't be hurried no matter how hungry we were.

One theory has it that chili was first invented by a cook in a Canary Island settlement close to what is now San Antonio. Supposedly, the cook substituted native chiles in his stewed beef after depleting his supply of curry. But another and more probable explanation is that chili originated among the cowboys, whose cooks had been preparing their own indigenous brand of Irish stew. In the absence of black pepper, some range cook used a large dose of red chiles instead. When the cowboys complained about the heat of the dish, the explanation was that it was "the chiles." As time went by, the dish itself became known as chili. I confess that the only time I make it at Routh Street is for staff meals. But it's a wonderful, almost nouvelle chili, made with beef tenderloin trimmings — I'm sure the late Frank X. Tolbert, the writer who popularized and mythologized chili, would never approve of my upmarket version!

Although the French, who briefly claimed Texas in the late seventeenth century, had more of an impact on neighboring Louisiana and its Creole-Cajun cookery, there is, nonetheless, a certain French influence in Texas cookery — especially on the Gulf Coast. This area proved ideal for growing rice and harvesting shellfish such as shrimp, crabs,

and oysters. I have distant relatives there in Port Arthur, Southeast Texas, and as a boy I remember eating fresh oysters and crawfish mounded on newspapers. At the time, I thought the crawfish were pretty strange looking and hard to eat, and I wondered what the big deal was! But I've long since learned the earthy pleasures of a crawfish boil.

In combination with the Spanish influence, the French Creole-Cajun influences gave birth to dishes such as jambalaya, shrimp Creole, and gumbo. Port Arthur, where it seems that everyone is close kin to someone on the bayou, is host to the annual Pleasure Island Music Festival. This Cajun-inspired event is where Texans go to hear "Gumbo-Stirring Cajun Fiddlin'." The Star Canyon menu usually includes Gulf Coast snapper or shrimp, and more occasionally, Gulf Coast Jambalaya, Gumbo Z'Herbs, and a Creole Sweet Potato Vichyssoise.

These, then, are the main strands that have been interwoven over many generations, through the process of "ethnic layering," to comprise Texas cuisine. These are the foods to which I have applied classic European techniques and influences in order to reinterpret the food with which I grew up.

Ω   Ω   Ω

The path I followed from my family's truck stop in Big Spring to Star Canyon has contained many unexpected twists and turns. I grew up in the food business, bussing tables and washing dishes. As a kid of seven or eight, I thought I was indispensible to the running of the restaurant, but my father was just letting me play. I also used to help my mother with the pastries. I remember the waitresses with beehive hairdos, Tammy Wynette playing on the jukebox, and the short-cut language the truckers would use to order. I was wide-eyed and very impressed by what seemed to be the cavernous kitchen, filled with wonderful equipment — the steam tables and commercial dishwashers (the rest was probably mostly can openers)!

I was always intrigued by the whole process of commercial cookery, and early on I wanted to be a cook. I thought it would be really cool to work in a floppy hat and a dirty apron, with a cigarette hanging out of my mouth! It didn't take long to get over that phase though, and I vowed that once I got out, I'd never return to the restaurant business.

I was never encouraged to stay in the business, and at that time, in the late 1960s, there weren't too many choices even if I had been interested: for the most part, you were either a fry cook in an American restaurant, or you were French or Italian. My parents wanted me to go to college, and I decided to study music, since it also played an important role in my family. I majored in piano and voice at East Texas State University at Commerce, and planned to teach music at the university level.

Then fate intervened. I had the opportunity to travel to France for three weeks in the summer of 1973, after I left college. Those three weeks turned into three months that changed my life. I fell in love with the French culture and French food; the street markets, the fresh produce, the smell of baking bread, the patisseries and charcuteries were all things I had never seen before, and which were a world away from Big Spring. At the same time, I recognized a correlation between the artistry and style of the food in France, particularly the fancy pastries, and the creativity inherent in music. This sparked my enthusiasm for learning more and reawakened my passion for cooking. I returned to the United States with the knowledge that food was the creative outlet I planned to pursue.

I settled in Dallas because I knew I didn't want to live anywhere but Texas — growing up I was instilled with the Texan pride that has always been in my blood — and I set about learning the business from top to bottom. I began as a waiter, and started collecting cookbooks to teach myself about food and cooking techniques. The most influential books from this period were by Julia Child, Dione Lucas, Alma Lach, and especially Jacques Pepin's *La Technique*.

Then I spent three years in the kitchen of a restaurant in Dallas called The Bronx, which still exists. I found it an exciting place for the mid-seventies; it was a simple café serving sandwiches, omelettes, wine by the glass, and daily specials like chicken Cordon Bleu and beef tournedos. I progressed from waiter to pastry chef to executive chef, and during this time I made an important contact with Michael James, who was then Director of The Great Chefs of France cooking school at the Robert Mondavi Winery in Napa Valley. I was asked to join the staff as a chef's assistant for four weeks a year, when I had the privilege of working twelve-hour days with three-star French chefs such as the Troisgros brothers, Georges Blanc, Michel Guerard, and Alain Chapel. This proved to be another turning point for me. The Great Chefs Program was a real stroke of luck.

Meanwhile, I made visits back to France to continue my informal education. This was the era during which the French nouvelle style reached its zenith, and I was amazed by its creativity and simplicity. As the name suggests, this was an altogether new culinary form, and I was deeply impressed by the colorful and artistic food presentation. Among the dishes that stand out in my mind were Michel Guerard's duck served with basil sauce and vegetables, served in a duck's foot; Roger Vergé's four courses of fish, which at the time I considered unusual; and Alain Chapel's chicken and black truffles cooked in a pig's bladder. This was food I had not encountered in any of the books I had read, and I found it inspirational. Later, in 1981, I studied pastry-making with Gaston Lenôtre.

In due course I left The Bronx restaurant to start my own catering business. But even while I catered small dinner parties in the French nouvelle style around Dallas, and

even though I would never have admitted it, I still yearned for the Texas food with which I had grown up. I was already planning to open my own restaurant, but being a "proud Texan," I wanted it to be American (specifically, Texan), and not French. For the early 1980s, this was a pretty radical departure, but when the circumstances occurred that allowed me to open Routh Street Cafe, it was a case of being in the right place at the right time, with the right concept: American regional cuisine.

Routh Street Cafe resulted from my business partnership with John Dayton, who was originally a client of my catering business. John, a scion of a prominent Minneapolis family, was a lawyer with a prestigious firm in Dallas for whom I arranged one particularly lavish event. It was clear to me that Routh Street Cafe should depart from the formal, clublike atmosphere of the leading restaurants in Dallas at that time, with their wood paneling and classic settings. I wanted a relaxed and less formal ambience, in a casually elegant setting, where dining could be really enjoyable. In keeping with this concept, Tony Foy designed a truly contemporary dining room that was the first of its kind in Dallas, and we opened our doors in November 1983 to glowing—even "rave"—reviews.

Since the first printing of this book, I dissolved my business partnership, which resulted in the closing of Routh Street Cafe. While disappointing at the time, it has allowed me the opportunity to fulfill a dream I've had for some time; to open a restaurant whose exciting design truly complements the food.

Star Canyon serves the lusty food from this book in a more rustic and therefore appropriate setting. The ambience is very lively, yet there is a comforting element that makes everyone feel at home. Perhaps most important, Star Canyon offers my food in a less intimidating environment and provides a more affordable dining experience than did Routh Street Cafe.

Some of the recipes that follow represent the food we serve at Star Canyon, and they include all our most popular dishes. There are also a number of recipes that appeared on the menu at Baby Routh in Dallas, and Tejas, the Southwestern restaurant we opened in Minneapolis. Other recipes are old Texas classics that have been given a new spin.

This New Texas Cuisine adapts the food drawn from the disparate cultures and historical eras of the Lone Star State, and reinterprets old favorites to create original dishes, and sometimes unexpected combinations. When I teach cooking classes, I tell people to try the recipes for the first time exactly as they're written. After that, I suggest they change one thing in the recipe each time they try it again. That way, you create something and learn at the same time. To me, that is one of the most exciting and rewarding aspects of cooking.

NOTES ON INGREDIENTS AND EQUIPMENT

In the recipes that follow, I am assuming at least a basic knowledge of ingredients and measurements. However, certain specific conventions are worth clarifying here, to avoid any possible confusion.

- All ingredients used are fresh. Do your best to avoid using frozen, canned, or dried ingredients unless specifically called for (one obvious exception is dried chiles). This applies especially to ingredients such as herbs, as well as vegetables, fruit, and meat. Ingredients should also be as ripe as possible and of the best quality. Cutting corners and making do with second best will inevitably lead to inferior results. A source list can be found in the Appendix.

- Ingredients are of medium size, unless stated otherwise. One exception: eggs are large.

- Onions, garlic, shallots, and carrots are always peeled, unless stated otherwise.

- "Onions" are yellow onions, unless stated otherwise.

- Chiles and bell peppers are always stemmed, unless stated otherwise. In recipes calling for "diced bell peppers," the peppers are also seeded.

- Fresh ginger is always peeled.

- Corn kernels are always cut from fresh cobs.

- Both green and white parts of scallions are used, unless stated otherwise.

- All citrus fruit juice is freshly squeezed.

- The recipes in this book assume you will be using regular table salt. Both sea salt and kosher salt are more flavor-intense, so when a quantity is given, adjust the quantity down slightly if you are using them. The clean flavor of sea salt naturally matches fish particularly well.

- Pepper is freshly ground, using a peppermill.

- Grated cheese is freshly grated.

- All butter is unsalted. Salt is added to butter as a preservative, and as the amount can vary from brand to brand, it can throw the correct amount of seasoning off. If you want to preserve unsalted butter, freeze it.

- All sugar is granulated, unless stated otherwise.

- All flour is unbleached all-purpose, unless stated otherwise.

Finally, as I counsel in cooking classes, don't be afraid to experiment with the recipes in this book. Change one or two ingredients each time you prepare a dish until you feel quite confident to improvise at will. Substitute ingredients that you know will work and taste good, and above all, have fun with the recipes.

The kitchen equipment called for in this book is standard. However, there are some points I think it is important to make about the equipment used:

- Certain sauces and purees are best prepared as indicated in the text, that is, in a blender rather than a food processor. Using a blender gives finer, smoother results, and you usually won't need to strain the sauce or puree. The consistency given by a food processor just isn't the same.

- Food processors are best used for grinding large amounts of nuts, making compound butters, or for combining ingredients that need a large amount of space. I generally prefer using the processor when incorporating ingredients, rather than pureeing.

- Spice or coffee grinders are best for grinding small amounts of nuts, seeds, peppercorns, and the like. They serve exactly the same purpose as a mortar and pestle, but take a fraction of the effort.

- A number of these recipes call for a fine mesh strainer or chinois. This is an essential piece of equipment for preparing certain delicate or smooth-textured sauces, for example. A chinois is available from restaurant supply stores, gourmet or specialty retail stores, or from mail-order sources.

CHAPTER ONE

TECHNIQUES AND INGREDIENTS

A number of techniques and specifically prepared ingredients recur frequently in the recipes that follow, and are described in this chapter. Most of these techniques are common to Southwestern as well as Mexican and other cuisines.

A glossary of ingredients is also provided in this chapter; it assumes a basic knowledge of the most common ingredients.

TECHNIQUES

SELECTING AND HANDLING FRESH CHILES

The fresh chiles most commonly used in these recipes are the Anaheim, which is closely related to and is, for all intents and purposes, similar to the New Mexico green chile; the fiery habanero; the staple of Texas cuisine, the jalapeño; the poblano; and the serrano. All of these chiles are generally available, although you may need to track down the habanero and poblano chiles in Latin or Hispanic markets. To facilitate identification, I recommend *The Great Chile Book* by Mark Miller (Ten Speed Press, Berkeley, California).

Buy chiles that have shiny, smooth skins, and are heavy for their size. They should be dry and firm to the touch, and smell fresh and clean. They should be kept dry and stored in the crisper section of the refrigerator; do not wrap them in plastic bags, where moisture could spoil them, and don't leave them out in the open.

When handling fresh chiles, I recommend using rubber gloves to protect your hands against capsaicin, the potent chemical in chiles responsible for their heat. About 80 percent of the capsaicin in chiles is contained in the seeds and internal ribs, and these are often removed to modify the fiery effects of capsaicin. Another method of protecting your hands is to rub your fingers with vegetable oil; this neutral oil helps prevent the capsaicin from penetrating the skin. In any event, be particularly careful not to touch your eyes or face when working with chiles, and always wash your hands thoroughly afterwards. You can neutralize capsaicin on your fingers by washing them in a mixture of 1 quart of water and 1 tablespoon of bleach.

Before use, wash fresh chiles under running water and pat them dry. In preparing

all fresh chiles (except when used as rellenos or stuffed chiles), remove the stem. In those recipes that call for raw chiles (salsas, for example), remove the seeds if called for. Where seeding the chiles is not specified, bear in mind that removing the seeds will reduce the heat by about one half; you may wish to use additional seeded chiles. Conversely, when pureeing fresh chiles, you may retain the seeds, but you should use only half as many as the number of seeded chiles called for.

For instructions on roasting and peeling chiles, see page 6.

SELECTING AND HANDLING DRIED CHILES

The recipes in this book call for dried chiles almost exclusively in sauces. The process of drying chiles concentrates their natural sugars and intensifies their flavors, which in turn gives sauces complex nuances of flavor as well as spiciness. The two most commonly used dried chiles in this book (and in Texas cooking in general) are the ancho (the dried poblano), which has mellow, sweet tones of chocolate, coffee, and dried raisin; and the chipotle (the dried, smoked jalapeño), which has a smoky flavor featuring chocolate and tobacco tones. Other dried chiles used here include the cascabel, with a smoky and nutty flavor; the guajillo, with tones of greenness and berry; the pasilla (or chile negro), which has berry and herbaceous flavors; and chile pequín, whose citrus and nut tones go particularly well in salsas.

Select dried chiles that are clean and not discolored; they should not be faded or dusty, and preferably, they should be unbroken. Freshly dried chiles will be relatively soft and supple, with a distinct aroma. Dried chiles are best used within a few months, and should be stored in airtight containers in a dry, cool place.

Most dried chiles are roasted and rehydrated before processing into a chile puree (see below).

PUREEING DRIED CHILES

A number of recipes in this book call for chile puree, most often in sauces.

The first step in this process is to wash and thoroughly dry the chiles. Cut off the stems and slit open the dried chiles with a knife and remove the seeds before roasting.

Heat the oven to 450° F., place the chiles in a single layer on a baking sheet, and roast for 1 minute. Alternatively, dried chiles may be dry-roasted over high heat in a skillet or on a comal until they puff up, about 30 seconds to 2 minutes, depending on the heat of the skillet.

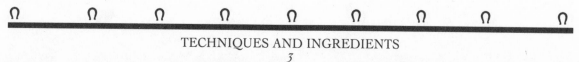

Transfer the chiles to a bowl, cover with warm water, and keep the chiles submerged for 30 minutes to rehydrate.

Strain the chiles, reserving the liquid, and place the chiles in a blender. Puree the chiles, adding just enough of the soaking liquid to make pureeing possible; you should have a thick paste. The puree can be passed through a medium or fine strainer at this point, or strained in the sauce or final product.

SELECTING AND PREPARING PURE CHILE POWDER

Many recipes in this book include "pure chile powder." This is to differentiate between commercial chile powder, which contains extraneous ingredients such as black pepper, salt, sugar, cumin, garlic, paprika, and cayenne, and the real thing, which is 100 percent ground dried chile.

If you buy pure chile powder, it should be a brick-red color and have a slightly lumpy texture, which shows that the natural oils are still present, and it should have an intense, earthy smell.

To prepare your own chile powder, take a mixture (or single type) of dried chiles (such as anchos, chipotles, and guajillos), and slit them open with a knife to remove the seeds before roasting.

Heat the oven to 300° F., place the chiles in a single layer on a baking sheet, and roast for 3 to 5 minutes, until they're thoroughly dry and stiff.

Remove from the oven and crumble the chiles in a bowl. Transfer to a spice grinder and grind them to a powder.

Chile powder should be stored airtight in a cool, dry place and preferably should be used within 1 month.

PREPARING THE GRILL

Grilling food over a fire is probably the oldest form of cooking. A modern grill cooks food both by direct heat and by heat transmitted through the metal bars of the grill itself.

Build a fire in a grill using charcoal briquettes or natural, lump charcoal. Briquettes, which are more readily available, are composed of charcoal, coal, and starch, and some chemical additives to enhance lighting and burning. Lump charcoal, processed from hard wood such as hickory, mesquite, cherry, maple, or pecan, is preferable as it contains no additives. Note that mesquite charcoal, which burns the hottest and lasts the longest, throws out showers of sparks and requires special care.

To start the fire in the grill, use wood kindling or an electric starter. The electric starter is basically an electric element loop similar to those fitted in ovens. You need an electric outlet to use it, of course, and you should remove it once the charcoal has started to burn well. I have strong feelings against using lighter fuel, which imparts unpleasant flavors in the smoke and can taint the flavor of the food being grilled. The case has probably been put most eloquently and amusingly by A. Cort Sinnes in his excellent *The Grilling Book* (Aris Books, Berkeley, California):

> If aliens from outer space landed in a typical suburban neighborhood around 6.00 P.M. on any given weekend, when the aroma of lighter fluid is at its most pervasive, they would surely conclude that ours is a volatile atmosphere. So ubiquitous is this odor that whole generations take one whiff of lighter fluid and immediately conjure up images of barbecued hamburgers, hot dogs, and playing outside after dark. . . . As embedded in our collective consciousness as lighter fuel is, the environmental movement of the 1960s made us all more aware of the effects of chemicals on our environment and in our bodies. Like it or not, lighter fluid is on the wrong side of the fence when it comes to a "natural" approach to life, and, quite frankly, most professional chefs abhor its use . . . if those with the power to change our minds have their way, objections to its odor (in the air and in the food) and concern for the effects of petroleum by-products on our insides will probably win out, and the familiar red-capped squeeze can will become another artifact of a culture in transition.

So far, then, we have lump charcoal (or briquettes), which should be stacked in a pyramid over kindling or an electric starter. Let the coals burn down until they are covered by a uniform whitish-gray ash, which should take 20 to 30 minutes, then spread the coals out. The grill should be hot (especially for cooking fish). Test for the hottest part of the grill by carefully holding your hand about 2 inches over the fire.

At this stage, before placing any food on the grill, you can add 6 to 8 hardwood chunks or chips to the fire (such as hickory, almond, cherry, apple, orange, or pecan), that have soaked in water for 20 minutes; this procedure will give an extra smoky flavor to the food.

It is important, especially for fish, to scrub the metal bars of the grill with a wire brush and then oil them with a towel or rag before and after use; doing this will help prevent the food from sticking to the grill. For best results, bring the meat or fish to room temperature before grilling; at room temperature the heat can penetrate to the center of the food more quickly without burning the outside.

While gas grills seem to be more prevalent today than those requiring charcoal or

wood, they simply don't impart the same flavor to foods. If you're using a gas grill, the same timing and technique discussed here would generally apply. A gas grill turned to high radiates the same heat as a medium-to-medium-hot charcoal fire.

ROASTING FRESH CHILES AND BELL PEPPERS

The word "pepper" in reference to chiles is a misnomer. It originated when Columbus was searching for a westward route to the spice islands in the East Indies and the source of the highly valued black pepper spice. Instead, he landed in the West Indies and discovered a plant bearing small red berries that resembled unripe black pepper berries. Columbus called these "peppers," whereas he had in fact encountered a type of chile which, like all others, is native to the New World. "Peppers" were brought back to Europe, and the botanically incorrect name (as pepper is a spice and chiles are fruits) has, confusingly, stuck ever since. Roasting chiles and bell peppers (which actually are also chiles) concentrates the natural sugars and thereby imparts a more intense, smoky flavor to these ingredients. A further purpose of roasting is to facilitate removing the skin of the chiles or bell peppers, which can give a bitter flavor, especially in the skin of green chiles.

The process of roasting chiles or bell peppers blisters and blackens the skin on all sides without burning through the flesh. If being prepared whole, they should be roasted quickly and turned frequently, and there are several methods to do it. They can be roasted on a grill (see above), under a broiler, or set on a wire rack over an open flame on top of the stove. They can also be halved, seeded, and roasted on a baking sheet lined with parchment or wax paper in a 400° F. oven for 20 minutes, until the skin blackens. If the primary purpose is to peel the chiles or bell peppers rather than to provide flavor (preferable for preparing rellenos, or stuffed chiles, for example), you can dip them in hot oil (about 375° F.) until the skin blisters and then place in ice water. This process allows the skin to be removed while keeping the texture intact for further use.

After roasting, place the chiles or bell peppers in a large paper bag and twist to secure, or in a bowl covered with plastic wrap. Let them "steam" for 20 minutes, until cool, when they will be ready to peel with your fingers or a sharp knife. Split open with a knife and remove the seeds and stem (unless preparing rellenos). Chiles and bell peppers can be roasted ahead of time and kept in the refrigerator for 2 to 3 days.

Bell peppers may also be sliced in half and seeded before roasting (it's actually easier to remove the seeds before roasting). Roast them cut side down.

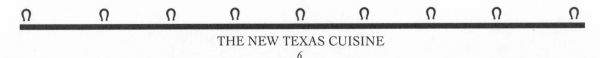

ROASTING GARLIC

Preheat the oven to 350° F. Cut 3 heads of garlic in half and place cut side up in a roasting pan. Pour 1 teaspoon of olive oil over each half head of garlic. Sprinkle the pan with 2 to 3 tablespoons of water, cover tightly with foil, and bake in the oven for 30 to 40 minutes.

Uncover the pan and continue baking for 5 to 7 minutes longer, until the garlic is golden brown. Remove from the pan and let cool. Squeeze the softened garlic into a blender and discard the skin. Add just enough olive oil to make pureeing possible. This yields about ⅓ cup.

Alternatively, peel individual cloves from 3 heads of garlic with a paring knife. Place the cloves on a baking sheet or in a roasting pan, pour 2 tablespoons of olive oil over, and toss to coat thoroughly. Sprinkle with water, cover with foil, and roast in the oven at 350° F. for 30 minutes. Remove the foil and roast for 5 to 7 minutes longer, until brown.

ROASTING CORN

Preheat the oven to 400° F. Remove the outer layer of husks from the ears of corn, leaving 1 or 2 layers intact. Pull these remaining husks back, exposing the kernels. Remove the corn silks, spread butter or olive oil over the kernels, and sprinkle with a little salt. Replace the husks over the kernels, place the ears on a sheet pan, and bake in the oven for 30 minutes.

OVEN-DRYING CORN

Oven-drying concentrates the sweetness and full flavor of corn. The dried corn can be used in salads, salsas, and soups, or ground as cornmeal.

Preheat the oven to 175° F. With a sharp knife, remove the corn kernels from the ears and spread evenly in a single layer on a sheet pan. Place in the oven and check every 30 minutes, turning the pan so the heat is evenly distributed. When the corn is free of moisture, about 2 to 2½ hours, the kernels will appear shriveled and almost dry. Continue to bake in the oven for an additional 1½ hours, until the kernels are completely dry. Remove from the oven and let cool.

PREPARING TOMATOES

To blanch, peel, and seed tomatoes, prepare a large bowl of ice water. With a sharp knife, make an "X" ¼ inch deep into the bottom of the tomato.

Bring a large pan of water (about 4 inches deep) to a rapid boil. Plunge in the tomatoes and cook for 20 seconds, making sure they are covered with water. Remove with a slotted spoon and place in the ice water.

When cool, peel the tomatoes, cut in half, and squeeze gently. Remove any remaining seeds with a blunt knife or with your fingers, and discard.

To prepare tomatoes that are not watery, but still have their skins on (for Pico de Gallo, for example), remove just the outer flesh from each tomato with a sharp paring knife, as you would remove the peel from an orange. Discard the pulp and seeds, or use for sauces or soups. Cut the tomato flesh into the desired-sized dice (usually ⅛ inch).

OVEN-DRYING CHERRY TOMATOES

As with corn, oven-drying, like sun-drying and roasting, accentuates and intensifies the flavors and sweetness of the tomatoes.

Preheat the oven to 200° F. Slice 8 pints of red cherry tomatoes (or a combination of yellow and red) in half, place cut side up on a sheet pan, and salt them lightly. Place in the oven and check every 45 minutes, turning the pan so the heat is evenly distributed. When the tomatoes are free of moisture, in 4 to 5 hours, remove from the oven and let them cool. This yields about 2 cups. If not using immediately, the tomatoes can be stored in vegetable oil or olive oil.

TOASTING SEEDS AND NUTS

As with roasting peanuts or coffee, toasting seeds and nuts brings out their full, rich flavor.

To toast seeds, place in a dry, hot skillet over medium-high heat for 2 to 3 minutes; stir occasionally with a wooden spoon until seeds have lightly browned. This is a practical method as the seeds are easy to watch. Alternatively, preheat the oven to 350° F. Place the seeds in a single layer on a sheet pan and toast in the oven for 15 to 20 minutes, until they're fragrant, stirring occasionally.

To toast nuts, place in a dry, hot skillet over medium-high heat for 5 to 7 minutes until lightly browned; stir occasionally with a wooden spoon. Smaller nuts, such as pine nuts, will take 3 to 5 minutes. Alternatively, preheat the oven to 325° F. Place the nuts in a single layer on a sheet pan and toast for 15 to 20 minutes, until lightly browned, stirring occasionally.

PREPARING THE SMOKER

Smoking, like grilling, is one of the oldest cooking methods, and was a means of preserving food, long before the advent of refrigeration. Now it is mostly used to impart flavor dimensions to meats, poultry, and fish, as well as to other ingredients such as vegetables. Smoking on a large scale was brought to Texas by German immigrants in the nineteenth century, who introduced smokehouses for sausage making, and the practice has remained an important part of the Texas culinary tradition and culture ever since. I started to experiment with smoking vegetables in the early 1980s and began a trend that is now widespread. I like to think this is my legacy not only to the New Texas Cuisine, but to a far broader audience as well.

Home smokers are available from specialty hardware stores and mail-order sources; they are relatively inexpensive, so they are well worth the investment. You can also adapt a barbecue by adding a pan of water to the bottom, sealing all but one vent, and following the method described here:

Soak 6 to 8 chunks of aromatic hardwood, such as hickory, mesquite, or apple in water for 20 minutes. Place a pan of water in the bottom of the smoker. Build a fire in the smoker with hardwood lump charcoal or charcoal briquettes and an electric starter (see Preparing the Grill, above, for notes on charcoal and starter). Let the charcoal burn down until it is covered by a uniform whitish-gray ash, which should take 20 to 30 minutes, and spread the coals out. Add the soaked hardwood chunks and let burn for 5 minutes. Place the ingredients to be smoked on the grill over the water pan and cover with the top of the smoker. Keep the fire stoked every 30 minutes, adding more charcoal and soaked wood chunks as necessary.

As a general rule, an average (2½ pound) chicken will take 1½ to 2 hours at a temperature of 250° F.; chicken or duck breasts will take 20 to 25 minutes; tomatoes will take 20 minutes; and chiles, bell peppers, and onions 25 to 30 minutes.

PREPARING AND COOKING DRIED BEANS

Historically, beans have always been an important element in the Southwestern diet. Black beans, pinto beans, and black-eyed peas are all used in the recipes in this book.

Always carefully sort through dried beans to remove imperfect beans and foreign particles such as twigs and (most dangerous of all) small stones. Black beans need special attention in this regard, as stones can be barely distinguishable but disastrous to dental health!

Once cleaned, the beans should be rinsed thoroughly in a colander, and soaked to "de-gas" them. Place the beans in a large pot, cover with enough water to come 2 inches above the beans, and soak overnight. The next day, drain and rinse the beans. Return them to the pot, cover with the same amount of water, and simmer until tender, 45 minutes to 1 hour. Never add salt until the last 15 minutes of cooking as it will toughen the beans.

I remember, as a child, that my grandmother would add one large chopped onion and a ham hock or two, and she only stirred up the beans two or three times while they were cooking so as not to break them up. She also swore by adding an aspirin to the beans. When I looked very confused by this one day, she looked at me and explained "No, they don't have a headache, son, I'm just de-gassing them." This is another way of minimizing their legendary effect on the digestive system. In Mexico, the same result is achieved by cooking the beans with epazote.

Incidentally, in her book *Julia Child & More Company* (Alfred A. Knopf, New York, 1979), the eponymous author writes an amusing note on "intestinal motility," which, she clarifies, "is polite gobbledegook for flatulence, which in turn means gas." She explains that this effect is caused by sugars that the body cannot easily digest. In corresponding with the head of something called the USDA bean study group, Julia discovered that the word "motility" was deemed inaccurate and so she has regretfully substituted "the more prosaic but possibly more safely descriptive 'trouble.' "

PREPARING CITRUS FRUIT

To achieve optimum results from juicing citrus fruit, place the lemon, lime, orange, or grapefruit on a work surface. With the palm of your hand, press down firmly on the fruit and roll forward and backward for about 20 seconds. Then cut in half and juice.

To cut citrus fruit into peeled slices, use a short paring knife to cut ½ inch off both ends of the fruit. Standing the fruit on a cut end, remove the skin and all the white pith to reveal the flesh, cutting downward with the knife. Turn the fruit on its side and cut into slices of desired thickness.

PREPARING AND BLANCHING ARTICHOKE BOTTOMS

⅓ cup flour
2 quarts cold water
½ teaspoon salt

4 lemons
6 large artichokes

Place the flour in a large saucepan and gradually whisk in 1 quart (4 cups) of the water. Bring to a boil and simmer while whisking to get rid of all lumps. Whisk in the remaining quart of water and the salt. Cut the lemons in half and squeeze 3 of the lemons into the water. Remove from the heat.

To prepare the artichokes, break the stem from the base so that any fibers are pulled out. Rub the bottoms of the artichokes with the halves of the reserved lemon to prevent discoloration. With a large knife, chop off the top one third of the artichoke. Remove and discard all the outer leaves to expose the bottoms, and rub the artichoke bottoms with the reserved lemon halves. Cut off the remaining inner leaves just above the artichoke bottoms.

With a paring knife, trim all the green parts of the artichoke bottoms to expose the white flesh around the bottoms and leaf ends. Rub with lemon and drop the prepared artichoke bottoms into the water and flour mixture. When all the artichoke bottoms are in the pan, bring the water to a boil, reduce heat, and simmer for 30 to 40 minutes, until the artichokes are tender when pierced with a knife. Keep the artichokes submerged if necessary by placing a wet towel on top of the water.

Remove the artichokes from the pan, let cool, and keep refrigerated until needed. Just before serving, scoop out the choke and discard.

RENDERING DUCK FAT

Place duck breasts skin side down in a skillet. Over low heat, sauté for 15 minutes until the skin is crisp and all the fat has been rendered. Drain the fat and let cool. The sautéed breast can be diced and used in salads or sandwiches.

Duck fat can also be rendered as part of the process of making duck cracklings.

Preheat the oven to 350° F. Remove the skin from the duck breasts, cut into small dice, and arrange in a baking dish. Roast in the oven for 30 minutes, stirring occasionally, until the cracklings are nicely browned and the fat is a clear yellow. Remove cracklings with a slotted spoon, drain on paper towels, and sprinkle with salt. Strain the warm duck fat into a jar and keep refrigerated.

Use rendered duck fat for sautéing or basting roast poultry or lean meats. Cracklings are a good accompaniment for salads or any dish that uses diced, crisp bacon.

HOME CANNING AND BOTTLING

Preparing pickles, jellies, jams, and preserves is rewarding and well worth the effort involved. The difference in flavor and quality between homemade and store-bought can be significant, and you are assured of the healthfulness of the ingredients. For the most part, home canning and bottling is straightforward and does not have to be a labor-intensive endeavor.

It is best to use standard-sized canning jars or glasses with matching lids that ensure an airtight seal. The components, including the rubber rings, should be washed and rinsed, and the jars or glasses must be hot when they are filled. Place them in a large pot, cover with water, and bring to a boil. Remove from the heat and keep hot until ready to fill.

Fill hot jars to within ¼ inch of the top, and seal quickly and securely with the ring and lid. If there is only enough to fill a jar or glass partly, do not seal. Instead, keep refrigerated and use as quickly as possible.

Paraffin must be used to seal the top of glasses, to keep the air out. Melt bars of paraffin in a double boiler; never melt over direct heat in a saucepan as it is highly flammable. Seal one jar at a time with a thin layer of melted paraffin.

GLOSSARY OF INGREDIENTS

ANNATTO (achiote)
The brick-red seeds of the tropical annatto or achiote tree are usually ground into a paste and used for coloring and seasoning. It is a common feature of the cuisine in the Yucatán region of Mexico and parts of the Caribbean. Annatto has an earthy, slightly acidic flavor rather like green olives. It is used commercially to dye dairy products.

ANTELOPE

Antelope have a rich, nutty, complex flavor and are highly nutritious. Those in Texas are lean, as they don't have to develop fat to keep warm in the winter. Mike Hughes at Texas Wild Game in Ingram probably knows more about antelope and other wild game than anyone. Eddie Rickenbacker, the Texan World War I fighter pilot, introduced **nilgai** and **black buck** antelope from Africa and India to Texas (as well as sika and axis deer) for hunting, and they have adapted well to the climate and terrain. For availability, see source list. Venison can be substituted.

ARTICHOKES

The ultimate spring vegetable. Globe artichokes are the bud of a type of thistle native to the Mediterranean, and were treated as a delicacy by the Romans. Mostly grown in the United States around Castroville in the mid-coastal region of California north of Monterey, artichokes have a unique subtle, nutty, and somewhat green flavor. They contain a substance — cynarin, an organic acid — unique to artichokes that affects the taste buds to make other foods (and wine) seem sweeter. It also forms the base of Cynar, the Italian aperitif. Buy artichokes that are heavy for their size and have a fresh, deep green appearance. For information on preparing artichokes, see page 11.

AVOCADOS

Avocados are indigenous to Mexico and have been cultivated in Central America for over seven thousand years. If possible, buy avocados when they are ripe, but not too soft; you should be able to barely indent them with your thumb (I prefer the bumpy-skinned **Hass** or **Mexican avocado,** which ripens to a purple-black color rather than the larger, green **Fuerte** variety). Use avocados as rapidly as possible, since they turn color quickly once they're peeled. You can preserve the green color of chopped or pureed avocado — in guacamole, for example — by adding the avocado pit and placing slices of lime over the top, and then covering with plastic wrap. Avocados are buttery in texture when ripe, mild and slightly nutty in flavor, rich in minerals, but they contain a high unsaturated fat content.

BACON

Side cut of a pig that is cured and smoked. At least half of the bacon should consist of fat, as this gives the bacon its flavor and crispness when cooked. Buy sliced or slab bacon; on average, there are about 15 to 20 regular slices per pound. Remove the rind of slab bacon before cutting into slices.

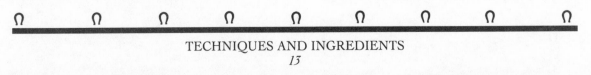

TECHNIQUES AND INGREDIENTS
13

BASIL

A member of the mint family that originated in the Middle East. There are a great many varieties of basil, and it's worth experimenting with different colors and types, especially the purple, opal basil that can give salads a decorative flair. They all have a rich, warm flavor with tones of clove and licorice that combine well with other herbs and spices, and tomatoes especially. Buy basil that is fresh-looking and brightly colored.

BEANS

Together with corn, dried beans were the most important staple of the Native Americans of the Southwest. Beans were cultivated in the region at least 1,500 years ago, and over 7,000 years ago in South America. They are rich in protein and high in minerals such as calcium, iron, and phosphorus. For information on preparing pintos, black-eyed peas, and black beans, the main types of beans used in this book, see page 10.

BELL PEPPERS

Actually members of the chile family, bell peppers (also called sweet peppers) can add a crisp texture and color to dishes as well as a sweet, mild, vegetable flavor. They come in a variety of colors, including red, green, orange, blond, yellow, violet, and purple. They are often used in Texan and Southwestern cooking in salads, stews, casseroles, and vegetable dishes. They should always be seeded before use; for instructions on roasting and peeling, see page 6.

BUTTERMILK

Traditionally, buttermilk was the liquid or whey left over from churning butter. It has always been a staple in Southern and cowboy cooking for marinating meat because of its tenderizing effect. Nowadays it is made by adding special bacteria to low-fat or skimmed milk, making it thicker and giving it a refreshing, tangy sourness.

CACTUS

Nopal, or prickly pear cactus, with its distinctive spiny, paddlelike leaves, is a big part of the scenery in West Texas and Hill Country. It has a similar texture to okra, with a flavor akin to green beans and asparagus or okra. Cactus makes a crunchy and succulent addition to salads or casseroles, or grilled as a vegetable. It should be twice boiled in salted water with tomatillo husks to minimize any sliminess. The smaller pads tend to be more tender. Wear thick gloves for extracting the spines, or for handling the prickly-pear fruit (cactus pear, or *tuna*). The egg-sized, barrel-shaped prickly pear is purple to red in

color, smells a little like watermelon, and has a fruity, earthy flavor similar to sour cherries; it is always peeled before use. Cactus is available at some Hispanic markets.

CAJETA

I have always compared the taste of cajeta, the Mexican goat's milk caramel, to sugar babies (I was addicted to these as a child!). Because of the acidic nature of the goat's milk, it seems less sweet than regular caramel, which I find welcome, and it can be flavored with ingredients such as chocolate or coffee to make delicious dessert sauces. While bottled cajeta is available in Hispanic markets, it is preferable to make your own; see page 364.

CAYENNE

I often use powdered cayenne chile as a seasoning to add piquancy to a variety of ingredients. Also known as the Ginnie pepper, the dried cayenne from which the powder is made is thin-fleshed, hot, and with a tart, somewhat smoky flavor. Other dried chiles, such as chile pequín or chile de arbol, can also be powdered and used instead.

CHAYOTE

Also called vegetable pear and mirleton, this pale-green, pear-shape vegetable native to the Southwest and Mexico has an earthy flavor similar to cucumber and zucchini (it is a member of the squash family). It grows on a vine and was much prized and widely used by the Aztecs. The crisp flesh makes it a good substitute for jicama; it can also be eaten raw, although in Mexican and South American cooking it is traditionally cooked as a vegetable, like squash. It can also be mashed or stuffed. The large pit is edible when cooked, but I prefer not to use it.

CHEESE

The technique of cheese-making (as well as the livestock to produce it) was brought to the New World and Texas by the Spanish. Cheeses (especially the softer varieties) readily absorb strong aromas and flavors, so be careful to wrap them in wax paper or plastic wrap, or store them in an airtight container. About 80 percent of the cheese I use comes from Paula Lambert's Mozzarella Company, which is not only the closest and freshest source, but also is of the highest quality. (See source list.) The recipes in this book call for several types of cheeses, and the main varieties used are:

- *Asiago:* like Monterey Jack, a semisoft cheese with a slightly tart flavor.

- *Buttero:* a hard-grating Italian sheep milk cheese similar to Parmesan.

- *Caciotta:* Italian cheese with similar characteristics to asiago or Monterey Jack.

- *Cambazola:* a creamy Italian blue cheese.

- *Cheddar:* semisoft cheese that is ideal for cooking, and grated in quesadillas and enchiladas. Can be mild or sharp in flavor.

- *Fontina:* a semisoft, creamy Italian cheese with a mild, nutlike flavor. Melts easily, and makes a good all-purpose cheese.

- *Goat cheese:* a soft, crumbly, moist cheese with a tartness and an earthy flavor. Excellent for salads, beans, chili, and enchiladas. Fresh goat cheese is much milder than the classic aged French chèvre, which is quite pungent.

- *Monterey Jack:* semisoft cheese with high moisture content that melts easily. A good mild, all-purpose cheese for this style of cooking, and a good base for flavored cheeses.

- *Mozzarella:* a soft, mild cheese that becomes stringy when cooked. Buy fresh mozzarella and use as quickly as possible as it's very perishable.

- *Queso fresco:* a fresh, moist, white Mexican cheese made from partially skimmed milk. Similar to farmer cheese or even feta, it has a slightly sharp, salty taste. Queso fresco goes well in salads and in enchiladas.

- *Parmesan:* a salty, sharp-tasting, hard cheese used for grating, especially over salads.

- *Ricotta:* a soft cheese best bought fresh, that takes well to other flavors such as herbs. Also a good cheese to use for desserts.

CHERIMOYA

Also known as the custard apple, and a cousin of the atemoya. A tropical native of the New World, cherimoyas are an amazingly complex fruit with a rich texture. They must be soft and mushy-ripe before the true variety of exotic flavors—which include mango, coconut, pineapple, and sometimes even vanilla—are brought out. Cherimoyas have large, watermelonlike seeds which should be discarded. They can be bought at specialty or Latin markets, and can be substituted by a combination of ripe mango and pineapple. Buy them heavy for their size, slightly soft, and dark green (rather than brown) in color.

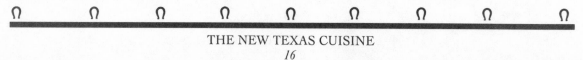

CHILES

Probably the world's most widely used seasoning. Chiles originated in the Amazon Basin and were cultivated in South America over eight thousand years ago. They are members of the nightshade family, which includes the tomato, eggplant, and potato. Historically, chiles were a staple of the cultures of Mesoamerica, and trade brought them northward into Texas and the Southwest. They were discovered by Columbus, who took them back to Europe, from where they rapidly spread around the world. For information on buying, handling, and preparing chiles, see pages 2 to 4 and 6.

CHOCOLATE

Cocoa beans, from which chocolate is made, originated in South America. The beans were used by the Mayans and Aztecs among other Mexican cultures, not only as food but also as a form of currency (the word itself is derived from the Aztec language). In pre-Hispanic times, the beans were ground with cinnamon, vanilla, and other spices and mixed with water to form a beverage. Columbus brought chocolate back to Europe where it quickly became popular. It is used in a wide array of Southwestern desserts as well as beverages.

CHORIZO

A spicy Spanish or Mexican-style sausage usually made from pork. Typically crumbled and used as a filling for tacos or enchiladas, or as an accompaniment for egg dishes. Most Mexican stores with meat departments make their own chorizo. The nearest substitute is hot Italian sausage, but the flavors are rather different. In the recipes that follow, you can also use andouille, a Cajun specialty, or Country Sausage (page 297).

CILANTRO

People seem to either love or hate cilantro (also known as Chinese parsley or fresh coriander). It's an indispensible ingredient in Texas cooking, as well as in Southwestern and Mexican cuisines (among others). Like chiles, I happen to find the aroma and pungent, cooling flavor rather addictive. In most recipes, you can use the upper stems as well as the leaves. The seeds of the cilantro plant are called coriander, but the two are not interchangeable.

CINNAMON

Available in stick and ground (powdered) forms. There are more than 150 varieties of cinnamon, which is the dried inner bark of an evergreen tree in the laurel family. True cinnamon (canela) grows in Sri Lanka and the islands of the East Indies, but the darker,

stronger-flavored Malabar cinnamon is most commonly used. Cinnamon is a useful ingredient in stews and marinades as well as desserts.

CLARIFIED BUTTER

This butter is ideal for high-temperature cooking such as frying or sautéing, as it has a higher smoking point than regular butter. It has a rich flavor that I like for searing meat and that matches most fish. It is made by heating butter so that the water content evaporates and the milk solids can be separated from the butterfat. To prepare, melt the butter in a pan over low heat, remove the pan from the heat, and let stand for 5 minutes. A milky residue, the milk solids, will collect in the bottom of the pan. Skim off the surface froth and carefully pour the liquid through a sieve lined with cheesecloth, leaving the solids in the pan. The clarified butter should be stored in an airtight jar in the freezer.

COCONUT

The influence of coconut on Texas cooking is particularly noticeable on the Gulf Coast, especially the farther southwest you go. Both the milky water and grated white meat can be used; you can freeze the white meat. I prefer using fresh coconut rather than the commercial products because it's difficult to find canned coconut that does not contain preservatives. Buy heavy coconuts that sound full of liquid when shaken.

CORN

Historically, corn is an important staple of Southwestern cuisine and was originally cultivated from a type of grass by pre-Hispanic Mexican cultures, as long as eight thousand years ago. Like subsequent Native American groups in North America, these cultures considered corn to be sacred, and referred to it as "Sacred Mother" and "Giver of Life." Use fresh corn whenever possible, as it's usually available year-round in most parts of the country. **Blue corn** is often used in Texas cuisine for cornmeal and in tortillas, and is not only attractive but also has a slightly sweeter flavor than yellow corn. For information on roasting and oven-drying corn, see page 7. **Corn husks** are essential for making tamales. They must be softened in warm water before use. Corn husks can be purchased in Hispanic markets in most large cities, but if they are unavailable, use fresh corn husks. You can dry your own corn husks by leaving them out at room temperature for several days until thoroughly dried.

COUSCOUS

Moroccan grits! A North African staple in the form of granular semolina, or durum wheat.

CRANBERRIES

Cranberries have been cultivated in North America long before the advent of European settlers. They are one fruit that doesn't seem to have geographical boundaries — cranberries are grown extensively in the northern United States, but are a culinary tradition in the South. They are cultivated on long vines in large, sandy bogs, and are most common in the fall. Dried cranberries are becoming increasingly available and important as an ingredient. Cranberries need plenty of sugar to counterbalance their natural tartness, and they have a natural affinity for the flavor of orange.

CRAWFISH

Not surprisingly, given the geographical proximity to Louisiana, crawfish are a staple in East and Southeast Texas. They resemble tiny lobsters, measuring 3 to 6 inches long, and weighing anywhere from 2 to 8 ounces.

CUMIN

Available in seed and ground (powdered) forms. It's hard to imagine Texas cooking without the warm, aromatic, nutty flavor of cumin. Cumin combines well with other spices and seasonings. It belongs to the carrot and parsley family, and is indigenous to the Southwest, as well as to Mexico and Asia — Iran is a major producer. It's best to buy fresh seeds and grind your own as needed in a coffee or spice grinder; you always run the risk, if you buy cumin in powdered form, that it might be stale.

DILL

This feathery-leaved herb that is a member of the parsley family imparts a delicate, refreshing flavor and is used most extensively in Scandinavian and Eastern European cuisines. It can be added to butters, sauces, and marinades, and complements the delicate flavors of fish well. Dried dill loses the character of the fresh, while heating dillseed brings out a more pungent flavor.

EPAZOTE

A Mexican herb, also known as wormseed or Mexican tea, that is gradually becoming better known. It is more commonly available dried rather than fresh, which is unfortunate as the flavor is much less pronounced when dried. It has large, pointed, jagged-edged leaves, grows very easily, and requires little care. Epazote has a pungent, eucalyptic flavor, and is used extensively in bean dishes — it has a reputation for combating their flatulent effect. It has a better flavor cooked, although it can be found occasionally in

salsas, and the younger leaves tend to have the most flavor. Epazote is available in Hispanic markets dried, and sometimes fresh. It grows wild in many unexpected parts of the country, such as Central Park in New York.

FLOUR
Most of the recipes in this book call for unbleached all-purpose flour, which is a blend of hard (high protein, high gluten) and soft (high starch, low gluten) flours. Hard flour has a gritty, coarse texture, suitable for making into bread flour, while soft flour is powdery and is usually processed into cake flour. There are regional differences in flour; soft wheat is grown mainly in the southern United States, and hard wheat in the North and in Canada.

GARLIC
Texas is a major grower of garlic. Originating in the Mediterranean region, garlic's name is derived from the Anglo-Saxon word for "spear plant," which refers to its shoots. Garlic figures prominently in most cuisines of the world, especially those from warm climates. I often prefer to use roasted garlic (page 7) in a recipe, as it naturally enhances other Southwestern flavors. If you have to chop garlic ahead of time, cover with olive oil to prevent it from oxidizing. Buy garlic that is firm, heavy for its size, unblemished, and with dry, papery skin. Avoid bulbs that are soft, moist, mouldy or discolored, or sprouting. Try to avoid using garlic powder or dried garlic.

GREENS
In the Southern tradition, it is typical to cook greens for a long time. In general, however, greens such as spinach, and collard, mustard, or turnip greens should be blanched for no more than 10 minutes or cooked with a vinaigrette. To really develop their flavor, cook or stew greens with pork or some other type of meat. **Spinach,** with its slightly bitter taste, was brought to the New World by the Spanish. **Collard greens,** whose name is derived from Anglo-Saxon, are a type of cabbage that originated in Africa and are grown almost exclusively in the South. **Mustard greens** are usually a rich green in color, with frilly edges. Their flavor is peppery and pungent, hence their name. **Turnip greens,** another Southern staple, have a somewhat sweet flavor, especially when young.

GRITS
Corn kernels soaked in lye water before the hulls are removed are called hominy; and dried and coarsely ground hominy is known as "grits." Grits are no longer processed by

means of lye, but the principle is the same. Grits are basically the same as polenta, but quintessentially Southern. A Texan once wrote that the best recipe for grits is to make them and then throw them away, but most Southerners I know are attached to this regional staple that is eaten as a hot cereal or as a side dish.

HOJA SANTA

An herb also known as "the root beer plant," because of its primary sassafras flavor; anise tones are also predominant. It has large, heart-shape, medium-green leaves which in Mexico are considered to stimulate the digestion and have other medicinal qualities. I discovered hoja santa some years ago in Oaxaca, where it is used extensively in salsas and moles, and also to wrap fish for steaming. I expect it to be used much more, and to become more widely available, in the next three to five years. It is growing in popularity, and more people are growing it in their gardens at home. It grows up to ten feet high along the river walk in San Antonio. I enjoy teaching about its virtues in my cooking classes.

HORSERADISH

A native of southeastern Europe, horseradish is the root of a plant in the cabbage family. It is related to mustard, and when its tissue is broken, it releases mustard oils. Horseradish is one of the five bitter herbs of the Jewish Passover seder. It is available year-round, but is particularly plentiful in the spring. It is used to enliven just about everything in Texas cuisine, from Bloody Marys to shrimp cocktails. Buy fresh roots that are plump, firm, and crisp, and avoid those that are limp, soft, or sprouting. As a general rule of thumb, use twice the amount of fresh horseradish than bottled or prepared. In choosing a bottled horseradish, make sure the ingredients other than horseradish are minimal — preferably, just vinegar and salt.

JICAMA

This crisp-textured, almost turnip-shaped tuber originated in the Amazon Basin and has long been indigenous to Mexico, hence its nickname, "the Mexican potato." It has a thin brown skin and white, crisp flesh that is slightly sweet in flavor, rather like water chestnuts, or a cross between apples and turnips. It is refreshing and cool, and has the perfect texture for salsas and relishes. It can be cooked as a vegetable, but I prefer it served raw, with a little freshly squeezed lime juice, cilantro, and pure chile powder or paprika sprinkled over it.

LARD

Formerly a key ingredient in Texas and Southwestern cuisine, and one of the few cooking fats available. Lard, which is usually rendered from pork fat, is much less popular now because of its high level of saturated fat and cholesterol and the large number of healthier alternatives (although the USDA reports that lard has less than half the cholesterol of butter). It's also hard to get good fresh lard because of the preservatives that are added to it. However, lard does add a distinctive flavor to items such as beans and tortillas. This is an ingredient where moderation makes more sense than abstinence.

LIMES

Buy the small Mexican limes (resembling Key limes) that are light green to yellow in color, as they tend to be much juicier and sweeter than the larger Persian limes.

MANGOES

These tropical fruits, which originated in India and Southeast Asia (where they are considered sacred), reach their peak season in late spring and early summer. Although best tree-ripened (like other tropical fruit), mangoes are usually picked green, and should be ripened in a paper bag at room temperature until they reach an orange-yellow hue and exude an exotic, heady perfume. They should be peeled with a paring knife and the flesh cut lengthwise from the large, fibrous pit. Mangoes are indispensible in salsas, relishes, and sauces in the cooking of the Southwest, and their sweet tropical coolness is a perfect foil for the heat of chiles. Mangoes also complement black beans very well.

MARIGOLD MINT

Very similar to tarragon, but more heady in flavor with anise tones, this herb goes well in salads, and with corn and squash. It is used as a medicinal tea in Mexico, and the flowers make an attractive garnish. For availability, see source list.

MARJORAM

I consider marjoram, a member of the mint family, to be one of the most underutilized herbs. Its aromatic, subtley sweet, perfumelike flavor adds a dimension to food that no other herb can. In Mexico, it is called wild oregano, and most resembles that herb.

MASA HARINA

Masa is the Mexican word for "(corn) dough," and *harina* means "flour." Masa harina is flour made from specially processed corn (posole), and is used to make tortilla and tamale dough. Brands such as Quaker can be bought in the flour section of many supermarkets, or it can be found in Latin markets. You can buy already prepared masa dough from tortilla factories in large cities. Substituting cornmeal for masa harina does not work, as it has sufficiently different qualities.

MELONS

Melons such as honeydews, cantaloupes, crenshaws and watermelons evoke midsummer and the peak growing season. In fact, this is by far the best time to enjoy them, when they are luscious and sweet. An extensive variety is grown in the southern Texas valley. Melons are a welcome addition to salsas; their soft texture and sweet flesh complement chiles very well. Melons are very low in calories. Buy melons that are fragrant when scratched at the stem end, and feel very heavy; the stem ends should yield to gentle pressure.

MINT

An herb that originated in the Mediterranean region and grows throughout the Southwest. It should always be used in its fresh form as the active oil, menthol, is present to a far greater degree than when mint is dried. Like basil, which belongs to the mint family, there are many varieties that offer a wide range of pungency; for example, **peppermint,** with its bright green leaves and purple-tinged stems, is more pungent and peppery than the gray-green-leaved **spearmint** (these are the two most common varieties of about thirty species of mint).

NOPAL

See CACTUS.

NUTS

The main types of nuts used in this book include:

- *Almonds:* very versatile and commonly used in Texas cooking (as well as in Mexican cuisine), in both savory and sweet sauces, fillings, and desserts.

- *Hazelnuts:* also known as filberts, hazelnuts were grown by the Chinese five thousand years ago. In the United States, these nuts are cultivated mostly in the Midwest and Northwest. Their bitter brown skin should be removed (see page 9).

- *Macadamia nuts:* the buttery, rich macadamia originated in Australia and grew on an evergreen tree named after a Scot, John Macadam, who cultivated them. They were introduced to Hawaii in the 1930s, where they have flourished and are an important crop. The trees take at least seven years before they bear any fruit. These nuts should be used rapidly, as they can turn rancid with age.

- *Pecan nuts:* related to walnuts and a Texas staple. In my opinion, the small, rich, sweet-meated pecans from San Saba in the heart of Texas are as good as any in the world.

- *Pine nuts* (or piñon nuts): derived from several types of pine tree, and harvested throughout the Southwest, especially in New Mexico and Arizona. However, much of the supply in the United States comes from China. The ivory-colored nuts can only be gathered by hand and extracted by means of a labor-intensive process involving heating the shells, which makes them rather expensive. Pine nuts have a delicate flavor, but like macadamia nuts, they should be used rapidly as they turn rancid quickly.

- *Walnuts:* related to pecans and hickory nuts, walnuts are highly versatile. They are the second most popular nut, in terms of consumption in the United States, after the almond. The rarer black walnuts native to the Appalachian region are even richer.

OILS

I like to cook with **olive oil** as it imparts a subtle but distinctive flavor to food. A good-quality brand is important when using olive oil raw in dressings or for tossing salads. **Peanut** and **canola oil** are good for frying as they withstand high temperatures without burning and are relatively flavorless. I use **vegetable oil** as a neutral, all-purpose cooking oil, and sometimes mix it with olive oil to tone down the flavor of the latter. **Nut oils,** such as hazelnut, walnut, and almond, add a marvelous flavor to salad dressings. They should be stored in the refrigerator as they spoil easily.

OKRA

A relative of the hibiscus and a Southern staple that originated in tropical Africa. Okra is used extensively in Cajun and Creole cooking; for example, in gumbo, and as a thickening agent. It is typically cooked in the South breaded with cornmeal and fried. Buy okra that is plump and green, and preferably less than 3 inches long (the shorter spears are more tender). Use rapidly, as it keeps poorly.

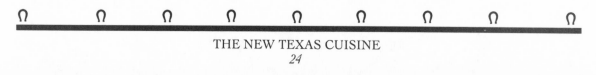

ONIONS

Surprisingly perhaps, onions are members of the lily family, like garlic, chives, scallions, leeks, and shallots. I love to cook with Texas **sweet onions** such as Noonday and Texas Spring Sweet. The more widely available **Vidalia** variety, from Georgia, is originally from Texan stock. Try and use them whenever they are available; they are delicious eaten raw in salads. The standard onion used throughout this book is the multipurpose **yellow onion,** which is sweeter than the **white,** and highly flavored. **Red onions** are generally mild, and used mostly for color. Buy onions that are firm, heavy for their size, unblemished, and that have dry, papery skins. Avoid those that are soft, mouldy, discolored, or sprouting.

OREGANO

Like cilantro, the intensely flavored oregano is a very important herb in Southwestern and Mexican cooking. **Mexican oregano** is stronger in flavor than the regular (Italian) oregano. Oregano, another member of the mint family, combines well with other herbs and tomato-based dishes.

OYSTERS

First cultivated over two thousand years ago by the Romans, oysters grow in estuaries and shallow bays where fresh water dilutes the salinity of sea water. The United States, Japan, and France, respectively, produce the most oysters. Their flavor is best in those months containing an "r"; in other months, their starch content makes them less palatable.

PAPAYA

Like mangoes, tropical papayas are picked green, and should be bought when green and yellow or rose colored. They should then be ripened in a paper bag at room temperature until mostly yellow in color and soft to the touch. The skin should be peeled with a paring knife and although the black seeds are edible, they can be removed. Most papayas available in the United States are grown in Hawaii and Florida.

PARSLEY

Although parsley can perk up heavier dishes, it is not widely used in Southwestern cooking, as cilantro is generally preferred. **Chinese parsley** is another name for cilantro. **Flat-leafed (or Italian) parsley** tends to be more flavorful than the curly-leafed variety.

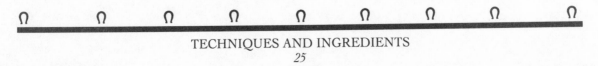

PASSION FRUIT

The rounded egg-sized passion fruit is native to Brazil and related to the papaya. It has an uneven, brown to dark purple skin, which contains a yellowish or golden mass of pulp and seeds. The pulp yields an exotic fragrance and a wonderful, tropical flavor and is usually extremely tart. This fruit makes delicious sauces and desserts, and can be used as an attractive garnish. Buy large fruit that is firm and heavy for its size.

PECTIN

Naturally occurring in certain fruits and vegetables, pectin is a water-soluble jelling agent used for thickening preserves, jellies, and jams. It is sold either in liquid or powdered form; I prefer the liquid, which usually sets up faster.

PLANTAINS

Related to bananas and used for cooking, ripe plantains are at their sweetest when dark or even black in color, and soft to the touch. They can be bought when deep green and firm, and ripened at room temperature. Unripe plantains taste rather like potatoes when cooked, and can be used as a vegetable. When peeling, remove the bitter strings that run along the plantain (the same is true for bananas).

POLENTA

Italian grits! Made from cornmeal, it's a staple of northern Italy, especially.

POMEGRANATES

The pomegranate (which is actually a berry) is a native of the Middle East that is now grown in the United States in Texas, California, and Arizona. The flavor is sweet but tart, with tones of berries and nuts. The brilliant pink seeds of the pomegranate make a wonderful garnish item as well as a colorful and tasty ingredient for salads, desserts, and sauces. Buy large, bright-looking, unblemished pomegranates. Avoid the bitter white pith, and take care, as any juice stains are very difficult to remove from clothing. This must be one of the most labor-intensive fruits to eat. Pomegranates are in season during the fall.

ROSEMARY

Another herb in the mint family that is native to the Mediterranean, rosemary grows wild as an evergreen shrub throughout the Southwest. Rosemary twigs make a great addition

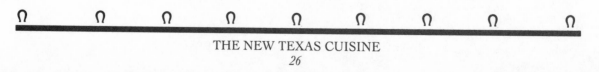

to the grill to flavor meats, and the pine needle–like leaves are also a flavorful addition to marinades. Use sparingly as its piney, lemony flavor can easily overwhelm delicate dishes.

SAFFRON
One of the most exclusive and expensive spices in the world, saffron threads are the dried stigmas of a crocus flower native to the eastern Mediterranean. The Spanish brought the pungent, bright orange saffron with them to Mexico, and it has remained an important element in the cuisine. It is used for its yellow coloring as well as its delicate flavor.

SAGE
Another herb that comes in a number of varieties, sage grows wild in parts of Texas and the Southwest. It was used extensively in ancient Greece and Rome for medicinal purposes. Today, it is most commonly used with pork, game, and poultry, especially in stuffings.

SCALLIONS
Also known as green onions and spring onions, scallions are members of the lily family and related to onions, garlic, and leeks. Their refreshing, subtle, peppery flavor and versatility make them an important ingredient in Texas cooking.

SHALLOTS
Middle Eastern in origin, and used extensively in French cooking, which is how I first made their acquaintance. Like scallions, shallots are members of the onion family. They have a subtle flavor that lies somewhere between onions and garlic. Buy shallots that are firm and heavy for their size, with dry, papery, reddish-brown skins. Avoid those that are soft, moist, or sprouting.

SHRIMP
Fishing for shrimp, the most popular shellfish consumed in the United States, is a major Gulf Coast industry. They almost always come frozen, and are often frozen on the boats. You'll have to live near a source to find fresh shrimp, but get them if you can, because they're a real treat. Small shrimp yield about 50 to 55 per pound; medium, 30 to 35; large, 15 to 20; and jumbo, 6 to 10.

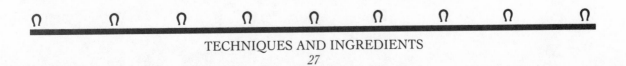

SQUASH BLOSSOMS

Squash blossoms, which can be picked from any squash, but typically from yellow, crooknecked squash, are greatly overlooked as a food item in this country. I think of them as a celebratory ingredient of the late spring and early summer. They are a wonderful package for stuffing, and are a flavorful addition to soups and salads. Use the same day you buy them, as they do not keep.

SWEET POTATOES

A real Southern staple, sweet potatoes should not be confused with yams, which are also tubers and similar in appearance and flavor, but are botanically quite different (sweet potatoes are members of the morning glory family). Sweet potatoes are so called because of their high (3 to 6 percent) sugar content; in general, the smaller potatoes are the most sweet and tender.

TAMARIND

Grown in Asia and Mexico, tamarind is the fruit of an evergreen tree which originated in Western Africa. The pods contain a bittersweet pulp and some hard seeds that are processed into a paste. Tamarind is used extensively as a flavoring in Southwestern and Mexican cuisines; in Mexico, for example, it is used to flavor the wonderfully refreshing drink, Agua Fresca. Its tartness complements most dried chiles well, and it is a great ingredient in marinades and glazes. It is available in paste form in Asian or Latin markets.

THYME

A multipurpose herb in the mint family that is widely used in Texas cooking. Its rich flavor enhances stocks, soups, and sauces, as well as meats. Like rosemary, it can be added to the grill to provide a fragrant flavor to meats and vegetables.

TOMATILLOS

The firm, green tomatillo resembles an unripe tomato and is related to it as a member of the nightshade family (thus it is also related to chiles, eggplants, potatoes, and tobacco). Tomatillos are a staple of Texas cooking, and their tart, acidic, and slightly lemony flavor has a natural affinity for serranos, garlic, and cilantro. They are now grown throughout the Southwest, mainly due to Mexican migration. Select unblemished tomatillos that completely fill their papery, parchmentlike husks. These must be removed before use, and the tomatillos should be rinsed as they have a sticky surface. They are good cooked, but I prefer them diced raw in salsas; to me, they are the very essence of Salsa Verde.

TOMATOES

Native to the New World (and believed to have originated in Peru), the word "tomato" is derived from the Aztec language. The tomato is a member of the nightshade family (see TOMATILLOS, above). Tomatoes were cultivated in Mexico and taken to Europe by the Spanish, but they have only become universally popular in this century. Use vine-ripened tomatoes whenever possible, as commercially grown tomatoes (especially out-of-season) are picked when green and ripened by exposure to ethylene gas. Do not refrigerate ripe tomatoes as this affects their flavor. If mushy, tasteless tomatoes are all that is available, use a premium-quality canned Italian tomato packed in juice instead, but strain the liquid and adjust the recipe accordingly. **Yellow tomatoes** tend to be sweeter fleshed and are becoming increasingly available; they make a striking presentation in salsas, relishes, soups, and sauces.

VANILLA

Vanilla is a native of the New World and a member of the orchid family. The black, shiny beans grow on climbing vines. Vanilla was cultivated by the Aztecs. Use fresh vanilla beans whenever possible, and choose large, plump, soft beans. The best-quality beans are usually from Tahiti, although Mexican Papantla vanilla is also excellent.

VENISON

Venison has always been an important element in meat consumption in Texas. Although it is usually regarded as a fall or winter item, reflecting the traditional hunting season, it is available year-round from range-raised sources such as Texas Wild Game. It is healthful and much lighter in both flavor and fat content than beef, for example. **Fallow deer** —from which the venison served in most restaurants is derived—as well as **sika** and **axis deer** have all been introduced relatively recently into Texas and the Southwest as game animals. They have proliferated to the point where they have almost overwhelmed the native **white-tailed deer,** which does not produce such high-quality venison.

VINEGARS

There are all kinds of flavored vinegars available now, and I recommend keeping a number on hand at all times; I also like to have aged sherry and balsamic vinegars available. As with olive oil, use the best quality vinegars, especially in salads and other dishes where vinegar is not cooked. Making your own fruit vinegars is a very simple process: pour a good-quality champagne or white wine over macerated fruit, and store in an airtight bottle or jar for at least one month.

CHAPTER TWO

STOCKS, MARINADES, CONDIMENTS, AND PICKLES

The recipes in this chapter are the flavor building blocks of Texas cooking, and most are used elsewhere in the book. Many are standards or classics in other cuisines, too, but for the most part, these recipes have been adapted for the foods of Texas.

Stocks are a cornerstone of many cuisines around the world. They freeze well, and they can easily be made up in large batches, so there's no excuse not to have stocks on hand at all times. For veal stock, you can save space in the freezer by reducing the liquid down to a demiglace, pour it into ice-cube trays, and cover well with plastic wrap until you need it.

Almost every soup in this book calls for a rich chicken or fish stock, and chicken stock is called for extensively in other recipes as well. If there's one thing that's worth taking the extra effort over, it's a good stock.

Many of the condiments and pickles are variations on Texas classics, and they too are well worth having on hand to add a little flair to just about any dish.

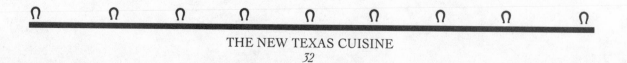

CHICKEN STOCK

Chicken stock is never far from reach at any of my restaurants. In fact, it's hard for me to imagine cooking without it — it is such an important all-purpose component and flavor ingredient for so many of my dishes. If you do use canned chicken stock instead, be sure to adjust for salt, as most canned stocks are quite salty.

ABOUT 3 QUARTS

½ large onion, unpeeled
3 cloves garlic, unpeeled
5 pounds raw chicken wings, backs, or necks (or a combination)
1 cup chopped carrots

1 cup chopped celery
6 to 8 sprigs thyme, or 1 teaspoon dried thyme
3 bay leaves
½ teaspoon black peppercorns
3 to 4 quarts water

Heat a nonstick skillet over high heat until extremely hot, about 7 minutes. Place the onion in the skillet, cut side down, and cook for 15 minutes, until completely charred. Add the garlic and cook until charred on both sides, about 5 minutes. (Charring the onion and garlic adds color and flavor but is not entirely essential).

Place the onion and garlic in a large stockpot and add all the remaining ingredients; if not submerged, add more water. Bring to a boil, reduce the heat, and let simmer for at least 2 hours, and up to 6 hours. Add water as necessary and let simmer for 20 minutes after the last addition.

Remove from the heat, let cool, skim off any fat, and strain the stock. For an even richer flavor, the stock may be reduced by half.

The stock will keep for 3 to 4 days in the refrigerator, and up to 2 months frozen.

BROWN CHICKEN STOCK

This stock is made with the same ingredients and can be used in the same recipes and in the same way as regular chicken stock. But the cooking method adds a darker color and yields a richer flavor. I often use this stock, simply reduced by one half or three quarters, as a sauce; this process intensifies and compounds the stock's essence.

ABOUT 1 QUART

5 pounds raw chicken wings, backs, or necks (or a combination)
½ large onion, chopped
3 cloves garlic, chopped
1 cup chopped carrots

1 cup chopped celery
6 to 8 sprigs thyme, or 1 teaspoon dried thyme
3 bay leaves
½ teaspoon black peppercorns
3 to 4 quarts water

Preheat the oven to 450° F. Place the chicken pieces in a roasting pan and bake in the oven until browned deeply on all sides, about 1 hour. Add the onion, garlic, carrots, and celery for the last 30 minutes.

Remove the pan from the oven, transfer the baked ingredients to a large stockpot, and add the seasonings. Place the roasting pan over high heat on the stove and deglaze with 2 quarts of the water by cooking for 2 minutes while scraping to dissolve any hardened brown particles. Pour into the stockpot and add 1 to 2 quarts additional water or enough to cover. Bring to a boil, reduce the heat, and simmer strongly for 3 hours. Reduce the heat further and simmer gently for an additional 2 hours. Add more water as necessary and let simmer for 1 hour after the last addition.

Remove from the heat, let cool, skim off any fat, and strain the stock into a clean pan. Reduce the stock by three quarters over medium heat, skimming and stirring occasionally, until the stock is very brown and rich.

The stock will keep for up to 1 week in the refrigerator, and up to 2 months frozen.

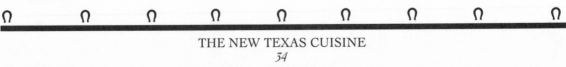

FISH STOCK

I know there are parts of the country where fish bones are not easy to buy. Bottled clam juice is a commonly called-for substitute for the stock, but it's always more salty. While it's not as desirable as fish stock, it's still the next best thing, but be sure to adjust downwards the quantity of salt in the recipe.

ABOUT 3 QUARTS

4 pounds fish bones and/or heads
1 tablespoon olive oil
1 large onion, diced
2 cloves garlic, chopped
1 small carrot, chopped

2 cups dry white wine
3 to 4 quarts water
1 teaspoon chopped thyme
2 bay leaves
1 tablespoon chopped parsley

Rinse the fish bones and if using heads, make sure they are thoroughly cleaned and that the gills are removed. Set aside.

In a large stockpot, heat the oil until lightly smoking and sauté the onion, garlic, and carrot over medium heat for 2 minutes. Add the fish bones, cover, and simmer for 10 to 15 minutes, stirring occasionally; the bones should fall apart.

Add the wine and water, and bring to a boil. Add the herbs, reduce to a simmer, and cook for 45 minutes. Strain, and let cool.

The stock will keep for up to 5 days in the refrigerator, and up to 2 months frozen.

BROWN VEAL STOCK

In areas where veal bones are not available, substitute beef soup bones in equal proportions.

ABOUT 2 QUARTS STOCK OR 1 QUART DEMIGLACE

6 pounds veal bones
2 pounds calves' feet (optional)
1 large onion, halved
½ head garlic
1 cup chopped turnips
1 cup chopped carrots
1 cup chopped celery
6 to 8 sprigs thyme, or 1 teaspoon dried thyme

6 bay leaves
1 cup chopped parsley
½ teaspoon black peppercorns
6 large tomatoes, chopped
6 ounces canned tomato paste
2 quarts (8 cups) red wine
6 quarts (1½ gallons) water or chicken stock

Preheat the oven to 450° F. Place the bones in a roasting pan and bake in the oven until browned deeply on all sides, about 2 hours. Add the onion, garlic, turnips, carrots, and celery for the last 30 minutes.

Remove the roasting pan from the oven, transfer the ingredients to a large stockpot, and add all remaining ingredients except red wine and water. Place the roasting pan over high heat on the stove and deglaze with the red wine by cooking for 2 minutes while scraping to dissolve any hardened brown particles. Pour into the stockpot and add enough water or chicken stock to cover. Bring to a boil, reduce the heat, and simmer strongly for at least 6 hours. Reduce the heat further and simmer gently for an additional 4 hours. Add more water or chicken stock as necessary and let simmer for 1 hour after the last addition.

Remove from the heat, let cool, skim off any fat, and strain the stock into a clean pan. Reduce the stock by one half over medium heat, skimming and stirring occasionally, to enhance and intensify the flavor.

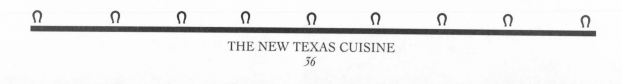

The stock will keep for up to 1 week in the refrigerator, and up to 2 months frozen.

NOTE: To make a demiglace, reduce the stock further by one half.

CREOLE VEGETABLE STOCK

This flavorful stock is a great medium for poaching chicken or fish, and makes a wonderful base for soups — it's an essential element in the Creole Sweet Potato Vichyssoise (see Index). If a pure vegetable stock is desired, replace the bacon with 3 tablespoons vegetable or olive oil; the chicken stock may be replaced by water.

ABOUT 1 GALLON

1 tablespoon olive oil	*2 heads garlic, unpeeled and sliced in half*
5 ounces (about 3 slices) bacon, chopped	*½ teaspoon black peppercorns*
6 green bell peppers, seeded and coarsely chopped	*½ teaspoon cayenne powder*
1 head celery, chopped	*2 bay leaves*
2 carrots, chopped	*¼ cup chopped thyme*
3 onions, chopped	*3 quarts Chicken Stock (see Index)*

In a large stockpot, heat the oil until lightly smoking, add the bacon, and sauté over medium-high heat for 2 minutes to render the fat. Add the remaining ingredients except the chicken stock and sauté for 10 minutes, stirring frequently.

Add the stock and bring to a boil. Reduce the heat and simmer for 45 minutes. Strain, pressing down hard with the back of a spoon to extract the vegetable essence.

The stock will keep for up to 1 week in the refrigerator, and up to 2 months frozen.

HAM HOCK BROTH

This is a great cooking liquid to have on hand at all times, and it can be frozen until needed. I particularly like the rich ham flavor it imparts to beans, and one of my all-time favorite comfort foods is black-eyed peas cooked with ham hock broth served alongside a mess of greens.

ABOUT 2 QUARTS

6 to 8 ham hocks
1 large onion, chopped
6 cloves garlic, chopped
1 carrot, chopped

1 stalk celery, chopped
2 jalapeño chiles, seeded and sliced
2 quarts Chicken Stock (see Index) or water

Place all the ingredients in a large stockpot, covering with chicken stock or water. Bring to a boil, reduce the heat, and simmer for 2 hours, adding more liquid as necessary.

Remove the ham hocks, strain the stock, and reserve. Remove the meat from the bones and reserve for another use, discarding the bones.

This broth becomes gelatinous when reduced or chilled; add more water if desired. Keep for up to 1 week in the refrigerator, or up to 2 months frozen.

ALL-PURPOSE BRINE FOR SMOKING MEATS AND POULTRY

This brine should only be made up and stored in an earthenware, glass, or plastic container; never use metal or wood. After it has cooled, stir the brine well to ensure the ingredients are evenly mixed. Make sure the meat or poultry is thoroughly submerged in the brine, weighting it down with a plate if necessary, and lightly rinse the meat after brining.

ABOUT 1 GALLON

4 quarts (1 gallon) water
1 cup kosher or sea salt
½ cup dark brown sugar
1 bay leaf
1 tablespoon chopped thyme, or 1 teaspoon dried thyme

½ teaspoon black peppercorns
2 cloves
1 clove garlic, crushed
1 teaspoon cayenne powder

Place all the ingredients in a large stockpot and bring to a boil over medium heat while stirring. Reduce the heat and simmer for 5 minutes. Remove from the heat and let cool.

THREE CITRUS MARINADE

This recipe is particularly suited to poultry such as chicken and quail, which should be submerged in the marinade for at least 2 hours or even overnight.

ABOUT 2⅓ CUPS

½ cup fresh lime juice
½ cup fresh lemon juice
½ cup fresh orange juice
½ cup olive oil

4 cloves garlic, minced
2 teaspoons coarsely ground black pepper
3 bay leaves, crushed
3 tablespoons chopped cilantro

Combine all the ingredients in a mixing bowl and let stand at room temperature for 30 minutes to allow the flavors to develop.

MOLASSES-GARLIC MARINADE

While this marinade is used for quail (see Index), it also lends a special flavor to other types of poultry, as well as pork.

ABOUT 1¼ CUPS

½ cup soy sauce
¼ cup dark beer
2 tablespoons molasses
Zest of 1 lemon, blanched
Zest of 1 orange, blanched

1 tablespoon chopped lemon verbena
or lemon thyme
4 tablespoons peeled and diced fresh ginger
2 cloves garlic, crushed

In a mixing bowl, thoroughly combine all the ingredients.

CATSUP

The name of this condiment is derived from the Chinese word ke-tsiap *meaning "brine of pickled fish" and used to describe a popular seventeenth-century condiment in that country. For those who wonder why you'd make your own when you can buy bottled catsup so easily, you only need to taste the homemade variety to realize that it's well worth the effort.*

ABOUT 3 CUPS

¼ cup sun-dried tomatoes
6 pounds very ripe tomatoes, cored and chopped
1 large onion, chopped
⅔ cup cider vinegar
½ cup brown sugar
1 cinnamon stick, 2 inches long

½ teaspoon cayenne powder
½ teaspoon ground allspice
¼ teaspoon ground cloves
Pinch of ground mace
Salt to taste

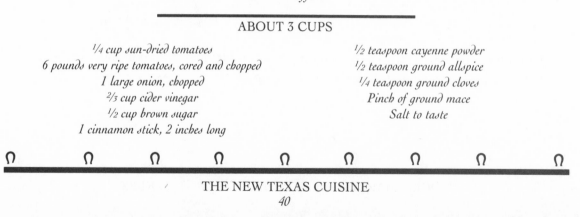

In a large saucepan, cook the tomatoes and onion over medium-high heat for 30 minutes. Remove from the heat and press through a sieve. Return to the pan, add the remaining ingredients, and simmer until quite thick, about 1½ to 2 hours.

Remove the cinnamon stick, transfer the sauce to a blender, and puree until smooth. Let cool and refrigerate for several weeks.

BARBECUE SAUCE #1 (simple)

This very basic, simple sauce can be thrown together in no time at all. It's the easiest of all three barbecue sauces to make, and is perfect for barbecuing chicken or steak.

ABOUT 2½ CUPS

1 teaspoon olive oil
2 onions, finely chopped
2 jalapeño chiles, seeded and diced
½ cup firmly packed dark brown sugar

½ cup white vinegar
¼ cup Worcestershire sauce
1 tablespoon dried mustard
2 cups Catsup (see opposite)

In a large enamel or stainless-steel saucepan, heat the oil and sauté the onions and jalapeños over medium-high heat for 2 minutes. Add the remaining ingredients and bring to a boil while stirring. Reduce the heat and simmer, uncovered, for 15 minutes. Strain the barbecue sauce through a medium strainer.

All three barbecue sauces will keep up to 1 week in the refrigerator.

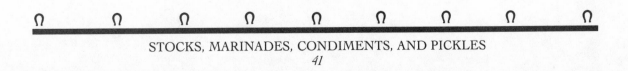

BARBECUE SAUCE #2 (medium)

This sauce is only more complicated than #1 because smoked vegetables are added. The additional depth of flavor that these provide make it worth the effort.

ABOUT 2 QUARTS

3 tablespoons unsalted butter
1 onion, chopped
3 cups Catsup (see Index)
½ cup Worcestershire sauce
⅓ cup A.1. sauce
3 tablespoons red wine vinegar
½ cup brown sugar

2 red bell peppers, smoked, roasted, peeled, seeded, and chopped (page 6 and 14)
2 onions, smoked and roasted (page 9)
3 tomatoes, halved and smoked (page 9)
2 tablespoons chipotle chile puree (pages 3 to 4)
Chicken or Veal Stock (optional, see Index)

Heat the butter in a skillet and sauté the chopped onion over medium-high heat for 5 minutes. Add the catsup, Worcestershire sauce, A.1. sauce, vinegar, and sugar, and cook for 2 minutes. Transfer to a food processor, add the smoked vegetables and chile puree, and blend for 3 minutes until smooth. Thin with a little chicken stock or veal stock, if desired.

BARBECUE SAUCE #3 (complex)

This refined barbecue sauce is the one we use at Star Canyon, and despite the extensive preparation, it's well worth the effort.

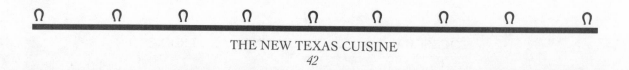

1 small ripe tomato, quartered	*2 dried chipotle chiles, halved and seeded*
1 small onion, quartered	*1 quart Brown Veal Stock (see Index)*
1 stalk celery	*2 teaspoons dried mustard*
1 red bell pepper, halved and seeded	*⅓ cup raspberry vinegar*
2 cloves garlic	*⅓ cup light brown sugar*
1 small turnip	*½ cup Catsup (see Index)*
1 small dried ancho chile, halved and seeded	*Salt to taste*
1 serrano chile, halved and seeded	

Smoke all the vegetables and chiles for 20 minutes (see page 9). Transfer the ingredients to a medium saucepan with the veal stock. Bring to a boil and reduce the liquid by one third. Whisk in the mustard, strain, and set aside.

In a small saucepan, whisk together the vinegar and sugar. Bring to a boil and continue cooking until the mixture becomes syrupy, about 3 minutes. Add to the strained veal stock mixture and whisk in the catsup. Strain the barbecue sauce through a fine strainer, and season with salt to taste.

ANNATTO OIL

Annatto or achiote seed is used commercially as a natural coloring for butter and cheese, and it's a useful ingredient to add when sautéing for imparting a vibrant yellow-orange tinge. This oil can be drizzled over meat or shellfish both for color and subtle flavoring or added to salad dressings.

ABOUT 1 CUP

¼ cup annatto seeds	*1 cup olive oil*

Heat the annatto seeds and oil in a saucepan until the oil becomes very hot. Remove from the heat and let infuse for 3 hours. Carefully skim off the colored oil, leaving the bottom layer undisturbed. May be stored in the refrigerator for up to 2 months.

CILANTRO OIL

Like the Annatto Oil, this infusion provides an attractive presentation as well as a subtle flavor. Other herbs, chiles, and vegetables can also be used to flavor oils.

ABOUT 1 CUP

¼ cup cilantro leaves   *1 cup olive oil*

Heat the cilantro leaves and oil in a saucepan until the oil becomes very hot. Remove from the heat and let infuse for 3 hours. Carefully skim off the colored oil, leaving the bottom layer undisturbed. May be stored in the refrigerator for up to 1 week.

ROUTH STREET VINAIGRETTE

This is a good all-purpose dressing for salads or for any recipe calling for a flavorful vinaigrette. The herbs can be interchanged with others and adjusted to taste.

ABOUT 2¼ CUPS

2½ tablespoons balsamic vinegar
2½ tablespoons red wine vinegar
1 cup olive oil
1 cup vegetable oil
1 teaspoon minced cilantro
1 teaspoon minced thyme
½ teaspoon minced sage

1 teaspoon minced basil
½ teaspoon ground cumin
2 teaspoons honey mustard
1½ tablespoons pureed roasted garlic (page 7)
½ teaspoon salt
Freshly ground black pepper to taste

Gulf Grouper with Smoked Tomato Salsa and Vegetable Escabeche

Left: Barbecue in West Texas

Right: Hill Country guard dog

Top: U.S. Post Office in Luckenbach, Texas, population 1–5

Middle: Johnny Nicholas performing after dinner at his Hill Top Cafe

Bottom: Prickly pear in bloom

Top: Crushing equipment at Fall Creek Winery

Bottom: Dallas skyline at dusk

Oil derrick in West Texas

Top: *Loin of Lamb with Gingered Fruit Couscous and Tomato-Eggplant Ragout*

Bottom: *Veal Medallions on Wilted Greens with Pinto-Wild Mushroom Sauce and Spicy Whipped Sweet Potatoes*

*P*umpkin–White Bean Chowder with Roasted Garlic Croutons and
Pomegranate Crème Fraîche

In a mixing bowl, combine the vinegars and drizzle in the oils while whisking. Whisk in the remaining ingredients. Alternatively, the procedure may be followed using a food processor or blender.

CRÈME FRAÎCHE

Because of the pasteurization regulations enforced by the FDA in the United States, it is impossible to get the true flavor and texture of the real thing. In France, crème fraîche has nearly the texture of sour cream and a much richer flavor. This recipe, however, is the next best thing.

3 CUPS

1 cup heavy cream *2 cups sour cream, buttermilk, or yogurt*

Place the ingredients in a mixing bowl and whisk together. Cover with plastic wrap and let sit in a warm place for 12 to 14 hours. If you have a gas oven with a pilot light, this is the ideal place to let it sit overnight. Transfer to the refrigerator and chill. May be stored in the refrigerator for up to 10 days.

MAYONNAISE

It really is worth the effort involved to make your own mayonnaise — there's a big difference between this recipe and store-bought. Since mayonnaise is an emulsion — the egg yolks are forced to absorb the oil and hold it in suspension — the oil must be added gradually. The thicker the mayonnaise gets, the more rapidly you can add the oil. As a general rule of thumb, each yolk can absorb as much as ⅔ cup of oil. This recipe can be stored in the refrigerator, wrapped tightly, for 4 to 5 days.

For those interested in how certain foods got their names, one theory is that mayonnaise was created in the mid-eighteenth century by the chef of the Duke of Richelieu, while the Duke's forces were laying siege to Port Mahon, the capital of the Balearic island of Minorca — hence "mahonnaise."

ABOUT 1½ CUPS

2 egg yolks
¾ teaspoon salt
Freshly ground black pepper to taste
1 teaspoon Dijon mustard
½ cup peanut, canola, or safflower oil

½ cup extra-virgin olive oil
2 teaspoons fresh lemon juice
¼ to ½ cup Chicken Stock (optional, see Index)
or water

Whisk together the egg yolks, salt, pepper, and mustard in a mixing bowl. Combine the oils and drizzle into the mixing bowl while whisking. Continue to whisk until thoroughly incorporated. Add the lemon juice, taste, and adjust the seasoning if necessary.

Alternatively, the mayonnaise can be made in a blender or food processor. Add 1 extra whole egg to the egg yolks, and process for 15 seconds. Add the salt, lemon juice, pepper, and mustard, and process for 15 seconds more. With the machine running, drizzle 1½ cups of the combined oils in a steady stream, making sure they are incorporated gradually. Stop the machine to check the consistency: if very thick, add a little stock or water. Taste for seasoning, and add a little vinegar or more lemon juice if desired. Add more oil with the machine running until the mixture is the desired consistency (you do not have to use all the oil). Thin with stock if desired.

NOTE: No one can consider themselves an expert cook until they have "broken" mayonnaise at least half a dozen times; this happens if the yolks do not absorb the oil quickly enough. Fortunately, there is a solution to reemulsifying the mixture; unfortunately, it must be done by hand:

Run the mixing bowl under warm water, dry with a towel, and place 2 teaspoons of prepared mustard in the bowl. Add 1 egg yolk and whisk together until smooth. Add 1 tablespoon of the broken mayonnaise while whisking. When creamy, add in 1 more tablespoon of the broken mayonnaise, and whisk thoroughly. When incorporated, begin to drizzle in the remaining broken mayonnaise, whisking until it is all incorporated.

CREAMY HORSERADISH SAUCE

ABOUT 1⅓ CUPS

2 tablespoons prepared horseradish
½ cup sour cream
½ cup Mayonnaise (see opposite)

3 tablespoons heavy cream
1 tablespoon fresh lemon juice
1 teaspoon salt

In a mixing bowl, whisk all the ingredients together.

AÏOLI

Aïoli is a term generally used to refer to garlic mayonnaise, but in the Languedoc region of southern France, aïoli is a complete dish of boned salt cod, squid, hard-cooked eggs, and vegetables such as carrots or artichokes, served with a sauce.

2¼ CUPS

2 cups Mayonnaise (see Index)   *4 tablespoons pureed roasted garlic (page 7)*

Place the mayonnaise in a mixing bowl and whisk in the roasted garlic.

SMOKED TOMATO AÏOLI

This aïoli is used with the Fried Catfish Sandwich (see Index), and can be served with other foods to provide a complex flavor contrast. It makes a good all-purpose dipping sauce for anything from boiled or fried shrimp to potato chips or tortilla chips.

ABOUT 3½ CUPS

8 ripe tomatoes, smoked (page 9)
2 tablespoons pureed roasted garlic (page 7)
1 cup Mayonnaise (see Index)

1 tablespoon chipotle chile puree (pages 3 to 4) or tomato paste
Salt to taste

In a saucepan, cook the tomatoes over high heat, stirring frequently, until reduced to a thick paste. Transfer to a blender and puree with the garlic, mayonnaise, and chipotle puree or tomato paste until very smooth. Season with salt if necessary.

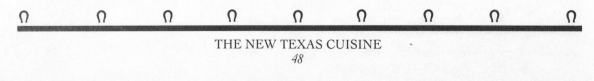

CASCABEL CHILE AÏOLI

Dried cascabel chiles are dark brown and round, and the seeds rattle when shaken. They have a subtle, slightly smoky flavor and a pleasant heat. Any other pureed chiles, such as ancho or chipotle, can be substituted. In Mexico at Christmastime, children sing "cascabel" instead of "jingle bells," to the same tune.

ABOUT 2 CUPS

2 cups Aïoli (page 48)
1 teaspoon cascabel chile puree (pages 3 to 4)
1 teaspoon paprika

½ teaspoon pure chile powder (page 4)
¼ teaspoon cayenne powder

Place the aïoli in a mixing bowl and whisk in the remaining ingredients.

SPICY COCKTAIL SAUCE

This tangy all-purpose cocktail sauce makes a good accompaniment for broiled crawfish, shrimp, or even oysters on the half shell.

ABOUT 1½ CUPS

1 cup Catsup (see Index)
4 tablespoons grated fresh horseradish
1½ teaspoons Worcestershire sauce
Zest of 1 lemon
1 tablespoon fresh lemon juice

¼ teaspoon cayenne powder
¼ teaspoon salt
2 teaspoons chipotle chile puree (pages 3 to 4)
½ teaspoon ground cumin

Mix all the ingredients together and keep refrigerated.

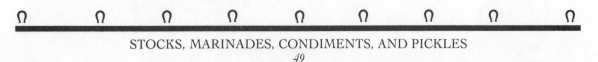

AGARITA JELLY

Agarita bushes grow mainly in the Hill Country and West Texas, and yield tart berries that ripen in May. The folks in this part of the world, by the way, usually slip in an "l" and pronounce them algeritas. I had an uncle who made agarita wine from the berries, and there was always a mason jar of it fermenting underneath his sink (I don't think Robert Mondavi has much to worry about). The harvesting of the berries is a real labor of love. Not only is it unorthodox, it can also be dangerous, as rattlesnakes have an affinity for the bushes. There was a joke, I remember growing up, that you need three items in gathering the berries: an old sheet that goes underneath the bushes to catch the fruit, a broom with which to beat the bushes, and a .22 pistol with which to "charm" the rattlers. For those of you in more remote places such as New York City or California, a good substitute for the "algeritas" is red currants or cranberries, when they're in season.

ABOUT 2 QUARTS

10 cups (2½ quarts) agarita berries
4 cups (1 quart) fruity white wine
(Gewürztraminer or Riesling)
4 cups (1 quart) water
2 cinnamon sticks

4 cloves
3 to 4 cups (1½ to 2 pounds) sugar
9 ounces liquid pectin
Paraffin

Wash the berries thoroughly. In a large stockpot combine the berries, wine, water, cinnamon, and cloves. Bring to a boil, reduce the heat, and simmer until the berries begin to burst. Continue cooking until the berries lose color.

Dampen a piece of cheesecloth and place inside a colander set over a large bowl (alternatively use a chinois). Strain the berry juice into the bowl; do not press the berries or the jelly will cloud. Add ½ cup sugar per cup of strained liquid.

Return the liquid to the pot, bring to a boil stirring continuously, reduce the heat, and simmer for 10 minutes, skimming foam. Stir in the pectin, boil for 1 minute, and remove from the heat. Pour into sterilized jars (see page 12) and seal with paraffin. (If using immediately, you do not need paraffin.) Keep refrigerated.

CACTUS PEAR JELLY

Cactus pears (tuna *in Spanish) are the fruit of the prickly-pear cactus, which, like agarita bushes, are found primarily in the Hill Country and West Texas. They are usually available at Hispanic or Latin markets, already dethorned, and the ripest fruit are a reddish purple color. Each year in the growing season, which is fall through late spring, my sister comes to visit me in Dallas from West Texas, and always brings two bushels of cactus pears she's picked at various spots along the way, using long tongs. Needless to say, the prep cooks at my restaurants don't like to see her coming! If you are able to pick your own, or in peeling them, wear thick gloves as the small, innocuous-looking, hairlike thorns can be irritating.*

2 TO 3 QUARTS

20 (3½ to 4 pounds) ripe cactus pears
3½ cups sugar
¼ cup fresh lemon juice

3 ounces liquid pectin
1 cup dry red wine
Paraffin

Using thick gloves, slice the cactus pears in half lengthwise and scoop out the pulp. Place in a food processor, whirl for 1 minute, then press the pulp and liquid through a food mill to remove the seeds (or press through a strainer).

Place the liquid in a saucepan and bring to a boil with the sugar and lemon juice. Reduce the heat and simmer for 5 minutes. Stir in the pectin and wine, bring to a boil, and remove from the heat after boiling for 30 seconds. Let stand for 30 minutes. Pour into 2 or 3 sterilized quart jars (see page 12) and seal with paraffin (if using immediately, you do not need paraffin). Keep refrigerated.

JALAPEÑO JELLY

This condiment has become a real staple in Texas, and is sold all across the state. It's a great souvenir item to take back home, or to send to other parts of the country. Although Jalapeño Jelly is a novelty item, it's also delicious. It makes a great snack mixed with an equal amount of cream cheese and served with Blue Corn Skillet Sticks (see Index).

2¼ QUARTS

3 cups cider vinegar
10 cups (5 pounds) sugar
14 jalapeño chiles, seeded and minced
3 large green New Mexico or Anaheim chiles, seeded and finely diced

1½ cups liquid pectin
Paraffin

In a large saucepan, bring the vinegar and sugar to a boil. Stir until the sugar has dissolved, and reduce the heat to a simmer. Add the chiles and simmer for 10 minutes, skimming foam. Stir in the pectin and return to a boil. Boil for 1 minute, remove from the heat, and let stand for 20 minutes. Pour into sterilized jars (see page 12) and seal with paraffin. (If using immediately, you do not need paraffin). Keep refrigerated.

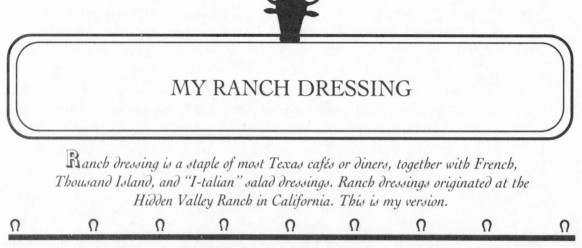

MY RANCH DRESSING

Ranch dressing is a staple of most Texas cafés or diners, together with French, Thousand Island, and "I-talian" salad dressings. Ranch dressings originated at the Hidden Valley Ranch in California. This is my version.

1 cup buttermilk, fresh if available
1½ cups Cascabel Chile Aïoli (see Index)
½ cup sour cream
1 tablespoon minced scallions
1 tablespoon chopped basil

1 teaspoon chopped marjoram
1 teaspoon chopped lemon zest
1 teaspoon balsamic vinegar
Salt and freshly ground black pepper to taste

Mix all the ingredients together and keep refrigerated.

PICKLED ONIONS

These are not the traditional onions pickled in vinegar, but instead, a chutney-style condiment cooked with vinegar and sugar. I originally made it for the Black-Eyed Pea Bisque (see Index), but it is a natural accompaniment for any sandwich in Chapter 12, and served warm with game dishes.

ABOUT 1 CUP

2 tablespoons unsalted butter
2 medium onions, julienned
1 cup light brown sugar

1 cup red wine vinegar
Salt and freshly ground black pepper to taste

In a large skillet, melt the butter and sauté the onions over medium heat until lightly browned, about 5 minutes. Add the sugar and vinegar, and simmer for about 15 minutes, stirring frequently. Season with salt and pepper. Serve warm or cold.

OKRA PICKLES

Okra, which is one of the gifts of the African-American heritage, makes great pickles, and no true Southerner would be caught at a picnic or barbecue without them on a relish tray. Use only okra pods that are less than 3 inches long, as these are the most tender. These crisp pickles will appeal to those folks who only think of okra as boiled and slimy.

1 QUART

1 pound okra pods
4 red serrano chiles
1 cup water
1 cup white wine vinegar

5 cloves garlic, minced
1 teaspoon ground turmeric
3 tablespoons freshly ground black pepper
2 tablespoons salt

Wash the okra thoroughly. Pack into 2 sterilized pint jars (see page 12), stem side up. Place 2 serranos in each jar.

In a large stainless-steel saucepan, combine the remaining ingredients. Bring to a boil, and pour over the okra, filling each jar to the top. Seal the jars immediately and store in a dark place for at least 3 weeks.

PICKLED JALAPEÑOS

One of the four major food groups in Texas cooking is pickled jalapeños. Jalapeño chiles are the most commonly used in America, and they have even made it into space, but somehow the word "jalapeño" is inextricably bound up in Texas lore. Perhaps this has most to do with Jalapeño Sam, a colorful character from San Angelo who has promoted jalapeño jelly, jalapeño lollipops, jalapeño jellybeans, and even jalapeño ice cream. Every year, he hosts the Great Jalapeño Lickoff, which any true Texan, at least, should attend at some point in their life.

1 QUART

12 large jalapeño chiles
1/2 cup olive oil
1 large onion, thinly sliced
4 large cloves garlic, minced
1 carrot, thinly sliced
1 cup cider vinegar

1/2 cup water
1 teaspoon sugar
2 teaspoons salt
1/4 cup chopped cilantro
2 bay leaves
1 teaspoon cuminseed

Place the jalapeños in 2 sterilized pint jars (see page 12). In a stainless-steel saucepan, heat the oil to lightly smoking. Sauté the onion, garlic, and carrot over medium heat for about 5 minutes. Add the vinegar, water, sugar, and salt, and bring to a boil. Remove from the heat. Add the cilantro, bay leaves, and cumin, and stir in.

Pour the liquid over the jalapeños, filling the jar to the top. Seal immediately and store in a dark place for at least 3 weeks.

VEGETABLE PICKLES

*These pickles make a good relish tray for picnics, and can be used with any sandwich.
We always keep a wide array of pickles (at least 8 to 10 different types) at Star Canyon
for our sandwiches. These pickles can be eaten immediately, but they are always better if
you allow them to mellow for 2 to 3 weeks.*

SPICY PICKLED CARROTS

1 GALLON

3 cups champagne vinegar
2 cups rice vinegar
2 cups water
4 jalapeño chiles, halved lengthwise
3 tablespoons lemon peel

½ cup fresh ginger, peeled and
sliced ½ inch thick
2 tablespoons salt
4 pounds medium (about 12) carrots,
sliced ¼ inch thick

Place all the ingredients, except the carrots, in a large stainless-steel saucepan
and bring to a boil. Add the carrots and cook for 2 minutes, until al dente. Pour
into 4 sterilized quart jars (see page 12), seal immediately, and store in a dark
place.

PICKLED BEETS

3 QUARTS

5 cups red wine vinegar
3 cups water
3 cups sugar
¼ cup kosher salt
1 clove garlic
12 black peppercorns

¼ cup fresh ginger, peeled and
sliced ¼ inch thick
1 cup basil leaves
1 cup thyme sprigs
2 pounds raw beets, washed, peeled, and
cut into ½-inch chunks

In a large stainless-steel saucepan, combine the vinegar, water, sugar, and salt, and bring to a boil. Reduce the heat and add the garlic, peppercorns, and ginger. Wrap the basil and thyme in cheesecloth, secure with string, and add to the saucepan. Simmer for 10 minutes and remove the herbs. Add the beets and continue to simmer about 15 minutes longer until al dente. Pour into 3 sterilized quart jars (see page 12), seal immediately, and store in a dark place.

DILL PICKLED CUCUMBERS

2½ QUARTS

3 pounds (about 6) medium cucumbers
3 tablespoons salt
4 cups (1 quart) champagne vinegar
1 tablespoon sugar
2 cloves garlic

½ teaspoon celery seeds
½ teaspoon mustard seeds
½ medium onion, thinly sliced
½ cup chopped fresh dillweed, or ¼ cup dried dill

Wash the cucumbers, slice ¼ inch thick or cut each lengthwise into 8 spears, and place in a colander. Sprinkle with 2 tablespoons of the salt and cover with a plate weighted with a heavy can or jar. Let stand for 1 hour. Rinse the cucumbers and drain well.

In a large stainless-steel saucepan, bring the remaining ingredients, except the dill, to a boil, simmer for 1 minute, and remove from the heat.

Place the cucumbers and dill in 5 sterilized pint jars (see page 12), and pour the liquid over, filling the jars to the top. Seal immediately, and store in a dark place.

BREAD AND BUTTER PICKLES

I remember three types of pickles when I was growing up: dill, sour, and sweet. Bread and butter pickles were the sweet kind, and of course as a child they were my favorite. I always thought the pickling process my mother went through in the late summer was fascinating, and just tasting the pickles during the winter would evoke that special time of year.

1 GALLON

5 pounds (about 10) medium cucumbers, washed
and cut into ½-inch slices
3 large onions, thinly sliced
4 tablespoons salt
4 cups crushed ice

3 cups sugar
3 cups white wine vinegar
2 teaspoons mustard seeds
1 tablespoon celery seeds
1 teaspoon ground turmeric

In a large stainless-steel pan, combine the cucumber and onion slices. Sprinkle with salt and add the ice. Cover, and let stand in the refrigerator for 3 to 4 hours. Drain and rinse with cold water.

Return the vegetables to the pan and add the remaining ingredients. Bring to a boil and remove from the heat. Pour into 4 sterilized quart jars (see page 12), seal immediately, and store in a dark place.

NOTE: Cucumbers can also be quartered lengthwise, for spears.

WATERMELON RIND PICKLES

Watermelon is another ingredient that was brought to America from Africa, so it's no surprise that this recipe probably originated in the South. These odd-sounding but delicious pickles can also be used on relish trays, as picnic or buffet items, and with sandwiches, burgers, and hot dogs.

---

1 GALLON

12 cups (3 quarts) peeled and cubed
watermelon rind
½ cup plus 1 tablespoon salt
8 cups (2 quarts) water

4 cups (1 quart) raspberry vinegar
4 cups (2 pounds) sugar
4 teaspoons cloves
4 cinnamon sticks

Place the watermelon rind in a large stainless-steel pan and cover with ½ cup of the salt and enough water to cover. Let soak overnight. Drain and rinse well.

Return the rind to the pan and add the 8 cups of water and the remaining tablespoon of salt. Bring to a boil, reduce the heat, and simmer for about 15 minutes, until the rind is tender. Drain and place the rind in ice water to stop the cooking process.

In the same pan, whisk together the vinegar and sugar. Bring to a boil, add the cloves, and continue to boil for 15 minutes. Add the blanched rinds and cook until the rinds are clear, about 4 to 5 minutes.

Pour into 4 sterilized quart jars (see page 12), add 1 cinnamon stick to each jar, and seal immediately. Store in a dark place.

AUNT JEAN'S CHOWCHOW

Jean is one of my favorite aunts and as a child I loved going to her house — she is a great cook who has always been aware of, and interested in, food and nutrition. She was the one who introduced me to the more interesting vegetables such as asparagus and mushrooms. Another reason that I liked to visit was that she and her husband Jack owned a boat, and they took me water-skiing in the summer. One of Aunt Jean's favorite activities was putting up jams, jellies, and pickles, and I fondly remember her chowchow. Like Slang Jang (see Index), it's served with beans, black-eyed peas, and chili, and as far as I'm concerned, the spicier it is, the better. We sometimes serve a tomatillo chowchow at Star Canyon alongside Pork Tenderloin with Dried Cherry Sauce and Creamed Pine Nuts (see Index).

2 QUARTS

3 pounds green tomatoes, cored and chopped
2 medium onions, chopped
1 large red bell pepper, seeded and chopped
1 large green bell pepper, seeded and chopped
1 head green cabbage, shredded
6 jalapeño chiles, seeded and chopped
3 cups cider vinegar

1½ cups sugar
¼ cup prepared horseradish
1 tablespoon mustard seeds
¼ teaspoon ground cloves
1 tablespoon ground cinnamon
2 teaspoons ground allspice
1 tablespoon salt

Combine all the ingredients in a large stainless-steel saucepan. Toss well and bring to a boil. Reduce the heat and simmer for 45 minutes to 1 hour, stirring occasionally, until most of the liquid has evaporated; the mixture should be quite thick. Pour into 2 sterilized quart jars (see page 12) and seal immediately. Store in a dark place.

PRESERVED LEMONS

I associate preserved lemons with a trip I made to Morocco. In all the tagines (long-simmered stews) I tasted from Essaouira to Marrakesh, I detected a certain tangy, almost mentholated flavor that I had trouble identifying, until I finally realized it was preserved lemon. It adds an extra, intriguing dimension to any sauce, stew, or ragout, which you can't get from using lemon rind alone.

1 QUART

10 *small lemons*
½ *cup salt*

Additional fresh lemon juice

Soak the lemons in lukewarm water for 5 days, changing the water daily. Quarter the lemons from the top to within ½ inch of the bottom. Sprinkle salt on the exposed flesh and then reshape the lemons closed.

Place 2 tablespoons of salt on the bottom of a sterilized quart jar. Pack in the lemons and push them down, adding more salt between the layers. Press on the lemons to release their juices and to make room for the remaining lemons. Cover the lemons with additional juice, leaving a ½-inch air space at the top of the jar. Cover tightly.

Let the lemons ripen in a warm place for 3 weeks, turning the jar upside down each day to distribute the salt and juice. When ready, rinse the lemons under running water. Remove lemons to use as needed; rinse under running water, and remove and discard the pulp. Once the jar is opened, there is no need to refrigerate. The preserved lemons will keep for up to 1 year.

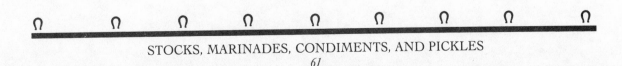

CHAPTER THREE

SALSAS, RELISHES, AND CHUTNEYS

Salsas, relishes, and chutneys can enliven even the dullest of dishes. It's hard to imagine eating most Texas food without one of these accompaniments. Although salsas are Mexican in origin and relishes are a Southern tradition, they are, for the most part, interchangeable. In Mexico, the four main building blocks for salsas are onions, garlic, chiles, and tomatoes, and regional variations of the same basic salsa may be considerable. Most salsas and relishes involve cooking, but some do not. Chutneys originate even farther afield — the Indian subcontinent — but they have been adapted here to the Texas style of cooking, where they fit in perfectly. All chutneys are cooked, and contain elements of sweet and sour flavors.

In these health-conscious days, salsas have gained popularity at least in part because they are low in cholesterol, fat, and calories. They also provide a great way to add depth and flavor dimensions to any dish, or a complexity to food served with a sauce. For example, at Star Canyon, we add a spoonful of the Pasilla-Corn Salsa to beef accompanied by chipotle barbecue sauce and Wild Mushroom Enchiladas (see Index); and Pico de Gallo to round out the flavor of chiles rellenos.

The recipes included in this chapter contain a wide variety of flavors and textures. Almost all of them can be mixed and matched with any of the recipes in this book. To think that salsas or relishes can only be made with tomatoes is to miss the crunchy sweetness of Jicama-Melon Relish, the tropical tones of Black Bean–Mango Relish, or the creamy tartness of Avocado-Tomatillo Salsa. Let your palate and tolerance level for spicy food guide you as to the degree of heat with which you infuse the recipes.

Remember that most of these recipes need nothing more than tortilla chips or good crusty bread to become a great hors d'oeuvre or tapas to accompany cocktails.

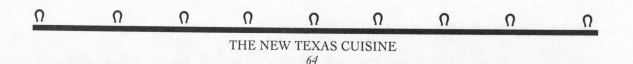

GRIDDLED SALSA ROJA

This is one of the few salsas in this chapter that is cooked, although not in the traditional Mexican style of pureeing the ingredients and then cooking in lard. Instead, the tomatoes are charred, and the blackened flecks of skin add to the appearance of the salsa. Like the Salsa Verde, this is a good multipurpose salsa that often appears in Mexican restaurants as a dipping sauce for tortilla chips. Among its many uses are as a sauce for Chilaquiles and Huevos Rancheros (see Index).

ABOUT 1 QUART

6 ripe tomatoes, halved
2 tablespoons olive oil
1 cup sliced onions
6 jalapeño chiles, seeded and sliced

4 cloves garlic, chopped
½ cup chopped cilantro
½ cup fresh lime juice
2 teaspoons salt

Place a large cast-iron skillet over high heat for 3 minutes, until smoking. Place the tomatoes in the skillet and char on both sides until black and somewhat soft. Remove from the skillet and lower the heat to medium. After 2 minutes, pour the olive oil into the skillet and immediately add the onions, jalapeños, and garlic. Cook for 3 minutes, stirring occasionally, until the vegetables are soft.

Remove the onions, jalapeños, and garlic from the skillet, and place in a food processor with the griddled tomatoes. Process until all the ingredients are blended. Transfer to a bowl and add the cilantro, lime juice, and salt.

SALSA VERDE

This deep green sauce is often used as a dipping sauce in Mexican restaurants. It's a good all-purpose salsa that goes well with most enchiladas or grilled chicken or fish.

ABOUT 2 CUPS

12 medium tomatillos (about 1 pound), husked, rinsed, and chopped
½ cup Chicken Stock (see Index)
2 cloves garlic, chopped
2 jalapeño chiles, seeded and chopped

1 teaspoon sugar
1 teaspoon fresh lime juice
½ cup chopped cilantro
2 teaspoons salt
Freshly ground black pepper to taste

Blend all ingredients until smooth. Adjust seasoning with salt and pepper.

SLANG JANG

Traditionally this is served with beans, and when I was growing up, we'd sometimes have it with pintos, and without fail on New Year's Day with black-eyed peas.

ABOUT 3 CUPS

2 ripe tomatoes, cored, seeded, and chopped
1 green bell pepper, seeded and chopped
1 small onion, chopped
2 stalks celery, chopped
1 jalapeño chile, seeded and diced

2 teaspoons sugar
½ cup cider vinegar
2 tablespoons olive oil
Salt and freshly ground black pepper to taste

In a mixing bowl, thoroughly combine all the ingredients. Let stand for 2 to 3 hours in the refrigerator. Serve chilled or at room temperature.

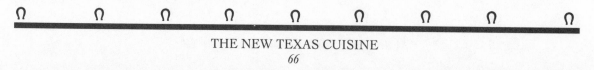

THREE TOMATO SALSAS

In addition to the refreshing quality of these salsas, the colors are vibrant and make for a striking presentation. The red tomato salsa is a staple in Southwestern cuisine; the addition of cilantro would make it the all-purpose Pico de Gallo. Yellow tomatoes are sweeter and softer-fleshed than the red, and the addition of mango and orange juice makes the salsa a wonderful accompaniment for fish. Tomatillos, the most acidic of the three, were known to have been cultivated in Aztec times, and are only now being grown in the Southwest. You can serve these salsas separately, or you can combine them into a three-tomato salsa.

TOMATILLO SALSA

ABOUT 2 CUPS

4 cloves garlic, minced
4 scallions, chopped
12 medium tomatillos (about 1 pound), husked, cored, and cut into ¼-inch dice

1 tablespoon chopped cilantro
3 serrano chiles, seeded and diced
2 teaspoons fresh lime juice
Salt to taste

RED TOMATO SALSA

ABOUT 2 CUPS

4 small (about 1 pound) red tomatoes, seeded and cut into ¼-inch dice
½ small red onion, diced
2 tablespoons red bell pepper, seeded and diced

2 cloves garlic, minced (½ tablespoon)
1 teaspoon fresh lime juice
1 red jalapeño chile, seeded and diced
Salt to taste

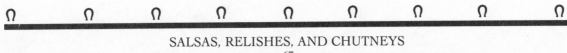

GOLDEN TOMATO SALSA

ABOUT 2 CUPS

*4 small (about 1 pound) yellow tomatoes, seeded
and diced, or 1 pint yellow cherry tomatoes, seeded
and cut into ¼-inch dice
2 serrano chiles, seeded and diced*

*2 tablespoons yellow bell pepper, seeded and diced
3 tablespoons diced mango
2 teaspoons fresh orange juice
Salt to taste*

Combine the ingredients for each salsa in 3 separate bowls. Let stand for at
least 30 minutes.

PICO DE GALLO

*Also known as "salsa fresca" or "salsa cruda," Pico de Gallo is used extensively in
Southwestern cooking. In Mexico, it's often made with oranges and jicama, and dusted
with chile powder. I once knew someone from Jalisco who made it with pineapple. At any
rate, Pico de Gallo in Spanish literally means "beak of the rooster" and there are at
least two theories about why it is so-called. One is that roosters chop up their food before
eating it, just as this salsa is chopped; another theory claims that in Mexico, the salsa is
eaten with the thumb and forefinger, mimicking the pecking action of a rooster.*

ABOUT 3 CUPS

*5 ripe tomatoes, outer flesh only, cut into
¼-inch dice
1 tablespoon chopped cilantro
1 clove garlic, minced*

*½ cup minced onion
Juice of ½ lime
2 small serrano chiles, seeded and minced
Salt and freshly ground black pepper to taste*

Combine all the ingredients in a bowl and let stand for 30 minutes before
serving. Serve at room temperature or chilled.

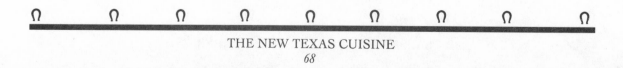

SMOKED TOMATO SALSA

I created this salsa in April 1984 for the first-ever festival of Southwestern cuisine that was held in Houston. It was around the time that I was experimenting with smoking bell peppers and onions. The festival raised a lot of questions about this burgeoning style of cooking, and it seems a long time ago now. Little did I think then I would be writing about Texas cuisine specifically. One of the issues brought up has since been asked of me more than any other question: what exactly is the difference between Tex-Mex and Southwestern food? Now I know how Paul Prudhomme or Emeril Lagasse feel when they're asked about the difference between Cajun and Creole food! Anyway, this salsa goes really well with grouper (see Index), other grilled fish, and chicken.

ABOUT 3 CUPS

4 small (about 1 pound) ripe tomatoes, halved
1 tablespoon olive oil
1 small red bell pepper, seeded and diced
1 small green bell pepper, seeded and diced
1 small yellow bell pepper, seeded and diced
(optional)

3 tablespoons diced scallions or white onion
3 small serrano chiles or jalapeños, seeded, deribbed, and minced
1 tablespoon tomato paste
2 tablespoons chopped cilantro
Salt and freshly ground black pepper to taste

Prepare the smoker (see page 9). Smoke the tomatoes, skin side down, for 10 minutes. Peel, seed, and dice the tomatoes, and set aside.

Heat the olive oil in a large skillet and sauté the bell peppers, scallions, and chiles over medium-high heat for 3 minutes. Add the smoked tomatoes and tomato paste, mix in, and warm through. Add the cilantro, remove from the heat, and season to taste.

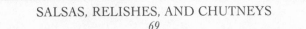

TROPICAL BLACK BEAN SALSA

This salsa is a warm version of a relish that I created with my friend Norman Van Aken in 1990 at an event at Fetzer Vineyards. Four sets of chefs from quite different regional cuisines were paired together; my partner Norman, from Miami, is a pioneer of the New World Cuisine which combines the foods and styles of Florida and the Caribbean. The other three interesting match-ups were the Midwest and Cajun; the Northwest and New England; and California and New York. This salsa goes well with meats, especially poultry and fish.

ABOUT 2 CUPS

¾ cup black beans, rinsed and soaked overnight (page 10)
3 cups Chicken Stock (see Index)
2 teaspoons olive oil
1 tablespoon chopped onion
1 large clove garlic, diced
1 tablespoon chopped carrot
1 tablespoon chopped celery
1 serrano chile, seeded and minced
2 tablespoons fresh lime juice

1 tablespoon diced mango
1 tablespoon diced pineapple
1 teaspoon diced tomato
1 teaspoon diced red bell pepper
1 teaspoon diced yellow bell pepper
1 teaspoon chopped basil
1 teaspoon chopped cilantro
½ teaspoon chopped Mexican oregano
Salt to taste

Drain the black beans, reserving the soaking liquid. Measure the liquid, which should be about 1 cup, and add enough chicken stock to make a total of 4 cups liquid. Set aside.

In a large saucepan, heat the oil until lightly smoking. Sauté the onion, garlic, carrot, celery, and serrano for about 3 minutes, stirring frequently. Add the lime juice and the 4 cups of reserved liquid. Bring to a boil and add the black beans. Reduce the heat and simmer for 45 minutes to 1 hour, until the beans are just tender.

Strain and reserve ¾ cup of the cooked bean mixture and set aside. Place the remaining bean mixture and liquid in a blender and puree. Pour back into a clean saucepan, add the reserved bean mixture and the remaining ingredients. Serve warm or at room temperature.

PASILLA-CORN SALSA

Pasilla chiles are dried, long, black chiles that are called chilacas in their fresh state (in California, fresh poblanos are erroneously referred to as pasillas). Pasillas are a common ingredient in mole sauces, especially in the Mexican state of Oaxaca. Robert del Grande cooked a mole sauce with lamb for 1,500 guests at the 1992 Napa Valley Wine Auction gala dinner that John Sedlar and I also prepared (the theme was Viva Napa Valley, which was their way of saying Southwestern). Many of the guests assumed Robert's mole sauce contained chocolate, as it was rich and dark; it didn't, and Robert explained it was because of the pasillas. We sometimes serve this salsa at Star Canyon with beef tenderloin and Wild Mushroom Enchiladas (see Index), and it accompanies the Seafood Cakes and the Chorizo Tamales (see Index).

ABOUT 2½ CUPS

1 tablespoon olive oil	1 tablespoon minced onion
1½ cups fresh corn kernels (2 ears)	1 tablespoon pureed roasted garlic (page 7)
Salt to taste	2 tablespoons pasilla chile puree (pages 3 to 4)
2 cups heavy cream	1 teaspoon chopped cilantro

Heat the oil in a skillet and sauté the corn over medium heat for 3 to 5 minutes. Season with salt and remove from the heat.

In a saucepan, bring the cream, onion, and garlic to a boil and reduce by half, whisking frequently. Remove from the heat, whisk in the chile puree and cilantro, add the sautéed corn, and adjust seasoning if necessary.

Serve warm. If reheating, do so gently so the cream does not "break."

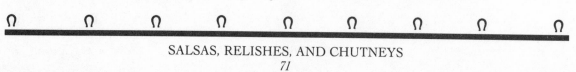

AVOCADO-TOMATILLO SALSA

*A*vocados, tomatillos, and cilantro have a natural affinity for each other, while the combination of olive oil and lime juice really livens up their flavors. Such an all-purpose salsa goes well with almost any savory dish, and it appears in several of the recipes in this book.

ABOUT 1½ CUPS

2 large avocados, peeled, pitted, and cut into medium dice
1 teaspoon diced red bell pepper
1 teaspoon diced green bell pepper
1 tablespoon diced scallion
4 tomatillos, husked, rinsed, and diced

1 clove garlic, minced
2 tablespoons cilantro leaves
2 serrano chiles, seeded and diced
2 teaspoons fresh lime juice
3 tablespoons olive oil
Salt to taste

Combine the avocados, bell peppers, scallion, and half of the tomatillos in a large mixing bowl. Place the garlic, cilantro, serranos, lime juice, and remaining tomatillos in a blender, and puree until smooth. Slowly drizzle in the oil. Pour the puree into the mixing bowl, combine thoroughly, and season with salt. Let sit for 30 minutes.

CRANBERRY SALSA

*N*eedless to say, this salsa is the perfect accompaniment for Thanksgiving dinner or Roast Turkey-Tostada Salad (see Index). It's also a great spread for leftover turkey sandwiches, and it's a good match for game in the fall. The salsa is best if it sits and macerates for several hours.

1 cup cranberries
Juice of ½ orange
⅓ cup sugar
2 red bell peppers, roasted, peeled, seeded and diced
(page 6)

3 tablespoons chopped cilantro
2 tablespoons chopped toasted pecans (page 9)
Zest of ½ lime
Zest of ½ orange
Salt to taste

In a food processor, blend the cranberries, orange juice, and sugar for 30 to 45 seconds. Transfer to a mixing bowl and add the remaining ingredients. Let sit for at least 30 minutes.

CHAYOTE–BLACK-EYED PEA RELISH

Chayote, a green squash about the same shape and size as a large pear, was a staple of the Aztecs and Mayans, and it is still used extensively in Mexican and South American cooking. In Louisiana and Florida, the chayote is known as "mirliton." It is more widely available during winter months and has a crisp, crunchy texture and an earthy flavor that suits salsas and relishes very well. This relish goes nicely with grilled chicken or fish.

ABOUT 2 CUPS

1 small chayote
1 cup cooked black-eyed peas (page 10)
1 small clove garlic, minced
1 serrano chile, deribbed, seeded, and minced
2 teaspoons chopped cilantro
4 tablespoons diced mango or papaya
2 scallions, thinly sliced (white parts only)

¼ cup roasted fresh corn kernels (page 7)
2 teaspoons fresh lime juice
2 teaspoons white wine, preferably Fall Creek
Emerald Riesling
2 tablespoons Routh Street Vinaigrette
(see Index)
Salt to taste

Peel the chayote, cut in half, and remove the seed with a knife. Cut into ¼-inch dice and place in a mixing bowl. Combine with the remaining ingredients. Let sit for at least 1 hour. Before serving, check the seasonings and adjust if necessary.

BLACK BEAN–MANGO RELISH

*B*lack beans and mangoes make a stunning combination. While this relish can be used with most dishes, it was originally created for the Blue Cornmeal Catfish (see Index). That dish, with the rich catfish, smoky peppers, and sweet mangoes provides one of the best flavor combinations I can think of.

ABOUT 2 CUPS

1 cup cooked black beans (page 10)
4 tablespoons diced mango
2 tomatillos, husked, rinsed, and diced
1 small clove garlic, minced
2 scallions, thinly sliced (white parts only)
1 serrano chile, seeded and minced
2 teaspoons chopped cilantro

¼ cup roasted fresh corn kernels (page 7)
2 teaspoons fresh lime juice
2 teaspoons fruity white wine
2 tablespoons Routh Street Vinaigrette (see Index)
Salt to taste

Thoroughly combine all the ingredients in a mixing bowl, and let sit for at least 1 hour.

PAULA'S "ROSY" RELISH

*T*his is one of the very few relishes in this chapter that is cooked. Although it is more like a chutney, I kept the name as the recipe was given to me by my friend Paula Lambert. It accompanies the Jalapeño-Stuffed Smoked Dove (see Index), a game bird that is prevalent in Texas. This relish also goes with other game and pork dishes.

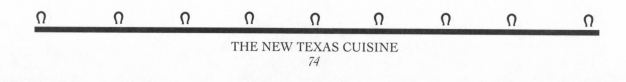

ABOUT 1¾ CUPS

2 ripe tomatoes, blanched, peeled, and chopped
(page 8)
2 large tart apples (pippin or Granny Smith),
peeled, cored, and chopped
½ cup chopped onion
½ cup chopped celery
½ cup chopped red bell pepper

1 tablespoon chopped and seeded red jalapeño chile
½ cup cider vinegar
1 cup sugar
½ cinnamon stick
1 tablespoon mustard seeds
4 cloves
1 teaspoon salt

Combine all the ingredients in a saucepan and bring to a boil. Reduce the heat
and simmer for 30 to 45 minutes, until the mixture is thick and clear. Serve
chilled.

MANGO-AVOCADO RELISH

*At first thought, mango and avocado may seem an odd combination, but in fact, they
enhance each other greatly. Their similar, soft texture is nicely offset by the crunchy
texture of the bell peppers. Use this relish with tortilla chips, on top of enchiladas, or
with fish.*

ABOUT 1⅓ CUPS

1 avocado, peeled, pitted, and cut into ¼-inch dice
1 mango, peeled, pitted, and cut into ¼-inch dice
1 teaspoon diced red bell pepper
1 teaspoon diced green bell pepper
1 tablespoon diced scallion

1 teaspoon fresh lime juice
3 tablespoons olive oil
1 teaspoon chopped cilantro
1 serrano chile, seeded and diced
Salt to taste

Combine the avocado, half of the mango, the bell peppers, and scallions in a
mixing bowl. Place the lime juice, olive oil, cilantro, serrano, and remaining
mango in a blender, and puree for 30 seconds. Drizzle over the avocado mixture. Season with salt and toss gently. Serve immediately.

JICAMA-MELON RELISH

This relish embodies the taste of summer, and it's really only worth making when melons are in peak season. Feel free to substitute whichever melons, such as Crenshaw, muskmelon, casaba, or Israeli, look ripest and best. If I had to choose one favorite salsa or relish, this is probably it. Serve with the Mixed Seafood Grill with Golden Tomato Salsa (see Index).

ABOUT 2 CUPS

1 small mango, peeled and pitted
1 serrano chile, seeded and deribbed
Juice of 1 lime
1½ tablespoons red bell pepper,
  cut into ⅛-inch dice
½ cup cantaloupe, cut into ¼-inch dice
½ cup honeydew, cut into ¼-inch dice

2 tablespoons cucumber, peeled, seeded and cut
  into ¼-inch dice
½ cup jicama, peeled and cut into ¼-inch dice
2 teaspoons chopped cilantro
¼ teaspoon salt
¼ teaspoon freshly ground black pepper
2 tablespoons sour cream

In a food processor or blender, puree the mango with the serrano chile and lime juice. Place the diced vegetables and fruit in a mixing bowl, add the puree, and thoroughly combine. Mix in the cilantro, salt, and pepper, and adjust seasoning to taste. Gently fold in the sour cream and serve immediately.

APPLE-BACON CHUTNEY

This smoky, sweet condiment goes well with grilled meat, especially quail. We also use it at Star Canyon with the Creole Sweet Potato Vichyssoise (see Index). You can add a little zip to the chutney by adding 1 or 2 seeded and diced serranos, or ½ teaspoon cayenne powder.

1½ cups apple cider vinegar
¾ cup dark brown sugar
1 cup diced smoked bacon
2 tart green apples (pippin or Granny Smith),
cored and diced

Juice of 2 lemons
¼ cup diced onion
2 tablespoons diced red bell pepper
2 tablespoons diced green bell pepper
Salt to taste

In a large saucepan, combine the vinegar and sugar and cook over high heat for 15 minutes, whisking for the first 30 seconds to dissolve the sugar.

In a small skillet, cook the diced bacon over medium-high heat for 3 to 5 minutes, until the fat renders. Drain the bacon.

Add the bacon and all the remaining ingredients, except the salt, to the vinegar mixture and cook for 10 minutes more. Remove from the heat, let cool completely, and season with salt.

TOMATILLO-JALAPEÑO CHUTNEY

This was one of the first condiments we developed at Routh Street Cafe, and we served it for some time with grilled quail and warm goat cheese, together with Chayote–Black-Eyed Pea Relish (see Index). This chutney goes well with any game dish.

ABOUT 2 CUPS

12 medium tomatillos (about 1 pound), husked,
rinsed, and chopped
2 small red bell peppers, seeded and diced
1 small green bell pepper, seeded, and diced
8 scallions, thinly sliced
4 jalapeño chiles, seeded and minced
⅔ cup red wine vinegar

½ cup fresh corn kernels (1 small ear)
¼ cup firmly packed light brown sugar
1 tablespoon chopped cilantro
1 teaspoon salt
1 clove garlic, minced
¼ teaspoon cayenne powder
¼ teaspoon ground cumin

In a large saucepan, bring all the ingredients to a boil, stirring frequently. Reduce the heat and boil gently until thick, stirring occasionally, 30 to 35 minutes. Let cool completely. Cover and refrigerate until ready to serve.

APRICOT-ALMOND CHUTNEY

Apricots and almonds are one of my favorite combinations. In fact, I have a general rule of thumb that any fruit with pits goes well with almonds. Because apricots have a natural affinity for pork, I created this chutney for the Tamarind-Glazed Pork Chop with Green Chile Spoon Bread (see Index), but it goes equally well with other grilled meats.

ABOUT 3 CUPS

11 ounces dried apricots, diced
1¼ cups boiling water
1 cup packed light brown sugar
2 small onions, thinly sliced
1 teaspoon ground ginger
1 cup red wine vinegar

2 tablespoons chopped cilantro
2 cloves garlic, chopped
¼ teaspoon salt
1 cup blanched sliced almonds, toasted and
coarsely chopped (page 9)

Place the apricots in a stainless-steel bowl and cover with the boiling water. Let stand for 1 hour.

Drain the apricots and reserve the soaking liquid. Transfer the liquid to a saucepan and reduce to about 2 tablespoons.

In a clean saucepan, combine the apricots, reduced liquid, and all the remaining ingredients, except the almonds. Bring to a boil, reduce the heat, and simmer for about 30 minutes, stirring occasionally. Remove from the heat and stir in the almonds. Let cool completely. Cover and refrigerate until ready to serve.

WARM CRANBERRY-ORANGE COMPOTE

This condiment, which was created for Baby Routh's opening menu, is a natural partner for turkey and game. It accompanies the Turkey-Yam Hash (see Index) and Venison Tamales (see Index), and we often serve it at Routh Street Cafe with smoked pheasant. With the pecans and cranberries, it embodies the taste of fall and the holiday season.

ABOUT 1 QUART

Juice of 2 large oranges
1 cup sugar
1 pound cranberries
Zest of 1 orange

½ cup toasted pecans (page 9)
1 tablespoon chopped mint
2 tablespoons Grand Marnier

In a saucepan, bring the orange juice and sugar to a boil. Add the cranberries and orange zest, reduce the heat, and simmer for about 5 minutes, until the cranberries burst their skins. Remove from the heat and stir in the pecans, mint, and Grand Marnier. Serve warm.

SALSAS, RELISHES, AND CHUTNEYS

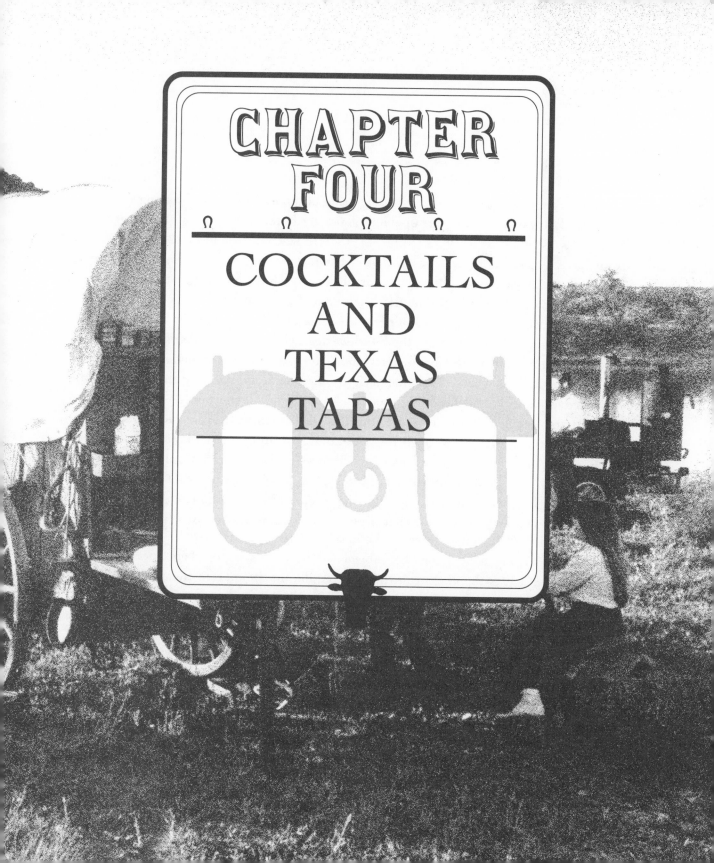

CHAPTER FOUR

COCKTAILS AND TEXAS TAPAS

I'll never forget a sign I once saw as I was getting off an elevator in a Washington, D.C., hotel. The sign was promoting the opening of a sister hotel in Texas, and to me, it said it all: GRACIOUS HOSPITALITY WAS INVENTED IN THE SOUTH AND PERFECTED IN TEXAS. Texans have long been known for their freewheeling entertaining and knack for having fun, and that's exactly what this chapter is all about. These recipes are a great way to sample the variety of flavors and the flair that make Texas food and drink unique.

You'll notice that at least one third of the cocktails in this chapter contain tequila, which is very popular in Texas and the Southwestern United States. Tequila is a regional Mexican liquor made from the maguey, or blue agave plant, and is named after the village in the state of Jalisco where it originated. Tequila is made by roasting the hearts of the mature agave plants, then shredding them and extracting all the juices, which are then fermented and distilled. Tequila right out of the still is white and referred to as *plata* or *blanco*; *reposado* is tequila that is aged for two months up to one year; and *añejo* is tequila that is aged at least one year, and usually for three to four years. While most Texans think of tequila as an ingredient for margaritas or as a liquor to be "shot" and "chased" with lime wedges, there is a growing following of connoisseurs who prefer to sip a well-aged tequila in much the same way that cognac or Scotch is appreciated by afficionados.

My good friend Lucinda Hutson, who knows everything that's worth knowing about tequila and is writing a book on the subject (to be published by Ten Speed Press in 1994), says that it was the margarita that put tequila on the map in the 1940s. She also reminds me that we shared a memorable tequila experience while searching for our friend Patricia Quintana's ranch for four hours in a blinding Mexican rainstorm. I was driving while Lucinda navigated and sang along with the lusty rancheras fading on the radio. She succeeded in talking the owner of a roadside cantina out of a bottle of tequila, which warmed our cold and drenched bodies and greatly lifted our spirits.

Lucinda writes: "Only a few regions in Mexico — most notably in the state of Jalisco — can produce tequila, just as only certain areas in France can produce cognac. It takes the silver-blue agave plant 8 to 12 years to reach its prime, at which time workers uproot the entire plant in order to harvest its 'heart'.

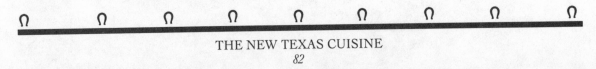

"Mexican law allows distillers to augment the naturally produced sugars with 49 percent of added sugars; however, 51 percent must come only from the blue agave variety. Naturally, 100 percent agave tequilas (with no added sugars) are much costlier to produce and leave the fruity flavor of the agave intact; a government seal certifies the authenticity. Now in great demand, these tequilas rival the price of a fine cognac."

Other cocktails and punches in this chapter include Texas wine, which is steadily becoming a significant force in the national market. It still amazes me when I talk to out-of-town guests at Star Canyon who are shocked to find Texas wines on our list. Obviously, other wines can be substituted in the recipes that follow, as the production of Texas wines is still limited and they can be hard to find outside the state. More information on Texas wines can be found in the Appendix.

Tapas fit into the tradition of hors d'oeuvres and Mexican *antojitos*, and I've adapted them here to the Texas style. *Tapa* is Spanish for "lid; cover." Tapas bars originated in Spain and were so called because the little bites of food were served on plates small enough to fit on top of a wine or beer glass so they could be eaten while standing up.

I vividly remember my first experience of tapas, which followed my induction into the (now defunct) *Cook's* magazine Who's Who of Cooking in America in 1985. The ceremony was held at The Palladium in New York, which at that time was the hottest disco/night spot in the city, and Julia Child and Craig Claiborne were the MC's. Afterwards, a group of about forty colleagues and friends went to eat at El Internacional, which was the fashionable new tapas place in town. The little plates of delicious food just kept coming out, and it was a terrific way to eat.

You can make the cocktails and tapas in this chapter the subject of a theme party, just as Wolfgang Puck has for years. Wolf and his wife, Barbara Lazaroff, host one of the most important fund-raising and social events in the country every fall in Los Angeles — the proceeds of which go toward Meals on Wheels. For the last few years, the event has been held on the Western set at Universal Studios, and the guests are invited to dress in Western style. Texana may come in and out of fashion, but this kind of theme makes for a great party, especially if you have the appropriate food and drink to go with it. Incidentally, one of the fun parts for me is to spot the difference between the drugstore, one-day cowboys who attend the Meals on Wheels event and the genuine article, in the form of Warren Clark's crew from Clark's Outpost restaurant in Tioga, Texas, which is about one and a half hours north of Dallas. They serve some of the best barbecue in the country, and it gives the guests at the fundraising event the opportunity of sampling the real thing.

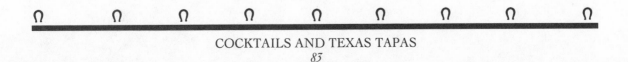

TEQUILA SOLO

Tequila is certainly Mexico's best-loved liquor, and its popularity crossed the Texas border centuries ago. It should not be confused with the more rustic mezcal, which is less distilled, a little rougher, and best known for the worm at the bottom of the bottle (a friend of mine jokes that the worm is there so you never have to drink alone). True tequila aficionados might balk at drinking a Tequila Solo because to them, a well-aged tequila is like a fine cognac or Scotch whisky which should be sipped and enjoyed at length. On the other hand, to write a book about Texas cuisine, culture, and customs without instructions on the pleasures of slamming back a shot of tequila would be heresy!

1 COCKTAIL

1½ ounces (1 jigger) aged tequila
1 lime wedge

Salt

Pour the tequila into a shot glass. Hold your left hand spread so the thumb and index finger shape an "L." Moisten the area between the thumb and index finger with your tongue or a little lime juice. Sprinkle salt on the moistened area. Bite into the lime, extracting the juice, lick the salt from your hand, and down the tequila in a single gulp. Chase with another bite of lime if necessary.

PRAIRIE FIRE

It seems as though every time I run into my friend Jasper White from Boston, he reminds me of a certain night in Dallas when a group of us gathered at Primo's after he had cooked at Routh Street Cafe to celebrate its fifth anniversary. The entire kitchen staff and Jasper held a Prairie Fire–consuming contest. This cocktail is also known as a "Desert Rose," because if the Tabasco sauce hits the tequila just right, it quickly forms a delicate rose shape in the glass. The more of these you drink, the easier it is to see the rose!

---

1 COCKTAIL

1½ ounces (1 jigger) tequila
2 drops of Tabasco sauce

Salt
1 lime wedge

Pour the tequila into a shot glass. Carefully add the Tabasco to the tequila. Hold your left hand spread so the thumb and index finger shape an "L." Moisten the area between the thumb and index finger with your tongue or a little lime juice. Sprinkle salt on the moistened area. Bite into the lime, extracting the juice, lick the salt from your hand, and down the tequila in a single gulp. Chase with another bite of lime if necessary.

PITCHER OF PERFECT 'RITAS

There are many stories about the origin of the margarita, and one of the most popular is that it was invented by Francisco Morales of Juarez, the twin city of El Paso, who named the cocktail after his wife Margarita. It's the classic Texas and Southwestern favorite, and just the thing to preface a dinner on a hot summer's evening.

---

12 TO 14 COCKTAILS

3 cups fresh lime juice
1¼ cups superfine sugar
3 cups Herradura gold tequila

⅓ cup Triple Sec
Ice cubes
Salt

Combine lime juice and sugar in a pitcher and let stand, stirring occasionally, until sugar has dissolved. Add tequila, Triple Sec, and ice cubes, and stir vigorously until thoroughly chilled. Strain into salt-rimmed martini glasses.

MANGO MARGARITA

This refreshing, tropical drink is a welcome variation on the classic margarita. One of the best mango margaritas to be had anywhere is made by Miguel Ravago at Fonda San Miguel in Austin. Fonda San Miguel is probably the finest example of Mexican cuisine that has crossed the border, and the food is served in a setting worthy of the wonderful flavors.

4 COCKTAILS

½ cup fresh lime juice
5 tablespoons superfine sugar
2 ripe mangoes, peeled, pitted, and chopped

¾ cup (4 jiggers) tequila
1½ ounces (1 jigger) Triple Sec
Crushed ice

Combine the lime juice and sugar in a large bowl, and let stand, stirring occasionally, until the sugar has dissolved. In a blender, puree the chopped mango, add the tequila and Triple Sec, and blend until smooth, about 30 seconds. Serve in margarita glasses over crushed ice.

LUCINDA'S MARGARITA PICOSITA

As I mentioned in the introduction to this chapter, my good friend Lucinda Hutson, author of The Herb Garden Cookbook, *is writing a book about tequila. She knows more about the subject than anyone, so I asked her for a recipe, preferably one using her chile-infused tequila. Here it is:*

"Although brands of pepper-flavored tequila are commercially available, I prefer to make my own. Simply place 2 to 4 chiles — such as jalapeños, serranos, or even the fiery habaneros — on wooden skewers, and place them in a bottle of tequila (I prefer Sauza

Hornitos tequila or a premium silver tequila). Taste after a few days; add or remove chiles to achieve desired piquancy. Serve in icy cold shots, Bloody Marys, or in margaritas, and use in marinades, salsas, stews, or with beans. Best of all, use the peppered tequila in this recipe; for a 'hotter' margarita, add more peppered tequila and less silver tequila."

3 COCKTAILS

1 lime wedge
Kosher salt
1½ ounces (1 jigger) peppered tequila (see note above)
3 ounces (2 jiggers) Herradura, El Tesoro, or another premium silver tequila

3 ounces (2 jiggers) fresh lime juice
1½ ounces (1 jigger) Grand Marnier
1½ ounces (1 jigger) Cointreau
Crushed ice

Chill 3 margarita glasses for 1 hour. Just prior to serving, rim the edges of the glasses with the lime wedge and dip into the salt. Place the remaining ingredients into a cocktail shaker and shake well. Strain into the chilled glasses. ¡Ay ay ay!

MEXI-DRIVER

This is a south-of-the-border twist on the old classic Screwdriver, and bears no reflection whatever on taxi drivers in Mexico!

4 COCKTAILS

4 cups (1 quart) fresh orange juice
3 ounces (2 jiggers) tequila
2 ounces (1⅓ jiggers) Triple Sec

1 ounce (⅔ jigger) vodka
Ice cubes
4 orange wedges, for garnish

Combine all the ingredients except orange wedges in a pitcher and stir vigorously until thoroughly chilled. Serve in highball glasses and garnish with an orange wedge.

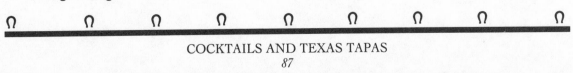

WEST TEXAS SUNSET

This recipe is not so different from the more familiar Tequila Sunrise — it uses fresh pomegranate juice rather than grenadine. Grenadine syrup used to be made from pomegranates grown on the Caribbean island of Grenada, but it now contains other fruit concentrates as well as colorings. I really think this cocktail is worth making only when pomegranates (preferably from Texas) are in season, in the fall and early winter. Its name reflects the fact that you are more likely to drink this at cocktail hour, as the sun is setting when the evenings are drawing in, than at sunrise! I've seen sunsets all over the world, and none are more spectacular than those in West Texas.

4 COCKTAILS

2 cups fresh orange juice
¾ cup (4 jiggers) tequila
Crushed ice
½ cup fresh pomegranate juice

3 tablespoons Simple Syrup (see Index), or
superfine sugar to taste
Pomegranate seeds, for garnish

In a cocktail shaker, combine orange juice, tequila, and ice. Shake well and strain into tall glasses filled with ice. Combine pomegranate juice and simple syrup, and carefully float on top of the cocktail. Garnish with pomegranate seeds.

SANGRITA

This is similar to a Bloody Mary, but you'll find the flavors rather different. The name is a contraction of the Spanish words sangre, *meaning "blood," and* grita, *meaning "uproar." If you want to increase the grita, add more jalapeños and Tabasco! This cocktail makes a good addition to any brunch item in Chapter 12.*

3 cups tomato juice
¼ cup cocktail onions
2 small cloves garlic, chopped
2 teaspoons Worcestershire sauce
1 teaspoon salt
2 jalapeño chiles, seeded and chopped
¼ teaspoon dillseed

½ teaspoon celery seed
¾ teaspoon prepared horseradish
Juice of 2 limes
6 ounces (4 jiggers) gold tequila
6 to 8 drops Tabasco sauce
Ice cubes
4 lime wedges, for garnish

Combine all the ingredients except ice and lime wedges in a blender. Puree until completely smooth, about 1 minute. Strain, and pour into tall ice-filled glasses. Garnish with the lime wedges.

ATHENS (TEXAS) PEA-TINI

Athens, Texas, claims to be the Black-Eyed Pea Capital of the Planet. Each year Athens holds a Black-Eyed Pea Jamboree. One event is a cookoff. Back in 1972, Bill Perryman emerged from the Cookoff with a Conviviality Award for his martini garnished with 2 black-eyed peas soaked in chile puree for 3 weeks. This is my version.

4 COCKTAILS

¼ cup dried black-eyed peas
6 jalapeño chiles, or 10 serrano chiles, sliced
(seeds not removed)
½ teaspoon salt

¾ cup (4 jiggers) gin
1½ ounces (1 jigger) dry vermouth
Crushed ice

Place the black-eyed peas, chiles, and salt in a small saucepan and cover with enough water to come 2 inches above the ingredients. Bring to a boil, reduce the heat, and simmer for 40 to 50 minutes, until the beans are tender. Remove the pan from the heat and let sit for 6 hours. Drain and reserve the beans.

In a cocktail shaker, combine the gin, vermouth, and ice, and strain into martini glasses. Garnish with several of the reserved black-eyed peas.

LAREDO GIN FIZZ

This cocktail originated in Nuevo Laredo, the Mexican border town across from Laredo in southern Texas. Enjoy this luscious, frothy white drink while you imagine relaxing in one of the Laredo bars. Flowerwater, which is commonly used in Moroccan and French cooking, can be obtained from specialty markets. This drink is refreshingly tart. If a sweeter drink is preferred, increase the amount of sugar.

4 COCKTAILS

1 tablespoon orange flowerwater
½ cup fresh orange juice
1 teaspoon orange zest
½ cup superfine sugar
¼ cup fresh lime juice
¼ cup fresh lemon juice

¾ cup (4 jiggers) gin
4 egg whites
½ cup heavy cream
2 cups crushed ice
4 orange slices, for garnish (optional)

Combine all the ingredients in a blender, and blend until frothy. Pour into tall glasses and garnish with an orange slice, if desired.

FERMENTED PINEAPPLE-RUM DAIQUIRIS

This cocktail is inspired by my friend Mark Miller, who serves a variation at both his restaurants — Coyote Cafe in Santa Fe, and Red Sage in Washington, D.C. The first time I ever tasted it was in Mark's Coyote Corral bar. A number of chef colleagues and friends were gathered, and I remember the daiquiri mixture in the large glass jar on the top of the bar dwindling rapidly as the evening wore on. I currently have a jar of this concoction that's been fermenting in my refrigerator at home for 10 months. Every month or so, a few friends gather to check its progress — they call it my science project.

2 cups Myers's dark rum
1 cup light rum
1 cup coconut-flavored rum (such as Malibu)
1 vanilla bean, split in half lengthwise
1 large ripe pineapple, peeled, cored, and cut into
1-inch dice

½ cup brown sugar
2 serrano chiles, halved lengthwise (seeds not
removed)
2 cinnamon sticks
½ cup crushed peppermint

Place all the ingredients in a large glass jar with a tight-fitting lid. Place in a warm-water bath and bring the rum to 100° F. to begin the fermentation process. Let cool, keeping the jar covered, and let stand at room temperature for at least 48 hours and preferably longer.

Store in the refrigerator. Ladle liquid into chilled martini glasses.

TROPICAL BANANA WHAM

Like the Hot Baby Routh, this could easily double as dessert, albeit a potent one. It's just the cocktail to drink lying poolside or on some tropical beach — or, come to think of it, in a hammock in your back yard. Don't forget the paper umbrellas!

2 COCKTAILS

½ cup Vanilla Bean Ice Cream (see Index)
1 very ripe banana, peeled and sliced
¼ cup passion fruit puree or juice
¼ cup canned sweetened coconut milk

1 ounce (2 tablespoons) light rum
2 ounces (4 tablespoons) banana liqueur
1 ounce (2 tablespoons) Myers's dark rum

Combine all the ingredients except for the dark rum in a blender, and blend until smooth. Pour into chilled glasses and carefully float ½ ounce (1 tablespoon) dark rum in each glass.

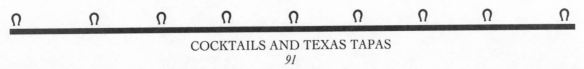

PADRE ISLAND COCONUT RUM PUNCH

For those who visualize Texas as nothing but flat, dry prairie, a visit to Padre Island and coastal far-south Texas will make you think again. Here you will find long, white, sandy beaches, coconut groves and tall palms . . . This is the cocktail of choice for many who spend spring break on Padre Island basking in the sun or dancing until dawn.

4 COCKTAILS

3 ounces (2 jiggers) light rum
4 tablespoons Simple Syrup (see Index)
¼ teaspoon vanilla extract
1 cup fresh coconut milk or canned, sweetened coconut milk (see Note)

1 cup finely crushed ice
Freshly grated nutmeg for garnish (optional)
4 slices pineapple for garnish (optional)

In a cocktail shaker, combine the rum, simple syrup, vanilla, coconut milk, and ice, and shake vigorously. Pour, unstrained, into 8-ounce goblets or wine-glasses. Garnish with the nutmeg and pineapple slices if desired.

NOTE: If using canned, sweetened coconut milk, decrease the simple syrup to 2 tablespoons.

HILL COUNTRY WINE SPRITZER

While some would say this is an adulteration of good wine, many would tell you that spritzers and coolers are a good introduction for those whose viticultural knowledge is limited to wines with high residual sugars or those fermented with strawberries. To transform this into a cooler, just substitute 7-Up or Sprite for the Artesia.

Crushed ice
Fall Creek Granite Blush (or other
Texas blush wine)

Artesia (or other sparkling water)
4 lemon slices, for garnish

Fill 4 highball glasses three quarters full of crushed ice. Half fill the glasses with wine, and top up with Artesia. Stir to combine, and garnish each glass with a lemon slice.

TEXAS SANGRIA

The essential idea behind this recipe is that all the ingredients, and especially the wine, must hail from Texas. In dire emergency you may substitute inferior out-of-state products, but the responsibility will be on your shoulders! ¡Viva La Tejas!

12 TO 14 COCKTAILS

³/₄ cup water
½ cup superfine sugar
2 cinnamon sticks
1 bottle dry red wine, such as Pheasant Ridge
Cabernet or Fall Creek Carnelian (must be
from Texas)
Juice of 2 oranges (from the Texas Valley)

Juice of 2 limes (may be from Mexico if not
available from Texas)
Juice of 1 grapefruit (must be ruby red from
the Texas Valley)
Crushed ice
12 to 14 orange slices, for garnish
12 to 14 mint sprigs, for garnish

In a saucepan, bring the water and sugar to a boil with the cinnamon sticks. Stir until the sugar has dissolved and then remove from the heat. Cover the pan and let the cinnamon infuse for 30 minutes.

In a large punch bowl or pitcher, combine the red wine, cinnamon-sugar mixture, and the fruit juices. Fill with crushed ice and stir until well chilled. Serve in well-chilled tumblers and garnish with orange slices and mint.

PEPPER-MINT JULEP

The mint julep, traditionally served ice cold in a silver mug, symbolizes the epitome of Southern hospitality. There is ardent debate about the authentic recipe, and in any event, I take things a step further here by introducing a controversial and Southwestern twist, in the form of a jalapeño chile.

4 COCKTAILS

⅔ cup mint sprigs (25 to 30), reserving 4 mint sprigs for garnish
2 tablespoons superfine sugar
1 jalapeño chile, sliced, seeded, and chopped

¼ cup ice-cold water
1½ cups (8 jiggers) bourbon
Shaved or finely crushed ice

Using a mortar and pestle, grind the mint together with the sugar and jalapeño, and transfer to a mixing bowl. Or, place the ingredients in a mixing bowl and crush with a wooden spoon. Cover with the ice-cold water and stir to dissolve the sugar. Add the bourbon and let sit in the refrigerator for at least 1 hour.

Fill 4 highball glasses with the ice. Strain the chilled mixture into the glasses, and place the glasses in the freezer for at least 20 minutes, until they become frosty. Serve with a straw, taking care not to wipe off the frost, and garnish each glass with a mint sprig.

LUCKENBACH LEMONADE

Luckenbach (population somewhere between 1 and 5) is located in the Hill Country not far from Fredericksburg. The hamlet consists of a general store, a dance hall, and several outbuildings, and was promoted tirelessly by Hondo Crouch, who bought Luckenbach in the early 1970s and coined the slogan "Everybody's somebody in Luckenbach." The Ladies' State Championship Chili Cookoff is held in Luckenbach every October, and the Texan country singer Jerry Jeff Walker recorded an album live there. Waylon Jennings added to Luckenbach's mystique with his classic song "Luckenbach, Texas." As my editor, John Harrisson, photographer Matthew Savins, and I traveled the highways and byways of Texas to bring you this book, Waylon's refrain became our official anthem.

This alliterative cocktail is a delicious cross between a whiskey sour and lemonade.

4 COCKTAILS

2 cups fresh lemon juice
1 cup Artesia (Texas sparkling water) or other sparkling water
³/4 cup superfine sugar

2 ounces (¼ cup) bourbon
2 ounces (¼ cup) vodka
Ice cubes
4 mint sprigs, for garnish

Combine all the ingredients except for the mint sprigs in a pitcher and stir to dissolve the sugar. Chill thoroughly. Pour into sugar-rimmed glasses filled with ice, and garnish with mint sprigs.

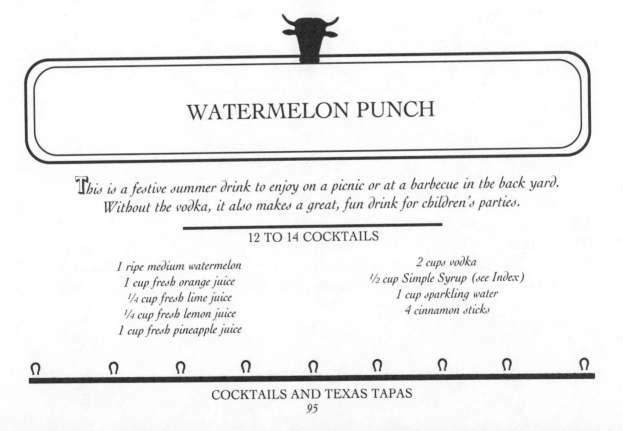

WATERMELON PUNCH

This is a festive summer drink to enjoy on a picnic or at a barbecue in the back yard. Without the vodka, it also makes a great, fun drink for children's parties.

12 TO 14 COCKTAILS

1 ripe medium watermelon
1 cup fresh orange juice
¼ cup fresh lime juice
¼ cup fresh lemon juice
1 cup fresh pineapple juice

2 cups vodka
½ cup Simple Syrup (see Index)
1 cup sparkling water
4 cinnamon sticks

Decoratively cut the watermelon in half, lengthwise or crosswise. Remove the flesh from both halves of the watermelon, and discard one of the empty halves. Slice a thin portion off the bottom of the other half so it will remain sturdy and not roll, and reserve. Press the watermelon flesh through a food mill or strainer to remove the seeds, reserving the juice in a large mixing bowl. Add the remaining ingredients, combine, and chill thoroughly. Pour the punch into the reserved watermelon half. Ladle into punch glasses.

HOT BABY ROUTH

This is one of the great, all-time, decadent, cold-weather, fireplace drinks. It could even suffice for dessert. Obviously, it's my hot and liquid rendition of the chocolate bar, in a glass. The hazelnut flavor of the Frangelico, the orangey essence of the Tuaca, and the almond-based amaretto make a perfect combination and match for the other ingredients.

6 COCKTAILS

3 ounces (2 jiggers) Frangelico
3 ounces (2 jiggers) Tuaca
3 ounces (2 jiggers) amaretto
2¾ cups freshly brewed hot coffee
6 tablespoons chocolate syrup or Hot Fudge Sauce
(see Index)

¾ cup whipped cream
6 tablespoons Caramel Sauce (see Index)
6 tablespoons peanuts, shelled, roasted, and
chopped (page 8)
¾ cup bittersweet chocolate shavings, for garnish

In a pan over low heat, gently warm the 3 liqueurs. Add the hot coffee and stir in the chocolate syrup or hot fudge sauce. Pour into wineglasses and top each cocktail with 2 tablespoons of whipped cream. Drizzle the caramel sauce over the cream and sprinkle with a tablespoon of the peanuts. Garnish with the chocolate shavings.

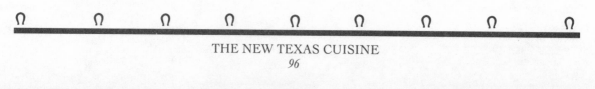

SMOKED CHICKEN NACHOS WITH AVOCADO-TOMATILLO SALSA AND ASIAGO

Nachos — quartered, crisply fried corn tortillas topped with cheese or a variety of ingredients — are definitely a Texan invention. They are a staple appetizer in Tex-Mex restaurants and at many sports arenas around the country. This particular version was created for the opening of Tejas in Minneapolis, and it immediately became a signature item there. Mark Haugen, the Executive Chef at Tejas, has asked, only partly in jest, for an additional "nacho room" — a preparation space just for nachos! He also thinks we should put up a sign, like a certain fast-food burger place, enumerating the millions we've sold. You can substitute Monterey Jack, white Cheddar, or any kind of soft grating cheese for the asiago, while the more readily available smoked turkey can be used instead of the chicken.

6 TO 8 SERVINGS

1 chicken, about 3 pounds
All-Purpose Brine for Smoking Meats and
Poultry (see Index)
1½ cups Avocado-Tomatillo Salsa (see Index)
3 cups Pico de Gallo (see Index)

Vegetable or canola oil, for frying tortillas
16 Corn Tortillas (see Index), cut into quarters
Salt to taste
4 cups grated asiago cheese
Sour cream, for garnish

Marinate the chicken in the brine overnight in the refrigerator.

Prepare the smoker (page 9). Remove the chicken from the brine, pat dry, and smoke for about 1½ hours, or until the breast meat is firm but springs back when squeezed. If necessary, finish cooking in a 350° F. oven until done.

Meanwhile, prepare the avocado-tomatillo salsa and Pico de Gallo, and set aside. Preheat the oven to 375° F.

Heat enough oil in a large skillet to come ½ inch up the sides. Fry the tortilla quarters until crisp. Drain thoroughly on paper towels and lightly salt.

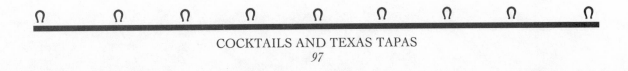

Remove the meat from the chicken and cut into ¼-inch dice. Spread the tortilla chips on a baking sheet and cover with the diced chicken. Cover with the salsa and then sprinkle the grated asiago over the top. Place in the oven and bake until the cheese has completely melted, about 15 minutes.

To serve, spoon the Pico de Gallo on top of the nachos and garnish with sour cream.

CHICKEN FLAUTAS

When I think of chicken flautas, I think of the early days at Routh Street Cafe when the kitchen staff would go next door to what was then Pepe's Cafe. Their favorite was the #2 on the menu: sour cream chicken enchiladas with chicken flautas and guacamole. Knowing my weakness for flautas, many of the staff would save me theirs so I could enjoy them as a midnight snack as I worked on the next day's menu. You can roast or grill the chicken, smoke it as in the previous recipe, or use the method given in Chapter 8 (Chicken–Sour Cream Enchiladas, page 208).

12 SERVINGS

1 tablespoon vegetable oil
½ cup finely chopped onion
2 cloves garlic, minced
1 jalapeño chile, seeded and minced
2 tomatillos, husked, rinsed, and minced
1 poblano chile, roasted, peeled, seeded, and diced (page 6)
½ cup Chicken Stock (see Index)

1 cup finely diced cooked chicken
1 tablespoon chopped cilantro
Salt and freshly ground black pepper to taste
2 tablespoons sour cream
Vegetable or canola oil, for softening and deep-frying tortillas
12 Corn Tortillas (see Index)

In a large skillet, heat the tablespoon of oil and sauté the onion, garlic, and jalapeño over high heat until the onions are translucent, about 2 minutes. Add the tomatillos and poblano, and cook for 30 seconds more. Add the stock and chicken, and continue cooking until the chicken stock is reduced to a glaze. Add the cilantro and season with salt and pepper. Stir in the sour cream, remove from the heat, and let cool slightly.

In another skillet, heat enough oil to come ½ inch up the sides. Over medium heat, bring the oil to 350° F. or just smoking. Submerge the tortillas in the oil one by one for 5 seconds each to soften. Drain the tortillas on paper towels and keep warm; do not stack the tortillas.

Divide the chicken mixture among the tortillas and roll them up. Secure the ends with toothpicks to ensure the flautas will not unroll when fried. Add more oil to the skillet to deep-fry the flautas. Reheat the oil to just smoking and deep-fry as many flautas as will fit at a time for about 30 seconds, until crisp.

Remove the flautas from the pan, take out the toothpicks, and drain the flautas on paper towels. Repeat for the remaining flautas. Cut them in half, if desired, and serve with any of the salsas or relishes from Chapter 3.

CHILE CON QUESO

I've been eating chile con queso, which literally means chile with cheese, for as long as I can remember. It is difficult for me to thoroughly enjoy a meal in any of my favorite Tex-Mex restaurants without a side of chile con queso for the tostadas. It's traditionally served with tortilla chips and pickled jalapeños, and don't make the horrible mistake of thinking that the only two ingredients used in the real thing are the processed cheese "food" that melts so easily and tomatoes canned with chiles. I mention no names!

4 SERVINGS

2 tablespoons vegetable oil
¾ cup chopped onions
3 cloves garlic, minced
2 tablespoons flour
1 cup milk
2 New Mexican or Anaheim green chiles, roasted, peeled, seeded, and diced (page 6)

3 jalapeño chiles, seeded and diced
2 medium tomatoes, blanched, peeled, seeded, and chopped (page 8)
6 ounces Monterey Jack cheese, grated
10 ounces Longhorn Cheddar cheese, grated
½ cup sour cream

In a skillet, heat the oil until lightly smoking. Sauté the onions and garlic over medium-high heat until the onions are translucent, about 2 to 3 minutes. Whisk in the flour and cook for 1 minute; when the mixture begins to darken, whisk in the milk to make a thick sauce.

Lower the heat to a simmer, stir in the chiles and tomatoes, and heat through for about 30 seconds. Stir in the cheeses. When the cheeses have melted, whisk in the sour cream and just heat through; you should have about 3½ cups. Serve immediately. Chile con queso can be kept warm in a double boiler or chafing dish. If reheating, do so gently in a double boiler.

CAJUN SPICED PECANS

These pecans can be absolutely addictive. While they were first developed as an accompaniment to the Creole Sweet Potato Vichyssoise (see Index), they make a great snack anytime and especially at cocktail hour. The pecans should be kept in an airtight container, where they will keep indefinitely.

ABOUT 3 CUPS

2 tablespoons unsalted butter	*2 teaspoons pure chile powder (page 4)*
3 cups pecan halves	*1 tablespoon ground cumin*
½ cup light brown sugar	*¼ cup cider vinegar*
1 teaspoon paprika	*Salt to taste*

Preheat the oven to 350° F. In a large skillet, melt the butter over medium heat. Add the pecans and sauté until lightly browned, about 3 minutes. Add the brown sugar and cook until lightly caramelized. Stir in the paprika, chile powder, and cumin. Add the vinegar and cook until all the liquid has evaporated. Season with salt.

Spread the pecans on a cookie sheet and bake in the oven until crisp, about 3 to 5 minutes.

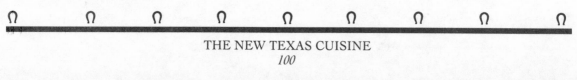

GUACAMOLE

What would a book on Texas cooking be without a recipe for guacamole? In my opinion, this is an item that shouldn't be improvised upon too much — it's simply great the way it is. There are a couple of schools of thought on the preparation of guacamole; some prefer it coarsely mashed and then mixed, while others prefer it pureed or blended. My personal preference is for the former. Whichever you choose, serve the guacamole with blue or yellow corn chips.

ABOUT 2 CUPS (4 TO 6 SERVINGS)

2 large very ripe avocados
1 large tomato, blanched, peeled, seeded, and diced (page 8)
¼ cup finely diced onion
2 cloves garlic, minced

2 serrano chiles, seeded and minced
1 tablespoon chopped cilantro
Juice of 1 small lime
Salt to taste

Peel and pit the avocados. Place in a bowl and mash with a potato masher or large fork. Fold in the remaining ingredients and season with salt.

Unless you serve guacamole immediately, it tends to lose its color. There are a couple of ways of preventing this. One is to submerge one of the avocado pits into the guacamole, and the other is to place thin slices of limes or lemons over the top and cover with plastic wrap. Refrigerate in either case.

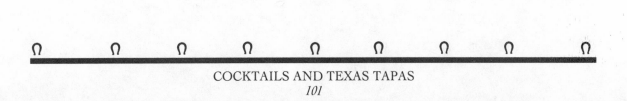

BEER BATTER SHRIMP
WITH CAYENNE REMOULADE

This is definitely a hybrid dish combining foods of the Gulf Coast and the Texas-Louisiana border region. It not only makes a great tapas dish, but you can also create an entire meal out of it, served with Jicama Coleslaw (see Index) and Jalapeño–Blue Corn Hush Puppies (see Index).

30 TO 40 SHRIMP (6 TO 8 SERVINGS)

CAYENNE REMOULADE:
1 cup Mayonnaise (see Index)
1 teaspoon dried mustard powder
1 teaspoon fresh lemon juice
1 clove garlic, finely minced
1 tablespoon capers, rinsed and finely chopped
1 tablespoon finely chopped tarragon
1 teaspoon finely chopped cilantro
1 egg, hard-cooked and finely chopped
1/2 teaspoon cayenne powder
1/2 teaspoon paprika
Salt to taste

2 pounds large raw shrimp

BATTER:
1 cup flour
2 teaspoons salt
Freshly ground black pepper to taste
3 eggs, separated
2½ tablespoons vegetable oil
1 cup dark beer, at room temperature

Vegetable or canola oil, for deep-frying

To prepare the remoulade, thoroughly combine all the ingredients in a large mixing bowl.

Wash, shell, and devein the shrimp, leaving the very tip of the tail intact if desired. Refrigerate while making the batter.

To make the batter, mix together the flour, salt, and pepper in a large mixing bowl. In a separate bowl, whisk together the egg yolks, oil, and beer. Gradually pour the liquid ingredients into the dry ingredients, whisking until completely free of lumps. Cover with plastic wrap and refrigerate for at least 1 hour or overnight.

Pour enough oil into a saucepan to come 2 inches up the sides. Over medium high heat, bring the oil to 375° F. or just smoking. Preheat the oven to 250° F. Place a baking sheet in the oven.

Meanwhile, beat the egg whites until stiff but not dry, and gently fold into the batter. (If the egg whites are chilled, place in a bowl set over warm water and whisk gently so they will stiffen properly). Hold the shrimp by their tails and dip one at a time into the batter. Cooking 4 to 6 shrimp at a time, lower them into the hot oil, and fry for 3 to 4 minutes, until brown and cooked through. Remove with a slotted spoon or tongs and keep warm in the oven while cooking the remaining shrimp. Serve with the remoulade.

JALAPEÑOS STUFFED WITH CHORIZO AND CREAM CHEESE

Having dinner at my dad's house would not be complete without a relish tray of stuffed jalapeños. His are always fresh from the garden, but if you prefer, you can use Pickled Jalapeños (see Index) or even canned jalapeños.

1 DOZEN WHOLE OR 2 DOZEN HALVED JALAPEÑOS (4 TO 6 SERVINGS)

1 tablespoon vegetable oil
1 tablespoon finely minced onion
1 clove garlic, finely minced
3 ounces Chorizo (see Index)
2 ounces cream cheese

1 tablespoon sour cream
Salt to taste
12 jalapeño chiles, halved, seeded, and deribbed;
or 12 Pickled Jalapeños (see Index)

Heat the oil in a skillet and sauté the onion and garlic over medium heat for 2 to 3 minutes, until translucent. Add chorizo and cook for 5 minutes, breaking up the meat with a fork as it cooks. When fully cooked, remove the skillet from heat and cool slightly. Stir in the cream cheese and sour cream, and season with salt. Spoon the mixture into the jalapeño halves and serve.

GULF COAST OYSTERS ON THE HALF SHELL WITH SERRANO CHILE MIGNONETTE

This recipe was first developed for a New York Times article entitled "Seafood of the Desert," which discussed Southwestern fish and shellfish dishes. When it comes to oysters, some of my fondest memories are of afternoon forays to the upstairs café at Chez Panisse, eating them with a classical black pepper mignonette. Of course, I'm partial to our delicious Texas Gulf Coast oysters, and they seem to have a perfect affinity for this dressing, which contains other Texas ingredients.

4 DOZEN OYSTERS (6 TO 8 SERVINGS)

4 dozen oysters
¾ cup champagne vinegar
½ cup dry white wine
¼ cup fresh lime juice
2 shallots, minced

2 serrano chiles, seeded and minced
¼ teaspoon freshly ground black pepper
1 teaspoon chopped cilantro
1 teaspoon minced red bell pepper
Crushed ice (optional)

With an oyster knife, shuck the oysters, keeping them curved side down to save their juices.

To make the sauce, combine all the remaining ingredients in a bowl and let stand for 10 minutes.

Place the oysters on an oversized platter with a bed of crushed ice, if desired. Serve the sauce on top of the oysters.

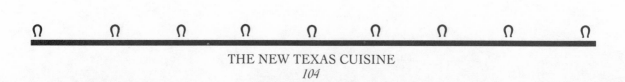

SCALLOP CEVICHE VERDE IN TORTILLA CUPS

We often served this dish as hors d'oeuvres with champagne at cocktail parties or wine dinner receptions at Routh Street Cafe. The softness of the scallops, the acidity of the lime, and the crunch of the fried tortilla make a tantalizing combination of textures and flavors.

4 TO 6 SERVINGS

CEVICHE:
8 ounces fresh sea scallops
1/4 cup fresh lime juice
3 medium tomatillos, husked, rinsed, and minced
1 clove garlic, minced
1/2 small tomato, seeded and diced
4 tablespoons diced scallions
1 tablespoon olive oil

3 serrano chiles, seeded and minced
1 small ripe avocado, peeled, pitted, and diced
1 tablespoon finely chopped cilantro
1 teaspoon finely chopped basil
Salt to taste

Vegetable oil, for deep-frying
4 to 6 Corn Tortillas (see Index)

In a stainless-steel or nonreactive bowl, marinate the scallops in the lime juice for 1 hour in the refrigerator. Drain, and reserve 1 tablespoon of juice to add back later. Add the remaining ceviche ingredients and the reserved lime juice, and mix well. Chill for at least 30 minutes.

If you do not want to go to the trouble of making the cups, the ceviche can be served with tortilla chips. However, the cups are the perfect serving container and make a great presentation.

Heat the oil in a deep-fryer or large pan to 375° F. Cut the tortillas with a 3-inch cookie cutter or use a 1½- or 2-ounce ladle as a guide for cutting the tortillas into circles. Place each tortilla circle inside a ladle and press down with a spoon or smaller ladle. Submerge the ladle and tortilla in the hot oil and deep-fry for about 30 seconds, until the tortilla is crisp and holds its cup shape. Remove and drain on paper towels.

Spoon the scallop ceviche into the tortilla cups and serve.

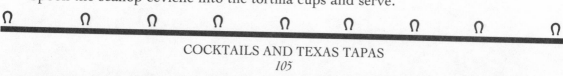

REFRIED BLACK BEAN DIP

This is a versatile dish which can be adapted very easily to make black bean nachos. Just spread the dip on fried tortillas, sprinkle with grated Monterey Jack cheese or queso fresco, and heat in a 375° F. oven for 10 minutes, until the cheese has melted.

2 CUPS (6 TO 8 SERVINGS)

1 cup black beans, soaked overnight and drained (page 10)
6 cups Ham Hock Broth or Chicken Stock (see Index)
3 tablespoons lard or vegetable oil
½ cup chopped onion
2 cloves garlic, minced

1 tablespoon chopped cilantro leaves
½ cup sour cream
2 tablespoons ancho chile puree (pages 3 to 4)
1 teaspoon ground cumin
Salt to taste
Tortilla chips

In a large saucepan, bring the soaked beans and broth or stock to a boil. Reduce the heat, cover, and simmer for about 1½ hours, adding more liquid if it evaporates too quickly. Drain, reserving the beans and liquid. In a clean pan over high heat, reduce the cooking liquid to a glaze, about 12 minutes, and set aside.

In a skillet, heat the lard or oil over medium-high heat until lightly smoking. Add the onion and garlic and sauté for 3 minutes. Add the beans and mash them with the back of a spoon or a potato masher. Lower the heat and let the beans simmer, stirring constantly, until they are quite thick. Whisk in the remaining ingredients.

Serve with tortilla chips.

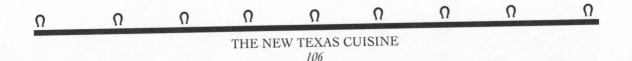

QUESO FUNDIDO WITH CHORIZO

My Spanish dictionary tells me that fundido nuclear means "nuclear meltdown." We are only talking about melted cheese here, but it ranks up there with nachos and chile con queso as a popular "antojito" in Mexican restaurants. You can make this dish with or without the chorizo, or you can use another type of sausage altogether. You can also experiment with different cheeses, but bear in mind that a somewhat stringy cheese is part of the fun of the dish.

ABOUT 2 CUPS (4 TO 6 SERVINGS)

2 tablespoons olive oil
½ small onion, chopped
1 clove garlic, minced
1 jalapeño chile, seeded and diced
1 small red bell pepper, roasted, peeled, seeded, and diced (page 6)

2 ounces Chorizo sausage (see Index)
4 ounces mozzarella cheese, cubed
4 ounces Monterey Jack cheese, cubed
3 ounces fresh goat cheese, crumbled
4 to 6 Flour Tortillas (see Index)

Preheat the oven to 400° F. Place an 8-inch ovenproof dish or casserole in the oven while preparing the fundido.

Heat the oil in a skillet over medium-high heat until lightly smoking. Sauté the onion, garlic, jalapeño, and bell pepper for 1 minute, stirring constantly. Add the chorizo and sauté for about 10 minutes, breaking up with a fork as it cooks. Pour off any excess oil and set aside.

Remove the dish or casserole from the oven and spread the cheeses over the bottom. Return to the oven and bake until the cheese is just melted, about 5 minutes. Remove from the oven and sprinkle the chorizo mixture over the top. Return to the oven and heat through for about 3 minutes. Serve with warm flour tortillas.

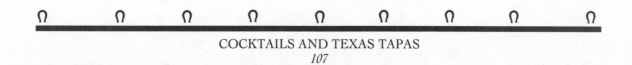

SOPES STUFFED WITH CRABMEAT

Sopes are silver dollar-sized, boat-shaped appetizers made from much the same dough as corn tortillas. They are indigenous to the Guadalajara region of Mexico, where they are eaten as street food. Typically, sopes are stuffed with cheese, salsa, chorizo, or some other meat, but they can also be fried and eaten plain.

ABOUT 48 SOPES (6 TO 8 SERVINGS)

2 cups masa harina
1¼ cups hot water
2 tablespoons lard or vegetable shortening
⅓ cup flour
½ teaspoon salt

1 teaspoon baking powder
1 pound crabmeat, shell and cartilage removed
Vegetable oil, for frying
1 cup Tomatillo-Jalapeño Chutney (see Index)

In a mixing bowl, combine the masa harina with the hot water, cover, and let stand for 30 minutes. Add the lard or shortening, flour, salt, and baking powder to the masa harina mixture, and mix together thoroughly.

Divide the dough into 12 balls, then the 12 balls into 24, and the 24 into 48. Place the masa balls on a cookie sheet and cover with a damp towel or plastic wrap.

Lightly oil your fingers and flatten one of the sopes by patting it between the fingers of one hand and the palm of your other hand. Place about 2 teaspoons of crabmeat in the middle and enclose it with the masa dough; form into a boat or diamond shape. Repeat the procedure for the remaining sopes.

Pour enough oil into a large skillet to come ¼ inch up the sides, and heat until lightly smoking. Fry the sopes over medium-high heat for 2 minutes per side. Serve with the tomatillo-jalapeño chutney.

*R*oast Wild Turkey with Blue Cornmeal–Chorizo Stuffing and
Thanksgiving trimmings

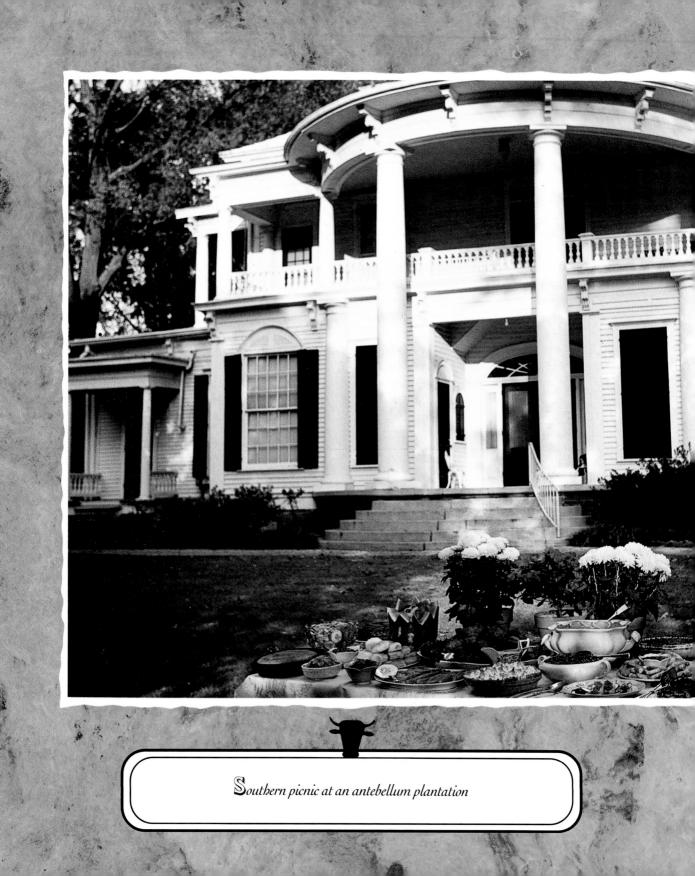

Southern picnic at an antebellum plantation

Top: Soft-Shell Crabs on Gumbo Z'Herbs with Chile Pequín Mayonnaise

Bottom: Fried Catfish Sandwich with Smoked Tomato Aïoli and Pickled Okra

Left: Crawfish boil in East Texas

Right: Caddo Lake, near the Louisiana border

Top: Clay Henry, the beer-drinking goat (mayor of Terlingua)

Middle: Springtime wildflowers in the Hill Country

Bottom: Terlingua Chili Cookoff chauffeurs

Top: Dunes near Monahans

Bottom: The general store at Terlingua

Top: Wine chilling for festivities at Pheasant Ridge Winery

Bottom: Cap Rock Winery

MELON WITH PROSCIUTTO AND HONEY-LIME CREAM

A while ago, my good friend Susy Davidson brought another friend, Julia Child, to Routh Street Cafe for a very special dinner to benefit a cause dear to Julia's heart, the American Institute of Wine and Food, which she cofounded with Robert Mondavi. We enjoyed this hors d'oeuvre with champagne before dinner, and sometime later, when Susy asked me to contribute an article for Food & Wine *magazine (of which she was Food Editor), she insisted I incorporate this recipe. While Italians know there's nothing new about prosciutto and melon, the honey-lime cream adds a new flavor dimension.*

8 TO 10 SERVINGS

1 honeydew melon, about 3 pounds	1 teaspoon lime zest
8 ounces prosciutto, very thinly sliced	1/2 teaspoon honey
1/2 cup sour cream	Salt to taste
1 teaspoon fresh lime juice	

Cut the melon into 2-inch-square pieces, about ⅓ inch thick. Cut or tear the prosciutto into 4-inch-long strips, about ½ inch wide.

In a mixing bowl, whisk together the sour cream, lime juice, zest, and honey. Season with salt.

Wrap a piece of melon with a strip of prosciutto and secure with a toothpick. Arrange the melon on a large platter, and top each piece with ¼ teaspoon of the honey-lime cream.

HELL'S EGGS

Growing up in West Texas, deviled eggs always seemed to be a feature of family reunions, picnics, or potluck dinners after church on Sunday evenings. I remember being drawn, as if by a magnet, to the deviled eggs that were the spiciest. I also recall feeling somewhat decadent whenever I ate deviled eggs at a church function!

10 SERVINGS

10 large eggs, hard-cooked, shelled
1 clove garlic, finely minced
2 serrano chiles, seeded and minced
½ cup Mayonnaise (see Index)
1 teaspoon fresh lemon juice
2 teaspoons dried mustard powder

¼ teaspoon cayenne powder
¼ teaspoon pure chile powder (page 4)
¼ teaspoon paprika
½ teaspoon salt
1 teaspoon chopped cilantro
1 teaspoon chopped chives

Cut a ⅛-inch slice off the bottom of each egg so that it stands upright. Slice off the top one third of each egg, and set aside. Carefully remove the yolks without breaking the egg white casings.

In a mixing bowl, mash the egg yolks together with all the remaining ingredients except the chives. Refill the eggs with the mixture, smoothing off the tops.

In another bowl, finely chop the reserved egg white scraps, mix together with the chives, and sprinkle over the tops of the eggs.

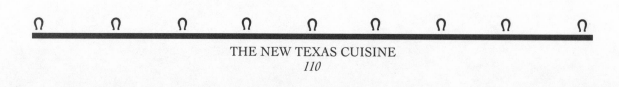

PICKLED EGGS

Pickled eggs in large glass jars have always been standard fare on counter tops of truck stops, cafés, filling stations, and stores all over Texas, and my dad's truck stops were no exceptions. You don't see these eggs so much nowadays, but they still make a good snack.

12 SERVINGS

3 tablespoons Dijon mustard
½ cup water
2 cups cider vinegar
1 cup sugar
1 tablespoon salt
1 teaspoon pure chile powder (page 4)
1 tablespoon ground cumin

1 tablespoon celery seeds
2 tablespoons mustard seeds
8 cloves
6 cloves garlic
4 serrano chiles
2 onions, thinly sliced
12 eggs, hard-cooked, shelled

In a large saucepan, combine the mustard, water, and vinegar, and blend until smooth. Add the sugar, salt, chile powder, cumin, and celery and mustard seeds. Bring to a boil, whisking to ensure the sugar dissolves. Reduce the heat, add the cloves, garlic, and serranos, and simmer for 10 minutes.

Remove the pan from the heat and let cool. Pack the onions and eggs in a glass jar and pour the cooled liquid over. Seal immediately and refrigerate for at least 10 days.

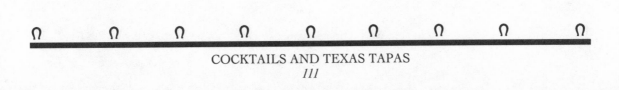

VENISON PICADILLO

Picadillo is a Mexican stew that seems to have resulted from the merging of Spanish and Aztec cuisines. Variations of this dish are found throughout Mexico, and picadillo has long been standard fare in Texas cooking. Traditionally, it's made from shredded or ground pork, but it can also be made with beef. It's a great item to have on hand for large parties, as it's easy to serve in bowls with flour tortillas. It also makes a wonderful stuffing for chiles (chiles rellenos) and bell peppers. For a tapas party, you can serve the picadillo in Tortilla Cups (see Index).

ABOUT 2 QUARTS (8 TO 10 SERVINGS)

3 tablespoons olive oil
2 small onions, diced
2 cloves garlic, minced
1½ pounds lean ground venison
8 ounces ground pork
3 medium ripe tomatoes, blanched, peeled, seeded, and diced (page 8)
2 red bell peppers, roasted, peeled, seeded, and diced (page 6)
3 jalapeño chiles, seeded and minced

1 apple, peeled, cored, and chopped
½ cup raisins, plumped in tequila
1 cup blanched slivered almonds, toasted (page 9)
½ teaspoon ground cloves
½ teaspoon ground cinnamon
1 teaspoon ground cumin
½ cup red wine
½ cup Chicken Stock (see Index)

In a large skillet, heat the oil to lightly smoking and sauté the onions and garlic for 2 to 3 minutes over medium-high heat, until translucent. Add the venison and pork, and continue to cook, breaking the meat up with a fork until the meat's cooked through, about 5 minutes. Add all the remaining ingredients except the wine and stock, and cook for 2 more minutes. Then add the wine and stock, reduce the heat, and simmer for 20 to 30 minutes.

OVEN-DRIED BEEF JERKY

The best I can tell, jerky originated in the days of the Western Movement, with its cattle drives and wagon trains. Jerky derived from the drying techniques used by the Pueblo Indians of the Rio Grande valley in New Mexico for preserving meat over the winter. The pioneers and cowboys would cut meat into thin strips, string them on a piece of cord, and dip them into a boiling brine solution until the meat lost its color. The strips would then be removed and hung up near the campfire to drip dry. Sometimes the meat would be dried in the sun, but the process would take longer and insects would have to be discouraged.

The procedure given here produces a result similar to the historical method. The jerky can be eaten as a snack or used in a sauce with veal stock to accompany beef dishes.

---

15 TO 20 STRIPS

1 pound beef top round
2 tablespoons kosher salt
2 tablespoons freshly ground black pepper

½ teaspoon cayenne powder
¼ teaspoon ground cumin

Place the beef in the freezer for at least 20 minutes, to facilitate slicing; ice crystals should form but the meat should remain pliable. Meanwhile, combine the remaining ingredients in a bowl and set aside. Preheat the oven to 175° F.

Remove the beef from the freezer and cut into paper-thin slices across the grain with a razor-sharp knife or a meat slicer. Dredge the beef slices lightly in the dry ingredients and place in a single layer on a rack in a baking dish or pan large enough to hold all the slices.

Place in the oven and cook for at least 10 hours, or until the jerky is dry and somewhat chewy. Turn the meat after 6 hours. Store the jerky in an airtight container in a dark place. Will keep for up to 1 month.

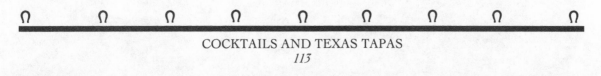

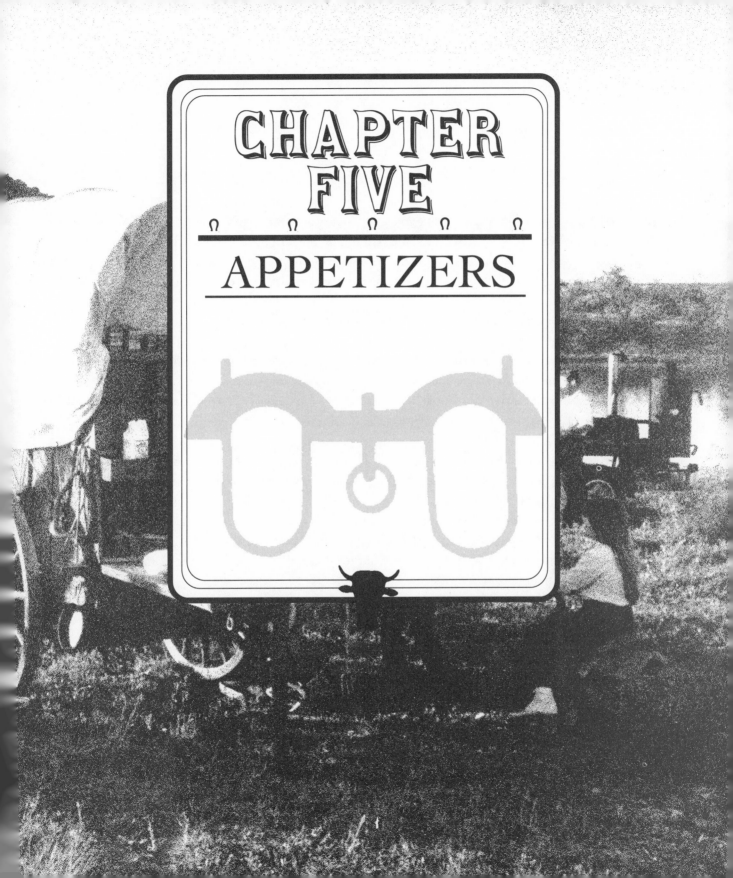

CHAPTER FIVE

APPETIZERS

If I had to single out one particular course as being more important than all the others, it would have to be appetizers. They set the stage for a meal and provide the diner with the first impression. Appetizers should stimulate the appetite, and with the first bite, affirm that the rest of the meal will be an enjoyable experience. I know this is true for me; it's going to be very hard to win me over if my appetizer isn't good, even if the entrée is great.

The importance I attach to the role of appetizers was demonstrated by the fact that during the first two years that Routh Street Cafe was open, I worked each evening as a line chef, in charge of executing the hot appetizers. Whenever I am devising a new menu, I most enjoy the challenge of coming up with exciting appetizers. I feel this is the area that allows most creativity, and perhaps that's why I enjoy this process particularly.

One side effect of switching from an exclusively "prix fixe" menu to an "à la carte" menu at Routh Street Cafe was that some diners have preferred to order two, three, or even four appetizers instead of an entrée. This "grazing" trend means that it is possible to get a much broader grasp of the repertoire of a restaurant, and can make for a more complete dining experience.

All of the recipes in this chapter can be used to create main courses; in that case, as a general rule of thumb, all of the ingredients should be doubled. Likewise the quantity given for most of the tapas contained in Chapter 4 can be increased to yield an additional choice of appetizers.

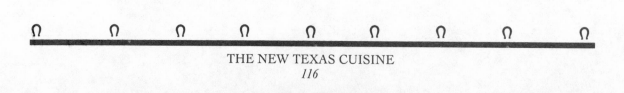

SEAFOOD CAKES WITH PASILLA-CORN SALSA

This is a good recipe for using up any leftover fish you may have, but that's not the only time you should try it. You can use different types of fish — for example, salmon instead of halibut, and for an interesting combination of flavors, serve this dish with Smoked Tomato Dressing (see Index).

8 TO 10 SERVINGS

SEAFOOD CAKES:
8 ounces fresh sea scallops, cleaned and chopped
8 ounces halibut, snapper, or other firm white fish, chopped
8 ounces medium raw shrimp, peeled, deveined, and chopped
1 tablespoon minced celery
1 tablespoon minced carrot
1 tablespoon minced onion
1 tablespoon seeded and minced red bell pepper
1 tablespoon seeded and minced green bell pepper
2 jalapeño chiles, seeded and minced
2 cloves garlic, minced
½ teaspoon chopped basil

½ teaspoon chopped thyme
½ teaspoon chopped rosemary
· ½ teaspoon ground cumin
½ teaspoon freshly ground white pepper
1 teaspoon dried mustard powder
1 teaspoon salt
½ teaspoon ground coriander
Juice of 1 lime
1 egg
¾ cup fresh breadcrumbs

4 tablespoons unsalted butter
1 to 1¼ cups Pasilla-Corn Salsa (see Index)
1 bunch chives, for garnish

Pass the scallops and halibut through the largest setting of a meat grinder or place in a food processor and process until smooth. In a large bowl, place the ground mixture with the chopped shrimp and remaining seafood cake ingredients. Form into 3-ounce patties.

Heat the butter in a large skillet until lightly smoking, and cook the patties over medium heat for about 4 minutes. Turn the patties, lower the heat, and cook for an additional 4 minutes.

Place 2 seafood cakes on each plate with 2 tablespoons of pasilla-corn salsa, and garnish with 2 whole chives.

SMOKED TROUT TORTA
WITH HABANERO-HORSERADISH CREAM

When Mark Haugen helped us open Tejas in 1987, he was probably the most talented chef in Minneapolis. However, his training was classical French and some Italian cuisine. To put it bluntly, he didn't know a sopaipilla from a quesadilla. Today, he's as adept as anyone in the country at interpreting and creating Southwestern dishes. This recipe is one of his recent inventions. If smoked trout is unavailable, or if you don't want to go to the trouble, substitute smoked salmon; use about 2 ounces per torta. And be warned: the habanero is just about the hottest chile around!

8 SERVINGS

TORTA:
1 pound prepared masa dough (page 324)
6 ounces Jack cheese, grated
2 tablespoons chopped cilantro
½ cup diced mango
1 each red, green, and yellow bell pepper, roasted, peeled, seeded, and diced (page 6)
1 tablespoon olive oil
½ cup diced onion
2 rainbow trout, about 8 ounces each, smoked, skinned, boned, and shredded (page 9)
Clarified butter, for brushing

HABANERO-HORSERADISH CREAM:
1 cup dry white wine
1 cup Fish Stock (see Index) or canned fish broth
2 tablespoons minced shallots
1 habanero or Scotch bonnet chile, chopped
4 cups (1 quart) heavy cream
½ cup freshly grated horseradish
1 teaspoon salt
½ teaspoon freshly ground white pepper
Juice of 1 lime
1 tablespoon unsalted butter

GARNISH:
4 tablespoons sour cream
4 tablespoons Pico de Gallo (see Index)
4 sprigs cilantro

Divide the masa dough evenly into 16 balls. Press the balls of dough between sheets of plastic wrap or wax paper with a heavy plate or pie pan to ¹⁄₁₆-inch thickness and about 4 inches across.

In a large mixing bowl, combine the cheese, cilantro, mango, and bell peppers. Heat the oil in a skillet and sauté the onion over medium heat until golden, about 5 minutes. Add the onion to the ingredients in the mixing bowl.

Evenly distribute the smoked trout on 8 of the flattened masa patties, and cover with the cheese mixture. Place the remaining 8 patties over the filling to form a sandwich or torta.

Brush each side of the tortas with clarified butter and place in a preheated skillet. Cook over medium heat until the bottom of each patty turns golden brown, about 1 minute. Turn the tortas over and continue cooking until the cheese is melted and the bottom on the second side turns golden brown.

To prepare the cream sauce, combine the wine, stock, and shallots in a saucepan and, over low heat, reduce to ¼ cup of liquid, about 15 to 20 minutes. Add the chile, cream, and horseradish, and reduce by half, about 30 to 35 minutes. Taste the sauce and adjust for spiciness by removing some or all of the chile. Transfer to a blender, add the salt, pepper, lime juice, and butter, and puree. Strain, and keep warm.

Spoon 6 tablespoons of the sauce onto each plate. Place one torta in the middle of each plate and garnish with sour cream, Pico de Gallo, and cilantro sprigs.

LINGUINE WITH AVOCADO, SHRIMP, AND CORN

Growing up in West Texas, the only pasta we ever knew was spaghetti. One of my great culinary discoveries was the wide array of Italian pastas. At Star Canyon, we always have a pasta appetizer on the menu. In the winter, I prefer a hearty pasta dish, such as this recipe, which combines some exciting flavors.

8 SERVINGS

3 cups Chicken Stock (see Index)
16 medium (about 12 ounces) raw shrimp, peeled and deveined
4 slices bacon, chopped
1 teaspoon olive oil
½ cup diced onion
½ cup diced red bell pepper
1½ cups fresh corn kernels (2 ears)
1½ cups heavy cream

1 tablespoon ancho chile puree (pages 3 to 4)
10 ounces uncooked fresh linguine
1 tablespoon snipped chives
1 tablespoon chopped basil
1 large avocado, peeled, pitted, and diced
1 large ripe tomato, blanched, peeled, seeded, and diced (page 8)
Salt and freshly ground black pepper to taste
1 tablespoon fresh lime juice

In a saucepan, bring the stock to a boil and reduce the heat to simmer. Add the shrimp and cook until opaque, about 2 minutes. Drain and reserve both the stock and shrimp. Over high heat, cook the bacon until all the fat is rendered. Reserve the bacon.

In a medium saucepan over high heat, heat the oil until lightly smoking. Add the onion and bell pepper, and cook until the onion is transparent, about 2 minutes. Set aside.

Return the reserved stock to a saucepan, add the corn kernels and cream, and bring to a boil. Lower the heat slightly and reduce the liquid by half. Add the ancho chile puree, transfer the mixture to a blender or food processor, and puree. Set aside.

Cook the linguine until al dente and drain. Return the linguine to the pan and add the pureed corn mixture, reserved shrimp, reserved onions and red pepper, the chives, basil, avocado, tomato, and reserved bacon. Toss together and heat through. Season with salt, pepper, and lime juice, and serve.

GOAT CHEESE–ALMOND CHILES RELLENOS WITH DRIED APRICOTS

This recipe is based on the Mexican classic chiles rellenos, or stuffed chiles. It makes a good party dish, and will really warm you up on a winter night. The Anaheim chiles, which are similar to New Mexico green chiles, can be substituted by poblanos, which are somewhat larger. Roasting the chiles gives a unique flavor, but the skins of the chiles can also be removed by immersing them in hot oil until they blister, and then transferring them to ice water. This recipe can be simplified by using either the apricot or almond sauce alone, or by foregoing both and using just the Pico de Gallo or another salsa from Chapter 3 instead.

8 SERVINGS

8 Anaheim chiles, roasted and peeled, with stems (page 6)
2 cloves roasted garlic, minced (page 7)
6 ounces goat cheese, crumbled
3 ounces caciotta or Monterey Jack cheese, grated
1 tablespoon chopped shallot
1 tablespoon chopped cilantro
1 tablespoon chopped basil
1 tablespoon chopped marjoram
½ cup diced dried apricots

2 tablespoons chopped toasted almonds (page 9)
Salt and freshly ground black pepper to taste
1 egg
2 tablespoons heavy cream
Yellow cornmeal, for dredging
Peanut or vegetable oil, for deep-frying
1 cup Almond Sauce (recipe follows)
1 cup Apricot Sauce (recipe follows)
1 cup Pico de Gallo (see Index), for garnish

Carefully slit the chiles down one side and remove the seeds, leaving the stem attached. Set aside.

In a large mixing bowl, combine the garlic with the goat cheese, caciotta, shallot, herbs, apricots, and almonds. Season with salt and pepper, and mix well. Stuff the chiles with the mixture, taking care not to overfill. Close the chiles and chill for at least 30 minutes before frying.

In a bowl, beat the egg into the cream and coat the stuffed chiles; then dredge in cornmeal that has been lightly salted. Heat at least 2 inches of oil in a heavy saucepan to 325° F. Fry the chiles, 1 or 2 at a time, for 3 to 5 minutes, until lightly browned. Remove and drain on paper towels.

Pour some of the almond sauce on each serving plate. Place a stuffed chile on the middle of each plate, and spoon some apricot sauce on the top of each chile. Garnish with the Pico de Gallo.

ALMOND SAUCE
ABOUT 1 CUP

1 cup heavy cream
½ cup toasted sliced almonds (page 9)
1 tablespoon roasted garlic puree (page 7)

2 tablespoons Chicken Stock (see Index)
Salt to taste

Place the cream in a large saucepan and over medium heat, reduce to ¾ cup, whisking frequently. Transfer to a blender, add the almonds, garlic puree, and chicken stock, and blend at high speed until smooth. Season with salt and strain through a fine strainer. Keep warm or reheat when ready to serve.

APRICOT SAUCE
ABOUT 1 CUP

1 cup Chicken Stock (see Index) or water
½ cup diced dried apricots
1 tablespoon sugar
¼ cup dry white wine

½ shallot, finely diced
8 tablespoons (1 stick) unsalted butter,
at room temperature
Salt to taste

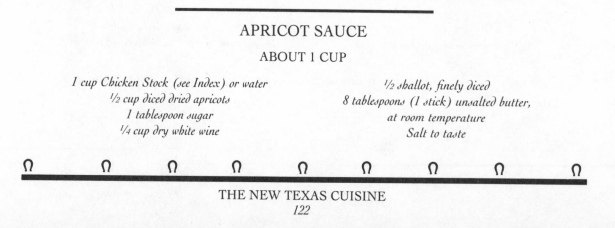

In a saucepan, bring the stock or water to a boil and reduce the heat to a simmer. Add the apricots and simmer over low heat until soft, about 10 minutes. Remove from the heat, stir in the sugar to dissolve, transfer to a blender, and puree. Reserve and keep warm.

Place the wine and shallot in a saucepan, and over high heat, reduce the liquid to 2 tablespoons. Reduce the heat to medium and whisk in the butter, 2 tablespoons at a time, until incorporated. Remove from the heat. Add the apricot puree, combine, and strain through a fine strainer; taste and season with salt. The sauce will be quite thick.

LOBSTER-PAPAYA QUESADILLAS WITH MANGO CREAM

Quesadillas make exceptional hors d'oeuvres and appetizers, and the variety of fillings is endless. In this version, lobster is paired with papaya and mango for an elegant tropical combination.

4 SERVINGS

2 ounces fresh goat cheese, crumbled
2 ounces Monterey Jack or caciotta cheese, grated
1 teaspoon pureed roasted garlic (optional, see Index)
1/4 cup chopped onion
1/2 poblano chile, roasted, peeled, seeded, and diced (page 6)
1/2 red bell pepper, roasted, peeled, seeded, and diced

1 teaspoon minced cilantro
1/3 teaspoon salt
1 teaspoon fresh lime juice
5 ounces cooked lobster meat, chopped
1 papaya, peeled, seeded, and chopped
4 Flour Tortillas (see Index), at room temperature
2 tablespoons unsalted butter, melted
1 cup Mango Cream (recipe follows)

In a large mixing bowl, combine the cheeses and stir in the garlic, onion, poblano, bell pepper, cilantro, salt, and lime juice. Carefully blend in the lobster and papaya.

Spread some of the lobster mixture over half of each tortilla and fold over. Brush each tortilla with the melted butter. Heat a large nonstick skillet over medium-high heat. Cook the quesadillas for 2 to 3 minutes, until golden brown on both sides. Cut each quesadilla into 3 triangles, and serve with the mango cream.

MANGO CREAM
ABOUT 1½ CUPS

2 mangoes
½ cup sour cream

Juice of ½ lemon

Peel the mangoes and cut the pulp from the seed. With your hands, squeeze the juice from the pulp into a bowl. Transfer the pulp to a blender and puree until smooth. Add the sour cream and lemon juice, and blend to incorporate, scraping down the sides of the blender with a spatula as necessary.

POBLANOS STUFFED WITH JERKED PORK, PINEAPPLE, AND PUMPKIN SEEDS

I love the tropical flavors of the Caribbean islands, and I am especially drawn to Jamaican food. Jerked pork is almost the national dish, and the best I've found there is at the Pork Pit at Montego Bay. Jerked pork (as well as chicken, goat, and fish) is traditionally prepared with a spicy dry marinade, and then smoked in a pit over green pimento wood and charcoal. The combination of flavors and textures in this dish is enough to tantalize even the most jaded of palates.

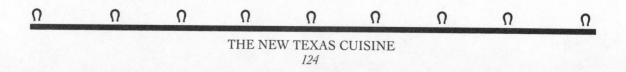

4 medium poblano chiles, roasted and peeled, with
stems (page 6)
2 tablespoons unsalted butter
¼ cup diced onion
2 cloves garlic, minced
1 red bell pepper, seeded and diced
1 green bell pepper, seeded and diced
2 tablespoons diced fresh pineapple
2 tablespoons toasted pumpkin seeds (pages 8 to 9)
¼ cup Gewürztraminer or Riesling wine
½ cup Brown Veal Stock (see Index)
¼ cup brown sugar
¾ cup red wine vinegar
12 ounces Jerked Pork (recipe follows)
1 teaspoon minced basil
1 teaspoon minced cilantro
Salt and freshly ground black pepper to taste

SAUCE:
4 tablespoons unsalted butter
2 tablespoons diced onion
3 tomatoes, seeded and diced
1 clove garlic, minced
2 cups Chicken Stock (see Index)
¼ cup dry white wine
Salt to taste

HABANERO-SAFFRON CREAM:
¼ cup water or Chicken Stock
1 teaspoon saffron threads
1 habanero chile, seeded and diced
½ cup sour cream

Preheat the oven to 200° F. Carefully slit the chiles down one side and remove the seeds, leaving the stem attached. Keep the chiles warm in the oven until ready to fill.

Heat the butter in a skillet and sauté the onion, garlic, and bell peppers over medium heat until translucent, about 3 to 5 minutes. Stir in the pineapple and pumpkin seeds. Add the wine and cook to a glaze. Add the stock, brown sugar, and vinegar, and cook until the liquid is syrupy, about 7 minutes. Add the jerked pork and just heat through. Add the herbs and season with salt and pepper.

To prepare the sauce, heat the butter in a saucepan and sauté the onion over medium heat until translucent, about 2 to 3 minutes. Add the remaining sauce ingredients except salt and reduce the liquid by three quarters. Transfer the sauce to a blender, purée, and strain through a fine strainer into a saucepan. Season with salt and keep the sauce warm.

To prepare the habanero-saffron cream, bring the water or stock to a boil in a saucepan. Add the saffron and habanero, reduce the heat, and simmer for 1

minute. Remove the pan from the heat and let infuse for 10 minutes. Strain the stock into a mixing bowl through a fine strainer, and whisk in the sour cream.

Remove the chiles from the oven and carefully stuff with the pork mixture, taking care not to overfill. Leave the chiles open to expose the stuffing. Spoon some of the sauce onto warm plates, and pour the remainder into a serving bowl. Place the chiles on the sauce and top with the habanero-saffron cream.

JERKED PORK
4 SERVINGS

DRY INGREDIENTS:
1 tablespoon chopped thyme
½ teaspoon chopped sage
1 teaspoon cayenne powder
1 teaspoon freshly ground black pepper
½ teaspoon grated nutmeg
½ teaspoon ground cinnamon
1 teaspoon ground allspice
1½ tablespoons salt
1 tablespoon brown sugar

LIQUID INGREDIENTS:
¼ cup olive oil

¼ cup fresh orange juice
2 tablespoons fresh lime juice
2 tablespoons soy sauce
½ cup balsamic vinegar

1 cup diced onion
1 tablespoon minced garlic
1 habanero chile, seeded and minced

1 pork tenderloin, 12 to 14 ounces, trimmed of fat

Combine all the dry ingredients in a large mixing bowl. Whisk in the liquid ingredients and add the onion, garlic, and habanero; mix the marinade thoroughly.

Place the pork tenderloin in a roasting pan just large enough to hold it and the marinade. Pour the marinade over and let stand in the refrigerator for at least 3 hours and preferably overnight.

Prepare a medium wood-burning grill (see pages 4 to 6). Remove the pork from the marinade and reserve the marinade. Grill the pork for 12 to 15 minutes, turning every 4 to 5 minutes to ensure even cooking, until its internal temperature reaches 160° to 170° F. on a meat thermometer. Baste with marinade every few minutes.

Remove the pork from the grill and let rest for 5 minutes. Dice the meat and set aside.

TAMALE TART WITH ROAST GARLIC CUSTARD AND GULF CRABMEAT

This dish has become a signature dish of mine. It combines the rustic flavors of tamales with the elegant silkiness of roast garlic custard. The ancho chiles, which are dried poblanos, are a staple in the cuisines of the Southwest and Mexico. They contribute smoky, chocolatey flavors and sweet tones, while the addition of Gulf crabmeat provides another good example of the rich diversity of the food resources of Texas. The masa harina used in the recipe is available at Latin markets and many supermarkets.

8 TO 10 SERVINGS

ROAST GARLIC CUSTARD:
1½ cups heavy cream
1½ tablespoons pureed roasted garlic (page 7)
2 egg yolks
1 teaspoon salt
⅛ teaspoon freshly ground white pepper

1 large red bell pepper, seeded and coarsely chopped
2 cups masa harina
¼ cup yellow cornmeal
¼ teaspoon cayenne powder
2 teaspoons ground cumin
2 teaspoons salt
6 tablespoons (3 ounces) vegetable shortening, at room temperature

6 tablespoons ancho chile puree (pages 3 to 4)
2 cups water
2 tablespoons olive oil
½ small onion, finely chopped
10 ounces fresh lump crabmeat (preferably Gulf Coast)
¼ cup red tomato, blanched, peeled, seeded, and diced (page 8)
¼ cup yellow tomato, blanched, peeled, seeded, and diced
2 tablespoons chopped cilantro
1 serrano chile, seeded and minced
2 teaspoons fresh lime juice
Salt to taste

Ω   Ω   Ω   Ω   Ω   Ω   Ω   Ω   Ω

To prepare the garlic custard, place the cream in a medium saucepan and over medium heat, reduce to 1 cup plus 2 tablespoons. Whisk in the roasted garlic. In a mixing bowl, whisk the egg yolks lightly while drizzling in the cream mixture, and season with salt and pepper. Cover and set aside to cool.

In a small saucepan, steam the red bell pepper over boiling water until soft, about 10 minutes. Drain and transfer to a blender or food processor; blend until smooth. You should have about ¾ cup puree; if necessary, add a little water to make up the quantity.

In a medium bowl, combine the masa harina, cornmeal, cayenne, cumin, and salt. In a large bowl, using an electric mixer at medium speed, whip the shortening until light and fluffy.

Gradually beat in the dry ingredients until smooth. Beat in the ancho chile puree and the red bell pepper puree. Form the dough into a disk, and pat into a 9-inch tart pan with a removable bottom, pressing the dough evenly over the bottom and up the sides. Fill the tart pan with the reserved garlic custard and cover with plastic wrap.

Place a round metal cooling rack inside a wok and pour in the 2 cups water. The rack should fit at least 3 inches above the water. Bring the water to a boil over high heat, then turn off the heat. Place the wrapped tart on the rack and reheat the water until it boils again. Lower the heat to simmer, cover the wok, and steam until the custard is set but still trembles slightly, 25 to 30 minutes. Using 2 pot holders, carefully lift the tart off the rack; remove the plastic wrap and the sides of the tart ring. Transfer to a serving platter.

In a large nonreactive skillet, heat the olive oil over high heat, until lightly smoking. Add the onion and cook, stirring for 1 minute. Stir in the crabmeat, tomatoes, cilantro, serrano, and lime juice, and cook until warmed through, about 2 minutes. Season with salt. Using a slotted spoon, cover the top of the tart with the crab mixture. Cut the tart into wedges and serve warm.

CATFISH MOUSSE WITH CRAWFISH SAUCE

The idea for this recipe came to me as I was preparing to open Routh Street Cafe. One of my favorite meals when I was growing up was fried catfish, and I was determined to find a way to elevate this humble creature. I devised a sauce using crawfish, which are in abundance in neighboring Louisiana. The combination of these two regional ingredients seemed both unusual and appropriate. If crawfish are unavailable, you can make a sauce with 2 cups of Fish Stock (see Index) reduced by half, and 1 cup of cream; then reduce by one third.

4 SERVINGS

8 ounces catfish fillets, skinned and chopped
Ice cubes
1 egg
1 egg yolk
1/4 cup milk

1/2 cup heavy cream
1/2 teaspoon salt
Pinch of cayenne powder
2 cups Crawfish Sauce (recipe follows)

Preheat the oven to 325° F. Grind the catfish through the finest blade of a meat grinder, or whirl until smooth in a food processor fitted with a metal blade. Press the fish through a medium strainer or sieve into a mixing bowl. Set over a bowl of ice.

In another bowl, lightly beat the egg, egg yolk, milk, and cream. Slowly drizzle into the fish while stirring vigorously with a wooden spoon. Add the salt and cayenne, and mix thoroughly.

Divide the mixture evenly among four ¾-cup buttered ramekins, filling each about three quarters full. Place the ramekins in a large baking pan and pour enough very hot water around them to reach halfway up the sides. Cover the pan with foil and bake in the oven until the mousses have set and are firm to the touch, about 20 minutes.

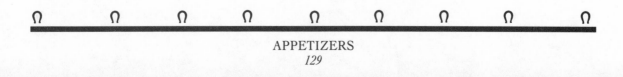

Unmold onto individual plates and top with the crawfish sauce. Divide the tail meat among the plates, placed around the mousse, and garnish with one whole crawfish per plate (see below).

CRAWFISH SAUCE
ABOUT 2 CUPS

3 tablespoons olive oil
3 tablespoons vegetable oil
2 pounds live crawfish
1 medium carrot, chopped
1 leek, cleaned and chopped (white part only)
1 stalk celery, chopped
1 clove garlic, crushed

3 tablespoons chopped parsley
2 sprigs fresh thyme, or ¼ teaspoon dried thyme
6 tablespoons bourbon
1 cup dry white wine
1½ tablespoons tomato paste
1½ cups heavy cream
Salt and freshly ground black pepper to taste

In a large skillet, heat both oils over medium-high heat. Add the crawfish, cover the skillet, and cook for 5 minutes, shaking often. Remove the crawfish from the pan, and set aside 4 of the most attractive for garnish.

Separate the crawfish tails from the bodies and remove the meat from the tails. Set the tails aside and reserve the meat for garnish. Place the bodies and tail shells in a food processor fitted with a metal blade and whirl to crush.

Reheat the skillet over medium heat and add the carrot, leek, celery, garlic, parsley, thyme, and crushed crawfish bodies and shells. Cook gently for about 5 minutes, stirring occasionally. Add the bourbon and cook over medium heat until reduced by half, about 2 to 3 minutes.

Add the white wine and stir in the tomato paste. Return to a boil and reduce by one third, about 4 to 5 minutes. Stir in the cream and reduce the heat. Simmer slowly for 7 to 10 minutes. Add salt and pepper to taste. Strain into a bowl, pressing on the mixture with a wooden spoon to extract as much liquid as possible. Reheat when ready to serve.

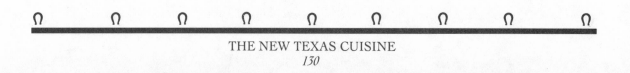

CARPACCIO OF BLACK BUCK ANTELOPE
WITH CASCABEL CHILE AÏOLI

Carpaccio was invented at Harry's Bar in Venice in 1950. It was named for Vittore Carpaccio, the Venetian Renaissance painter, whose work was on display in the city that year at a major exhibition. I can think of nothing more civilized than sipping Bellinis and eating carpaccio and saffron risotto at Harry's Bar. Carpaccio has been duplicated all over the world, and I've brought this version by way of Texas. The delicate flavor of the antelope, which is raised in the Texas Hill Country, is heightened by the cascabel chile aïoli.

---

6 TO 8 SERVINGS

2 pounds antelope loin, trimmed of fat
¼ cup Cilantro Pesto (optional, recipe follows)
1 cup Cascabel Chile Aïoli (see Index)

Juice of 1 lemon
¼ cup grated pecorino, Parmesan, or other hard cheese

Place the antelope loin in the freezer for at least 20 minutes, to facilitate slicing; ice crystals should form but the meat should remain pliable.

Remove the antelope from the freezer and cut into paper-thin slices across the grain with a razor-sharp knife or a meat slicer. Place the slices symmetrically on serving plates so the plates are covered and all spaces are filled.

With a pastry brush, moisten the meat with the cilantro pesto. Thin the aïoli by whisking in a little milk, chicken stock, or water, until it reaches a drizzling consistency. Drizzle over the antelope slices, squeeze lemon juice over, and sprinkle cheese on top.

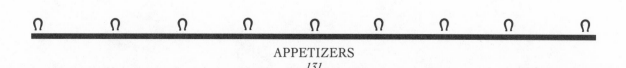

CILANTRO PESTO

ABOUT 2 CUPS

1 clove garlic, chopped
1½ cups cilantro leaves
¾ cup grated Parmesan cheese
½ cup toasted pine nuts (pages 8 to 9)

½ teaspoon salt
¼ teaspoon freshly ground black pepper
¼ cup extra-virgin olive oil

Place all the ingredients, except the olive oil, in a blender. Blend while adding the olive oil in a steady stream. Continue to blend until smooth. Leftover pesto can be stored in the refrigerator or frozen.

BLUE CORN POLENTA WITH GULF OYSTERS AND ANCHO CREAM SAUCE

This recipe demonstrates the versatility of blue cornmeal. Polenta is that great hearty Italian dish that's not so different from the old Southern tradition, grits. While polenta is usually found in fine restaurants and grits in truck stops, the distinction reminds me of an old culinary joke that defines the difference between spaghetti and pasta: about $5! This robust dish, together with a salad, makes an entrée for lunch. You can substitute almost any shellfish for the oysters, especially shrimp or scallops.

6 TO 8 SERVINGS

POLENTA:
5 cups Chicken Stock (see Index)
3 jalapeño chiles, seeded and minced
2 tablespoons pureed roasted garlic (see Index)
2 cups blue cornmeal
½ cup grated Parmesan or pecorino cheese
Salt and freshly ground black pepper to taste

ANCHO CREAM SAUCE:
1 cup dry white wine
1 cup Fish Stock (see Index)
1 red bell pepper, roasted, peeled, seeded, and diced
(page 6)

1 yellow bell pepper, roasted, peeled, and seeded,
and diced
2 shallots, minced
2 dried ancho chiles, rehydrated, seeded, and
julienned (pages 3 to 4)
3 cups heavy cream, reduced by one third
3 tablespoons unsalted butter
Juice of 1 lime
1 tablespoon chopped cilantro
48 fresh oysters, shucked
2 tablespoons sour cream
Salt and freshly ground black pepper to taste
6 scallions, thinly sliced, for garnish

To prepare the polenta, bring the chicken stock to a boil in a saucepan. Add the jalapeños and garlic, and slowly stir in the cornmeal. Lower the heat and simmer, stirring frequently, for 15 minutes; the polenta should be the consistency of mashed potatoes. Thin with a little chicken stock if necessary. Add the cheese and stir until melted. Keep the polenta warm in a double boiler and thin with more chicken stock if necessary. Add salt and pepper to taste.

For the oysters and sauce, place the wine and fish stock in a saucepan and bring to a boil. Lower the heat to medium and add the bell peppers, shallots, anchos, and cream. Reduce the sauce until it coats a spoon, about 10 minutes. Whisk in the butter, lime juice, and cilantro. Add the oysters and cook just until they begin to curl. Remove from the heat and whisk in the sour cream. Season with salt.

To serve, spoon the polenta on the center of each plate and spoon the oysters and sauce around the polenta. Garnish with freshly ground black pepper and the scallions.

SMOKED RABBIT–BLACK BEAN TOSTADAS WITH GOAT CHEESE–ROAST GARLIC CREAM

If you have difficulty in obtaining rabbit for this recipe, you can substitute smoked, roasted, or grilled chicken. Apart from the overnight brining and the smoking process, which is well worth the effort, this is a relatively simple recipe to assemble, and ideal for a quickly prepared dinner. To simplify the recipe even more, forego the smoking procedure. Season the rabbit pieces with salt and pepper, sauté until browned (about 3 minutes per side), and add to the braising liquid.

---

4 SERVINGS

2 whole rabbits, about 3 pounds each, cut into 8 pieces each
All-Purpose Brine for Smoking Meats and Poultry (see Index)
1 cup red wine
½ cup Chicken Stock (see Index)
6 sprigs thyme
1 tablespoon chopped oregano
8 cloves garlic, coarsely chopped
Vegetable or peanut oil, for frying
4 Corn Tortillas (see Index), 6 inches in diameter

½ cup pureed cooked black beans (page 10)
5 tablespoons sour cream
1 tablespoon ancho chile puree (pages 3 to 4)
1 teaspoon ground cumin
1 teaspoon pure chile powder (page 4)
½ teaspoon salt
¼ cup diced onion
¼ cup diced roasted red bell pepper (page 6)
¼ cup diced tomato
1 cup grated Monterey Jack cheese or caciotta
¼ cup Pico de Gallo (see Index), for garnish
1⅓ cups Goat Cheese Sauce (recipe follows)

After brining the rabbits overnight, prepare the smoker (see page 9) and smoke the rabbits at 200° to 225° F. for 1 hour, rekindling the fire and adding more chips as necessary. Preheat the oven to 350° F. Remove the rabbits from the smoker and set aside.

In a large pot or casserole, bring the wine, stock, herbs, and garlic to a boil; add the rabbits, cover, and bake in the oven for about 45 minutes. Remove the rabbits, let cool, and then shred the meat.

Pour enough oil in a skillet to come ½ inch up the sides, and heat until lightly smoking. Fry the tortillas for about 30 seconds, until crisp. Press down on the tortillas with a metal spatula to keep them flat while frying. Drain the tortillas on paper towels and set aside.

In a bowl, thoroughly combine the black bean puree with 1 tablespoon of the sour cream, the chile puree, cumin, chile powder, and salt. Spread the mixture on the tortillas.

In a skillet, heat a tablespoon of the vegetable oil until lightly smoking, add the onion, and cook for 2 minutes, or until translucent. Sprinkle the onion over the black bean mixture on each tortilla, together with the bell pepper and tomato. Then sprinkle half of the cheese on top of the tortillas and cover evenly with the shredded rabbit. Cover the tortillas with the remaining cheese.

Place the tostadas on a sheet pan and place in the oven for 10 minutes. Remove from the oven and garnish with the remaining 4 tablespoons of sour cream and the Pico de Gallo.

Ladle about ⅓ cup of the goat cheese sauce on each plate, and place a tostada on top of the sauce.

GOAT CHEESE SAUCE
ABOUT 1¾ CUPS

1 cup heavy cream
¾ cup fresh goat cheese, at room temperature

1 tablespoon pureed roasted garlic (see Index)
Salt to taste

In a saucepan, bring the cream to a boil. Remove from the heat. Whisk in the goat cheese and garlic. When blended, season with salt and strain.

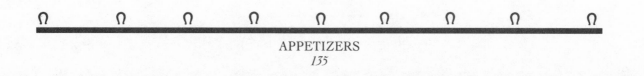

DUCK CONFIT EMPANADAS WITH WILD MUSHROOMS, GOLDEN RAISINS, AND KALAMATA OLIVES

Traditionally, empanadas are made from corn or flour tortillas that are stuffed with meat, cheese, nuts, or some combination of the three and then fried. In this version, phyllo pastry is used to enclose the filling, a combination that was inspired by a trip to Morocco, and then baked. Duck confit is extremely versatile, and only continues to improve in flavor the longer it is kept. It is best made at least one week in advance.

4 SERVINGS

1 tablespoon olive oil, plus extra for brushing
2 tablespoons diced onion
2 cloves garlic, minced
1 tablespoon diced yellow bell pepper
1 tablespoon diced red bell pepper
¼ cup chopped mixed wild mushrooms, such as shiitakes, chanterelles, pleurottes (oyster mushrooms)
½ ounce prosciutto (or Smithfield ham), julienned
2 tablespoons golden raisins
½ cup Marsala
2 tablespoons diced Kalamata olives

1 teaspoon orange zest
1 teaspoon plus 1 tablespoon chopped marjoram
1 teaspoon chopped chives
¼ teaspoon chopped rosemary
1 ounce fresh goat cheese, crumbled
½ cup diced or shredded Duck Confit (recipe follows)
Salt to taste
4 sheets phyllo pastry dough
¼ cup dried breadcrumbs
3 cups Brown Chicken Stock (see Index)
4 sprigs marjoram, for garnish (optional)

Preheat the oven to 450° F. In a skillet over medium heat, heat the tablespoon of olive oil until lightly smoking. Sauté the onion, garlic, and bell peppers for 1 minute. Add the wild mushrooms and prosciutto, and cook for 1 minute longer.

Soak the raisins in the Marsala, and add both, together with the olives, to the skillet. Cook until the Marsala has evaporated. Add the orange zest, 1 teaspoon marjoram, chives, rosemary, cheese, and Duck Confit. Stir to combine thoroughly, and season with salt to taste.

To make an empanada, place 1 sheet of the phyllo pastry dough on a work surface with the long side facing you. Brush the dough lightly with olive oil. Sprinkle evenly 1 tablespoon of the dried bread crumbs over the phyllo. Fold one third of the phyllo pastry (from the top edge) over to make 2 layers. Fold the bottom edge (one layer) up over the folded 2 layers to form 3 layers. Spoon a quarter of the duck mixture in the left hand corner of the pastry. Begin folding the pastry triangularly (as if folding a flag) to encase the duck mixture. Trim off any phyllo that is left after the empanada is formed. Repeat the procedure with the other empanadas.

Brush the empanadas with olive oil and place on a baking sheet. Place in the oven and bake for 8 to 10 minutes, until golden brown.

In a saucepan, bring the chicken stock to a boil and reduce to ¾ cup, about 15 minutes. Add the tablespoon of marjoram and let infuse at a simmer for 3 minutes. Ladle 3 tablespoons of stock onto each plate and serve the empanadas on top of the stock. Garnish with sprigs of fresh marjoram if desired.

DUCK CONFIT

4 TO 6 SERVINGS

1 duck, about 4 pounds
3 tablespoons coarse salt
1 teaspoon freshly ground black pepper

3 sprigs thyme
2 bay leaves, crumbled
4 cups olive oil, or more if needed

Cut the duck into 8 pieces, trimming the neck and wings and removing the backbone; reserve these bones for stock. Rub each piece of duck with some of the salt and place in a baking dish just large enough to hold the duck pieces in one layer; it is preferable that the pieces fit snugly. Sprinkle with pepper and the remaining salt, and add the thyme and bay leaves. Cover and refrigerate for 6 to 12 hours, turning the duck pieces occasionally.

When ready to cook, wipe the excess salt from the duck pieces. Heat the oven to 300° F. Place the duck pieces, skin side down, back in the dish and cook on

top of the stove over low heat for 15 to 20 minutes, or until the fat runs and the duck browns lightly.

Add enough olive oil to cover the browned duck, cover, and cook in the oven for 2 hours, or until the duck is very tender and has rendered all its fat.

To preserve the duck, pour a layer of rendered duck fat in the base of a small terrine and leave until set. Pack the pieces of duck on top and pour over enough fat to cover them completely; cover the terrine and refrigerate at least a week for the flavor to mellow.

SQUASH BLOSSOMS STUFFED WITH DEVILED CRAB

This recipe is a terrific way to celebrate the arrival of summer. While deviled crab has always been an American favorite, the squash blossom packaging puts a sophisticated spin on this down-home classic. If squash blossoms are unavailable, form the deviled crab into cakes any size you wish and use the same cooking method; you'll need an additional ½ cup of breadcrumbs to bread the cakes before frying.

8 SERVINGS

1 pound fresh lump crabmeat (preferably Gulf Coast)
8 tablespoons (1 stick) unsalted butter
¼ cup chopped onion
¼ cup chopped celery
2 tablespoons diced red bell pepper
2 tablespoons diced yellow bell pepper
1 large clove garlic, minced
1 teaspoon minced thyme
2 tablespoons snipped chives
½ teaspoon Worcestershire sauce
¼ cup grated Romano cheese
½ cup unseasoned breadcrumbs

5 large eggs, lightly beaten
Pinch of cayenne powder
2 teaspoons dried mustard powder
1 tablespoon chopped basil
Salt to taste

32 squash or zucchini blossoms
1½ cups milk
½ tablespoon baking powder
1 cup flour
1 teaspoon salt
Vegetable oil, for frying
1 cup Smoked Tomato Aïoli (see Index)

Carefully pick over the crabmeat to remove all cartilage and shells. Set aside. Heat the butter in a large skillet, and over medium heat sauté the onion, celery, bell peppers, garlic, and thyme until the onion is translucent, about 5 minutes.

Add the crabmeat, chives, and Worcestershire sauce. Combine thoroughly but gently. Remove from the heat and add the cheese, breadcrumbs, 2 eggs, cayenne, mustard, and basil. Season with salt.

Carefully stuff each of the squash blossoms with about 1½ tablespoons of the crab mixture. Gently press the blossoms together to completely enclose the mixture, and refrigerate.

Preheat the oven to 200° F. In a mixing bowl, whisk together the 3 remaining eggs and the milk. Sift in the baking powder, flour, and salt, while continuing to whisk. Set the batter aside.

In a large skillet, add enough vegetable oil to come ½ inch up the sides, and heat until just smoking. Lightly dredge the squash blossoms in the flour, and then dip into the batter. Shake to remove the excess batter, and then cook in the hot oil until golden brown, about 3 minutes per side. The blossoms should be cooked in batches, and then kept warm in the oven while the others are being cooked.

Serve 4 squash blossoms per person, with 2 tablespoons of the smoked tomato aïoli.

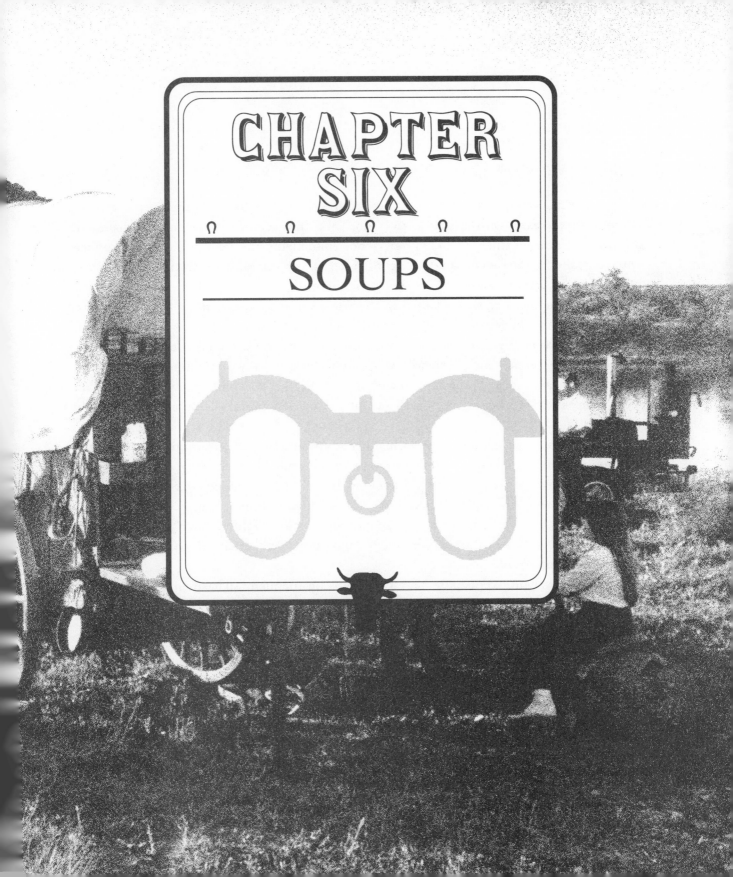

CHAPTER SIX

SOUPS

Soups are marvelous starters that transcend the seasons. I like nothing better than to begin a winter meal with a hearty, rich, hot soup that sets the stage for the dishes to follow. In warm weather, a chilled gazpacho, epitomizing the best of summer produce with its really ripe tomatoes and fresh garden herbs, is a refreshing dish that cleanses the palate. Cold soups are also ideal summer picnic fare.

Texas soups are strongly rooted in the Mexican and Southern cooking traditions. They tend to be hearty rather than subtle. They have strong flavors and plenty of character. Back in Big Spring, it seemed like I grew up on Campbell's soup, though my mother made a great chicken noodle soup, and chicken with dumplings. When I first tasted soups in France, I was immediately struck by the different, distinct flavors that were like eating the ingredients fresh out of the garden (and, of course, they usually were).

All the basic techniques I use in making soups are French in origin, especially the technique of stock making. One of the soups in this vein I'll never forget was a potage, or pureed vegetable soup, made by Raymond Blanc, at Le Manoir Aux Quat' Saisons, just outside Oxford in England. It was so fresh-tasting, it seemed like the essence of ripe vegetables at their peak, treated very simply and cooked lightly. Such treatment is in keeping with the French tradition of potages and purees, which are prepared and cooked in a delicate, unaffected manner.

At Star Canyon, we usually have two soups on the menu. These change seasonally and sometimes daily, and in summer we offer a choice of either a cold soup or a warm soup.

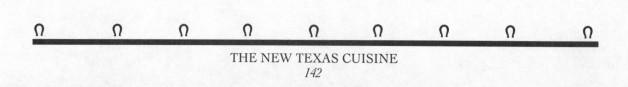

CREOLE SWEET POTATO VICHYSSOISE WITH APPLE-BACON CHUTNEY AND SPICED PECANS

When I first opened Routh Street Cafe in 1983, my good friend Joe Middleton moved from New Orleans to help me for about a year. Joe has an incredible touch with ante-bellum Southern food and anything Creole or Cajun. We developed this dish together as one of the very first menu items at the restaurant, and it has completed its evolution over the years with the addition of the chutney and pecans. Vichyssoise refers to any cold creamy soup using a potato or some type of vegetable base.

8 SERVINGS

2 slices (2 to 3 ounces) bacon, diced
1 large onion, diced
1 carrot, diced
1 green bell pepper, seeded and diced
5 stalks celery, diced
1 head garlic, minced
2 medium (12 ounces to 1 pound) sweet potatoes, peeled and diced
2 to 3 (about 4 ounces) new potatoes, peeled and diced

6 cups Creole Vegetable Stock (see Index)
1 cup fresh orange juice
2 tablespoons maple syrup
½ teaspoon cayenne powder
Salt and freshly ground black pepper to taste
1 cup Apple-Bacon Chutney (see Index), for garnish
1 cup Cajun Spiced Pecans (see Index), for garnish

In a large pan, sauté the bacon over medium heat for 2 minutes to render the fat. Add the onion, carrot, bell peppers, celery, and garlic, and sauté for 5 to 7 minutes, stirring frequently. Add the potatoes and stock, bring to a boil, reduce the heat, and simmer until the potatoes are tender, about 30 minutes.

In a small saucepan, reduce the orange juice over high heat to a thick syrup (about ¼ cup). Add to the large pan together with the maple syrup and cayenne. Puree and strain. Chill, and season to taste with the salt and pepper. If the soup is too thick, thin with a little chicken stock or water.

Serve chilled, and garnish with the chutney and pecans.

CORN AND RED PEPPER SOUPS WITH SOUTHWESTERN CREAMS

This soup is visually striking, with the colors of the Southwest represented: the earthy, brick tones of the red peppers and the ancho chile cream, the rich yellow of the corn, and the lush, green tones of the cilantro cream. A while back, multicolored soups were in vogue, but now they are not quite as popular. I think they are still a great way to impress your guests at a dinner party, and with a little practice, it's easy to become adept at preparing all kinds of attractive presentations. It's important to follow the recipe closely so that the soups and creams are of a similar consistency; that way, they don't run into each other. If necessary, you can thin one of the soups with a little chicken stock. This dish can be prepared the day before and then reheated.

---

4 TO 6 SERVINGS

CORN SOUP:
4 cloves roasted garlic (page 7)
1¾ cups fresh corn kernels (2 large ears)
1½ cups Chicken Stock (see Index)
½ cup chopped onions
¼ cup chopped carrots
¼ cup chopped celery
1 jalapeño chile, seeded and chopped
1 cup heavy cream
Salt to taste

RED PEPPER SOUP:
3 medium red bell peppers, roasted, peeled, and
seeded (page 6)

1½ cups Chicken Stock (see Index)
½ cup chopped onions
¼ cup chopped carrots
¼ cup chopped celery
¼ teaspoon cayenne powder
1 cup heavy cream
Salt to taste

⅓ cup Ancho Chile Cream (recipe follows)
⅓ cup Cilantro Cream (recipe follows)

To prepare the corn soup, place the roasted garlic, corn kernels, chicken stock, onions, carrots, celery, and jalapeño in a medium saucepan. Bring to a boil, reduce the heat, and simmer for 10 minutes to blend the flavors. Transfer to a blender and puree thoroughly. Strain through a fine sieve back into the saucepan. Add the cream and simmer until thickened, about 5 minutes. Season with salt. (If preparing ahead, cool, cover, and refrigerate).

To prepare the red pepper soup, combine all the ingredients except cream and salt in a medium saucepan and bring to a boil. Reduce the heat and simmer for 10 minutes to blend the flavors. Transfer to a blender and puree thoroughly. Strain through a fine sieve back into the saucepan. Add the cream and simmer until thickened, about 5 minutes. Season with salt. (If preparing ahead, cool, cover, and refrigerate).

To serve, gently reheat both soups in separate pans. Simultaneously ladle some of each into warm bowls, and drizzle with the ancho chile and cilantro creams in a zigzag or abstract pattern of your choice (follow your instincts!).

ANCHO CHILE CREAM

ABOUT ⅓ CUP

*1 small dried ancho chile, roasted and rehydrated
(pages 3 to 4)
3 tablespoons milk or half and half*

*2 tablespoons sour cream or Crème Fraîche
(see Index)*

Place the rehydrated roasted ancho in a blender with the milk. Blend until smooth. Pass the mixture through a fine strainer into a mixing bowl and whisk in the sour cream or Crème Fraîche.

CILANTRO CREAM

ABOUT ⅓ CUP

*2 cups water
5 large spinach leaves, stems removed
1 cup loosely packed cilantro leaves*

*3 tablespoons milk or half and half
2 tablespoons sour cream or Crème Fraîche
(see Index)*

Bring the water to a boil, add the spinach leaves, and cook for 1 minute. Drain the liquid and place the leaves in ice water for 1 minute. Place the cilantro, milk, and spinach in a blender, and blend until smooth. Pass the mixture through a fine strainer into a mixing bowl and whisk in the sour cream or Crème Fraîche.

BLACK-EYED PEA BISQUE WITH PICKLED ONIONS

This soup originated at Routh Street Cafe one New Year's Eve. I always try to incorporate the Southern tradition of black-eyed peas bringing good luck into our special annual celebration at Routh Street. We try to pull out all the stops on New Year's Eve, and usually feature such delicacies as caviar, truffles, and foie gras, so this dish was an attempt at introducing some Southern reality into the proceedings! It turned out to be a big hit, so we occasionally bring it back onto the menu. Bisques involve a smoothing, pureeing process, and traditionally (but not necessarily) include shellfish. The name originally derives from the Biscay province of Spain, where this style of soup originated.

6 SERVINGS

2 cups (about 1 pound) dried black-eyed peas
¼ cup olive oil
1 pound smoked ham, diced
1 cup diced celery
1 cup diced onions
4 cloves garlic, chopped
2 serrano chiles, halved and seeded

3 quarts Chicken Stock (see Index)
1 teaspoon minced thyme leaves
2 tablespoons minced cilantro
Salt and freshly ground black pepper to taste
Tabasco sauce to taste
1 cup Pickled Onions (see Index), for garnish

Soak the peas overnight in enough water to cover. Drain and rinse. In a large pan, heat the oil over medium heat until lightly smoking. Add the ham, celery, onion, garlic, and serranos, and cook until the onions become translucent, 3 to 5 minutes. Add the chicken stock, black-eyed peas, and thyme, and bring the liquid to a boil. Reduce the heat and simmer for 1 to 1½ hours, stirring periodically. When the peas are tender, add the cilantro.

Transfer to a blender and puree for about 3 minutes until smooth. Return to the pan, season with salt, pepper, and Tabasco sauce, and bring the soup to a simmer over low heat. Ladle into warm bowls and garnish with pickled onions on the center of the soup.

NOTE: If the bisque is made ahead of time and refrigerated, it will probably be necessary to thin with a little water or chicken stock before reheating.

CHILLED YELLOW PEPPER SOUP WITH SCALLOP CEVICHE VERDE

This soup really hits the spot during the hot Texas summer. There is very little cooking involved, and what there is can be done up to 3 days in advance. The sweetness of the roasted yellow peppers contrasts dramatically with the acidity of the ceviche. Served with bread or tortilla chips and a simple salad, this soup can make a whole summer luncheon.

4 SERVINGS

SOUP:
¼ teaspoon saffron threads
1 tablespoon warm water
3 medium yellow bell peppers, roasted, seeded, and peeled (page 6)
½ cup chopped onion
¼ cup chopped carrot
1 clove garlic, chopped
½ serrano or jalapeño chile, seeded

1½ cups Chicken Stock (see Index)
½ cup heavy cream
½ cup milk (or half and half)
Salt to taste

GARNISH:
Scallop Ceviche Verde (see Index)
4 tablespoons sour cream

Soak the saffron in the warm water for 10 minutes. Transfer to a medium saucepan and combine all the soup ingredients except the cream, milk, and salt. Bring to a boil, then immediately reduce the heat to low. Simmer gently for 5 minutes.

Transfer the ingredients to a blender and blend for 1 minute. Scrape down the sides with a spatula and blend again for 1 minute longer, until smooth. Strain the mixture into a mixing bowl and chill. When cold, blend in the cream and milk, and season with salt.

Ladle the soup into chilled bowls, and garnish each bowl with a generous portion of the scallop ceviche verde and a tablespoon of sour cream.

CHICKEN AND CORN DUMPLING SOUP

$\mathfrak{C}$hicken and dumplings are a very Southern combination, and during my childhood my mother would make them at least every couple of weeks. Each year, my family would travel from Big Spring to Dallas to visit my grandmother, who was originally from Mississippi, and her chicken and dumplings were something I would daydream about. This is a "cleaned-up," lighter version of her recipe. I find it interesting that dumplings are common to many different cultures: Italy has its gnocchi, France its quenelles, Mexico its albondigas, and China its potstickers. In this country, the English settlers learned from the Indians in Virginia the practice of using corn dumplings in soups, and the tradition has remained in Southern cooking ever since.

---

8 TO 10 SERVINGS

CHICKEN:
1 stewing chicken, about 4½ to 5 pounds
1 cup sliced carrots
1 cup chopped onion
1 cup chopped celery
Salt to taste
1 bay leaf
6 sprigs thyme
2 sprigs rosemary

SOUP:
2 tablespoons olive oil
1 carrot, diced
1 medium onion, diced
3 cloves garlic, minced
6 scallions (white and green parts), finely sliced
1 red bell pepper, seeded and diced
1 yellow bell pepper, seeded and diced
2 poblano chiles, roasted, peeled, seeded, and diced (page 6)

2 medium ripe tomatoes, blanched, peeled, seeded, and diced (page 8)
5 tomatillos, husked, rinsed, and diced
1 cup heavy cream
1 tablespoon chopped basil
1 teaspoon chopped tarragon

DUMPLINGS:
1 cup water
4 tablespoons unsalted butter
2 teaspoons salt
1 cup flour
1 teaspoon pureed roasted garlic (page 7)
¾ cup fresh corn kernels (1 ear)
4 eggs
¼ cup chopped chives

Salt and freshly ground black pepper to taste

To prepare the chicken, rinse thoroughly inside and out. Cut downwards from the neck on both sides and remove the backbone. Cut the chicken in half and cut

Ω   Ω   Ω   Ω   Ω   Ω   Ω   Ω   Ω

off the legs. Place the chicken pieces in a large stockpot, add the vegetables and enough water to cover by 3 inches. Add 1 teaspoon salt for each quart of water.

Bring the pot to a boil, reduce the heat to a simmer, skim off the residue for several minutes, and then add the herbs. Continue to simmer, partially covered, for about 2 hours, or until the meat is tender.

Remove the chicken from the pot and separate the meat from the bones. Shred or chop the chicken meat and reserve. Return the bones to the partially covered pot and simmer for 1½ to 2 hours more. Strain the stock, let cool, remove the fat from the surface, and set aside for future use.

To prepare the soup, heat the oil in a large saucepan until lightly smoking, and sauté the carrot, onion, garlic, scallions, and bell peppers over medium heat for 2 minutes. Then add the poblanos, tomatoes, tomatillos, and the reserved chicken stock. Bring to a boil, reduce the heat to a simmer, and add the cream and herbs. Simmer for another 20 minutes.

Meanwhile, prepare the dumplings. In a saucepan, bring the water, butter, and salt to a boil. Sift in the flour and mix with a wooden spoon until the mixture pulls away from the pan and no longer clings to a spoon. Add the garlic and corn, and cook for 1 minute more. Remove the saucepan from the heat and beat in the eggs one at a time. Mix to incorporate completely, and then fold in the chopped chives. Separate the dough into 1 tablespoon pieces and form into dumplings.

Drop each dumpling into the simmering soup. Cook for about 3 minutes, until the dumplings are no longer doughy. Add the reserved shredded chicken and simmer for 3 to 5 minutes. Season with salt and pepper before serving.

GOLDEN GAZPACHO WITH SERRANO CHILES AND BAY SCALLOPS

Each spring, my friends Anne Lindsay Greer, Dean Fearing, Robert Del Grande, and I prepare a dinner together at the Texas Hill Country Food and Wine Festival in Austin. We each prepare a course, and in 1985, the first year we took this event on, this soup was my contribution to the meal. Soon afterwards, Craig Claiborne printed the recipe in the New York Times as part of a profile he wrote about me. The recipe can be made with red tomatoes if yellow ones are unavailable, and red bell pepper instead of yellow. The soup will not have its distinctive golden color, but it will still taste good. You can also substitute shrimp for the scallops. Chill the soup for at least 1 hour before serving.

---

4 SERVINGS

4 oranges
5 or 6 golden or yellow tomatoes, blanched, peeled, seeded, and diced (page 8)
¼ cup diced yellow bell pepper
¼ cup diced cantaloupe
¼ cup diced papaya
¼ cup diced mango
⅓ cup diced chayote
1 cucumber, peeled, seeded, and diced (about ½ cup)

6 scallions (white part only), finely chopped
3 serrano chiles, seeded
2¾ cups Chicken Stock (see Index)
¼ teaspoon powdered saffron
2 tablespoons fresh lime juice
½ teaspoon salt
1 tablespoon chopped cilantro
8 ounces fresh bay scallops

Zest one of the oranges, finely chop the zest, and reserve. Juice all of the oranges. Place the juice in a saucepan and reduce over high heat to about ¼ cup. Reserve the reduced juice.

In a large mixing bowl, combine the tomatoes, bell pepper, cantaloupe, papaya, mango, chayote, cucumber, and scallions. Set aside.

In a blender, puree the serrano chiles in ¾ cup chicken stock. Transfer to a bowl, add the saffron, and allow to infuse for about 10 minutes.

Ω   Ω   Ω   Ω   Ω   Ω   Ω   Ω   Ω

In a blender or food processor, puree one half of the reserved tomato mixture. Return to the remaining tomato mixture in the bowl. Strain the chicken stock mixture into the bowl and stir in the lime juice, reserved orange juice, and salt. Let the soup chill for at least 1 hour. Meanwhile, place the cilantro and reserved orange zest in a bowl and mix together. Lightly poach the scallops in the remaining 2 cups of chicken stock for 1 minute. Remove the scallops, let cool, and coat in the cilantro and orange zest.

To serve, divide the soup into 4 chilled bowls and garnish each serving with 2 ounces of the scallops.

CHILLED SHRIMP AND JICAMA SOUP WITH FRESH GOAT'S BUTTERMILK AND BASIL

This simple, do-ahead soup lends elegance to any meal, yet also is ideal for picnics. The contrast of flavors and textures is created by the acidity of the buttermilk, sour cream, and vinegar; the crunchiness of the jicama; and the floral nuttiness of the basil. Our source for goat's buttermilk is Paula Lambert's Mozzarella Company in Dallas, but the buttermilk can be made like crème fraîche by adding cultured buttermilk to goat's milk and allowing it to sit at room temperature overnight. Goat's milk is usually available at health food stores, but you can substitute regular buttermilk if necessary.

4 TO 6 SERVINGS

1 medium (about 8 ounces) cucumber, peeled, seeded, and chopped
¼ cup raspberry vinegar
1½ pounds jicama, peeled and cut into ¼-inch dice (about 3 cups)
1 tablespoon plus 2 teaspoons sugar
2 teaspoons salt, plus extra
8 ounces small raw shrimp, peeled and deveined
½ teaspoon cayenne powder

2 tablespoons olive oil
2 cups goat's buttermilk or cultured buttermilk
1 cup heavy cream
1 cup sour cream
½ cup packed chopped basil leaves
1 medium red bell pepper, roasted, peeled, and cut into ¼-x-1-inch strips (page 6)
1 yellow bell pepper, roasted, peeled, and cut into ¼-x-1-inch strips

In a food processor, puree the cucumber with the raspberry vinegar for about 30 seconds, until smooth. In a large bowl, toss the jicama and cucumber puree together. Mix in the sugar and 1 teaspoon of the salt. Let the mixture stand while preparing the shrimp.

Place the shrimp in a medium bowl and sprinkle with the remaining teaspoon of salt and the cayenne. In a large skillet over high heat, heat the olive oil until lightly smoking. Add the shrimp and cook until they turn pink, about 2 minutes. Remove the shrimp and set aside.

In a large bowl, combine the buttermilk and heavy cream, then whisk in the sour cream. Add the jicama-vinegar mix, the reserved shrimp, the basil, and the roasted bell peppers, and combine. Season with salt to taste, and serve.

SQUASH BLOSSOM SOUP WITH CANDIED LIME

Some years ago, my friend Zarela Martinez and her mother Aida visited me from New York. It was the middle of summer and my garden was full of squash blossoms. Aida, like her daughter, is a terrific cook, and before I knew it she had harvested the entire crop of squash blossoms and was in the kitchen preparing a wonderful soup. This version is inspired from that memorable evening.

6 TO 8 SERVINGS

1 tablespoon unsalted butter
1 tablespoon olive oil
1 yellow crookneck squash, diced
⅓ cup finely chopped onion
2 cloves garlic, minced
2 serrano chiles, seeded and diced
½ cup chopped yellow cherry tomatoes
1 poblano chile, roasted, peeled, seeded, and diced
(page 6)

15 to 20 squash blossoms
6 cups Chicken Stock (see Index)
8 to 10 epazote leaves
1 teaspoon chopped oregano
1 teaspoon chopped basil
Candied Lime Peel (recipe follows), for garnish

In a large saucepan, heat the butter and olive oil over medium heat. When the butter has melted, add the squash, onion, garlic, and serranos. Cook for 3 to 5 minutes, until the onions are translucent. Add the cherry tomatoes, poblano, and the squash blossoms and cook, stirring, for 1 minute more. Add the chicken stock and bring to a boil. Lower the heat and add the herbs. Simmer gently, covered, for 10 minutes. Garnish each bowl with 3 or 4 candied lime slices.

CANDIED LIME PEEL
ABOUT 3 CUPS

3 to 4 medium (about ½ pound) limes   *½ cup sugar*

Place the limes on a cut end and, using a sharp paring knife, cut downward to remove the peel in strips, leaving a little of the lime flesh attached. Cut into ½-inch lengths. Place the peel in a large pot, add cold water to cover well, and slowly bring to a boil. Boil rapidly, uncovered, for 3 minutes. Drain the peel in a colander. Repeat this procedure 3 times, beginning with cold water each time (this blanching process removes all but a pleasing trace of bitterness from the peel).

Return the peel to the same (drained) pot. Add the sugar and cook, uncovered, over the lowest possible heat, stirring the peel frequently with a wooden spoon. The cooking procedure must be done gradually over a period of 1 to 1½ hours, in order to avoid rapid evaporation of the liquid, resulting in insufficiently cooked peel.

When the peel is glazed, remove from the pot, and arrange on racks set over wax paper, so excess syrup drains away. After the peel has cooled, about 30 minutes, chop the peel into ¼-inch slices.

BLACK BEAN SOUP WITH EPAZOTE AND PICKLED JALAPEÑOS

There is something mysteriously satisfying about bean soups, and I think of them as a real comfort food. Like lasagne and meat loaf recipes, people tend to regard their black bean soup recipe as better than anyone else's! When I was growing up in West Texas, we used to have pintos or black-eyed peas or refried beans, but rarely black beans, which are indigenous to Mexico and Central America rather than Texas. Black bean soup has now become a popular item in the Southwestern repertoire, and this is my version. Epazote is a pungent herb with a camphorlike odor used in Mexican cooking and typically added to bean dishes. It lends a very earthy flavor to this rustic soup.

4 TO 6 SERVINGS

8 ounces bacon, diced
1 small onion, chopped
1 small carrot, chopped
2 stalks celery, chopped
1 poblano chile, seeded and chopped
4 cloves garlic, chopped
2 teaspoons chopped thyme leaves
1 tablespoon chopped epazote
3 cups black turtle beans (about 1 pound),
soaked overnight and drained (page 10)

1 dried chipotle chile (optional)
6 to 8 cups Ham Hock Broth or Chicken Stock
(see Index)
2 teaspoons pure chile powder (page 4)
1 tablespoon ground cumin
1 tablespoon chopped cilantro
Salt to taste
1/2 cup sour cream, for garnish
Pickled Jalapeños (see Index), for garnish

In a large pot, sauté the bacon for 2 minutes over medium heat. Add the onion, carrot, celery, poblano, garlic, thyme, and epazote, and cook for 3 more minutes, or until the onions are translucent. Add the soaked beans and chipotle chile, and enough ham hock broth or chicken stock to cover the beans. Bring to a boil and skim the surface to remove any residue. Reduce the heat and simmer for 2 hours, loosely covered and stirring occasionally, until the beans are tender. Add more broth or stock if the level of liquid falls below the surface of the beans.

When the beans are cooked, transfer all the ingredients in batches to a blender, and puree. Return each batch to a clean pan. Whisk in the chile powder, cumin, cilantro, and salt. Add more broth or stock to thin if necessary, and reheat the soup. Ladle the soup into warm bowls and garnish with sour cream and the pickled jalapeños.

POBLANO-BUTTERO CHEESE SOUP WITH CRISP TORTILLAS

This was a very popular soup at Baby Routh when Rex Hale was the chef. The smoky flavor of the poblano chiles, the acidity of the tomatillos, and the sweetness of the cream and cheese make a delightful combination. Although the Pico de Gallo is optional, it adds depth to the dish. The extra effort of frying the tortilla is worth it; the crunchy texture is a welcome counterbalance to the smoothness of this soup. Buttero cheese is a pasteurized hard sheep's cheese, and parmesan or romano can be substituted.

4 TO 6 SERVINGS

¼ cup flour
4 tablespoons unsalted butter, at room temperature
3 poblano chiles, roasted, seeded, peeled, and chopped (page 6)
1 medium onion, chopped
10 to 12 tomatillos, husked, rinsed, and chopped
3 cloves garlic, minced
1½ cups Chicken Stock (see Index)
½ cup heavy cream

2 cups milk
1 cup chopped cilantro leaves
¾ cup chopped rinsed spinach leaves
10 ounces buttero cheese, grated
Salt and freshly ground white pepper to taste
Vegetable or peanut oil, for frying
4 Corn Tortillas (see Index), cut into ⅛-inch strips, for garnish
½ cup Pico de Gallo (optional, see Index), for garnish

In a mixing bowl, incorporate the flour and butter with a fork. Place the poblanos, onion, tomatillos, garlic, chicken stock, cream, and milk in a heavy pan and bring to a boil. Whisk in the flour and butter mixture and continue to whisk until all the lumps disappear. Cook over medium heat until the mixture thickens.

Add the cilantro, spinach, and cheese, and continue to cook for 30 seconds, while stirring. Transfer to a blender in batches, and blend until completely smooth. Strain through a medium strainer back into the heavy pan, season with salt and pepper, and keep warm.

Place 1 inch of vegetable oil in a skillet and heat until lightly smoking. Fry the tortilla strips until crisp.

Ladle the soup into warm bowls and garnish with tortilla strips and Pico de Gallo, if desired.

CLAM CHOWDER WITH SWEET POTATOES, SAFFRON, AND ORANGE

Clam chowder was one of the few Yankee dishes I was exposed to growing up in West Texas. We served it at one of our family restaurants and it took me the longest time to realize that clams came in something other than cans. I've brought this dish a little farther south by using sweet potatoes instead of white potatoes, and adding a good dose of hot sauce. The saffron and orange round out this dish and give it a deliciously complex layering of flavors.

6 TO 8 SERVINGS

30 raw littleneck clams (about 2 to 2½ pounds), or 10 to 12 cherrystone clams
2½ cups dry white wine
1 tablespoon minced thyme
2 cups water
2 medium (about 1¼ pounds) sweet potatoes, peeled and diced
3 ounces salt pork or bacon, diced
4 tablespoons unsalted butter
1 red bell pepper, seeded and diced

1 green bell pepper, seeded and diced
1 medium onion, diced
2 cups heavy cream
3 cups milk
1 teaspoon saffron threads
Juice of 6 oranges (about 1½ cups)
1½ teaspoons salt
½ teaspoon freshly ground black pepper
¼ teaspoon Tabasco sauce
6 to 8 cilantro leaves, for garnish

Clean the clams thoroughly and reserve 6 to 8 for garnish. Place the remaining clams in a large pot and add 2 cups of the white wine and the thyme. Cover the pot with a lid and steam the clams just until they open. Separate the clams from the shells. Remove the tough meat surrounding the center of each clam and finely chop. Coarsely chop the rest of the meat and set all of the clam meat aside.

Strain the cooking liquid through a double layer of cheesecloth and add the water. Bring the liquid to a boil and cook the sweet potatoes until al dente, about 3 to 5 minutes. Reserve the sweet potatoes and broth separately.

Cook the salt pork or bacon in a large pot with 1 tablespoon of the butter until the pork is lightly browned. Remove with a slotted spoon and reserve. In the same pot, cook the bell peppers and onion for 5 minutes or until softened. Remove from the heat.

Strain the reserved broth into the pot with the vegetables. Add the pork, cream, and milk. Bring back to a boil and add the saffron. Immediately lower the heat, cover the pot, and simmer for 10 minutes.

Meanwhile, in a saucepan over high heat, reduce the orange juice to 2 table-spoons. Whisk in the remaining 3 tablespoons of butter, 1 tablespoon at a time, until melted and fully incorporated. While simmering, steam the reserved clams in the remaining ½ cup of wine and keep warm.

When the broth and pork mixture has simmered, add the orange and butter mixture, reserved potato, clams, salt, pepper, and Tabasco. Return to a simmer and stir thoroughly. Ladle the chowder into warm bowls and garnish with the cilantro leaves and reserved clams in their shells.

SMOKED TOMATO SOUP WITH PAN-FRIED MOZZARELLA AND BASIL CRÈME FRAÎCHE

Soups such as this one were among the first dishes I made when I began smoking vegetables in the early 1980s. This particular recipe has gone through several evolutionary changes since then. It's based on the classic combination of tomatoes, mozzarella, and basil, and makes a great savory dish on a cold winter's night. The addition of beet may seem unusual, but it adds a sweetness and brilliant color. This soup can be made without smoking the vegetables, but you'll appreciate the difference if you taste the final smoked version. A home smoker costs less than $100, and will prove to be one of the best investments you'll ever make! At Star Canyon, we use just a small smoker, and even though it seems to be in constant use, we only need to replace it about every 2 years.

4 TO 6 SERVINGS

1 pound large ripe tomatoes
½ small onion, cut into eighths
2 large cloves garlic, chopped
½ red bell pepper, seeded
1 small beet, peeled and cut into eighths
1 small turnip, peeled and cut into eighths
1 cup heavy cream
2½ cups Chicken Stock (see Index)
6 sun-dried tomatoes
1 tablespoon ancho chile puree (pages 3 to 4)

1 tablespoon tomato paste

Peanut oil, for pan frying
1 egg
1 tablespoon milk
Flour, for dredging
8 ounces fresh mozzarella, cut into 4 rounds
Yellow cornmeal, for dredging
⅓ cup Basil Crème Fraîche (recipe follows)
4 basil leaves (optional)

Prepare the smoker (see page 9). After about 20 minutes, place the tomatoes, onion, garlic, bell pepper, beet, and turnip on the grill over a water pan and cover with the top of the smoker. Smoke the vegetables for 20 to 30 minutes.

Remove the vegetables from the smoker and place them in a large saucepan or stockpot. Add the cream, chicken stock, and sun-dried tomatoes. Bring to a boil and stir in the ancho chile puree and tomato paste. Reduce the heat and simmer for 15 minutes. Place the ingredients from the pan in a blender, and blend until completely smooth. Strain through a medium sieve, return to the pan, and keep the soup warm while frying the mozzarella.

Place just enough peanut oil in a skillet to come halfway up the sides of the mozzarella. Heat the oil over medium heat until lightly smoking. Meanwhile, beat the egg with the milk to form a wash, dredge the mozzarella slices in the flour, dip in the egg wash to coat thoroughly, then dredge in the cornmeal. Fry quickly on both sides until lightly browned.

To serve, ladle the soup into warm bowls and place a cheese slice in the center of each bowl. Streak with the Basil Crème Fraîche and garnish with the basil leaves, if desired.

BASIL CRÈME FRAÎCHE

ABOUT ⅓ CUP

2 cups water
5 large spinach leaves, stems removed
1 cup basil leaves, stems removed

3 tablespoons milk or half and half
2 tablespoons Crème Fraîche (see Index)
or sour cream

Bring the water to a boil, add the spinach and basil leaves, and cook for 30 seconds. Drain the liquid and place the leaves in ice water for 1 minute. Place the spinach, basil, and milk in a blender and blend until smooth. Pass the mixture through a fine strainer into a mixing bowl and whisk in the Crème Fraîche or sour cream.

PUMPKIN–WHITE BEAN CHOWDER WITH ROASTED GARLIC CROUTONS AND POMEGRANATE CRÈME FRAÎCHE

This is a hearty soup that celebrates the flavors of autumn. You can't help but be stimulated by the combination of flavors, textures, and colors: the headiness of garlic, the crunch of crouton, and the tartness and vivid color of the pomegranate. You can substitute sweet potatoes for the pumpkin, and the juice of an orange reduced to 2 tablespoons for the pomegranate. Note that the beans need to be soaked overnight.

6 TO 8 SERVINGS

2½ quarts Chicken Stock (see Index)
1½ cups white beans, soaked overnight and drained (page 10)
1 medium (5 to 6 pounds) pumpkin
1 tablespoon corn oil
8 ounces bacon, diced
1 medium onion, diced
2 stalks celery, diced
1 carrot, diced
1 red bell pepper, seeded and diced
1 yellow bell pepper, seeded and diced

2 cloves garlic, finely minced
2 tablespoons chopped thyme
¼ cup white wine
Salt to taste

GARNISH:
1 cup Roasted Garlic Croutons (recipe follows)
¾ cup Pomegranate Crème Fraîche (recipe follows)
¼ cup chopped chives

Preheat the oven to 350° F. Bring ½ quart (2 cups) of the chicken stock to a boil, and add the soaked beans. Lower the heat and simmer for 30 to 45 minutes, until tender. Set aside.

Meanwhile, slice the pumpkin into 4 pieces and remove the seeds. Place 3 pieces, skin side down, on a cookie sheet and bake in the oven for 30 minutes. Have a bowl of very cold water ready. Peel the reserved piece and cut it into ¼-inch dice. Bring a pan of water to a boil and cook the diced pumpkin until tender, about 1 minute. Drain, and plunge the boiled, diced pumpkin into the bowl of cold water. When cold, drain and set aside.

Heat the oil in a large saucepan over medium heat. Add the bacon and cook for 1 minute. Add the onion, celery, carrot, bell peppers, garlic, and thyme. Cook for 3 to 5 minutes, or until the vegetables become translucent. Add the white wine and remove the pan from the heat.

Remove the skin and seeds from the roasted pumpkin. Cut into pieces and add to the vegetables. Return the pan to the heat, add the remaining 2 quarts of chicken stock, and simmer for 45 minutes. Ladle the soup into a blender and puree. Pass through a strainer and return to a clean saucepan. Add the reserved diced pumpkin and the white beans. Heat through, and season with salt.

To serve, ladle the soup into warm bowls and garnish with the croutons, Pomegranate Crème Fraîche, chives, and a few of the reserved pomegranate seeds.

ROASTED GARLIC CROUTONS
ABOUT 1 CUP

4 slices French or sourdough bread
3 tablespoons olive oil

Salt to taste
1 tablespoon pureed roasted garlic (page 7)

Preheat the oven to 350° F. Cut the crust off the bread and slice the bread into ½-inch strips. Cut the strips into ½-inch cubes. Combine the olive oil, salt, and roasted garlic in a mixing bowl, and add the bread cubes. Mix thoroughly so the croutons are well seasoned. Place on a sheet pan and bake in the oven until the croutons are golden brown, 5 to 7 minutes.

POMEGRANATE CRÈME FRAÎCHE

Be sure not to spill or splatter the pomegranate juice on your clothing — it's one of the most difficult stains to remove!

ABOUT ¾ CUP

1 pomegranate
½ cup Crème Fraîche (see Index)

1 tablespoon heavy cream

Cut the pomegranate into quarters and reserve one for garnish. Squeeze the other 3 into a saucepan and reduce to a syrupy glaze over medium heat (about 5 minutes). Cool, then in a mixing bowl whisk together with the Crème Fraîche and heavy cream. Use the seeds from the reserved quarter for garnish.

CHAPTER SEVEN

SALADS

I like the fact that salads are versatile, and they can play a variety of roles in a meal. They can be a creative appetizer; they can be paired with a meat or fish course for a main meal; or they can serve to cleanse the palate after a sophisticated four-course meal.

Salads are my favorite food to eat at home in the summer. I particularly enjoy playing with the variety of textures and colors that salads provide: the crunch of jicama, the tropical taste and color of mango or papaya, and the sharp tang of citrus. Even the simplest combination of fresh garden salad greens, with a slice of vine-ripened tomato dressed with good-quality olive oil and balsamic vinegar makes a wonderful, simple, and refreshing meal.

I didn't always feel this way about salads, though. Growing up, I used to dread the all-too-familiar iceberg lettuce, tomatoes, and mayonnaise dressing. Other common salads would be pea or three bean salads, tuna or chicken salad, or fruit salad. Since those days, however, there has been a tremendous growth in the availability of new and exciting salad ingredients.

I first got to appreciate some of these ingredients when I traveled to France after graduating from college. Until then, I didn't know that any other lettuces existed: they just weren't grown in Texas back then. Even Bibb and romaine lettuce are relatively recent alternatives to the traditional iceberg in Texas and the South.

Salads are very important in Southwestern cuisine, and many different vegetables and salad ingredients grow across the region. They act as a perfect foil for spicy foods, or as interludes between substantial courses. Salads made with lettuce are not a feature of the Mexican culinary tradition, and instead they are composed primarily of ingredients such as beans, chiles, fruit, and citrus juice.

I always stress the importance of using the best-quality salad greens. As with any dish which includes ingredients that are not cooked, the quality of the raw materials is paramount. At Star Canyon, we use at least fifteen different kinds of salad greens — one salad uses eight varieties alone. Be adventurous and don't be afraid to try out new ingredients. If you live in an area where it is difficult to obtain a good array of unusual lettuces but you have the capability of growing them yourself, it's well worth tracking down a catalog from a good seed company (such as Shepherd's) so you can raise your own.

GARDEN SALAD WITH SMOKED
TOMATO DRESSING

This salad shows the diversity of smoked vegetables, although unsmoked tomatoes can be used just as well. In that case, the tomatoes should be blanched and peeled first. The bacon will provide a slight smokiness, but smoking the tomatoes gives a far greater depth of flavor. Use whichever lettuces are available; I like to use different types with a wide range of textures and flavors.

4 TO 6 SERVINGS

2 slices bacon, diced
1 large ripe tomato
2 teaspoons tomato paste
1 clove roasted garlic (page 7)
1 shallot, diced
1 teaspoon balsamic vinegar
2 teaspoons raspberry vinegar

¼ cup corn oil
¼ cup olive oil
Salt to taste
12 cups (about 7 to 8 ounces) assorted young lettuce leaves, such as romaine, Bibb, arugula, and oak leaf, rinsed and dried

In a skillet, cook the bacon until all the fat is rendered; reserve the bacon and fat separately. Smoke the tomato for 15 minutes (see page 9). Remove from the smoker, peel, slice in half, and squeeze the juice from the tomato into a small saucepan. Reserve the tomato. Add the tomato paste to the saucepan and cook over medium heat for 2 minutes to thicken, stirring often.

Place the tomato and paste in a blender with the garlic, shallot, and vinegars. Puree for 30 seconds. Combine the bacon fat and oils, and with the blender on low, drizzle into the puree. Season with salt.

Place the lettuces in a large mixing bowl. Add the blended dressing and toss gently but thoroughly. Divide among 4 or 6 plates and top each salad with some of the reserved bacon.

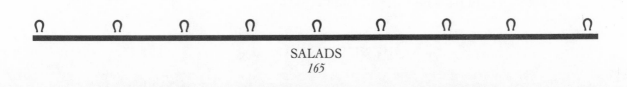

SMOKED PHEASANT SALAD WITH JICAMA AND TEXAS GOAT CHEESE

This salad was on the menu at Routh Street Cafe, off and on, almost from the day we opened in 1983. Smoked chicken can be used as a less expensive substitute for the pheasant. Jicama is the fleshy tuber of a leguminous plant indigenous to Mexico and the Amazon Basin. It is very versatile and is now widely available, especially in cities with Latin and Oriental markets. In Mexico, jicama is eaten as a simple street snack, sprinkled with fresh lime juice and a little chile powder.

4 TO 6 SERVINGS

DRESSING:
2 tablespoons minced cilantro
1 tablespoon minced thyme leaves
1 clove garlic, minced
2 shallots, minced
1 tablespoon dry white wine
3 tablespoons white wine vinegar
½ cup olive oil
¼ cup vegetable or corn oil
Salt to taste

6 ounces Smoked Pheasant breast (recipe follows), thinly sliced
4 ears baby corn, blanched and halved lengthwise

½ cup julienned yellow bell pepper
½ cup julienned red bell pepper
½ cup julienned carrot
½ cup julienned jicama
½ cup julienned chayote
½ cup diced mango
2 ounces (about ⅓ cup) toasted pine nuts (page 9)
4 to 6 rounds of fresh goat cheese, 2 ounces each
2 tablespoons olive oil
¼ cup dried corn-bread crumbs
6 ounces mixed greens, such as arugula, lamb's-lettuce, oak leaf, and radicchio, rinsed and dried

In a mixing bowl, combine the cilantro, thyme, garlic, and shallots and mix well. Whisk in the wine and vinegar, and then slowly drizzle in both oils while still whisking. Season with salt and set the dressing aside.

In a separate mixing bowl, toss the sliced pheasant with the baby corn, peppers, carrot, jicama, chayote, mango, and pine nuts. Set aside.

Heat the oven to 350° F. Moisten the goat cheese rounds with the olive oil and coat with the corn-bread crumbs. Place on a baking sheet and warm in the oven for about 3 minutes while assembling the salad.

In another mixing bowl, combine the lettuces and toss with a quarter of the reserved dressing. Divide the lettuces equally among 4 to 6 chilled plates. Toss the reserved pheasant mixture with the remaining dressing, and arrange the mixture evenly on top of the lettuces. Remove the cheese from the oven and place one round centered at the top of the plate.

SMOKED PHEASANT

FOR 2 PHEASANTS

2 pheasants, 2 to 2½ pounds each
All-Purpose Brine for Smoking Meats and
Poultry (see Index)

Arrange the pheasants in a nonmetallic container. Pour the brine over, adding water if necessary to cover the pheasants. Weight them with a large nonmetallic object to keep submerged. Cover and refrigerate for 12 hours.

Drain the pheasants and pat dry. Let stand at room temperature until dry. Build a fire in a smoker, repeating the procedure used for smoking vegetables (see page 9). Grease the grill rack and arrange the pheasants breast side up on the rack. Cover and smoke for 25 minutes. Turn the pheasants over, cover, and smoke until the breast meat is firm but springs back when touched, about 10 minutes. Serve immediately, or cool completely and refrigerate. Bring to room temperature before using.

PASTA SALAD WITH SMOKED CHICKEN AND OVEN-DRIED TOMATOES

This salad makes a perfect summer luncheon and a wonderful picnic item. Roasted or stewed chicken can be substituted for the smoked chicken to simplify the recipe, although it will not have nearly the same depth of flavor. The good news is that smoked chicken is becoming increasingly available in grocery stores. One thing I've noticed about this salad is that after it sits for several hours it absorbs the seasoning as though it was never applied and tastes bland; so you may want to season the salad again with salt, lemon juice, or vinaigrette.

6 TO 8 SERVINGS

2 tablespoons chopped cilantro
1 tablespoon chopped thyme
2 tablespoons chopped basil
2 cloves garlic, minced
2 shallots, minced
1 tablespoon dry white wine
2 tablespoons white wine vinegar
1 tablespoon balsamic vinegar
½ cup plus 3 tablespoons olive oil
¼ cup corn oil
Salt and freshly ground black pepper to taste

9 ounces dried pasta, such as fusilli or penne
½ cup cooked black beans (page 10)
½ medium red bell pepper, seeded and cut into ¼-inch strips
½ medium yellow bell pepper, seeded and cut into ¼-inch strips
1 small carrot, coarsely chopped
5 tomatillos, husked, rinsed, cored, and diced
4 ounces fresh mozzarella, diced
8 ounces smoked chicken breast, diced
1 cup oven-dried cherry tomatoes (page 8)

In a mixing bowl, thoroughly combine the cilantro, thyme, 1 tablespoon of basil, half of the minced garlic, and the shallots. Whisk in the wine and both vinegars. Slowly drizzle in the ½ cup olive oil and all the corn oil, whisking constantly. Season the vinaigrette to taste with salt and pepper, and set aside.

Cook the pasta in a large pot of boiling salted water until al dente. Drain and place in a large serving bowl. Add the remaining 3 tablespoons olive oil and toss well. Set aside to cool.

When the pasta is thoroughly cool, add the black beans, vegetables, mozzarella, smoked chicken, dried tomatoes, and the remaining basil and garlic. Toss with the reserved vinaigrette and season to taste. Cover the salad and refrigerate to chill slightly, about 20 minutes.

GRILLED CHICKEN SALAD WITH CILANTRO-PESTO MAYONNAISE

This salad was on the opening menu at Baby Routh and is a permanent feature at Tejas in Minneapolis. It's a new twist on an old classic. The cilantro-pesto mayonnaise was inspired by my good friend Anne Lindsay Greer, who likes to serve it with oysters on the half shell. This salad can be served with a mixture of greens, or as a sandwich with your favorite bread.

6 SERVINGS

1½ pounds skinless, boneless chicken breasts
1 to 2 tablespoons vegetable oil
Salt and freshly ground black pepper to taste
5 tablespoons Cilantro-Pesto (page 132)
3 tablespoons Mayonnaise (see Index)
¼ cup green bell pepper, roasted, peeled, seeded, and julienned (page 6)
¼ cup yellow bell pepper, roasted, peeled, seeded, and julienned

½ cup red bell pepper, roasted, peeled, seeded, and julienned
¾ cup diced celery
½ cup diced, unpeeled Granny Smith apples
¾ cup chopped cilantro leaves
1 tablespoon salt
1 tablespoon sugar
1 tablespoon freshly ground black pepper
Juice of 3 limes

Brush the chicken breasts with the oil, and season with salt and pepper. Grill the chicken on a medium-hot charcoal grill, about 3 minutes per side. Remove from the grill and let cool. Slice each breast in half lengthwise, and then julienne. Set aside.

Combine the cilantro-pesto with the mayonnaise and set aside. In a large serving bowl, combine the julienned chicken with the remaining ingredients. Dress with the cilantro-pesto mayonnaise, mix thoroughly, and adjust the seasonings.

ARUGULA–POACHED PEAR SALAD WITH CAMBAZOLA, WALNUTS, AND PORT VINAIGRETTE

This is a perfect salad following a multicourse meal and before dessert. It combines the classic flavors of port, blue cheese, and walnuts, while bringing together the traditional courses of salad and cheese. Cambazola is a creamy blue cheese from Italy, and any similar cheese can be substituted.

4 SERVINGS

2 ripe Anjou or Bartlett pears
2 cups dry red wine
1/2 cup good-quality port
2 cloves
1/2 cup sugar
2 tablespoons raspberry vinegar
1 small shallot
1 small clove roasted garlic (page 7)

6 tablespoons walnut oil
2 tablespoons vegetable oil
Salt to taste
2 ounces Cambazola cheese
4 croutons, about 2 inches long x 1/4 inch wide
4 to 6 cups arugula, rinsed and dried
1 ounce (3 tablespoons) walnut halves

Preheat the oven to 400° F. Peel and core the pears, and cut them in half. In a saucepan just large enough to hold the 4 pear halves, bring the wine and port to a boil with the cloves and sugar. Reduce the heat to low and add the pears, cut side down, into the pan. Let simmer for 10 to 15 minutes; the pears should be tender when pierced with a knife. Remove the pears and set aside.

Pour off all but 1 cup of the poaching liquid and reduce it over a high heat to 2 tablespoons. Place the reduced liquid in a blender and add the raspberry vinegar, shallot, and garlic. Blend until smooth, and then add the oils in a steady drizzle. Taste the vinaigrette and season with salt.

Spread the Cambazola evenly on the 4 croutons and place on a sheet pan in the oven just long enough to melt slightly.

Dress the arugula with the vinaigrette and divide between 4 plates. Serve each salad with half a poached pear at the top of the plate (cut into a fan if desired), the Cambazola crouton at the bottom, and some walnuts sprinkled over.

WILTED SOUTHERN GREENS WITH BACON, PECANS, AND CRANBERRIES

This salad utilizes the flavors of fall. Every week when I was growing up, my mother would cook up a big pot of greens with a ham hock, red onion, and a big clove of garlic. As is typical with preparing any vegetables in the South, these greens would be cooked for much longer than they needed to be! In this recipe, the greens are quickly wilted in the bacon vinaigrette. The crunch of apple and the tartness of the cranberries play off the pungent greens.

4 SERVINGS

³/₄ cup fresh cranberries
¹/₄ cup sugar
4 ounces bacon, diced
2 shallots, minced
2 cloves garlic, minced
¹/₄ cup corn oil
¹/₄ cup olive oil
2 tablespoons balsamic vinegar

2 tablespoons red wine vinegar
2 sprigs rosemary, chopped
¹/₂ cup chopped toasted pecans (page 9)
2 green apples, cored and coarsely chopped
8 ounces assorted greens, such as turnip, collard, and mustard greens, rinsed and dried
Salt and freshly ground black pepper

Coarsely chop the cranberries, add to a blender with the sugar, and blend for 30 seconds. Set aside.

In a large skillet, cook the bacon until all the fat is rendered. With a slotted spoon, remove the bacon from the pan and reserve. Using the bacon fat, sauté the shallots and garlic until soft. Add both oils and vinegars to the skillet and whisk. Add the rosemary, pecans, apples, and macerated cranberries, and cook for 1 minute.

Add the greens, toss until just wilted, about 20 to 30 seconds, and season with salt and pepper. Divide evenly between 4 plates, and sprinkle the reserved bacon on top.

BLACK-EYED PEA–CRAB SALAD WITH RUBY GRAPEFRUIT

This easy, do-ahead salad is a perfect entrée for a summer lunch or picnic. Black-eyed peas, crab, and grapefruit may not exactly be an orthodox combination, but they are all staples of Texas cookery and go well together. I always knew that Texas ruby grapefruit was a great product, but I became thoroughly convinced while I was a chef's assistant at the Mondavi Great Chefs Program. Many of the guest three-star French chefs demanded the ruby variety from Texas whenever grapefruit was included in their repertoire.

4 TO 6 SERVINGS

1½ cups black-eyed peas, soaked overnight and drained (page 10)
1 quart Ham Hock Broth (see Index) or water
Salt to taste
4 slices bacon, diced
1 pound fresh lump crabmeat (preferably Gulf Coast)
1 red bell pepper, seeded and finely diced
1 yellow bell pepper, seeded and finely diced
1 green bell pepper, seeded and finely diced

1 purple onion, minced
3 scallions, thinly sliced
1 tomato, flesh and skin only, diced (page 8)
1 teaspoon chopped thyme
1 teaspoon chopped marigold mint or tarragon
1 teaspoon chopped chervil
1 cup Grapefruit Vinaigrette (recipe follows)
4 ruby grapefruit, peeled with a knife and sections removed (pages 10 to 11)
8 to 10 cilantro sprigs, for garnish

Place the drained black-eyed peas in a saucepan with the ham hock broth or water, and bring to a boil. Reduce the heat and simmer until tender, 45 minutes to 1 hour. Toward the end of the cooking time, taste the peas and season with salt. Drain and set aside.

In a skillet, cook the bacon over medium-high heat until all the fat is rendered. Transfer the bacon to a large mixing bowl and add the crabmeat, vegetables, peas, and herbs. Mix together until thoroughly combined.

Combine the salad with the vinaigrette. Mound the tossed salad on a large serving platter, leaving at least 2 inches around the edge of the platter. Arrange the grapefruit sections around the salad, and garnish the grapefruit sections with the cilantro sprigs.

GRAPEFRUIT VINAIGRETTE
1 CUP

Juice of 1 grapefruit (about ¼ cup)
Juice of 1 lemon
Juice of 1 orange (about 2 tablespoons)
1 teaspoon sugar
1 tablespoon grapefruit zest

2 tablespoons champagne vinegar
¼ cup corn oil
¼ cup olive oil
Salt to taste

In a small saucepan over medium-low heat, reduce the citrus juices and sugar to 2 tablespoons. Transfer to a mixing bowl, and add the zest and champagne vinegar. Whisk together while drizzling in the combined oils, and add the salt.

JICAMA–BELGIAN ENDIVE SALAD WITH TEQUILA-ORANGE VINAIGRETTE

This cool and refreshing salad is the perfect summer luncheon item. It first appeared on the menu at Tejas and has since made the rounds to the other restaurants in some form or other. Jicama, Belgian endive, and orange always make a great combination, but the addition of tequila really perks it up.

---

4 TO 6 SERVINGS

¼ cup fresh orange juice
2 tablespoons tequila
1 tablespoon white wine vinegar
½ shallot
½ cup corn oil
¼ cup olive oil
Salt and freshly ground white pepper to taste

2 heads Belgian endive, rinsed, dried, and leaves separated
3 oranges, peeled by knife and sections removed (pages 10 to 11)
2 medium jicamas, peeled and julienned
12 chives, snipped, for garnish

Ω   Ω   Ω   Ω   Ω   Ω   Ω   Ω   Ω

Place the orange juice, tequila, vinegar, and shallot in a blender, and blend at high speed. Slowly add the oils while still blending. Season with the salt and white pepper.

Arrange the endive leaves in a spoke pattern around the outside of each plate, and place an orange section on each leaf. Toss the jicama with some of the dressing and mound in the middle of each plate. Ladle the rest of the dressing onto each plate and sprinkle with chives.

SOUTHWESTERN CAESAR SALAD WITH POLENTA CROUTONS

Originally served at Routh Street Cafe, this salad was featured on the opening menu at Baby Routh and Star Canyon. The basic version of the Caesar salad was created in Mexico in the 1920s by Caesar Cardini, an Italian by origin with a thriving restaurant in Tijuana. It's a classic salad that has been in and out of fashion with regularity. It is currently in vogue, especially in this Southwestern style. This version has collected chiles from Mexico and the Southwest, mustard from France, and tamarind from the Orient. I prefer the visual presentation of red and green romaine, but not to worry if only green romaine is available — it'll taste just as good!

8 SERVINGS

DRESSING:
1 teaspoon ground cumin
4 teaspoons Dijon mustard
2 tablespoons pureed roasted garlic (page 7)
1 teaspoon tamarind paste
2 tablespoons chipotle chile puree (pages 3 to 4)
4 anchovy fillets
1 tablespoon balsamic vinegar
2 tablespoons fresh lemon juice
1 small shallot, minced
3 egg yolks

1 teaspoon pure red chile powder
2/3 cup extra-virgin olive oil
1/3 cup vegetable oil
Salt and cayenne powder to taste

SALAD:
2 heads red romaine lettuce, rinsed and dried
2 heads green romaine lettuce, rinsed and dried
4 ounces pecorino or Parmesan cheese, shaved

2 cups Polenta Croutons (recipe follows)

Place all the dressing ingredients, except the oil and seasoning, in a blender, and blend until smooth. With the machine running, slowly drizzle in the oil and incorporate thoroughly. Season with salt and cayenne powder, and set aside.

Derib the inside leaves of each head of the romaine, and then tear into bite-sized pieces. In a large salad bowl, toss the romaine with the dressing and half of the cheese. Divide the tossed greens evenly among 8 plates and top with the remaining cheese and the hot croutons.

POLENTA CROUTONS

3 TO 3½ CUPS

4 serrano chiles, seeded and minced
½ teaspoon cayenne powder
1½ teaspoons salt

2¾ cups milk
1½ cups yellow cornmeal
6 cups peanut oil

In a medium saucepan, combine the serranos, cayenne, and salt to the milk, and bring to a rapid boil. Slowly add 1 cup of the cornmeal while stirring constantly. Cook over medium heat for 3 to 5 minutes, until the mixture pulls away from the sides of the pan and forms a ball. Press the mixture into a 9-inch pie pan lined with plastic wrap. Place in the refrigerator, uncovered, to cool. Remove from the pan and dice into ½-inch cubes.

In a medium saucepan, heat the peanut oil to 350° F. Dredge the polenta cubes in the remaining ½ cup of cornmeal. Fry the croutons until crisp, about 1 to 2 minutes. Remove from the oil with a slotted spoon, drain on paper towels, and keep warm.

ARUGULA–FRIED OKRA SALAD WITH ROAST CORN VINAIGRETTE

This salad combines the sophisticated flavor of arugula with the Southern passion for fried okra and corn. The pungent arugula is a perfect foil for the silky vinaigrette and the sweet acidity of ripe tomatoes.

6 SERVINGS

2 large ears fresh corn, shucked
½ large shallot, minced
1 clove garlic, minced
1 tablespoon white wine vinegar
½ cup Chicken Stock (see Index)
¼ cup olive oil
¼ cup corn oil, plus more for frying
Salt to taste
1 egg

1 tablespoon milk
12 large (about 6 ounces) okra spears, cut into
⅓-inch rounds
½ cup cornmeal
1 pound arugula, large stems removed, rinsed, and dried
1 medium tomato, blanched, peeled, seeded, and diced (page 8)

Preheat the oven to 400° F. Using a sharp knife, cut the corn kernels off the cobs. On a large, heavy baking sheet, spread the kernels in an even layer. Roast in the oven for about 20 minutes, stirring occasionally, until the corn is lightly browned but still moist. Set aside to cool. Reduce the oven temperature to 300° F.

In a blender or food processor, combine the cooled corn kernels with the shallot, garlic, vinegar, and chicken stock; process until the corn is pureed. With the machine running, slowly drizzle in the olive oil and ¼ cup corn oil. When thoroughly incorporated, strain the vinaigrette into a bowl and season with salt. Thin with a little chicken stock or water if necessary. Cover and set aside.

In a medium cast-iron skillet, heat ¼ inch of corn oil over medium-high heat until lightly smoking. Meanwhile, in a bowl, beat the egg with the milk. Working in 2 batches, dip the okra rounds in the egg wash and then dredge in the cornmeal to coat thoroughly. Fry in the hot oil, stirring occasionally, until golden brown and crisp, about 2 minutes. Using a slotted spoon, transfer the okra to a baking sheet lined with paper towels to drain. Keep the fried okra warm in the oven while you fry the rest.

Place the arugula on a large serving platter. Drizzle with the corn vinaigrette and toss thoroughly. Garnish the salad with the fried okra and diced tomato, and serve at once.

SMOKED DUCK SALAD WITH CHAYOTE, MANGO, AND FRIED CAYENNE PASTA

This is another salad that I created in the early days of Routh Street Cafe, although the recipe has evolved quite a bit since then. It has become one of our most popular salads, and something of a trademark dish that I often prepare at events. A small amount of this salad on toasted brioche also makes a great appetizer. Although the cayenne pasta really adds an interesting element to this dish, it is not absolutely essential. If you live in a community with a sizable Chinese population, smoked duck is likely to be readily available.

4 TO 6 SERVINGS

SALAD:
6 ounces skinless duck breast, smoked and diced
(see Preparing the Smoker)
1 tablespoon diced red bell pepper
1 tablespoon diced yellow bell pepper
1 tablespoon diced carrot
2 tablespoons diced jicama
3 tablespoons diced mango
1 tablespoon diced chayote

2 tablespoons red seedless grapes, cut into eighths
3 tablespoons blanched podded sugar snap or English peas
4 tablespoons toasted pine nuts (page 9)

1/3 cup Herbed Mayonnaise (recipe follows)
Salt and freshly ground black pepper to taste
1 quart peanut oil
4 ounces Cayenne Pasta (recipe follows)

In a large mixing bowl, combine the diced duck breast with the remaining salad ingredients.

Stir the mayonnaise into the salad and season with salt and pepper. Set aside.

Heat the peanut oil (there should be at least 2 to 3 inches in the pan) to 375° F. Fry the cayenne pasta for 10 to 15 seconds and remove with a slotted spoon. Drain the pasta on paper towels. Divide the pasta evenly among 4 to 6 plates and place the duck salad on top of the pasta.

HERBED MAYONNAISE

A smaller amount of mayonnaise cannot be made successfully. The remaining mayonnaise will keep for up to a week in the refrigerator.

1 GENEROUS CUP

1 egg yolk
¼ teaspoon salt
Juice of ½ lemon
½ cup olive oil
½ cup rendered duck fat (pages 11 to 12) or vegetable or corn oil
1 small shallot, diced

1 tablespoon chopped cilantro
1 tablespoon chopped basil
1 teaspoon chopped marjoram
1 teaspoon chopped chives
1 teaspoon chopped parsley
Salt and freshly ground black pepper to taste

In a mixing bowl, whisk together the egg yolk, salt, and lemon juice until blended. In a small bowl, combine the oil and duck fat, and slowly drizzle into the mixing bowl while continually whisking. After all the oil is incorporated, continue whisking for 15 seconds. Add the remaining ingredients and incorporate thoroughly.

CAYENNE PASTA

This recipe makes a very spicy pasta. For a milder version, reduce the cayenne by one third.

ABOUT 12 OUNCES

1 cup flour
½ cup semolina flour
2 tablespoons Hungarian sweet paprika
1 tablespoon cayenne powder

¾ teaspoon salt
2 eggs
1 tablespoon tomato paste
½ tablespoon olive oil

Combine the flours, paprika, cayenne, and salt in a food processor or blender. In a small bowl, beat the eggs, tomato paste, and oil and blend thoroughly. With the processor running, add the egg mixture to the dry ingredients and blend until the dough is evenly moistened; do not form into a ball. Turn the dough out onto a lightly floured surface, gather into a ball, and pat into a disk. Cover and let stand at room temperature for 1 hour.

Cut the dough into 2 pieces. Flatten 1 piece of the dough, keeping the remainder covered, and then fold into thirds. Using a pasta machine, turn to widest setting and run the dough through several times until it's smooth and velvety, folding before each run and dusting with flour if sticky. Adjust the machine to the next narrower setting. Run the dough through the machine without folding. Repeat, narrowing the rollers after each run, until the pasta is 1/16 inch thick, dusting with flour as necessary.

Hang the dough sheet on a drying rack or place on kitchen towels. Repeat with the remaining dough. Set aside until the sheets look leathery and the edges begin to curl, about 10 to 30 minutes, depending on the dampness of the dough.

Cut the pasta at this stage, or the dough will become too brittle. Run the sheets through the linguine blade of the pasta machine. Arrange on a towel, overlapping as little as possible, until ready to cook.

MARINATED BEAN SALAD WITH TEXAS SWEET ONIONS

This dish reminds me of Nancy Silverton, the former pastry chef at Spago who, with her husband, Mark Peel, now owns Campanile in Los Angeles. When we first met, we discovered we both had a passion for beans, and we agreed that any restaurant which did not feature beans in several dishes was simply not worth frequenting! While my affinity for beans came from being raised on pintos, black beans, and black-eyed peas in West Texas, Nancy's was derived from her love of Tuscany. This is a perfect dish for a large buffet, and it makes an excellent accompaniment to a summer barbecue or grill-out since all the work can be done ahead of time. If the salad is marinated overnight, check the seasonings the next day, as they tend to dissipate.

¾ cup (4 ounces) black turtle beans, soaked overnight and drained (page 10)

¾ cup (4 ounces) pinto beans, soaked overnight and drained

¾ cup (4 ounces) white navy beans, soaked overnight and drained

About 2 quarts Ham Hock Broth (see Index) or water

1 large sweet onion, such as Noonday or Texas Spring Sweet, as thinly sliced as possible

¼ cup cider vinegar

2 teaspoons sugar

½ teaspoon salt, plus extra to taste

1 red bell pepper, roasted, peeled, seeded, and diced (page 6)

1 yellow bell pepper, roasted, peeled, seeded, and diced

1 large ripe tomato, blanched, peeled, seeded, and chopped (page 8)

½ cup chopped pitted ripe black olives

3 tablespoons chopped cilantro

¾ cup Routh Street Vinaigrette (see Index)

1½ cups Roasted Garlic Croutons (optional, see Index)

8 cups (about 5 to 6 ounces) assorted young lettuce leaves, such as romaine or chicory, rinsed and dried

Place the drained beans in separate pans and cover each with ham hock broth or water. Bring to a boil, then reduce the heat and let the beans simmer until tender, 45 minutes to 1 hour. Drain the beans completely in a large colander, reserving the broth (if using) for further use. Mix the beans together in a large bowl and refrigerate until cool.

In another bowl, toss the onion with the vinegar, sugar, and ½ teaspoon salt, and reserve.

When the beans are chilled, add the bell peppers, tomato, olives, and cilantro. Drizzle with ½ cup of the vinaigrette, toss well, and refrigerate for 1 hour. Remove from the refrigerator, add the croutons, season with salt, and toss thoroughly.

In another bowl, toss the lettuces with the remaining ¼ cup of vinaigrette. Arrange the lettuces around the edge of a large platter and mound the bean salad in the middle. Garnish with the reserved sliced onions.

SOUTHWESTERN COBB SALAD

The original Cobb salad was created in 1936 at Hollywood's famous Brown Derby restaurant by Robert Cobb, who was then the proprietor. This version is given a distinctive Texan flair by the addition of ancho chile, jalapeño cheese, avocado, and tortillas. If blue or red corn tortillas are unavailable, just use the regular yellow tortillas.

4 TO 6 SERVINGS

½ small onion
½ cup Chicken Stock (see Index)
½ cup dry white wine
1 serrano chile, seeded and diced
2 cloves garlic, minced
1 teaspoon marigold mint or tarragon
1 pound chicken breast
Salt and freshly ground black pepper to taste
1½ cups Routh Street Vinaigrette (see Index)
8 slices bacon, diced
1 ripe avocado, peeled, pitted, and diced
Juice of ½ lemon
1 small head chicory, rinsed and dried
1 bunch watercress, rinsed and dried
1 head Belgian endive, rinsed and dried

½ cup cilantro leaves
3 eggs, hard-cooked and chopped
2 medium ripe tomatoes, blanched, peeled, seeded, and diced (page 8)
3 ounces jalapeño Jack cheese, or similar flavored cheese, grated
4 scallions, finely chopped (green and white parts)
1 dried ancho chile, seeds removed and very finely sliced
2 blue corn tortillas
2 red corn tortillas
2 yellow Corn Tortillas (see Index)
Peanut oil, for frying

Place the onion, stock, wine, serrano, garlic, and mint marigold in a large saucepan, bring to a boil, and reduce the heat to simmer. Season the chicken with salt and pepper, add to the saucepan, and cover. Poach for about 20 minutes, until just done.

Remove saucepan from the heat and allow to cool. Remove the chicken from the broth, cut into ½-inch dice, and set aside. Return pan to medium heat, and reduce the stock to 2 tablespoons. When cool, whisk into the vinaigrette.

Sauté the bacon until crisp and the fat is rendered. Drain on paper towels and set aside. Place the diced avocado in a bowl and gently mix with the lemon juice.

Slice the chicory into shreds and chop crosswise. Remove the stems from the watercress and separate the endive leaves. Place the greens and cilantro in a large bowl and toss gently to combine. Transfer the tossed greens to a large platter. In circles, rows, or in decorative patterns, place the chicken, avocado, eggs, tomatoes, and cheese over the greens. Then sprinkle the bacon, scallions, and ancho chile over the salad.

Cut the tortillas into Southwestern shapes or motifs, such as arrows, lightning bolts, cacti, coyotes, or cowboy boots (use cookie cutters if available). Pour enough peanut oil in a large skillet or pan to come ½ inch up the sides. Heat until lightly smoking and fry the tortilla shapes for 30 to 40 seconds, until crisp. Remove from the pan, drain on paper towels, sprinkle with salt, and transfer to a basket for service.

Bring the salad platter to the table, pour the vinaigrette over the salad, and toss well. Serve with the basket of tortilla shapes.

ROAST TURKEY–TOSTADA SALAD WITH RANCH DRESSING AND CRANBERRY SALSA

This is the perfect salad for using up leftover Thanksgiving turkey. It's a far cry from the beef taco salad my mother made when I was growing up, but nevertheless that was the inspiration. Leftover chicken can be substituted for the turkey, and if it's not cranberry season, try using another fruit such as fresh or dried cherries, or fresh berries; either will also require less sugar.

Vegetable oil, for frying
6 Corn Tortillas (see Index)
Salt to taste
2 cups chopped roast turkey (white and/or dark meat)
½ cup diced onion
1 small tomato, blanched, peeled, seeded, and chopped (page 8)
¼ cup toasted pecans (page 9)
1 avocado, peeled, pitted, and sliced
¼ cup pitted black olives

¾ cup My Ranch Dressing (see Index)
¾ cup grated caciotta or Jack cheese
1 head romaine lettuce, rinsed, dried, and shredded with a knife
1 head radicchio or red cabbage, rinsed, dried, and shredded with a knife
½ cup Routh Street Vinaigrette (see Index)
4 tablespoons sour cream
1 cup Cranberry Salsa (see Index)
2 Pickled Jalapeños, sliced (optional, see Index), for garnish

Preheat the oven to broil. Pour enough oil in a large skillet or pan to come 1 inch up the sides. Heat until lightly smoking, and fry 4 of the tortillas over medium heat for about 2 minutes until crisp, keeping the tortillas as flat as possible by holding them down with 2 spatulas. Remove from the pan, drain on paper towels, and sprinkle with salt. Transfer to a baking sheet.

Cut the remaining 2 tortillas into strips ⅛ inch thick and fry until crisp. Remove from the pan, drain on paper towels, and sprinkle with salt.

In a large mixing bowl, combine the turkey, onion, tomato, pecans, avocado, and olives. Add the ranch dressing and toss to thoroughly combine.

Divide the turkey mixture into 4 equal amounts, and place on top of the 4 tostadas (fried tortillas). Sprinkle the cheese over the turkey mixture and place the tostadas under the broiler. Broil for about 1 minute, just until the cheese melts. Remove and transfer the tostadas to plates.

In a mixing bowl, toss the shredded lettuces with the vinaigrette. Place the tossed lettuces around the tostadas on the plates, and sprinkle with the reserved tortilla strips. Place 1 tablespoon of sour cream on the center of each tostada, and top with a dollop of cranberry salsa (the remaining salsa should be placed in a serving bowl). Sprinkle the sliced jalapeños over the tostadas and lettuces, if desired, and serve.

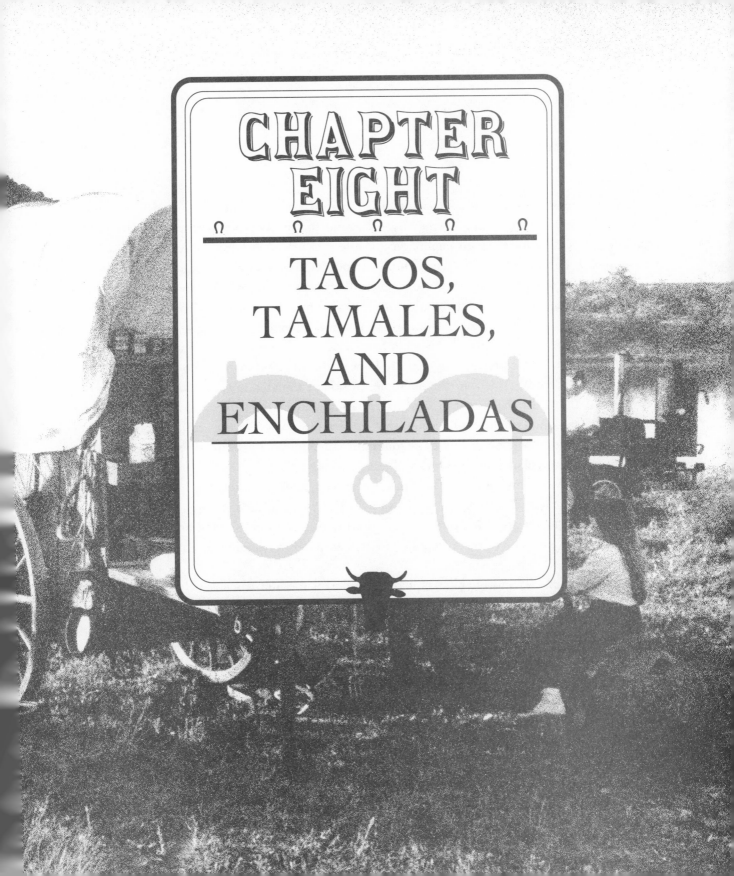

CHAPTER EIGHT

TACOS, TAMALES, AND ENCHILADAS

Perhaps more than any other food, tacos, tamales, and enchiladas epitomize the new style of Texas cooking. They have evolved beyond the predictable beef tacos, plain corn tamales, or cheese or chicken enchiladas. While these delicious mainstays are still common, new ground has been broken with the introduction of exotic and exciting ingredients and fillings. It would have been unthinkable, fifteen years ago, to find tuna or duck tacos, shellfish tamales, or lobster enchiladas on Texas menus, but these and other interesting combinations have all become established in the new cuisine.

Tacos, tamales, and enchiladas stem from a rich tradition that originates well beyond Tex-Mex food. There are literally hundreds of different regional variations of tamales in Mexico and Central America, for example, although tamales may not necessarily have originated there. In the fifteenth century, missionaries in East Texas witnessed Native Americans making tamales and learned that this tradition was centuries old. In any event, these foods have long been staples throughout Mexico, and are an integral part of the influence of that cuisine on the food of Texas.

When I was growing up in Big Spring, the best tacos, tamales, and enchiladas were to be found in the Mexican restaurants in town. But even the steakhouses seemed to have them on their menu as a "Mexican plate," usually offering one of each as a combination dish. This remains true of restaurants and truck stops in the smaller Texas towns outside the major cities.

Tacos, tamales, and enchiladas are a wonderful medium for creativity and expression. They are extremely versatile and can be served as appetizers, accompaniments, or entrées, and for breakfast, brunch, lunch, or dinner; they can even be served as dessert. We serve a different enchilada special every day for lunch at Baby Routh. Even though the fillings always change, ranging from beef to pork, venison, seafood, chicken, turkey, or mushrooms, there is one thing in this world of which I can be certain: whenever my editor comes to town to work with me, he will unfailingly order the *enchilada del día* for lunch.

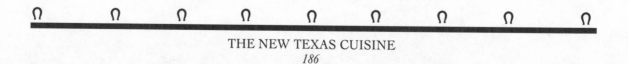

DAD'S TRUCK STOP TACOS

My father excels at Tex-Mex cooking, and I remember these tacos from my earliest childhood. They were always on the menu at his Big Spring Truck Stop Cafe, and the truckers would say that they were some of the best tacos west of the Mississippi. Dad still makes them for special occasions. They differ from tacos you find nowadays, at least in Dallas, in that they are fried with the meat inside them, secured with toothpicks. We would make an entire meal out of these tacos and garnish, but they can be served with a myriad of accompaniments, including the Black Bean–Prosciutto Refrito (see Index) and any number of the salsas and relishes included in Chapter 3.

6 SERVINGS (18 TACOS)

2 tablespoons vegetable oil, plus extra for frying and softening tortillas
2 medium onions, finely chopped
6 cloves garlic, minced
2 pounds ground chuck
2 teaspoons pure chile powder (page 4)
2 teaspoons ground cumin
2 teaspoons oregano

½ teaspoon cayenne powder
Salt and freshly ground black pepper to taste
18 Corn Tortillas (see Index)
2 cups grated Monterey Jack cheese
1 head romaine lettuce, shredded
1 cup sour cream, for garnish
1 cup Pico de Gallo (see Index), for garnish

Heat the 2 tablespoons oil in a large skillet over medium heat until lightly smoking. Add the onion and garlic, and sauté for 2 minutes, until translucent. Add the chuck and press with the back of a fork to crumble. Cook for about 10 minutes or until browned. Stir in the seasonings and continue cooking for 2 minutes more.

Pour enough oil in another skillet to come ½ inch up the sides. Over medium heat, bring the oil to 350° F. or just smoking. Submerge the tortillas in the oil one by one for 5 seconds each to soften. Drain the tortillas on paper towels and keep warm; do not stack the tortillas.

Fill each tortilla with about 3 tablespoons of the meat mixture, fold over, and secure the tacos with toothpicks.

Adding more oil to the skillet if necessary to come ½ inch up the sides and heating to just smoking, fry the tacos until crisp and light brown. Remove the tacos from the pan and drain on paper towels. Remove the toothpicks and push the grated cheese into each taco. Serve on top of the shredded lettuce and garnish with a dollop of sour cream and Pico de Gallo.

BARBECUED DUCK TACOS WITH BLACK BEAN–ORANGE SAUCE

Tacos vary in form, especially in Texas. Most people probably think of them as the rigid corn tortilla shell fried in a "U" shape to hold the filling (as used in the next recipe). But in the Lone Star State they more usually take the form of "soft" tacos — warmed tortillas softened in oil and rolled up with a filling inside, as in this recipe. This is another of Mark Haugen's innovations, and it's almost Asian in concept and in its flavor combinations. You can substitute chicken for the duck; a good accompaniment for this dish is the Annatto Rice (see Index). Use whichever barbecue sauce you have time for, although the complex version is worth the effort involved.

6 SERVINGS (12 TACOS)

1 duck, about 5 pounds
3 cups Barbecue Sauce #1 or #2 (see Index)
2½ cups Black Bean–Orange Sauce
(recipe follows)
1 red bell pepper, roasted, peeled, seeded, and diced
(page 6)
1 green bell pepper, roasted, peeled, seeded, and diced
1 yellow bell pepper, roasted, peeled, seeded, and diced

1 medium onion, minced
10 tomatillos, husked, rinsed, and cut into
¼-inch dice
1 teaspoon salt
½ teaspoon freshly ground white pepper
Vegetable oil, for softening tortillas
12 Corn Tortillas (see Index)

Preheat the oven to 250° F. Coat the duck with 1½ cups of the barbecue sauce and roast in the oven for 3 to 3½ hours, or until the legs pull away easily from the body. Baste the duck every 15 minutes. (While the duck is roasting, you can prepare the black bean–orange sauce.)

When the duck is done, remove from the oven and cool. Carefully remove all of the meat from the bones and cut into dice. In a large skillet or saucepan, reheat the duck with the remaining 1½ cups of barbecue sauce and the vegetables. Season with the salt and pepper.

Pour enough vegetable oil in a skillet to come ½ inch up the sides. Over medium heat, bring the oil to 350° F. or just smoking. Submerge the tortillas in the oil one by one for 5 seconds each to soften. Drain the tortillas on paper towels and keep warm; do not stack the tortillas.

Divide the duck mixture evenly among the tortillas and roll them up to form tacos. Spoon about 6 tablespoons of the black bean–orange sauce onto each plate and serve 2 tacos per person.

BLACK BEAN–ORANGE SAUCE

ABOUT 2½ CUPS

1 tablespoon olive oil
½ cup chopped onions
1 cup cooked black beans (page 10)
2 teaspoons chopped epazote (or cilantro)
1 teaspoon fresh lime juice

1 teaspoon ground cumin
2 cloves garlic, minced
Zest of 1 orange, blanched
2 cups Chicken Stock (see Index)
Salt and freshly ground black pepper to taste

Heat the olive oil in a sauté pan over medium heat, and sauté the onions for 2 minutes, until translucent. Transfer to a saucepan, add all the remaining ingredients except salt and pepper, and bring to a boil. Reduce the heat and simmer for 10 minutes. Transfer the mixture to a blender, puree, and season with salt and pepper to taste. Return to a clean saucepan and keep warm.

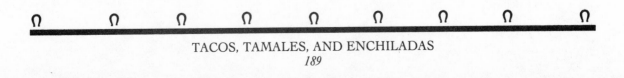

TUNA ESCABECHE TACOS WITH
JICAMA-ENDIVE SALAD

This is an excellent summer dish, as there is very little cooking involved and it can be prepared in advance. The recipe uses crisp taco shells, and the crunchy texture sets off the soft tuna perfectly. In addition, the richness of the tuna is complemented by the highly seasoned coating and the brine. Escabeche refers to the pickling or marinating process for preserving and flavoring foods such as fish, seafood, or vegetables. The technique originated in Spain, was brought to the New World, and is widely used throughout the South, as well as in Central and South America. If you want to avoid the trouble of making the aïoli, combine store-bought mayonnaise with ancho or cascabel chile puree.

4 SERVINGS (8 TACOS)

2 tablespoons ground cumin
1 tablespoon pure chile powder (page 4)
1 teaspoon paprika
1 teaspoon salt
2 tablespoons ancho chile puree (pages 3 to 4)
2 tablespoons olive oil
8 ounces tuna center-cut fillet, preferably yellowfin, about 1 inch thick
2 ripe tomatoes, blanched, peeled, seeded, and diced (page 8)
1 small onion, chopped
2 tablespoons pureed roasted garlic (optional, page 7)

½ cup Fish Stock or Chicken Stock (see Index)
Juice of 2 limes
3 tablespoons white wine vinegar
Vegetable oil, for softening tortillas
8 Corn Tortillas (see Index)

½ cup Avocado-Tomatillo Salsa (see Index)
½ cup finely shredded sorrel or romaine lettuce, for garnish
1 recipe Jicama-Belgian Endive Salad (see Index)

In a mixing bowl, combine the cumin, chile powder, paprika, and salt. Spread the ancho chile puree on the tuna, and then coat in the spice mixture.

Heat the olive oil in a skillet over medium heat until lightly smoking. Sear the tuna for 30 to 45 seconds per side; it should still be very dark on the outside but rare in the center. Transfer to a nonreactive or ceramic dish just large enough to hold the fillet.

In a blender, puree the tomatoes, onion, and garlic with the stock, lime juice, and vinegar. Pour the puree over the tuna and marinate for 6 to 8 hours in the refrigerator, turning the fish occasionally if it's not completely covered with the marinade. Remove the marinated tuna, cut into 4 strips lengthwise, and then finely slice each strip.

Pour enough vegetable oil into a skillet to come ½ inch up the sides. Over medium heat, bring the oil to 350° F. or just smoking. Submerge the tortillas in the oil one by one for 5 seconds each to soften. Holding the tortillas with tongs, fold in half and fry in a "U" shape until crisp. Drain on paper towels and keep warm.

Divide the tuna evenly among the tacos, top each taco with 1 tablespoon of the salsa and garnish with the sorrel or romaine. Serve 2 tacos per plate, together with the jicama–Belgian endive salad.

RICK'S BLUEBERRY COLESLAW TACOS

Rick (Rosemary) O'Connell and I first met in the late 1970s when we were both chef's assistants at the Robert Mondavi Great Chefs of France program in California. "The Great Schleps of Chance," as we called ourselves, was the most exciting food happening in America at the time. Rick's food is always brilliant and has a certain sense of whimsy. She served this dish at Rosalie's in San Francisco, but unfortunately the restaurant has since closed. It stemmed from a family tradition of tossing blueberries in coleslaw, made with a good garlic mayonnaise. While the whole dish may sound a bit odd, it's actually quite satisfying and a perfect item for a late spring or summertime lunch. The coleslaw is fine without the taco shells, but the tortillas add an appealing, crisp texture. This dish is a good accompaniment to grilled fish or chicken.

4 cups (1¼ pounds) finely shredded red cabbage
2 cups (10 ounces) finely shredded white cabbage
1 cup finely julienned celery
1 cup thinly sliced red onion
2 cups Mayonnaise (see Index)
¼ cup red wine vinegar

⅓ cup ancho chile puree (pages 3 to 4)
Salt to taste
1 cup fresh blueberries
1 cup roasted peanuts
Vegetable oil, for frying tortillas
12 Corn Tortillas (see Index)

In a mixing bowl, combine the vegetables. In a separate bowl, combine the mayonnaise, vinegar, chile puree, and salt. Fold the mayonnaise into the vegetables. Add ¾ cup of blueberries and ¾ cup of peanuts to the slaw.

Pour enough vegetable oil in a skillet to come ½ inch up the sides. Over medium heat, bring the oil to 350° F. or just smoking. Submerge the tortillas in the oil one by one for 5 seconds each to soften. Holding the tortillas with tongs, fold in half and fry in a "U" shape until crisp. Drain on paper towels and keep warm.

Stuff the taco shells with half of the slaw. Place the tacos on serving plates and garnish with the remaining slaw and remaining ¼ cup each of blueberries and peanuts.

FRESH CORN TAMALES

This basic tamale is usually served as an accompaniment, and also forms the foundation for flavored tamales that are stuffed with various fillings (see the recipes following). The word "tamale" is derived from the Aztec language, and there are countless regional variations of tamales in Mexico alone. Tamales are great do-ahead items, and will keep for at least 2 days in the refrigerator; they also freeze well. All *tamales are cooked by steaming, preferably in a bamboo Chinese steamer. The water must be kept lightly boiling or the tamales will become heavy. If cooked ahead, they can be reheated over steam for 5 minutes.*

---

6 TAMALES

DOUGH:
1½ cups fresh corn kernels (2 ears)
8 tablespoons vegetable shortening, at room
temperature
1 cup masa harina
⅔ cup cornmeal
¼ teaspoon cayenne powder

¼ teaspoon ground cumin
¾ teaspoon salt
1 teaspoon baking powder
¾ cup warm water (105° to 110° F.)
14 corn husks, soaked in water for 30 minutes
6 cilantro leaves, for garnish

To make the dough, in a food processor, grind half the corn kernels until completely smooth. In a mixing bowl, whisk the vegetable shortening until light and fluffy. In another bowl, combine the dry ingredients. Gradually pour in the water to make the masa dough. Add the dough to the shortening, whisking. Add the ground corn and remaining corn kernels to the dough and combine thoroughly with a wooden spoon; the mixture will be quite sticky.

Drain the corn husks and pat dry. Tear 12 strips ⅙ inch wide from 2 of the husks for tying the tamales. Place 2 husks together with the large ends overlapping by 2 inches. Repeat for the remaining husks. Divide the tamale dough evenly among the 6 double-husks, and spread in the center, leaving 1 inch at each end uncovered. Roll the corn husks so that the dough is completely enclosed. Twist and tie each end with the ⅙-inch strips already torn off.

Steam the tamales in a conventional steamer or in a strainer or vegetable basket set in a saucepan and covered with a tight-fitting lid. It is important that little or no steam escapes while cooking. Steam for 30 to 35 minutes; the water should always be lightly boiling. The tamales are done when the dough comes away easily from the husk.

When cooked, slice the tamales from end to end with a knife. Push the ends gently together, as for a baked potato, and garnish each tamale with a cilantro leaf.

SWEET POTATO TAMALES

This is one of the first innovative dishes for which I became known, and the recipe was originally published in COOK'S magazine in 1984. It has become something of a standard in Southwestern cuisine ever since. These light tamales make an excellent accompaniment to game, and we still serve them from time to time at Star Canyon.

6 TAMALES

2½ cups Chicken Stock (see Index)
1 small (12 to 14 ounces) sweet potato, peeled and cut into ¼-inch dice (about 2 cups)

DOUGH:
10 tablespoons vegetable shortening, at room temperature
2 cups masa harina
½ cup cornmeal
1 teaspoon baking powder
¼ teaspoon cayenne powder
¼ teaspoon ground cumin
1½ teaspoons salt
1½ cups warm water (105° to 110° F.)
¼ cup reserved potato cooking liquid

14 corn husks, soaked in water for 30 minutes

SAUCE:
2¼ cups reserved stock used for cooking sweet potatoes
1 cup heavy cream
2 tablespoons diced red bell pepper
2 tablespoons diced yellow bell pepper
2 tablespoons diced onion
1 clove garlic, minced
1 tablespoon chopped cilantro
1 teaspoon pure maple syrup
Salt to taste

6 cilantro leaves, for garnish

Bring the chicken stock to a boil in a saucepan. Add the sweet potatoes, and return to a boil. Reduce the heat and simmer for about 3 minutes, until the potatoes are just tender. Strain the sweet potatoes and reserve the cooking liquid for the sauce. Plunge the potatoes into ice water to stop them cooking; when chilled, strain again and set aside.

To make the dough, in the bowl of an electric mixer, whisk the vegetable shortening until light and fluffy. Scrape down the sides of the bowl as necessary. In another bowl, combine the dry ingredients. Gradually add the warm water and mix to form a soft dough. Add the dough to the shortening, while whisking. Add ¼ cup reserved potato cooking liquid and incorporate thoroughly; the mixture will be quite sticky.

Drain the corn husks and pat dry. Tear 12 strips ⅙ inch wide from 2 of the husks for tying the tamales. Place 2 husks together with the large ends overlapping by 2 inches. Repeat for the remaining husks. Divide the tamale dough evenly among the 6 double-husks, and spread in the center, leaving 1 inch at each end uncovered. Place the reserved sweet potatoes on top of the masa dough. Roll the corn husks so that the filling is completely enclosed. Twist and tie each husk end with the ⅙-inch strips already torn off.

Steam the tamales in a conventional steamer or in a strainer or vegetable basket set in a saucepan and covered with a tight-fitting lid. It is important that little or no steam escapes while cooking. Steam for 30 to 35 minutes; the water should always be lightly boiling. The tamales are done when the dough comes away easily from the husk.

Meanwhile, prepare the sauce. In a saucepan, bring to a boil the remaining 2¼ cups reserved cooking liquid. Add the cream, bell peppers, onion, and garlic. Return to a boil and reduce the liquid to 1 cup. Add the cilantro, maple syrup, and salt. Keep warm or reheat when the tamales are done.

When cooked, slice the tamales from end to end with a knife. Push the ends gently together, as for a baked potato. Pour the sauce onto plates and garnish each tamale with a cilantro leaf.

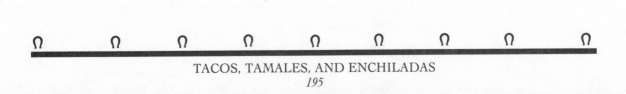

SHELLFISH TAMALES WITH ANCHO CREAM

This dish was on the opening menu at Baby Routh, and it became an instant hit. The tamales are especially light and flavorful because of the combination of the shellfish with the pureed sweet potatoes in the masa dough. You can substitute firm-fleshed fish or other seafood for the shrimp and scallops; it's always best to use whatever produce looks the freshest.

8 TAMALES

1 small (12 to 14 ounces) sweet potato, peeled and cut into ¼-inch dice (about 1½ cups)
4½ cups Chicken Stock (see Index)
½ teaspoon salt
1 tablespoon pure maple syrup

DOUGH:
10 tablespoons vegetable shortening, at room temperature
2 cups masa harina
½ cup cornmeal
1 teaspoon baking powder
¼ teaspoon cayenne powder
¼ teaspoon ground cumin
2 teaspoons salt
1½ cups warm water (105° to 110° F.)
½ cup reserved potato cooking liquid

18 corn husks, soaked in water for 30 minutes
1 quart heavy cream
3 tablespoons clarified butter or corn oil
1 pound medium raw shrimp, peeled, deveined, and diced
1 ancho chile, seeded and julienned
½ cup fresh corn kernels (1 small ear)
8 ounces bay scallops
3 tablespoons diced red bell pepper
3 tablespoons diced green bell pepper
3 tablespoons diced yellow bell pepper
2 tablespoons ancho chile puree (pages 3 to 4)
1 tablespoon chopped basil
1 tablespoon chopped cilantro
Salt to taste

8 sprigs cilantro, for garnish

Place the sweet potatoes in a saucepan and cover with the chicken stock. Add the salt and maple syrup, and bring to a boil. Reduce the heat and simmer for 4 minutes, and then strain the sweet potatoes; reserve the stock. Plunge half of the potatoes into ice water to stop them cooking; when chilled, strain again and set aside. Puree the other half of the potatoes in a blender or food processor, and set aside.

To make the dough, in the bowl of an electric mixer, whisk the vegetable short-ening until light and fluffy. Scrape down the sides of the bowl as necessary. In another bowl, combine the dry ingredients. Gradually pour in the warm water and mix to form a soft dough. Add the dough to the shortening, while whisking. Add the sweet potato puree and gradually add the ½ cup potato cooking liquid. Whisk for 1 minute more.

Drain the corn husks and pat dry. Tear 16 strips ⅛ inch wide from 2 of the husks for tying the tamales. Place 2 husks together with the large ends overlap-ping by 2 inches. Repeat for the remaining husks. Divide the tamale dough evenly among the 8 double-husks, and spread in the center, leaving 1 inch at each end uncovered. Roll the corn husks so that the dough filling is completely enclosed. Twist and tie each end with the ⅛-inch strips already torn off.

Steam the tamales in a conventional steamer or in a strainer or vegetable basket set in a saucepan and covered with a tight-fitting lid. It is important that little or no steam escapes while cooking. Steam for 30 to 35 minutes; the water should always be lightly boiling. The tamales are done when the dough comes away easily from the husk.

Meanwhile, prepare shellfish. In a saucepan, reduce the quart of cream to 2 cups. In a separate saucepan, reduce the reserved cooking stock to 1 cup. In a sauté pan, heat the clarified butter or corn oil over medium heat until lightly smoking. Add the shrimp, ancho, and corn, and sauté for 1 minute. Add the remaining ingredients (except garnish) including the reduced cream, reserved sweet potatoes, and reduced cooking stock. Bring to a boil, reduce the heat, and simmer for 1 minute. Season to taste with salt.

When the tamales are cooked, slice them from end to end with a knife. Push the ends gently together, as for a baked potato. Transfer to serving plates, pour the shellfish mixture over, and spoon the remaining shellfish and sauce around the tamales. Garnish with the cilantro sprigs.

CHORIZO TAMALES WITH PASILLA-CORN SALSA

The combination of the spicy chorizo, the subtle tones and heat of the pasilla chiles, and the texture of the masa make this an interestingly complex dish. The chorizo is available from Latin markets, or you can use hot Italian sausage.

6 TAMALES

1 tablespoon vegetable oil
1 small onion, chopped
6 ounces uncooked Chorizo sausage (see Index)

DOUGH:
10 tablespoons vegetable shortening, at room temperature
2 cups masa harina
1/2 cup cornmeal

1 teaspoon baking powder
1/4 teaspoon cayenne powder
1/4 teaspoon ground cumin
2 teaspoons salt
1 cup Chicken Stock (see Index)

14 corn husks, soaked in water for 30 minutes
3/4 cup Pasilla-Corn Salsa (see Index)

Heat the oil in a sauté pan and cook the onion over medium-high heat for 2 minutes, until translucent. Add the chorizo and continue cooking for 5 minutes, or until it is cooked through. Drain the oil and reserve the chorizo and onions.

To make the dough, in the bowl of an electric mixer, whisk the vegetable shortening until light and fluffy. Scrape down the sides of the bowl as necessary. In another bowl, combine the dry ingredients. Gradually add the stock and mix to form a soft dough. Add the dough to the shortening while whisking; the mixture will be quite sticky.

Drain the corn husks and pat dry. Tear 12 strips 1/6 inch wide from 2 of the husks for tying the tamales. Place 2 husks together with the large ends overlapping by 2 inches. Repeat for the remaining husks. Divide the tamale dough evenly among the 6 double-husks, and spread in the center, leaving 1 inch at each end uncovered. Place the chorizo mixture on top of the dough and roll the corn husks so that the filling is completely enclosed. Twist and tie each end with the 1/6-inch strips already torn off.

Steam the tamales in a conventional steamer or in a strainer or vegetable basket set in a saucepan and covered with a tight-fitting lid. It is important that little or no steam escapes while cooking. Steam for 30 to 35 minutes; the water should always be lightly boiling. The tamales are done when the dough comes away easily from the husk.

When the tamales are cooked, slice them from end to end with a knife. Push the ends together, as for a baked potato. Serve with the salsa.

VENISON TAMALES WITH CRANBERRIES AND PECANS

This is another recipe that celebrates the flavors of fall. I think of eating this dish in front of a roaring fireplace on a chilly autumnal or winter evening. Unfortunately (or perhaps, fortunately), we don't get too many opportunities to indulge that way in Dallas, but during the brief cold snaps we sometimes get in wintertime, I try to put these tamales on the menu at Star Canyon.

6 TAMALES

1 pound venison meat, cut from the leg or loin
1 tablespoon vegetable oil
1 medium onion, chopped
1 cup red wine
1½ cups reduced Brown Veal Stock (see Index)
Salt to taste

DOUGH:
1½ cups fresh corn kernels (2 ears)
8 tablespoons vegetable shortening, at room temperature
1 cup masa harina

⅔ cup cornmeal
¼ teaspoon cayenne powder
¼ teaspoon ground cumin
¾ teaspoon salt
1 teaspoon baking powder
¾ cup warm water (105° to 110° F.)

14 corn husks, soaked in water for 30 minutes
¾ cup Warm Cranberry-Orange Compote (see Index)
½ cup chopped toasted pecans (page 9)

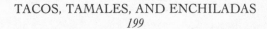

Slice the venison into very thin strips, and then finely dice the strips. Heat the oil in a skillet until lightly smoking, and sauté the onion over medium-high heat for 2 minutes, until translucent. Add the venison and continue cooking for 5 minutes, stirring occasionally. Add the red wine and reduce to a glaze. Add the stock and reduce once more to a glaze. Season with salt and set aside.

To make the dough, in a food processor, grind half the corn kernels until completely smooth. In a mixing bowl, whisk the vegetable shortening until light and fluffy. In another bowl, combine the dry ingredients. Gradually pour in the water to make the masa dough. Add the dough to the shortening, and whisk until smooth. Add the ground corn and remaining corn kernels to the dough and combine thoroughly with a wooden spoon; the mixture will be quite sticky.

Drain the corn husks and pat dry. Tear 12 strips ⅙ inch wide from 2 of the husks for tying the tamales. Place 2 husks together with the large ends overlapping by 2 inches. Repeat for the remaining husks. Divide the tamale dough evenly between the 6 double-husks, and spread in the center, leaving 1 inch at each end uncovered. Place the venison mixture on top of the dough and roll the corn husks so that the filling is completely enclosed. Twist and tie each end with the ⅙-inch strips.

Steam the tamales in a conventional steamer or in a strainer or vegetable basket set in a saucepan and covered with a tight-fitting lid. It is important that little or no steam escapes while cooking. Steam for 30 to 35 minutes; the water should always be lightly boiling. The tamales are done when the dough comes away easily from the husk.

In a saucepan, warm the cranberry-orange compote and fold in the pecans. When cooked, slice the tamales from end to end with a knife. Push the ends gently together, as for a baked potato, transfer to serving plates, and pour 2 to 3 tablespoons of the compote mixture over each tamale.

LOBSTER ENCHILADAS WITH RED PEPPER CRÈME FRAÎCHE AND CAVIAR

If all the recipes in this chapter, this is the most unconventional. The humble flour tortilla is paired with the rich lobster, cream stock, and caviar (the caviar is optional, but don't skimp now that you've gone this far!). This enchilada was an innovation from the earliest days of Routh Street Cafe. In looking back over the menus, I found that it originated in March of 1984. It has been imitated in many forms by many chefs since then. Although this dish has not been on the menu for several years, we still serve it on request for special parties.

4 SERVINGS (8 ENCHILADAS)

3 gallons water
4 live lobsters, about 1 pound each
5 tablespoons olive oil
1 medium carrot, chopped
1 leek, cleaned and chopped (white part only)
1 stalk celery, chopped
1 clove garlic, crushed
3 tablespoons chopped parsley
2 sprigs thyme
2 sprigs marigold mint or tarragon
6 tablespoons bourbon
1 cup dry white wine
1 quart Fish Stock (see Index) or water
2 tablespoons tomato paste

1 small onion, chopped
2 cups heavy cream
1 red bell pepper, roasted, peeled, seeded, and chopped (page 6)
1 yellow bell pepper, roasted, peeled, seeded, and chopped
1 serrano chile, seeded and minced
3 tablespoons sour cream
Salt to taste
8 Flour Tortillas (see Index)
½ cup Red Pepper Crème Fraîche (recipe follows)
2 tablespoons caviar, such as beluga or sevruga (optional)

In a large stockpot, bring the water to a boil and plunge in the lobsters head first. Cook for 2 minutes. Remove the lobsters and separate the tails and claws from the bodies. Cut the bodies in half lengthwise, remove the stomach sac, and then cut crosswise. Reserve the liver (tomalley) and roe if desired.

Heat 4 tablespoons of the oil in a large saucepan over medium-high heat. Add the lobster tails and claws and sauté until they turn red, about 5 minutes. Remove the tails from the pan and sauté the claws for 2 to 3 minutes longer. Set aside to cool.

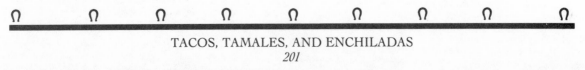

When cool enough to handle, remove the tail and claw meat from the shells. Chop the tail meat and 4 of the claws. Reserve the remaining 4 claws and the chopped meat.

Add a little more oil to the pan, if necessary, and sauté the vegetables and herbs over medium heat for 5 minutes. Crush the lobster bodies, add to the pan, and sauté for 5 minutes more.

Add the bourbon to the pan and ignite. Let the flames subside and add the wine, the fish stock or water, and tomato paste. Gently simmer for 15 minutes.

Transfer the lobster bodies to a food processor, grind, and return to the saucepan. Continue to cook for another 10 minutes.

Meanwhile, in a sauté pan, heat 1 tablespoon of olive oil over medium heat. Add the onion and cook until translucent, 2 to 3 minutes. Set aside. In a separate pan, reduce the heavy cream to ⅔ cup.

Strain the stock into a clean saucepan and reduce by two thirds, to about ½ cup. Stir in the ⅔ cup reduced cream and add the reserved chopped lobster meat and claws, the reserved onions, the bell peppers, and serrano chile. Cook for 1 minute and then add the sour cream and salt to taste. Remove the lobster claws and reserve.

Heat the tortillas and divide among 4 plates. Spread the lobster mixture down the middle of the tortillas. Roll the tortillas and spoon the red pepper crème fraîche over. Garnish with caviar and the reserved lobster claws.

RED PEPPER CRÈME FRAÎCHE

⅔ CUP

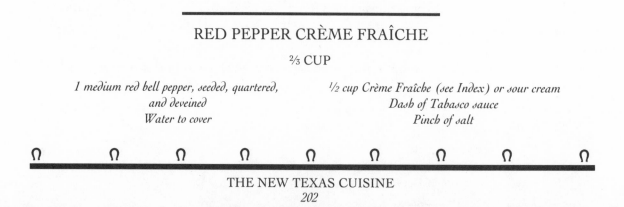

1 medium red bell pepper, seeded, quartered, and deveined
Water to cover

½ cup Crème Fraîche (see Index) or sour cream
Dash of Tabasco sauce
Pinch of salt

In a small saucepan, bring the bell pepper and water to a boil, reduce the heat, and simmer until very soft, about 5 minutes. Transfer to a blender with a tablespoon of the cooking water, and puree. Return to a clean saucepan and cook over high heat, while stirring, until the liquid has evaporated and only a paste remains. Allow to cool.

In a mixing bowl, combine the bell pepper paste with the remaining ingredients. Reserve in the refrigerator.

TURKEY MOLE ENCHILADAS WITH FRIED RIPE PLANTAINS

This is another great recipe for leftover turkey, especially during the holiday season. Try this recipe instead of the ubiquitous sandwiches! In Mexico, there are many variations of mole sauce, and most of them date from pre-Columbian times. In this recipe, chicken or smoked duck can be substituted for the turkey.

4 SERVINGS (8 ENCHILADAS)

MOLE SAUCE:
1 cup Chicken Stock (see Index)
1 large ripe tomato, blanched, peeled, seeded, and quartered (page 8)
2 tomatillos, husked, rinsed, peeled, and quartered
½ cup minced onions
2 cloves garlic, minced
¼ cup sesame seeds
½ teaspoon coriander seeds
2 tablespoons pumpkin seeds
¼ cup sliced blanched almonds
¼ cup raisins

¼ teaspoon ground cloves
½ teaspoon ground cinnamon
¼ teaspoon freshly ground black pepper
4 tablespoons pasilla chile puree (pages 3 to 4)
2 tablespoons ancho chile puree
1 ounce bitter chocolate, chopped
½ cup vegetable oil

2 cups diced cooked turkey meat
Vegetable or canola oil, for softening tortillas
12 Corn Tortillas (see Index)
Fried Ripe Plantains (recipe follows)

Preheat the oven to 350° F.

To make the sauce, in a saucepan, bring the chicken stock to a boil, reduce the heat, and add the tomato, tomatillos, onions, and garlic. Simmer for 10 minutes. Transfer to a blender, puree, and set aside.

In a skillet or pan, toast the sesame, coriander, and pumpkin seeds with the almonds (see pages 8 to 9). Combine the raisins, cloves, cinnamon, pepper, chile purees, and chocolate in a saucepan, add the toasted seeds and nuts, and the pureed tomato mixture. Cook over low heat until the chocolate melts. Transfer to a blender and puree; the yield should be about 2 to 2½ cups.

Heat the vegetable oil in a skillet until lightly smoking, and fry the puree for 3 to 5 minutes over medium-high heat, until dark and thick. Reserving ½ cup of the mole sauce, pour the remainder into a mixing bowl, add the diced turkey meat, and mix thoroughly.

Pour enough vegetable or canola oil in a skillet to come ½ inch up the sides. Over medium heat, bring the oil to 350° F. or just smoking. Submerge the tortillas in the oil one by one for 5 seconds each to soften. Drain the tortillas on paper towels and keep warm; do not stack the tortillas.

To assemble the enchiladas, divide the turkey-mole mixture among the tortillas, spreading evenly down the middle. Roll up the tortillas and place seam side down on a baking pan or in an ovenproof baking dish, placing them snugly together. Pour the reserved ½ cup of mole sauce over the tortillas, and cover with foil. Bake in the oven for 10 minutes. (Meanwhile, you can prepare the plantains.) Serve with 2 plantain pieces alongside.

FRIED RIPE PLANTAINS

In Mexico, Central America, and the Caribbean, this accompaniment is commonly served with any meat or fish dish. Plantains are ripe when their skins are quite black, and they must still be cooked before they can be eaten.

2 large ripe plantains, peeled   Vegetable oil, for deep-frying
¼ cup confectioners' sugar

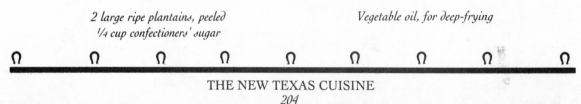

Cut the plantains in half lengthwise and in half again crosswise, dredge in the sugar, and set aside. Heat the oil in a deep-fryer to 350° F. and deep-fry the plantains until browned (about 1 to 2 minutes). Drain on paper towels.

SHRIMP AND PAPAYA ENCHILADAS WITH AVOCADO-TOMATILLO SALSA

This is another good example of using enchilada fillings other than the stereotypical beef or cheese you find in most Southwestern or Mexican restaurants. I have always been fond of the combination of seafood and tropical fruit, and it's a natural pairing that occurs throughout the coastal regions of the Gulf, the Caribbean, and Central America. Mango or even pineapple can be substituted for the papaya.

6 SERVINGS (18 ENCHILADAS)

2 tablespoons olive oil
2 onions, diced
2 tablespoons minced garlic
2 pounds medium raw shrimp, peeled, deveined, and cut into ½-inch dice
3 tablespoons chopped cilantro
6 tablespoons ancho chile puree (pages 3 to 4)
1 papaya, peeled, seeded, and diced
4 poblano chiles, roasted, peeled, seeded, and diced (page 6)

14 ounces grated Chihuahua or Monterey Jack cheese
Salt and freshly ground pepper to taste
Vegetable or canola oil, for softening tortillas
18 Corn Tortillas (see Index)
3 tablespoons water
1 cup Avocado-Tomatillo Salsa (see Index)

Preheat the oven to 350° F. Heat the oil in a large skillet until lightly smoking, and sauté the onions and garlic for 2 minutes, until lightly browned. Add the shrimp and continue to cook until they just begin to turn pink. Add the cilantro, 4 tablespoons of ancho puree, the papaya, and poblanos. Cook for 30 seconds, then remove from the heat and add 6 ounces of the cheese. Season with salt and pepper and mix all the ingredients thoroughly. Set aside.

Pour enough vegetable or canola oil in a skillet to come ½ inch up the sides. Over medium heat, bring the oil to 350° F. or just smoking. Submerge the tortillas in the oil one by one for 5 seconds each to soften. Place the tortillas on paper towels to drain and keep warm; do not stack the tortillas.

In a bowl, combine the remaining 2 tablespoons of ancho chile puree and the water. Dip the tortillas one at a time into the mixture, lightly coating both sides.

To assemble the enchiladas, divide the shrimp and papaya mixture among the tortillas, spreading evenly down the middle. Roll up the tortillas and place seam side down on a baking sheet or in an ovenproof baking dish, placing them snugly together. Sprinkle the remaining cheese on top and cover with foil. Bake in the oven for 3 to 5 minutes, or until the cheese has melted. Serve 3 enchiladas per plate, together with the avocado-tomatillo salsa.

GRILLED SIRLOIN–SWEET POTATO ENCHILADAS WITH QUESO FRESCO AND BLACK BEAN–MANGO RELISH

This meat-and-potatoes dish was another of Kevin Rathbun's Enchiladas del Día at Baby Routh. It represents very well the flexibility of enchiladas, as any leftover cooked meat — from roast beef to lamb or pork — can be used instead of the sirloin. Queso fresco ("fresh cheese"), a very typical generic Mexican cheese with a pleasant salty tartness, is available in most Mexican or Latin markets. Greek feta cheese is a great substitute.

4 SERVINGS (8 ENCHILADAS)

1 pound sirloin, about ¾ inch thick, trimmed of fat
1 tablespoon vegetable oil
Salt and freshly ground black pepper to taste
½ cup peeled and diced sweet potato
3 tablespoons olive oil
1 medium onion, minced
1 tablespoon minced garlic
2 poblano chiles, roasted, peeled, seeded, and diced (page 6)

1½ tablespoons chopped cilantro
3 tablespoons ancho chile puree (pages 3 to 4)
¾ cup plus 2 tablespoons grated queso fresco or feta cheese
Vegetable or canola oil, for softening tortillas
8 Corn Tortillas (see Index)
¼ cup fresh orange juice
1 cup Black Bean–Mango Relish (see Index)

Preheat the oven to 350° F. Prepare the grill (see page 4). Lightly oil the sirloin with the vegetable oil and season with salt and pepper. Grill the sirloin to medium rare, 4 to 5 minutes per side. Remove from the heat and let stand for 5 minutes before thinly slicing.

In a saucepan, blanch the sweet potato in boiling water for 2 minutes. Drain and set aside. Heat the olive oil in a sauté pan and cook the onion, garlic, and poblanos over medium heat for about 3 minutes, until the onions become translucent. Add the cilantro, 1 tablespoon of ancho puree, and the blanched sweet potatoes. Stir to combine and remove the pan from the heat. Mix in the ¾ cup queso fresco and season with salt and pepper to taste.

Pour enough vegetable or canola oil in a skillet to come ½ inch up the sides. Over medium heat, bring the oil to 350° F. or just smoking. Submerge the tortillas in the oil one by one for 5 seconds each to soften. Drain the tortillas on paper towels and keep warm; do not stack the tortillas.

In a bowl, combine the remaining 2 tablespoons of ancho puree and the orange juice. Dip the tortillas one at a time into the mixture, lightly coating both sides.

To assemble the enchiladas, divide the sliced sirloin evenly among the tortillas, placing the meat down the middle. Top with the poblano-cheese mixture. Roll up the tortillas and place seam side down on a baking sheet or in an ovenproof baking dish, placing them snugly together. Sprinkle with the remaining 2 tablespoons of queso fresco and cover with foil. Bake in the oven for 5 minutes, until heated through. Serve 2 enchiladas per plate, together with the black bean–mango relish.

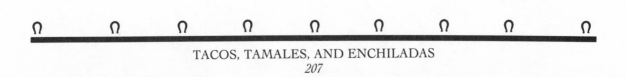

CHICKEN–SOUR CREAM ENCHILADAS WITH SALSA VERDE

I can say with great pride that there is absolutely nothing innovative whatsoever about this tried-and-true Texas dish. I judge the quality of Tex-Mex restaurants by their chicken enchiladas, just as truckers judge truck stops by their coffee. Chicken enchiladas are one of my favorite foods, and I try to track some down every 2 weeks or so. The Chicken Flautas (see Index) make a good combination with this dish, together with a bean accompaniment such as Drunken Beans, Ranch-Style Beans, or Black Bean–Prosciutto Refrito (see Index).

4 SERVINGS (12 ENCHILADAS)

1 chicken, 2 to 2½ pounds
1 carrot, diced
1 small onion, diced
2 stalks celery, diced
5 peppercorns
1 bay leaf
¼ cup olive oil
6 scallions, sliced
3 cloves garlic, minced
2 large ripe tomatoes, blanched, peeled, seeded, and chopped (page 8)

2 poblano chiles, roasted, peeled, seeded, and chopped (page 6)
1 teaspoon chopped basil
1 teaspoon chopped oregano
1 teaspoon ground cumin
1 teaspoon salt
2 cups grated Monterey Jack cheese
2 cups grated Cheddar cheese
12 Corn Tortillas (see Index)
2 cups sour cream
1 cup Salsa Verde (see Index)

Place the chicken in a large pot, cover with water, and add the carrot, onion, celery, peppercorns, and bay leaf. Bring to a boil, reduce the heat, and simmer for 30 minutes. Remove the chicken and let cool; reserve the stock, reduce to 2 cups, and set aside. Remove the chicken meat from the bones and cut into ¼-inch dice.

Preheat the oven to 350° F. Heat the oil in a large skillet until lightly smoking and sauté the scallions and garlic for 2 minutes over medium heat. Puree the tomatoes in a blender and add to the skillet, together with the 2 cups of reduced chicken stock, the poblanos, herbs, cumin, and salt. Reduce the heat to low and simmer for 5 minutes.

Mix together the cheeses in a bowl and set aside.

Dip the tortillas one by one into the hot tomato mixture to soften, and place on a baking sheet or in an ovenproof dish. Divide the diced chicken among the tortillas and top with 2 tablespoons cheese per tortilla. Roll up the tortillas and place seam side down on the baking sheet or in the dish, placing them snugly together. Combine the sour cream with the tomato mixture and pour over the tortillas, and top with the remaining cheese. Cover with foil and bake for 30 minutes. Serve 3 enchiladas per plate, together with the salsa verde.

BLACK BEAN–GOAT CHEESE ENCHILADAS WITH MANGO RELISH

This recipe was published in Parade *magazine in 1987 in an article commissioned by my friend Sheila Lukins, coauthor of the bestselling* Silver Palate Cookbook. *Black beans, goat cheese, and mango have become a popular combination in the new Texas cooking, and once you've tasted these enchiladas, you'll understand the appeal. Although at first glance this combination may not seem very Texan, one only has to realize that the Gulf Coast is subtropical and that some of the best goat cheese in the country is made here in Dallas by the Mozzarella Company.*

4 SERVINGS (8 ENCHILADAS)

SAUCE:
1 cup Chicken Stock (see Index)
8 to 10 tomatillos, husked, rinsed, and chopped
4 cloves garlic
1 cup chopped onions
2 serrano chiles, seeded and chopped
2 tablespoons chopped cilantro
Salt to taste

FILLING:
¼ cup Chicken Stock
2 cups cooked black beans (page 10)

1 clove garlic, minced
2 serrano chiles, seeded and minced
½ cup diced mango or papaya
4 scallions, thinly sliced (white parts only)
½ cup roasted corn kernels (optional, page 7)
8 ounces fresh goat cheese, crumbled
Salt to taste

Vegetable oil, for softening tortillas
8 Corn Tortillas (see Index)
1 cup Mango Relish (recipe follows)

Preheat the oven to 350° F.

To make the sauce, in a saucepan, cook the chicken stock, tomatillos, garlic cloves, onions, and serranos over medium-high heat for 10 minutes, stirring frequently. Transfer the mixture to a blender, add the cilantro, and puree until smooth. Season with salt and set aside.

To make the filling, in another saucepan, bring all the filling ingredients except the cheese and salt to a boil. Remove from the heat, whisk in 4 ounces of the goat cheese, and season with salt. Keep warm.

Pour enough of the oil in a skillet to come ½ inch up the sides. Over medium heat, bring the oil to 350° F. or just smoking. Submerge the tortillas in the oil one by one for 5 seconds each to soften. Drain the tortillas on paper towels and keep warm; do not stack the tortillas.

To assemble the enchiladas, divide the black bean–goat cheese mixture evenly among the tortillas, spreading evenly down the middle. Roll up the tortillas and place seam side down on a baking sheet or in an ovenproof baking dish, placing them snugly together. Pour the reserved tomatillo sauce over the enchiladas, and top with the remaining 4 ounces of the goat cheese. Cover with foil and bake in the oven for 10 minutes. Serve 2 enchiladas per plate, together with the mango relish.

MANGO RELISH

ABOUT 1 CUP

1 ripe mango, peeled, pitted, and diced
2 tablespoons finely diced peeled red bell pepper
3 tablespoons diced jicama
1 tablespoon chopped cilantro

1 tablespoon minced serrano chile
Juice of 1 lime
½ teaspoon salt

In a mixing bowl, combine all the ingredients. Keep refrigerated.

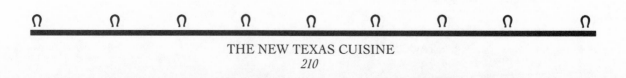

WILD MUSHROOM ENCHILADAS

These are not so different from the huitlacoche enchiladas prevalent in many parts of Mexico. Huitlacoche is a fungus that grows on corn, and is often referred to as the "truffle of Mexico." Huitlacoche is so hard to find in this country, but these enchiladas are a good alternative. At Star Canyon we usually serve them to accompany beef dishes, but they can also be served as an appetizer or with a salad for lunch.

6 SERVINGS (6 ENCHILADAS)

1 cup heavy cream
5 tablespoons ancho chile puree (pages 3 to 4)
2 cloves garlic, minced
2 teaspoons fresh lime juice
Salt to taste
1 tablespoon unsalted butter
1/2 onion, diced
6 ounces wild mushrooms, preferably a mixture of morels, shiitakes, oysters, and portobellos, sliced

1/2 avocado, peeled, pitted, and cut into 1/4-inch dice
3 ounces queso fresco or feta cheese, crumbled
1 tablespoon chopped cilantro
1 tomato, blanched, peeled, seeded, and diced (page 8)
6 Corn Tortillas (see Index)

In a skillet, bring the cream, ancho chile puree, and garlic to a boil, and simmer for 2 minutes. Transfer to a blender and puree. Add the lime juice, and season with salt. Strain the puree into a bowl and set aside.

Heat butter in a large skillet and sauté onion and mushrooms for 2 minutes over medium heat, until onion is translucent and mushrooms are soft. Add avocado, cheese, cilantro, and tomato, and just heat through. Add 2 tablespoons of reserved cream puree and stir gently. Add salt to taste and simmer 3 minutes.

Heat the remaining reserved cream puree in a skillet until simmering. Place the tortillas one at a time into the puree for 15 seconds to soften, and place on a sheet pan while filling. Divide the mixture in the skillet among the tortillas, spreading evenly down the middle. Roll up the tortillas and with a metal spatula place seam side down on serving plates. If not serving immediately, cover enchiladas on sheet pan with foil, and reheat at 350° F. for 10 minutes.

CHAPTER NINE

FISH AND SEAFOOD

When most people think of Texas ingredients, the foods that commonly spring to mind are beef, pork, and typical dishes such as chili, barbecue, chicken fried steak, and enchiladas. Fish and seafood tend to be low on such a list, but in actuality, they have long played an important role in Texas cooking. Texas, after all, is adjacent to Louisiana, and shares the same seafood that helped make Cajun and Creole cooking famous. The Gulf of Mexico has one of the most abundant seacoasts in the United States, with many busy fishing ports.

Seafood is one type of ingredient that defines the regional breakdown of cuisine in the state. In Southeast Texas and all along the Gulf Coast, seafood is a major staple. On the other hand, in West Texas, the only fresh fish we ate when I was growing up came from local lakes — catfish and bass, and occasionally, shrimp. Today, with state-of-the-art refrigerated transportation, the freshest seafood from all over the world can be found in the major cities of Texas.

Seafood consumption has increased dramatically over the last decade, corresponding with the trend toward healthier lifestyles. Statistics from the National Marine Fisheries Service show that per capita consumption of fish in the United States has grown from 11.8 pounds in 1970 to 15.1 pounds in 1985 and 15.5 pounds in 1990.

Fish is low in unsaturated fat and calories, high in protein, and rich in vitamins and minerals. However, with the quality and purity of seafood now becoming a major health issue, it seems strange that there is still no government agency that supervises the catching and processing of seafood, and controls quality in the same way that the USDA grades beef and other meat products. Certainly, the industry seems to be in favor of such a development so that public confidence can be maintained.

Fish keeps better on the bone, rather than filleted. When buying fresh whole fish, make sure the eyes are bright, clear, and shiny; the cloudier the eyes, the older the fish. The lungs under the gills should be a bright pinkish-red; a white color also indicates aging. The skin should be clear and bright, and there should be no fishy odor. Buy fillets that are displayed on ice rather than prewrapped, as the air trapped inside the package may make the fish smell unpleasant. Fillets should be fresh-looking; curled or browned

edges indicate age. Lean fish fillets should be bought skinless, while fattier fish like salmon should have their skin, as it holds the meat together better when cooked.

In general, lean fish, which have little fat, are best deep-fried, steamed, poached, or cooked in a moist heat to prevent them from drying out. Alternatively, they can be marinated and basted on a grill. Fattier fish, which tend to have stronger flavors, can be grilled, broiled, or baked, as they dry out less.

BLUE CORNMEAL CATFISH WITH SMOKED PEPPER–MARIGOLD MINT SAUCE AND CHAYOTE–BLACK-EYED PEA RELISH

One of my favorite meals growing up was fried catfish and hush puppies. In this recipe, the catfish gets a new look with blue cornmeal rather than the traditional yellow, while the smoked pepper sauce adds an extra flavor dimension. I created this dish in early 1984 when I was experimenting with smoked meats and fish. One day, I decided to see what bell peppers would taste like smoked over hickory, and found they were incredibly flavorful. Then I began smoking garlic, tomatoes, and almost every kind of vegetable. This recipe, with the smoked tomato salsa, was printed in COOK'S *magazine that same year. It's pretty commonplace now to see smoked tomato vinaigrettes and salsas on menus around the country; I like to think this could be my legacy to American cuisine. You can substitute tarragon if the marigold mint is unavailable.*

4 SERVINGS

SMOKED PEPPER–MARIGOLD MINT SAUCE:
- *½ red bell pepper, seeded*
- *½ yellow bell pepper, seeded*
- *¼ cup white wine vinegar*
- *¾ cup dry white wine*
- *1 clove garlic, finely diced*
- *1 shallot, finely diced*
- *12 ounces (3 sticks) butter, at room temperature*
- *1 tablespoon finely chopped marigold mint leaves*
- *Salt to taste*

- *3 cups vegetable oil*
- *2 eggs*
- *½ cup buttermilk*
- *4 catfish fillets, 4 to 6 ounces each*
- *Salt and freshly ground black pepper to taste*
- *Blue cornmeal, for dredging*
- *1 cup Chayote–Black-Eyed Pea Relish (see Index)*

Prepare the smoker (see page 9). Smoke the bell peppers for 20 to 30 minutes. Meanwhile, preheat the oven to 400° F. Remove the bell peppers from the smoker and roast in the oven for an additional 10 minutes. Remove the peppers, peel, chop, and set aside.

To prepare the sauce, place the vinegar, wine, garlic, and shallot in a medium saucepan. Reduce the liquid over high heat to 2 tablespoons. Reduce the heat to medium-low and begin whisking in the butter in 1-ounce increments, until all the butter is incorporated. Remove the pan from the heat and add the peppers and marigold mint. Season with salt and keep the pan warm in a water bath while cooking the catfish.

Heat the vegetable oil in a large skillet to 325° F. In a mixing bowl, whisk together the eggs and buttermilk. Dip the catfish fillets in the egg wash and season on both sides with salt and pepper. Place the cornmeal on a large plate and dredge the fillets. Fry the catfish in the skillet for 3 to 4 minutes on each side.

Serve with the chayote–black-eyed pea relish.

WHOLE FRIED CATFISH WITH ANCHO TARTAR SAUCE AND JALAPEÑO–BLUE CORN HUSH PUPPIES

This is the most Southern of dishes and, like barbecue, it's cooked as a social event; catfish fries are very typical at family reunions in Texas. These days, catfish are farm-raised in many states, and their flavor is far less earthy than those fish I ate growing up. Catfish caught in the wild—mostly in Southern and Central states—are also known as "mudsuckers" and, like other scavenging fish, eat whatever is on the bottom of the water they're in. It's been remarkable to witness the transformation of catfish from "trash" fish status in the 1970s to a vogue item during the 1980s.

ANCHO TARTAR SAUCE:
1 cup Mayonnaise (see Index)
1 small clove garlic, minced
½ shallot, minced
1 tablespoon ancho chile puree (pages 3 to 4)
⅛ teaspoon cayenne powder
⅛ teaspoon paprika
1 egg, hard-cooked and chopped
1 tablespoon chopped Pickled Onions or Bread and
Butter Pickles (see Index)
1 tablespoon chopped fresh herbs, such as basil,
cilantro, or chives, or a combination
1 tablespoon minced rinsed capers

1 teaspoon fresh lemon juice
Salt to taste

4 whole catfish, about 8 ounces each, head and
fins removed, cleaned, and skinned
2 eggs
½ cup milk
Salt and freshly ground black pepper to taste
Cornmeal, for dredging
Peanut or canola oil, for deep-frying
1 recipe Jalapeño–Blue Corn Hush Puppies
(see Index)

To prepare the sauce, whisk together the mayonnaise, garlic, and shallot in a mixing bowl. Add the remaining sauce ingredients and combine thoroughly.

Lay the catfish flat on a work surface. Insert a knife in the back of the fish at the head end and cut down on one side of the backbone, as if filleting, but keeping the meat attached on the other side of the fish at the belly. Repeat on the other side of the backbone to create a pocket.

In a mixing bowl, whisk together the eggs and milk. Dip the catfish in the egg wash and season on both sides with salt and pepper. Place the cornmeal on a large plate and dredge the catfish, making sure the fillets are coated.

Heat enough oil in a large frying pan to come 3 inches up the sides or to cover the catfish, to 325° F. Deep-fry the catfish for 3 to 5 minutes, until golden brown. Remove and drain on paper towels.

Serve with the ancho tartar sauce and jalapeño hush puppies.

SALMON IN HOJA SANTA WITH PECAN SAUCE AND PASILLA-ORANGE GLAZE

I discovered hoja santa (or yerba santa) on a trip I made to Oaxaca in Mexico with my friend Zarela Martinez. It has one of the most incredible flavors I've ever tasted — rather like sassafras, which explains why it's nicknamed "the root beer plant." The combination of salmon, hoja santa, toasted pecans, orange, and pasilla chiles is one you'll never forget, and it's also absolutely addictive. The frustrating thing is that hoja santa is hard to find and there really is no substitute. However, I predict that it will become much more readily available in the next few years. In the meantime, if you're curious about the flavor, it's worth the trip to Dallas and Star Canyon.

4 SERVINGS

4 hoja santa leaves
4 salmon fillets, about 4 ounces each and ½ inch thick
Salt to taste

PASILLA-ORANGE GLAZE:
Juice of 5 oranges
2 tablespoons pasilla chile puree (pages 3 to 4)

PECAN SAUCE:
½ cup finely chopped toasted pecans (page 9)

3 tablespoons unsalted butter, softened
2 tablespoons finely chopped onion
1 tablespoon finely chopped celery
2 teaspoons finely chopped serrano chiles
¾ cup Fish Stock or Chicken Stock (see Index)
½ cup dry white wine
3 tablespoons white vinegar
1 shallot, minced
8 tablespoons unsalted butter
Salt and freshly ground black pepper to taste

Place the hoja santa leaves in very hot water for 30 seconds. Drain the leaves and pat dry. Season the salmon fillets with salt and wrap with the hoja santa leaves. Set aside and keep refrigerated.

To make the glaze, in a small saucepan, reduce the orange juice by three quarters over high heat (leaving about ¼ cup). Whisk the pasilla chile puree into the reduced orange juice. Strain through a fine mesh strainer and set the glaze aside.

To make the sauce, grind the pecans with a mortar and pestle, or in a spice or coffee grinder, and combine in a mixing bowl with the butter, onion, celery, and serrano. Add just enough stock to make a paste; you should have about ¼ cup.

In a heavy saucepan, boil the remaining stock, wine, vinegar, and shallot until the liquid is reduced to 2 tablespoons. Remove the pan from the heat and whisk in 2 tablespoons of the butter. Set the pan over low heat and whisk in the remaining 6 tablespoons of butter, 1 tablespoon at a time, removing the pan from the heat briefly if drops of melted butter appear. Whisk in the pecan mixture and season with salt and pepper. Keep the sauce warm in a water bath.

The salmon must be steamed. Place the fillets in a traditional bamboo steamer placed over a pan of simmering water, and steam for 6 to 7 minutes.

Spoon some of the pecan sauce onto the serving plates and add a salmon fillet to each plate. Pour some of the pasilla-orange glaze over each fillet.

GULF GROUPER WITH SMOKED TOMATO SALSA AND VEGETABLE ESCABECHE

Grouper, a member of the sea bass family, is found not only in the Gulf but also on the Eastern seaboard from the Carolinas to Florida. With its lean, firm, and moist flesh that is similar to sea bass and halibut (sturgeon is also a good substitute in this recipe), grouper is a versatile fish that can either be prepared whole or filleted, and can be cooked in any number of ways. Note that the escabeche should be prepared the day before and allowed to set at least 2 to 3 hours ahead of time.

4 SERVINGS

4 grouper fillets, 4 to 6 ounces each
Vegetable oil, for brushing
Salt and freshly ground black pepper to taste

1 cup Smoked Tomato Salsa (see Index)
Vegetable Escabeche (recipe follows)

Prepare the grill (see pages 4 to 6). Brush the grouper with oil and season with salt and pepper. Grill for 3 minutes per side. Serve with the smoked tomato salsa and vegetable escabeche.

Ω　　Ω　　Ω　　Ω　　Ω　　Ω　　Ω　　Ω　　Ω

VEGETABLE ESCABECHE

This delicious side dish makes a good accompaniment to any grilled or roasted fish or meat. It is also a vegetarian's delight on its own. The only vegetable you may have trouble locating is the Peruvian blue potato. If it's unavailable, add an extra white or sweet potato.

4 TO 6 SERVINGS

1 small white baking potato
1 small sweet potato
1 medium to large blue potato
1 red bell pepper, roasted, peeled, and seeded (page 6)
1 yellow bell pepper, roasted, peeled, and seeded
1 small onion, cut into 1/2-inch slices
1 small zucchini, cut into 1/2-inch diagonal slices
2 oranges, zested, halved, and juiced
1/2 cup olive oil
1 cup white wine vinegar

1 cup dry white wine
3 allspice seeds
1 cinnamon stick
2 tablespoons lightly toasted cuminseed (pages 8 to 9)
1 teaspoon black peppercorns
1 bay leaf
1 teaspoon dried thyme
4 pequín chiles, or 1/4 teaspoon cayenne powder
1 tablespoon kosher salt
1 tablespoon sugar

In a saucepan, boil the baking potato and sweet potato together until tender but firm, about 25 to 30 minutes. In another saucepan, boil the blue potato likewise, about 15 minutes. Peel all the potatoes and cut into 1/4-inch slices. Cut the roasted peppers in half lengthwise and then crosswise, and reserve with the potatoes, onion, and zucchini.

Place the orange zest and juice, and 1/4 cup of the olive oil in a saucepan and combine with all the remaining ingredients (except the vegetables). Bring to a boil and simmer for 5 minutes. Remove from the heat and let stand for at least 6 hours and preferably overnight.

Prepare the grill (see page 4). Brush the reserved vegetables with the remaining 1/4 cup of olive oil, grill until tender, and set aside in a large dish or bowl. Meanwhile, return the reserved liquid to a boil and pour over the grilled vegetables. Let stand for 2 to 3 hours.

PECAN-CRUSTED RED SNAPPER WITH POTATO–GOAT CHEESE CASSEROLE AND FENNEL-ORANGE SAUCE

In 1990, when the Soviet leader Mikhail Gorbachev visited Minneapolis, our restaurant Goodfellow's was asked to prepare a luncheon in his honor at the Governor's Mansion. We prepared this snapper for the main course. Other nuts, such as walnuts or almonds can be used instead of the pecans. Cooking the snapper in the oven rather than finishing it in a skillet prevents the pecans from burning.

The casserole accompaniment goes well with any fish or poultry dish, and for an even more elegant presentation, you can layer the potatoes and cheese so they overlap the edges of a flan ring and then cut around the edges with a knife to make it perfectly round.

---

6 SERVINGS

FENNEL-ORANGE SAUCE (OPTIONAL):
1 tablespoon clarified butter or olive oil
½ onion, diced
1 cup chopped fennel bulb
¼ cup toasted fennel seeds (pages 8 to 9)
¼ cup chopped fennel greens
2 cups Fish Stock (see Index)
½ cup dry white wine
1½ cups heavy cream
4 oranges

Juice of ½ lemon
2 tablespoons unsalted butter
Salt and freshly ground black pepper to taste

6 red snapper fillets, 4 to 5 ounces each
2 cups chopped toasted pecan nuts (page 9)
¼ cup flour
6 tablespoons clarified butter or olive oil
1 teaspoon salt
Potato–Goat Cheese Casserole (recipe follows)

To prepare the sauce, heat the clarified butter in a saucepan over medium-high heat until lightly smoking. Add the onion and sauté for 1 minute. Add the fennel, fennel seeds, and greens, and sauté for 3 minutes, stirring constantly. Add the stock and wine, lower the heat to medium, and let boil gently until the liquid is reduced by half. Reduce the heat to low and simmer for 20 minutes. Strain through a fine strainer into a clean pan, pressing down with the back of a spoon to extract all the juices. Over medium-high heat, reduce the liquid to about ½ cup. Add the cream and reduce the liquid by half again, stirring constantly.

Meanwhile, place the zest of 1 orange and the lemon juice in a separate pan. Cut all of the oranges in half and squeeze the juice into the pan. Reduce the liquid over medium-high heat to a thick syrup, about ¼ cup. When the fennel sauce has reduced and thickened, whisk in the reduced orange juice mixture and the butter, and season with salt and pepper.

To prepare the snapper, first make sure all the bones are removed. Combine the nuts and flour in a food processor and mix for 15 seconds; take care not to overmix or the mixture will become oily. Scrape down the sides and mix again for 5 to 10 seconds; the crust should be the consistency of very coarse sand.

Preheat the oven to 400° F. Heat the butter in a large cast-iron skillet over medium-high heat.

Moisten the fish under cold running water, season with the salt, and dredge in the pecan crust, covering completely and packing the crust onto each fillet. Place the snapper skin side up in the hot skillet and brown for about 30 seconds while lightly shaking the pan. Turn the snapper over and place the skillet in the oven. Bake for 4 to 5 minutes, depending on the thickness of the fish.

Remove from the oven and transfer the snapper to serving plates. Serve with the potato–goat cheese casserole and the fennel-orange sauce, if desired.

POTATO–GOAT CHEESE CASSEROLE

6 SERVINGS

2 baking potatoes, peeled and cut into ¼-inch slices
2 slices bacon
Salt to taste
¼ cup Routh Street Vinaigrette (see Index)

3 tablespoons chopped chives
1¼ pounds fresh goat cheese, at room temperature
2 tablespoons heavy cream
4 eggs

Preheat the oven to 400° F. In a saucepan, boil the potatoes about 3 to 5 minutes until just tender when pierced with a knife. In a skillet, sauté the bacon over low heat until crisp, drain well, and discard the rendered fat. Dice the bacon.

Lightly oil a 9-x-9-inch ovenproof casserole. Layer the bottom of the casserole with the potatoes, arranging them so they slightly overlap, and sprinkle with salt. Drizzle with the vinaigrette and sprinkle with the bacon and 1 tablespoon of the chives.

In a food processor, combine the goat cheese, cream, and eggs, turning the machine on and off quickly. Mix until just combined, taking care not to over-mix. Spread this mixture over the potatoes.

Place the casserole in the oven and bake for 15 minutes, or until light brown and firm in the center. Sprinkle the remaining 2 tablespoons of the chives over the top.

ROASTED STUFFED RED SNAPPER WITH FRITTER FRIED OKRA

Red snapper is one of the most important fish harvested from the Gulf of Mexico. With its firm, lean flesh, I think that it's every bit as good as the highly-prized French rouget de roches that is erroneously called red mullet. This is another typically Southern dish, and it's best when fresh Gulf crab and red snapper are in peak season during the summer. For an even more pronounced Southern flair, substitute catfish for the snapper. The okra accompaniment makes a good side for other fish dishes.

6 SERVINGS

STUFFING:
1½ cups lump crabmeat, shell and cartilage removed
1 large egg
½ cup finely chopped scallions
2 tablespoons Dijon mustard
¼ cup finely crumbled fresh breadcrumbs
2 tablespoons chopped parsley
2 tablespoons chopped cilantro

1 teaspoon pure chile powder (page 4)
Salt and freshly ground black pepper to taste

6 red snapper fillets, about 4 ounces each
Salt to taste
4 tablespoons unsalted butter
2 tablespoons chopped shallots
¼ cup dry white wine
Fritter Fried Okra (recipe follows)

Preheat the oven to 450° F.

To make the stuffing, in a mixing bowl, combine and blend all the ingredients.

With a knife, make a slit along the length of each snapper fillet ½-inch deep, stopping 1 inch from each end. With the knife parallel to the work surface, make another slit from the center cut outwards on both sides, stopping an inch from the side of the fish, to make a pocket in each fillet for the stuffing. Then stuff each fillet with equal amounts of the crabmeat filling, and season both sides with salt.

Use 1 tablespoon of the butter to coat the bottom of a flameproof baking dish large enough to hold the fillets in one layer, and place the snapper fillets in the dish. Sprinkle the chopped shallots around the fillets.

Melt the remaining in a small pan, brush it over the fillets, and pour the wine around. Place the baking dish on top of the stove and bring the wine to a boil over high heat. Transfer to the oven for 8 to 10 minutes, basting occasionally with the cooking liquid; the fillets should be white and not translucent.

Preheat the broiler, and when hot, transfer the dish to the broiler, placing it 7 to 8 inches from the heat. Broil for 2 minutes.

Place the snapper fillets on serving plates and serve with the fritter fried okra.

FRITTER FRIED OKRA

6 SERVINGS

Vegetable or canola oil, for frying
1½ cups flour
1 tablespoon baking powder
½ tablespoon baking soda
1 teaspoon salt

1 large egg
1½ cups beer
1 tablespoon lemon zest
24 okra spears, about 3 inches long,
quartered lengthwise

Heat enough oil in a saucepan to come 1 inch up the sides. In a mixing bowl, sift together the dry ingredients. Set aside.

In another mixing bowl, beat together the egg, beer, and lemon zest. Sprinkle in the dry ingredients while whisking. Dip the okra strips into the batter, then let all but a thin film run off the strips. Fry in the hot oil until lightly browned.

SWORDFISH WITH TROPICAL BLACK BEAN SALSA AND COCONUT-CURRY CREAM

The curry cream, which provides the perfect contrast to the salsa, is an influence borrowed from the Pacific Rim. The impact of Asian cuisines in Texas cooking is stronger now than ever before, and there seems to be a very interesting fusion of cuisines emerging from the Vietnamese and Cambodian communities in Houston. This is a relatively new development, reflecting these groups' recent arrival, mostly as "boat people." It will be interesting to see how this culinary trend evolves over the next few years. The swordfish can be substituted by most seafood in this recipe; for example, at Star Canyon, we often sauté large sea scallops dredged in cornmeal. When buying the coconut, shake it to make sure it is full of liquid.

4 SERVINGS

4 center-cut swordfish steaks, about 4 ounces each and ½ inch thick	1 cup Tropical Black Bean Salsa (see Index)
Vegetable oil, for brushing	Coconut-Curry Cream (recipe follows)
Salt to taste	Grated coconut, for garnish
	Cilantro leaves, for garnish

Prepare the grill (see pages 4 to 6). Lightly brush the swordfish steaks with oil and season with salt. Grill the swordfish for about 2 minutes per side.

Heat the salsa and ladle onto warm serving plates. Place the swordfish steaks on top of the salsa, and drizzle about 2 tablespoons of the curry cream over each serving of swordfish and salsa. Sprinkle with grated coconut and garnish with cilantro leaves. Serve the remaining curry cream in a sauce boat at the table.

COCONUT-CURRY CREAM

ABOUT 1¼ CUPS

1½ cups heavy cream	1 large coconut
1 teaspoon olive oil	1 tablespoon fresh lime juice
¼ onion, chopped	1 teaspoon unsalted butter, at room temperature
1 serrano chile, seeded and chopped	Salt to taste
1 tablespoon curry powder	

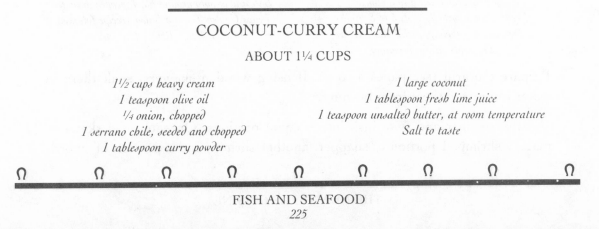

In a saucepan, reduce the cream by one third. In another saucepan, heat the olive oil until lightly smoking and sauté the onion and serrano for 1 minute. Whisk in the curry powder and cook for 1 minute longer. Crack the coconut and add the milk (about 1 cup), reserving the flesh. Add the lime juice and reduce the liquid by three quarters, whisking occasionally.

Add the reduced cream and simmer for 1 to 2 minutes. Strain the liquid into another pan and whisk in the butter. Season to taste with salt.

MIXED SEAFOOD GRILL WITH GOLDEN TOMATO SALSA AND JICAMA-MELON RELISH

This is another seasonal dish that is best prepared in the summer when the tomatoes are at their ripest, melons are fresh from the vine, and everyone is in the mood for an outdoor grill. You can substitute the seafood used; for example, scallops for the shrimp, tuna for the swordfish, or catfish for the snapper. Bear in mind that fattier fish work best for grilling, as they hold together well and stick less to the grill. You can also use red tomatoes instead of the golden in the salsa, but you will lose some of the colorful effect. For an additional layer of flavoring, marinate the seafood in the Three Citrus Marinade (see Index) for 20 minutes before grilling. While you are grilling the seafood skewers, you can also grill bell peppers, squash, or other vegetables to accompany this dish.

4 SERVINGS

1 red snapper fillet, 6 to 8 ounces
1 center-cut swordfish fillet, 6 to 8 ounces
8 medium raw shrimp, peeled and deveined
Vegetable oil, for brushing

Salt and freshly ground black pepper to taste
3 cups Golden Tomato Salsa (recipe follows)
Jicama-Melon Relish (see Index)

Prepare the grill (see pages 4 to 6). If using wooden skewers, soak them in water to prevent them from burning.

Cut the snapper and swordfish into 4 equal portions. On each of 4 skewers, place 1 shrimp, 1 portion of snapper, another shrimp, and a portion of swordfish. Brush the skewers with oil and season with salt and pepper. Clean the grill with a stiff wire brush and oil the bars with a lightly oiled towel or rag. Place the skewers on the grill and cook for 2 to 3 minutes per side.

Transfer the skewers to serving plates and serve with the golden tomato salsa and jicama-melon relish.

GOLDEN TOMATO SALSA

4 SERVINGS (ABOUT 3 CUPS)

1 pound ripe yellow tomatoes, halved, seeded, and diced
2 tablespoons diced red bell pepper
2 tablespoons diced green bell pepper
2 tablespoons diced yellow bell pepper
2 tablespoons diced chives

2 serrano chiles, seeded, deribbed, and minced
1 tablespoon fruit vinegar
1 tablespoon fresh lime juice
Salt and freshly ground black pepper to taste
1 tablespoon chopped cilantro

In a mixing bowl, combine the tomatoes, bell peppers, chives, and serranos. Toss and season with the vinegar, lime juice, salt, pepper, and cilantro. Serve slightly warmed.

GRILLED SOFT-SHELL CRABS ON CORNMEAL-BASIL FRIED TOMATOES

All crabs must shed their shells, and most commercial soft-shell crabs are blue crabs — these are what we serve at Star Canyon. Soft-shell crabs are most commonly caught in the Chesapeake Bay area and in the estuaries of the Gulf Coast. They are in season for only a short period, from late spring to midsummer. Serve this dish with Basil Crème Fraîche (see Index), or any salsa or relish from Chapter 3.

---

4 SERVINGS

4 fresh jumbo soft-shell crabs, 4 to 5 ounces each
1 tablespoon olive oil
1 tablespoon fresh lemon juice

Salt and freshly ground black pepper to taste
1 recipe Cornmeal-Basil Fried Tomatoes (recipe follows)

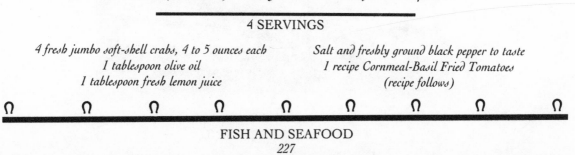

Prepare the grill (see pages 4 to 6). Place the crabs on a cutting board and cut off the protruding eyes. Turn the crabs over onto their backs and pull down to remove the triangular-shaped aprons. Lift the flaps on each side and remove the spongy gill tissue underneath. Rinse thoroughly in cold water and pat dry.

In a bowl, combine the olive oil and lemon juice and brush the crabs. Season with salt and pepper, and grill for 1 to 2 minutes per side, until the crabs turn red.

Transfer to serving plates and serve with the cornmeal-basil fried tomatoes.

CORNMEAL-BASIL FRIED TOMATOES

4 SERVINGS

4 ripe tomatoes, cut into ½-inch slices
1 tablespoon salt
Freshly ground black pepper to taste

1 cup basil leaves, cut into thin strips
1 cup cornmeal
¼ cup olive oil

Preheat a heavy skillet over medium-high heat for about 1 minute. Season the tomato slices on both sides with salt and pepper and press the basil onto both sides. Dredge the tomato slices in the cornmeal, making sure the basil is not dislodged. Add the oil to the skillet and cook the tomato slices for about 1 minute per side, until golden brown.

Main St. Big Springs, Texas.
1907

SOFT-SHELL CRABS ON GUMBO Z'HERBS WITH CHILE PEQUÍN MAYONNAISE

To me, soft-shell crab is as much a seasonal celebratory ingredient for the late spring and early summer as pumpkins, pomegranates, and cranberries are for the fall. Perhaps it's because they have such a short season that these crabs seem to taste so good. Gumbo z'herbs is a Cajun dish from Louisiana that's not so different from a mess of Southern greens. The chile mayonnaise is thinner than others in this book, so that it runs smoothly over the crabs. It can be served with any grilled fish or shellfish.

---

4 SERVINGS

4 fresh jumbo soft-shell crabs, 4 to 5 ounces each
2 eggs
1/3 cup buttermilk
1 cup flour
1 cup breadcrumbs
1 teaspoon chopped thyme
1 tablespoon chopped basil

1 teaspoon freshly ground black pepper
1/4 teaspoon cayenne powder
1/8 teaspoon ground cumin
Salt to taste
Peanut oil or canola oil, for deep-frying
Gumbo Z'Herbs (recipe follows)
1 cup Chile Pequín Mayonnaise (recipe follows)

Place the crabs on a cutting board and cut off the protruding eyes. Turn the crabs over onto their backs and pull down to remove the triangular-shaped aprons. Lift the flaps on each side and remove the spongy gill tissue underneath. Rinse thoroughly in cold water and pat dry.

In a mixing bowl, whisk together the eggs and buttermilk. In a separate bowl, combine the dry ingredients, except the salt. Dip the crabs in the egg wash, season with salt, and dredge in the flour mixture.

In a skillet large enough to hold all the crabs, heat enough oil to come 2 inches up the sides. Heat the oil to 360° F. and deep-fry the crabs until well-browned, 3 to 5 minutes. Drain on paper towels.

Divide the gumbo z'herbs between 4 serving plates, place the crabs on top, and serve a dollop of the chile mayonnaise on top of the crabs.

GUMBO Z'HERBS

Originally, this was a Cajun Lenten dish, and it was made without meat. An old Bayou saying is that gumbo z'herbs must have at least 7 greens; for every type of green in excess of 7, you make a new friend. One theory is that this soup of stewed greens is derived from a German dish; the German influence on Cajun and Creole food is significant but little recognized.

4 TO 6 SERVINGS

1 bunch collard greens
1 bunch turnip greens
1 bunch mustard greens
1 bunch watercress
1 bunch beet tops
1 bunch carrot tops
1 bunch radish greens
6 scallions, chopped
3 cups Chicken Stock (see Index)
1 tablespoon unsalted butter

8 ounces cooked sausage, such as tasso or andouille, diced
1 small white onion, chopped
2 cloves garlic, minced
1 tablespoon chopped basil or parsley
1 bay leaf
1 teaspoon chopped thyme
Salt and freshly ground black pepper to taste
Cayenne powder to taste
1 teaspoon filé gumbo

Wash all the greens thoroughly. Place in a large saucepan with the scallions and stock, and simmer for 10 minutes. Strain the greens and reserve the stock. Finely chop the greens and set aside.

Heat the butter in a large skillet and sauté the sausage over medium-high heat for about 10 minutes. Add the onion, garlic, and basil or parsley, and sauté until the onion and garlic turn golden brown. Add the greens and simmer for 15 minutes. Transfer to a large pan with the reserved stock and add the greens and all the remaining seasonings. Cover and simmer for 20 minutes.

CHILE PEQUÍN MAYONNAISE

ABOUT 2 CUPS

⅔ cup plus 1 tablespoon corn oil
1 tablespoon chopped shallot
½ cup dry white wine
12 pequín chiles, halved lengthwise
4 egg yolks
½ teaspoon dried mustard
1 tablespoon fresh lime juice

⅓ cup olive oil
1 tablespoon diced roasted red bell peppers (page 6)
1 teaspoon chopped chervil
1 teaspoon chopped marigold mint
Salt and cayenne powder to taste

Heat 1 tablespoon of corn oil in a skillet and sauté the shallot for 1 minute over medium-high heat, or until translucent. Deglaze with the white wine and reduce the heat to low. Add the chiles and reduce the mixture until almost dry. Remove the chiles and let the mixture cool.

In a small stainless-steel bowl, whisk together the egg yolks, mustard, lime juice, and reduced shallot mixture. Combine the remaining ⅔ cup of corn oil with the olive oil and slowly drizzle into the bowl while whisking. Continue to whisk until all the oil is incorporated; the mayonnaise should be smooth and silky. Add the remaining ingredients, and mix well.

SEARED SEA SCALLOPS ON BLACK BEAN CAKES WITH RUBY GRAPEFRUIT–SERRANO SAUCE

Sea scallops are harvested mostly in northeastern waters, and especially off the coast of Maine. This recipe combines the soft, sweet, white scallop flesh with rustic black beans and the spicy tartness of the sauce. They should be cooked quickly so they retain their natural juices; do not overcook, or the scallops will dry out and lose their flavor. A little sour cream and Pico de Gallo (see Index) rounds this dish out nicely.

6 SERVINGS

2½ cups dried black beans, cooked, drained, and cooled (page 10)
2 tablespoons duck fat, bacon fat, or lard
1 teaspoon ancho chile puree (pages 3 to 4)
2 tablespoons pure chile powder (page 4)
1 tablespoon ground cumin

2 tablespoons chopped cilantro
½ teaspoon salt, plus extra to taste
24 fresh sea scallops, washed and dried
2 tablespoons olive oil
Ruby Grapefruit–Serrano Sauce (recipe follows)

Preheat the oven to 350° F. Prepare the grill (see pages 4 to 6).

Place the beans and duck fat in a food processor and puree. Add the ancho chile puree, chile powder, cumin, cilantro, and ½ teaspoon salt, and puree for 1 minute longer.

Cut twelve 6-inch squares from parchment or wax paper and lightly oil. Form the mixture into 6 balls and flatten slightly between your hands. Place on 6 of the oiled squares and place the remaining squares on top, oil side down. Press evenly with a metal spatula to make cakes ¼ inch tall and about 4½ inches across. Place on a greased baking sheet and bake in the oven for 7 to 8 minutes or until the cakes are warm. Keep warm while preparing the scallops.

In a mixing bowl, toss the sea scallops with the olive oil, season with salt, and grill for 2 minutes per side.

Remove the top layer of paper from each cake and invert onto serving plates. Remove the remaining paper. Pour the sauce around the cakes and place 4 scallops on top of each bean cake.

RUBY GRAPEFRUIT–SERRANO SAUCE
ABOUT ¾ CUP

Juice of 2 grapefruit
Juice of 6 oranges
Juice of ½ lemon
4 serrano chiles, seeded and chopped
2 tablespoons chopped spearmint or peppermint

1 tablespoon chopped marjoram
8 tablespoons (1 stick) unsalted butter, at room temperature
Salt to taste

Place the citrus juices in a saucepan and reduce to ⅓ cup over high heat. Remove the pan from the heat, add the serranos and herbs, cover, and let infuse for 20 minutes.

Strain the mixture into a clean pan, pressing down firmly with the back of a spoon to extract all the juice. Reheat to a simmer and whisk in the butter 1 tablespoon at a time, until it is thoroughly incorporated. Season with salt.

SAUTÉED GULF SHRIMP WITH GARLIC-BOURSIN CROUTONS

This is a recipe that Rex Hale developed when he was the chef at Baby Routh, and it was always one of my favorites. It's incredibly rich but also extremely satisfying.

4 SERVINGS

SEAFOOD SEASONING:
1/2 teaspoon cayenne powder
1/2 teaspoon freshly ground black pepper
1 tablespoon paprika
1 1/4 teaspoons onion powder
1 1/4 teaspoons garlic powder
1 1/4 teaspoons dried thyme
1 1/4 teaspoons dried oregano

SHRIMP:
3 tablespoons corn oil
1/3 cup finely diced onion
4 teaspoons minced garlic
16 medium raw shrimp, peeled and deveined

1/2 cup heavy cream
2 tablespoons fresh lemon juice
2 tablespoons Worcestershire sauce
4 tablespoons chopped scallions
12 tablespoons (1 1/2 sticks) unsalted butter
Salt to taste

GARLIC-BOURSIN CROUTONS:
4 slices French bread
2 tablespoons Boursin cheese
1 tablespoon unsalted butter
1 tablespoon finely chopped chives
1 teaspoon minced garlic

To prepare the seafood seasoning, place the ingredients in a mixing bowl and combine thoroughly.

To prepare the shrimp, heat the oil in a large skillet and sauté the onion, garlic, and shrimp over medium heat until the shrimp are half-cooked. Add the seafood seasoning, cream, lemon juice, and Worcestershire sauce, and over high heat, reduce the mixture by half. Add the scallions, and whisk in the butter in tablespoon increments. Incorporate well, and season with salt.

To prepare the croutons, toast the bread. In a mixing bowl, thoroughly combine the remaining ingredients and spread on the toasted bread. Warm slightly.

Divide the shrimp and sauce evenly among 4 soup bowls, and garnish with the croutons. Serve hot.

GULF COAST JAMBALAYA

Jambalaya is a quintessential Cajun dish. Its name is derived from the Arcadian French for ham (jambon), "in the style of" (à la) and an African word for rice (ya). It's not difficult to find jambalaya along the Texas Gulf Coast, especially in cities bordering Louisiana. Since andouille sausage can be spicy, you might want to adjust the cayenne accordingly.

4 TO 6 SERVINGS

¼ cup olive oil
¾ cup chopped tasso or other smoked ham
⅔ cup chopped andouille sausage
2 cups finely chopped onion
6 scallions, chopped
6 cloves garlic, minced
1 large green bell pepper, seeded and finely chopped
1 large red bell pepper, seeded and finely chopped
6 stalks celery, finely chopped
8 (about 2 pounds) ripe tomatoes, blanched, peeled, seeded, and chopped (page 8)
1 tablespoon chopped oregano
2 teaspoons chopped basil

1 tablespoon chopped cilantro
1 teaspoon chopped thyme
3 bay leaves
1 teaspoon ground cumin
2 teaspoons cayenne powder
3 cups Fish Stock or Chicken Stock (see Index)
3 cups uncooked rice
24 medium raw shrimp, peeled and deveined
24 fresh Gulf Coast oysters, about 1 pound, shucked, with their liquor
8 ounces fresh Gulf Coast crabmeat, shell and cartilage removed
Salt to taste

Preheat the oven to 350° F. In a large saucepan, heat the olive oil until lightly smoking, add the tasso and andouille, and sauté over medium heat until crisp, 6 to 8 minutes. Add the onion, scallions, garlic, bell peppers, and celery, and sauté for 5 minutes more.

Add the tomatoes and seasonings, stir thoroughly, and cook for 5 minutes. Stir in the stock and bring to a boil. Add the rice, stir well, and remove from the heat. Transfer to a large baking dish, cover with foil, and bake in the oven until the rice is just tender, about 15 minutes.

Stir in the shrimp, oysters, and crabmeat. Cover, and bake for 15 minutes more. Remove the bay leaves, taste, and season with salt. Serve immediately.

SHELLFISH PAN ROAST WITH GUAJILLO CAPELLINI CAKES

This recipe is another inspiration from my dear friend Rick O'Connell, who lives in San Francisco. She has a unique way of combining ingredients with confidence and wit to create extraordinary dishes.

6 SERVINGS

1 cup dry white wine (more if necessary)
12 fresh clams, scrubbed
12 fresh mussels, scrubbed and beards removed
12 medium raw shrimp, peeled and deveined
1/3 cup heavy cream
1 tablespoon diced celery
1 tablespoon diced red bell pepper
1 tablespoon diced onion

1 teaspoon chopped basil
1/2 teaspoon Worcestershire sauce
1/2 teaspoon paprika
1 tablespoon Catsup (see Index)
1 tablespoon unsalted butter
Salt and freshly ground white pepper to taste
6 Guajillo Capellini Cakes (recipe follows)

In a large saucepan, bring the wine to a boil over high heat. Place the clams in the pan, cover, and steam for about 2 minutes. Add the mussels, cover the pan, and steam for 2 minutes more, or until the shells have opened. Discard any shells that do not open. Add the shrimp and more wine if it has all evaporated. Cook uncovered until the shrimp turn pink, about 30 to 45 seconds. Remove all the seafood with a slotted spoon and keep warm while finishing the sauce.

Strain the steaming broth into a clean saucepan. Add the cream, vegetables, basil, Worcestershire sauce, and paprika, and simmer for 2 to 3 minutes. When the sauce has thickened slightly, whisk in the catsup and butter, and season with salt and pepper; you should have about 1 cup.

Place the capellini cakes on serving plates. Arrange 2 of each of the shellfish around each capellini cake, pour the sauce over the shellfish, and serve.

GUAJILLO CAPELLINI CAKES

6 LARGE CAKES

3 eggs, lightly beaten
¼ cup half and half
3 tablespoons catsup
½ teaspoon Worcestershire sauce
1 tablespoon pureed roasted garlic (page 7)
6 tablespoons guajillo chile puree (pages 3 to 4)
4 tablespoons chopped basil

1½ cups grated pecorino or Parmesan cheese
8 ounces capellini (angel hair pasta), cooked al dente, drained, cooled, and oiled
Salt to taste
2 tablespoons vegetable oil
2 tablespoons olive oil

In a large mixing bowl, thoroughly combine the eggs, half and half, catsup, Worcestershire sauce, garlic, guajillo puree, basil, and pecorino. Add the pasta and season with salt. Mix well and form into 6 round cakes, 2 to 3 inches wide and about ¾ inch thick.

Combine the oils in a large, heavy skillet and heat until lightly smoking. Add 3 of the capellini cakes and cook for about 2 minutes over medium heat until golden brown on the bottom. Carefully turn the cakes and cook for 2 minutes longer; the cakes should be crisp on the outside and moist on the inside. Keep warm while cooking the remaining cakes.

SOUTHWESTERN BOUILLABAISSE WITH RED POBLANO ROUILLE

This recipe puts a Southwestern spin on the classic Mediterranean seafood stew. The original bouillabaisse uses monkfish, scorpion fish, John Dory, haddock, or flounder, whereas this version features fish and shellfish abundant on the Texas Gulf Coast. Although this stew hasn't appeared on any of my menus for a while, it has been published in magazines and is well worth the effort. Rouille is the French word for "rust," referring to the color of the highly flavored sauce. To achieve an even ruddier hue, add 1 tablespoon of tomato paste; for a milder flavor, leave out the chile powder and use red bell peppers instead of the poblanos. For a spicier taste, add more chile powder or cayenne.

Top: Tamale Tart with Roast Garlic Custard and Gulf Crabmeat

Bottom: Poblano Stuffed with Jerked Pork, Pineapple, and Pumpkin Seeds

Texas tapas spread

Top: *Shrimp and Papaya Enchiladas with Avocado-Tomatillo Salsa*

Bottom: *Lace Cookie Dessert Taco with Raspberries and Caramel*

Rattlesnake roundup in Big Spring

Top: *Fried rattlesnake for sale
at the festivities*

Bottom: *Cowboy in Alpine*

Shellfish Tamale with Ancho Cream

1 tablespoon unsalted butter
2 ounces salt pork or bacon, diced
1/2 red bell pepper, diced
1/2 yellow bell pepper, diced
1/2 green bell pepper, diced
1 serrano chile, seeded, deribbed, and diced
1/2 cup chopped onion
1/2 cup chopped celery
1/4 cup bourbon
1 cup dry white wine
1 quart Fish Stock or Chicken Stock (see Index)
1 small sweet potato, peeled and cut into 1/2-inch dice
1/2 cup fresh corn kernels (1 small ear)
8 live crawfish

6 ounces redfish or red snapper fillets, cut into
1-inch dice
2 ripe tomatoes, blanched, peeled, seeded, and
chopped (page 8)
24 fresh Gulf Coast oysters, shucked
2 teaspoons salt
2 teaspoons fresh lime juice
2 tablespoons chopped cilantro
1/2 cup jicama, cut into 1/2-inch dice
2 to 3 tablespoons Red Poblano Rouille
(recipe follows)
4 to 6 slices French bread, about 3 inches long
x 1 inch wide x 1/4 inch thick
Lime wedges, for garnish

In a saucepan, melt the butter and sauté the salt pork or bacon over high heat for 1 minute. Add the bell peppers, serrano, onion, and celery, and continue cooking for 3 minutes, stirring constantly. Deglaze with the bourbon, then add the wine, and reduce the liquid by one third.

Add the stock and bring to a boil. Add the sweet potato and corn, and simmer for 3 minutes. Add the crawfish, redfish or snapper, and tomatoes. Cover, and simmer for another 1½ minutes. Add the oysters and simmer for 1 minute more. Season with salt and stir in the lime juice, cilantro, and jicama.

Ladle the bouillabaisse into large bowls. Spread the rouille on the bread slices and float 1 crouton in each bowl. Garnish with lime wedges.

RED POBLANO ROUILLE

If red poblanos are unavailable, use 2 red bell peppers and 4 jalapeños instead.

ABOUT ¾ CUP

2 ripe red poblano chiles, roasted, peeled, seeded,
and diced (page 6)

1/4 teaspoon pure chile powder (page 4)
1/2 cup Aïoli (see Index)

Place the poblanos in a blender with the chile powder and puree until smooth. Place the aïoli in a mixing bowl, and whisk the puree into the aïoli. Strain through a fine strainer.

GRILLED BREAST OF CHICKEN WITH PEANUT–ANCHO
CHILE SAUCE   241

ROAST CHICKEN IN ADOBO SAUCE WITH BLACK BEAN–
PROSCIUTTO REFRITO   242

HONEY-FRIED CHICKEN WITH THYME-MINT
CREAM SAUCE   244

TORTILLA-CHILE–CRUSTED CHICKEN BREAST WITH
ANNATTO RICE   246

CHICKEN STUFFED WITH HERBED FRESH RICOTTA   247

COWBOY CHICKEN CASSEROLE   249

ROAST WILD TURKEY WITH BLUE
CORNMEAL–CHORIZO STUFFING   250

ROAST TURKEY STUFFED WITH FRESH CORN TAMALES   252

ROAST PHEASANT WITH OYSTER-PECAN DRESSING   252

PHEASANT BRAISED IN TEQUILA WITH PEACHES   254

MOLASSES-GRILLED QUAIL WITH HORSERADISH-TURNIP
PUREE AND TOMATILLO-JALAPEÑO CHUTNEY   255

SEARED QUAIL WITH SWEET POTATO PANCAKES, MUSCAT
WINE, AND JICAMA-ORANGE RELISH   256

JALAPEÑO-STUFFED SMOKED DOVE WITH DRUNKEN BEANS,
THREE POTATO SALAD, AND ROSY RELISH   259

GRILLED SQUAB WITH CARAMELIZED BANANAS AND
MANGO QUESADILLAS   260

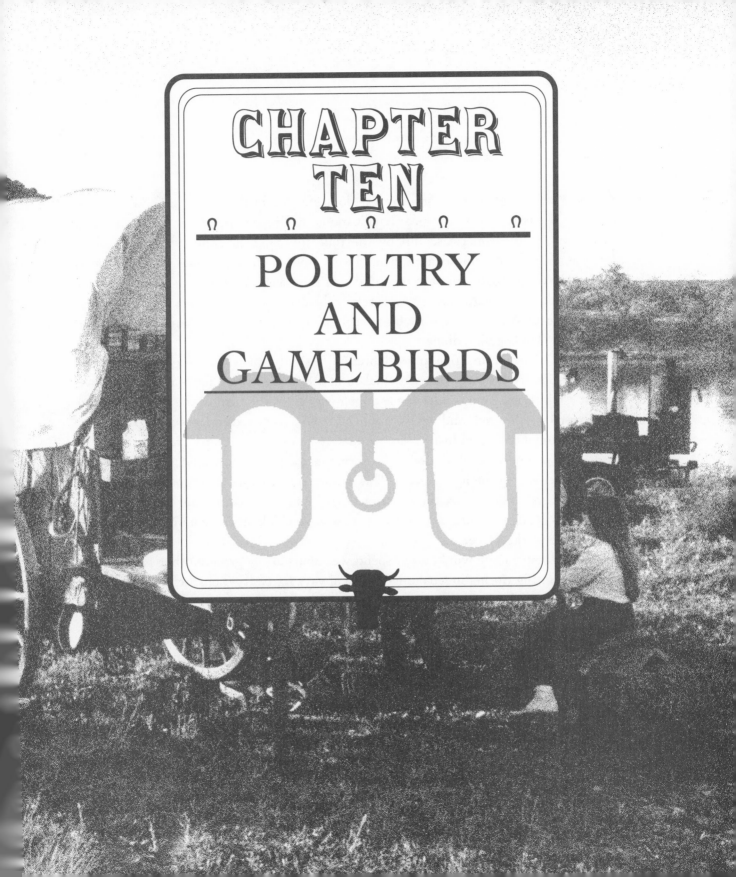

CHAPTER TEN

POULTRY AND GAME BIRDS

The Chinese were probably the first to raise domesticated birds for use as food, and the practice was brought to the European civilizations of Greece and Rome. Wild turkeys are indigenous to the Americas, and by the time the Spanish conquistadors reached Mexico, the Aztecs had domesticated them. These "Indian chickens" were taken back to Europe by Cortez in 1519, and it is recorded that they were served in the French court in 1570. Within fifty years, turkey was relatively common fare in Europe. The first colonists in North America were saved from famine in part by wild turkey, hence its significance at Thanksgiving dinners.

In fact, it's hard to imagine any celebration, festivity, or holiday in Texas without some kind of poultry — turkey or fried chicken at a Sunday social, for example, or dove or quail at a barbecue. Things have come a long way since the turn of the century, when poultry was mostly hunted, and we have moved from a very natural process to a highly streamlined assembly-line industry. Unfortunately, most commercial chicken today is purpose-bred, pampered and stuffed with hormones, kept in controlled, cramped environments, never seeing the light of day. This is one reason why I recommend free-range chicken; other good reasons are the superior flavor, which is meatier and less bland, and the firmer, less spongy texture. Fortunately, free-range chicken is becoming more widely available in the marketplace.

As a child, our family would often spend weekends at my grandmother's house, ten miles away from Big Spring in Coahoma. She'd always fix us fried chicken, and it wasn't hard to tell there was something different about Grandma's compared to my mother's. I associated it with the surroundings — she lived in a big, rather intimidating two-story home that somehow reminded me of a haunted house. Later, I realized she was using chicken that ran wild in the yard; they were grain-fed, but their diet was supplemented by the occasional earthworm and cricket, and their flavor was distinctively superior. I'll never forget the ease with which she would grab a chicken and swing it over her head to wring its neck — I'd always look the other way after the first time!

In Texas there are still plenty of wild turkeys — they can scare the hell out of you as they fly out of trees and flutter from roost to roost, squawking fiercely. Together with

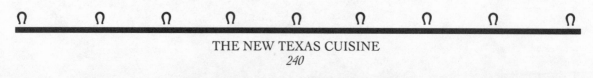

quail and dove, they make popular hunting quarry throughout most of the state come the fall. At Star Canyon, we always have free-range chicken and at least one game bird on the menu.

GRILLED BREAST OF CHICKEN WITH PEANUT–ANCHO CHILE SAUCE

This dish is inspired by Tim Anderson who was my opening sous-chef at Routh Street Cafe. Tim was at Goodfellows in Minneapolis for five years, and he's developing a style all of his own. He has recently been recognized by Food and Wine *magazine as one of the "rising star chefs" in the country, and it's good to see he's getting the acclaim he deserves. This recipe is a good example of how Southwestern cuisine combines to great effect with the Southern tradition; the combination of ancho chiles and peanuts works really well. A good accompaniment for this dish is the Cilantro Rice Ring (see Index).*

4 SERVINGS

PEANUT–ANCHO CHILE SAUCE:
¾ cup smooth peanut butter
1 cup Chicken Stock (see Index)
2 tablespoons soy sauce
¼ cup sesame oil
1 tablespoon minced garlic
1 tablespoon peeled and minced ginger

1 tablespoon dark brown sugar
6 tablespoons ancho chile puree (pages 3 to 4)
⅔ cup heavy cream

4 large skinless, boneless chicken breasts
Vegetable oil, for brushing
Salt to taste

Prepare the grill (see pages 4 to 6).

To prepare the sauce, place all the ingredients, except the cream, in a blender. Blend together, and with the machine running, add the cream; blend until smooth. Pass through a fine strainer into a saucepan. Bring to a boil, reduce the heat, and keep warm. Adjust the seasoning and thin with a little more chicken stock if necessary.

Ω   Ω   Ω   Ω   Ω   Ω   Ω   Ω   Ω

Meanwhile, lightly oil and salt the chicken breasts on both sides and grill over a medium-hot fire until just done, about 4 minutes per side. Remove and slice the chicken breasts diagonally. Place on serving plates in a fan and spoon the sauce around.

ROAST CHICKEN IN ADOBO SAUCE WITH BLACK BEAN–PROSCIUTTO REFRITO

Adobo is a spicy, rich marinade that usually contains vinegar and can also be used for pickling. The refrito is a recipe that my friend and onetime sous-chef at Routh Street Cafe, David Garrido, developed for a July 4 party at my house. We never really served it at the restaurant because it's a little too rustic in style, but it's one of the most satisfying accompaniments you'll ever have. It works well with any of the enchiladas in Chapter 8, or on its own with tostadas and a dollop of sour cream.

4 SERVINGS

2 chickens, 2 to 3 pounds, halved, backbones removed
Salt and freshly ground black pepper to taste
Melted butter, for basting (optional)

ADOBO SAUCE:
½ cup ancho chile puree (pages 3 to 4)
2 serrano chiles, halved (with seeds)
6 cloves garlic, minced
1½ cups Chicken Stock (see Index)
½ medium onion, diced

2 teaspoons sugar
¼ cup red wine vinegar
½ cup fresh orange juice
1 tablespoon fresh lime juice
½ teaspoon ground cumin
½ teaspoon chopped thyme
1 teaspoon chopped oregano
2 bay leaves
Salt to taste

Black Bean–Prosciutto Refrito (recipe follows)

Preheat the oven to 450° F. Place the chicken halves on a rack in a roasting pan, season with salt and pepper, and roast in the oven for 10 minutes. Lower the oven temperature to 400° F. and roast for an additional 20 minutes, basting occasionally with the melted butter, if desired.

Meanwhile, to prepare the sauce, place all the ingredients, except the bay leaves and salt, in a blender, and blend together until smooth. Pass through a strainer into a saucepan and add the bay leaves. Bring just to a boil, taste, and season with salt, and remove from the heat. Do not overseason, as the liquid will be reduced later. Place the chicken in a casserole or baking dish so that it fits snugly in a single layer. Pour the sauce over, cover, and bake for 20 minutes more.

Remove the chicken and keep warm. Place the cooking liquid in a large skillet and reduce over high heat to 1 cup. Divide the chicken between serving plates and pour the sauce over. Serve with the black bean refrito.

BLACK BEAN–PROSCIUTTO REFRITO

4 TO 6 SERVINGS

1 cup black beans, soaked overnight and drained (page 10)
6 cups Ham Hock Broth or Chicken Stock (see Index)
½ cup red wine (Burgundy or Cabernet)
½ cup chopped onions
2 cloves garlic, minced

3 tablespoons vegetable oil or lard
⅓ cup julienned prosciutto
3 Pickled Jalapeños (see Index), seeded and diced
Salt to taste
2 tablespoons chopped cilantro leaves
Sour cream (optional)

Rinse the beans in cold water. In a large saucepan, bring the broth or stock and wine to a boil. Add the beans, onions, and garlic. Bring the liquid back to a boil, lower the heat, and simmer for 1½ hours. Drain the beans and transfer the cooking liquid to a clean pan. Over high heat, reduce the liquid to ½ cup and set aside.

In a skillet, heat the oil or lard over medium-high heat until lightly smoking. Add the cooked beans, prosciutto, and pickled jalapeños, and mash with the back of a spoon or a potato masher until the beans have a rough puree texture. Add the reserved ½ cup liquid and bring to a boil. Reduce the heat and let the beans simmer for a few minutes, stirring constantly, until they are a little bit thinner than the desired consistency; they thicken as they sit.

Since prosciutto releases salt, taste before seasoning with salt. Add the cilantro and the reserved cooking liquid glaze, and mix thoroughly. Serve with a dollop of sour cream, if desired.

HONEY-FRIED CHICKEN WITH THYME-MINT CREAM SAUCE

I have been asked more than once what my last meal would be, and my reply comes readily: fried chicken, and specifically, this one, which is a variation on the classic Southern dish. The sauce is a lighter version of the typical heavy gravy; Spicy Whipped Sweet Potatoes (see Index) and Mable's Buttermilk Biscuits (see Index) are the perfect accompaniments. When Craig Claiborne tasted this dish at Routh Street, he liked it so much he included it in his book Craig Claiborne's Southern Cooking. *This chicken is wonderful served cold for picnics.*

4 TO 6 SERVINGS

1 chicken, about 3 to 3½ pounds
½ cup honey
2 tablespoons raspberry or other fruit vinegar
½ cup flour
2 tablespoons whole-wheat flour
2 teaspoons cayenne powder
2 eggs
¼ cup buttermilk
1 cup vegetable oil
Salt and freshly ground black pepper to taste

THYME-MINT CREAM SAUCE:
½ cup dry white wine
½ cup Chicken Stock (see Index)
1½ cups heavy cream
1½ tablespoons chopped mint
1 tablespoon chopped thyme
1 teaspoon lemon zest
1 tablespoon reserved marinade
Salt and freshly ground pepper to taste

Cut the chicken into serving pieces (preferably 6), and place in a mixing bowl, reserving the backbone, neck, and wings for the stock. Stir the honey and vinegar together and pour over the chicken. Let marinate for at least 2 hours, mixing occasionally.

In a separate mixing bowl, combine the flours and cayenne and set aside. In another mixing bowl, whisk together the eggs and buttermilk. Preheat the oven to 200° F.

In a large skillet, heat the oil over medium-high heat to 300° F.; cooking at a low temperature will prevent the honey from caramelizing too quickly and burning. Remove the chicken from the marinade and drain on paper towels. Dip the chicken in the egg wash, season with salt and pepper, and dredge in the flour-cayenne mixture, coating thoroughly. Strain the marinade and reserve 1 tablespoon for the sauce.

Starting with the dark meat first, gently drop the chicken pieces into the hot oil for 5 to 6 minutes on the first side until browned. Turn the pieces, add the white meat, and continue cooking, adjusting the heat so that the chicken browns evenly on both sides without burning. Turn once more and cook until well browned, and tender when pierced with a fork. The dark meat should cook for 15 to 18 minutes, and the white meat 10 to 12 minutes. Transfer the chicken to the oven and keep warm while making the sauce.

To prepare the sauce, pour the oil off from the skillet, leaving any bits on the bottom. Deglaze the pan with the white wine and add the chicken stock. Reduce the liquid by half over medium-high heat, 3 to 4 minutes. Add the cream, mint, thyme, lemon zest, and reserved marinade, and reduce until the sauce is thick enough to coat the back of a spoon, 5 to 6 minutes. Strain the sauce and season with salt and pepper.

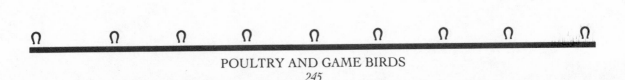

TORTILLA-CHILE–CRUSTED CHICKEN BREAST WITH ANNATTO RICE

It seems as though chefs all over the country are coating or crusting everything from oysters to buffalo. I keep expecting to come across potato-crusted chocolate cake! This recipe was partly inspired by Brendan Walsh in his early days at Arizona 206 in New York. We cooked together at an event in San Diego where he prepared a chile-rubbed chicken that I particularly liked. The annatto rice was another inspiration from David Garrido, formerly sous-chef at Routh Street Cafe, and a dish he brought to a party at my home.

4 SERVINGS

8 Corn Tortillas (see Index), fried until crisp and drained
⅓ cup cornmeal
⅓ cup flour
1 teaspoon ground cumin
¼ teaspoon cayenne powder
1 teaspoon pure chile powder (page 4)
2 teaspoons salt, plus salt to taste
2 eggs

2 tablespoons milk
4 skinless, boneless chicken breasts
3 tablespoons vegetable or canola oil
¼ cup dry white wine
½ cup Chicken Stock (see Index)
¼ cup sour cream
2 tablespoons ancho chile puree (pages 3 to 4)
Annatto Rice with Wild Mushrooms and Queso Fresco (recipe follows)

Break up the fried tortillas and place in a food processor together with the remaining dry ingredients, including the 2 teaspoons salt. Process until thoroughly ground and transfer to a mixing bowl. In another bowl, whisk together the eggs and milk. Dip the chicken breasts in the egg wash, then dredge in the tortilla crusting and coat thoroughly.

Heat the oil in a skillet until lightly smoking, and sauté the crusted chicken over medium heat for about 3 minutes per side. Remove the chicken and set aside, and pour off the oil. Deglaze the skillet with the wine and reduce to 1 tablespoon. Add the stock, bring to a boil, and reduce to 2 tablespoons. Whisk in the sour cream and ancho puree. Strain through a fine mesh sieve, season with salt, and serve with the chicken and annatto rice.

ANNATTO RICE WITH WILD MUSHROOMS AND QUESO FRESCO

4 SERVINGS

1 cup uncooked long-grain white rice
½ cup Annatto Oil (see Index)
2 cloves garlic, finely diced
½ medium onion, finely diced
1 small carrot, finely diced
1 stalk celery, finely diced
1½ cups thinly sliced wild mushrooms, such as morels or chanterelles

½ cup fresh corn kernels (1 small ear)
1 teaspoon ground cinnamon
2½ cups boiling Chicken Stock (see Index)
Salt to taste
½ cup crumbled queso fresco
2 tablespoons chopped cilantro
Freshly ground black pepper to taste

Rinse the rice in cold water and drain. In a large saucepan, heat the oil and sauté the garlic, onion, carrot, and celery over medium heat for 2 minutes, stirring occasionally. Add the mushrooms and corn, and cook for 2 minutes longer. Add the rice and cinnamon, and stir for 1 to 2 minutes, until the rice is well coated with the oil. Add the boiling stock and salt, reduce the heat, and simmer for 15 minutes, uncovered. Cover the pan and continue cooking for 5 minutes more. Remove the pan from the heat and let stand, covered, for 5 minutes.

When the rice has steamed, mix in the queso fresco and cilantro, and season with salt and pepper.

CHICKEN STUFFED WITH HERBED FRESH RICOTTA

I've been cooking this dish for so long — since my days at The Bronx restaurant — that I can't remember where it came from or how it originated. We served it at Routh Street Cafe, off and on, ever since we opened. It was one of our more popular dishes, perhaps because there's something very comforting about its simplicity. For best results, use fresh ricotta if available. Serve with a side dish from this chapter, such as Annatto Rice, Sweet Potato Pancakes, or Horseradish Turnip Puree.

4 SERVINGS

2 chickens, 3 to 4 pounds each
1 pound ricotta cheese
2 tablespoons pureed roasted garlic (page 7)
1 teaspoon minced basil
1 teaspoon minced chives
1 teaspoon minced oregano

1 teaspoon minced dill
1 teaspoon minced rosemary
1 teaspoon minced sage
1 teaspoon salt
⅛ teaspoon freshly ground black pepper
2 cups Brown Chicken Stock (see Index)

Preheat the oven to 350° F. Loosen the skin of the chicken from the breast meat by running your finger underneath, starting at the neck, taking care to leave the skin intact. Make a slit in the chicken legs with a knife, just large enough to loosen the drumstick skin with your finger.

Thoroughly combine all the remaining ingredients, except the stock, in a mixing bowl. Transfer to a pastry bag, and using a straight tube, pipe the mixture under the skin of the chicken, or use a spoon and work it between the skin and meat with your fingers.

Place the chicken in a roasting pan and roast in the oven for 1¼ to 1½ hours. Pierce the thigh with a knife or skewer to ensure the juices run clear. Remove the chicken from the oven and let rest for at least 20 minutes before serving. Slice with a sharp knife, removing the breast meat together with the skin from the bone so the stuffing remains intact. Carve the leg from the carcass and serve with the breast.

Place the stock in a saucepan and reduce to 1 cup. Serve as a sauce with the chicken.

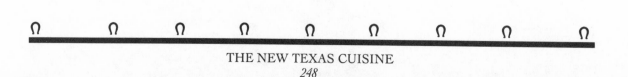

COWBOY CHICKEN CASSEROLE

I've enjoyed variations of this dish ever since I was a child, mainly at family reunions, Sunday church socials, or potluck dinners. It's probably a Texan invention, inspired by Chilaquiles (see Index), which also makes this a perfect brunch dish or a great do-ahead item.

6 TO 8 SERVINGS

2 chickens, 2 to 3 pounds
2 carrots, diced
3 small onions, diced
4 stalks celery, diced
10 peppercorns
2 bay leaves
2 tablespoons olive oil
6 cloves garlic, minced
1½ cups fresh corn kernels (2 ears)
2 medium ripe tomatoes, blanched, peeled, seeded, and diced (page 8)
2 poblano chiles, roasted, peeled, seeded, and diced (page 6)

1 cup cooked black beans (optional, page 10)
2 tablespoons chopped cilantro
1 teaspoon ground cumin
¼ cup unsalted butter
¼ cup flour
1 cup milk
Salt and freshly ground black pepper to taste
2 cups grated Monterey Jack cheese
2 cups grated sharp Cheddar cheese
12 Corn Tortillas (see Index)

Place the chickens in a large stockpot, cover with water, and add the carrots, 2 onions, celery, peppercorns, and bay leaves. Bring to a boil, reduce the heat, and simmer for 30 minutes. Remove the chicken and let cool, strain and reserve the stock, and discard the vegetables. Remove the chicken meat from the bones, roughly chop, and set aside. Place the reserved stock in a saucepan and reduce by half.

In a large skillet, heat the oil and sauté the remaining onion and the garlic until translucent, 3 to 5 minutes. Add the corn and cook for 1 minute more. Then add the tomatoes, poblanos, beans, cilantro, and cumin; sauté briefly, and remove from the heat.

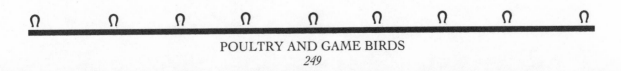

In a large saucepan, melt the butter over medium heat, add the flour, and stir constantly until lightly browned and smooth. Gradually add 1 cup of the reserved reduced stock and the milk, and stir until the sauce is thick and smooth. Remove from the heat, season with salt and pepper, and stir in the sautéed vegetables and the remaining stock.

In a mixing bowl, combine the cheeses. Dip the tortillas in the saucepan one at a time to soften, and cut into 2-inch strips. Preheat the oven to 350° F.

Place one third of the tortilla strips in the bottom of a 9-x-13-inch ovenproof casserole, and cover with half of the reserved chicken. Pour half of the vegetable-sauce mixture over the chicken and sprinkle half of the combined cheese on top. Place one third of the tortilla strips over the cheese, cover with the remaining chicken, and then cover with the remaining vegetable-sauce mixture. Top with the remaining tortilla strips, sprinkle the remaining cheese over, and cover the casserole with foil.

Bake the casserole in the oven for 20 minutes, remove the foil, and cook for 15 to 20 minutes longer.

ROAST WILD TURKEY WITH BLUE CORNMEAL–CHORIZO STUFFING

I used this recipe for the PBS series, Great Chefs of the West, which aired in the mid-1980s. It's a Southwestern adaptation of a very Southern Thanksgiving dish; the cornbread and pecans are matched with blue corn, chorizo, and chiles. Use regular turkey if the wild variety is unavailable, and be sure to buy it fresh rather than packaged or fresh-frozen. The Warm Cranberry-Orange Compote (see Index) is the perfect accompaniment.

BLUE CORNMEAL–CHORIZO STUFFING:
1 tablespoon vegetable oil
1 pound Chorizo sausage meat, crumbled
(page 17)
½ cup (1 stick) unsalted butter
1 cup chopped onions
¼ cup diced celery
¼ cup diced carrot
4 serrano chiles, deribbed, seeded, and minced
6 cloves garlic, minced
¼ cup chopped chayote (optional)
¼ cup bourbon whiskey

1 teaspoon minced thyme
1 teaspoon minced sage
2 teaspoons chopped cilantro
8 cups coarsely crumbled Blue Corn Skillet Sticks
(see Index)
½ cup Chicken Stock (see Index) or turkey stock
1 to 2 teaspoons salt

1 wild turkey, 8 to 10 pounds
Salt and freshly ground black pepper to taste
Unsalted butter, at room temperature

Preheat the oven to 350° F.

To make the stuffing, heat the vegetable oil in a skillet and sauté the chorizo over medium heat until cooked through, about 5 minutes. Drain and set aside.

In a large skillet, melt the butter and sauté the onions, celery, carrot, serranos, garlic, and chayote over high heat for 2 to 3 minutes. Deglaze the vegetables with the bourbon, and continue cooking over high heat for 1 minute, or until the liquid evaporates. Remove the skillet from the heat and add the thyme, sage, cilantro, chorizo, and crumbled blue corn sticks. Moisten with the stock and season with salt. Stir to combine.

Wash the turkey well and season the cavity with salt and pepper. Stuff the turkey and truss with a needle and string. Rub the turkey generously with the softened butter, and season the outside of the turkey with more salt and pepper.

Place the turkey on a rack in a roasting pan, cover tightly with foil, and roast in the oven for 2¾ to 3¼ hours. Baste well with butter periodically. Remove the foil in the last hour of cooking to allow the turkey to brown.

When done, transfer the turkey to a platter and let it rest for 10 to 15 minutes before carving. Remove the string and serve the turkey with the stuffing and a gravy made from the giblets.

Ω   Ω   Ω   Ω   Ω   Ω   Ω   Ω   Ω

ROAST TURKEY STUFFED WITH FRESH CORN TAMALES

This is a traditional Hispanic presentation for Christmas dinner, and although it can be enjoyed at any time, it goes best with the seasonal dishes of sweet potatoes and cranberries. The corn tamales make an unusual and tasty stuffing.

---

8 TO 10 SERVINGS

1 domestic turkey, 12 to 15 pounds	24 Fresh Corn Tamales (see Index)
Salt and freshly ground black pepper	Unsalted butter, at room temperature

Preheat the oven to 350° F. Wash the turkey well and season the cavity with salt and pepper. Stuff the turkey with the tamales and mold the foil over the cavity to allow the tamales to steam. Rub the skin generously with the softened butter and season the outside of the turkey with more salt and pepper.

Place the turkey on a rack in a roasting pan, cover tightly with foil, and roast in the oven for 3½ to 4 hours. Baste well with butter periodically. Remove the foil in the last hour of cooking to allow the turkey to brown.

When done, transfer the turkey to a platter and let it rest for 10 to 15 minutes before carving. Remove the tamales and serve with the carved turkey.

ROAST PHEASANT WITH OYSTER-PECAN DRESSING

This recipe makes a good alternative to the traditional Thanksgiving turkey, especially as Gulf Coast oysters are coming into season during the holiday period at the end of the year. The all-purpose dressing adapts very well to chicken or turkey. Pheasant is becoming more readily available throughout the country, although it is usually frozen.

Ω   Ω   Ω   Ω   Ω   Ω   Ω   Ω   Ω

2 pheasants, about 2½ pounds each
Salt and freshly ground black pepper to taste

OYSTER-PECAN DRESSING:
½ cup (1 stick) unsalted butter
1 cup chopped onions
2 tablespoons diced celery
2 tablespoons diced carrot
2 serrano chiles, deribbed, seeded, and minced
4 cloves garlic, minced
¼ cup peeled and chopped chayote
¼ cup bourbon whiskey

4 cups coarsely crumbled Mexican Corn Bread
(see Index)
1 teaspoon chopped thyme
1 teaspoon chopped sage
2 teaspoons chopped cilantro
¼ cup Chicken Stock (see Index)
8 ounces fresh shucked oysters (about 2 dozen in
the shell)
½ cup chopped toasted pecans (page 9)
Salt to taste
Unsalted butter, at room temperature

Preheat the oven to 425° F. Wash the pheasants well and season the cavity with salt and pepper. Set aside.

To make the stuffing, in a large skillet, melt the butter and sauté the onions, celery, carrot, serranos, garlic, and chayote over high heat for 2 to 3 minutes. Deglaze the vegetables with the bourbon and continue cooking over high heat for 1 minute, or until the liquid evaporates. Remove the skillet from the heat and add the corn bread and herbs. Moisten with the stock and fold in the oysters and pecans. Season with salt.

Dress the pheasants, placing any extra dressing in a casserole, and truss with a needle and string. Rub the pheasants generously with the softened butter, and season with more salt and pepper.

Place the pheasants on a rack in a roasting pan and roast in the oven for 10 minutes. Lower the oven temperature to 350° F. and roast for an additional 30 minutes, basting every 5 to 10 minutes.

When done, transfer the pheasants to a platter and allow to rest for 10 to 15 minutes before carving. Remove the string and serve the birds with the dressing.

PHEASANT BRAISED IN TEQUILA
WITH PEACHES

Although hunting for pheasant in Texas takes a back seat to dove and quail, pheasant is a significant game bird in the Panhandle region where the climate is drier. Pheasants are being reintroduced into other parts of Texas with mixed success. The birds we serve at Star Canyon are farm-raised. Pheasants can be difficult to cook at home, as they can turn out stringy and tough. However, the braising technique used in this recipe ensures that the birds stay moist, and the combination of flavors works well. Chicken can be substituted for the pheasants, but the cooking time should be increased a little, as pheasants are much leaner.

4 SERVINGS

2 pheasants, about 2½ pounds each,
rinsed and patted dry
2 small oranges, peeled
Salt and freshly ground black pepper to taste
½ cup unsalted butter (1 stick) or olive oil
1 teaspoon chopped rosemary
1 tablespoon chopped thyme
2 bay leaves
6 peaches, blanched, peeled, halved, and pitted

1 small onion, finely chopped
6 cloves garlic
2 tablespoons flour
1½ cups gold tequila
½ cup Chicken Stock (see Index)
1 cup dry red wine
3 cloves
¼ cup sugar

Preheat the oven to 450° F. Stuff the pheasants with the oranges, truss lightly with needle and string, and season with salt and pepper. In a large pan or skillet, heat the butter or oil until lightly smoking, and brown the pheasants for 10 to 15 minutes, turning and basting on the upper side continuously. Transfer to a large ovenproof casserole and sprinkle the herbs over the pheasants. Snugly fit 6 peach halves around the 2 birds and set the casserole aside.

In the oil remaining in the pan or skillet, sauté the onion and garlic for 2 minutes over medium heat. Add the flour and cook for 1 minute, taking care that the flour does not brown. Add ½ cup of the tequila and the stock, stirring as the sauce thickens. Pour the braising liquid over the pheasants, cover the casserole with foil, and cook in the oven for 40 to 50 minutes.

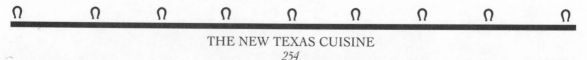

About 15 minutes before the pheasants are ready, place the remaining 1 cup of tequila, the wine, the cloves, and sugar in a saucepan just large enough to hold the remaining 6 peach halves in a single layer. Bring to a boil, reduce the heat to low, and add the peach halves, cut side down, to the pan. Simmer for 7 to 10 minutes, until the peaches are tender when pierced with a knife. Remove the saucepan from the heat. When ready to serve, slice the peach halves, into a fan if desired.

Remove the casserole from the oven and transfer the pheasants to a serving platter. Strain the braising liquid into a pan, pressing down on the peach halves to extract their essence. Reduce the sauce a little, if desired, to thicken. Carve the pheasants and serve with the reduced sauce and peach slices.

MOLASSES-GRILLED QUAIL WITH HORSERADISH-TURNIP PUREE AND TOMATILLO-JALAPEÑO CHUTNEY

Bobwhite quail are commonplace in West Texas, and quail hunting is a sport that's taken quite seriously in those parts. When I was growing up, my dad took me hunting for quail, and we'd either barbecue them over mesquite or smoke them in a big converted oil drum. You can buy boned-out quail, or if unavailable, you can remove the breastbone yourself by cutting down the bone with a sharp knife, and pulling it away from the carcass. The turnip accompaniment goes well with any poultry dish.

4 SERVINGS

8 quail, 4 to 5 ounces each, breastbones removed
1¼ cups Molasses-Garlic Marinade (see Index)
1 cup Tomatillo-Jalapeño Chutney (see Index)
Horseradish-Turnip Puree (recipe follows)

2 cups Brown Chicken Stock (optional, see Index)
Salt to taste

Place the quail in the marinade and let marinate for at least 1 hour, and up to 3 hours. (Meanwhile, you can prepare the chutney and turnip puree.) In a saucepan, reduce the stock to 1 cup and keep warm.

Prepare the grill (see pages 4 to 6). Remove the quail from the marinade and season with salt on both sides. Place breast side down on the grill, and cook for 2 to 3 minutes, brushing with the marinade. Turn over and cook for 2 minutes longer. The molasses from the marinade may look burned, but it is only caramelized, and actually has a pleasant flavor.

Place a spoonful of turnip puree in the center of each plate. Cut each quail down the center and arrange 4 halves around the turnip puree. Serve with the chutney and some reduced stock, if using.

HORSERADISH-TURNIP PUREE

ABOUT 3 CUPS

*2 medium turnips, peeled and diced
(about 2 cups)
2 medium new potatoes, peeled and diced
(about 1 cup)*

*1 tablespoon unsalted butter
1 teaspoon sugar
1 teaspoon prepared horseradish
Salt to taste*

Bring a saucepan of lightly salted water to a boil. Cook the turnips and potatoes for 6 to 8 minutes, until tender. Drain thoroughly and place in a food processor with the butter, sugar, and horseradish. Puree for 1 minute, until very smooth. Taste and season with salt. The puree may be made ahead and reheated.

SEARED QUAIL WITH SWEET POTATO PANCAKES, MUSCAT WINE, AND JICAMA-ORANGE RELISH

This dish incorporates a terrific combination of flavors: the sweet potatoes, orange, and quail. I recommend using Quady Essencia, which is a very rich orange muscat dessert wine made in Napa Valley by Andy Quady. If this or another orange dessert wine is unavailable, the quail is almost as good with just the pancakes and relish. As an alternative, the quail can be broiled for 3 to 4 minutes per side.

1 quart quail stock or Brown Chicken Stock
(see Index)
½ cup flour
2 tablespoons yellow cornmeal
1 teaspoon ground cumin
½ teaspoon cayenne powder
1 teaspoon salt, plus extra to taste
8 quail (4 to 5 ounces each), breastbones removed
¼ cup clarified butter
¼ cup vegetable oil or clarified butter
1 carrot, chopped
1 stalk celery, chopped

½ onion, chopped
4 cloves garlic, minced
8 sprigs fresh thyme
2 cups orange muscat wine
Juice of 2 oranges
Juice of 1 lemon
6 tablespoons unsalted butter, at room
temperature
Freshly ground black pepper to taste
Sweet Potato Pancakes (recipe follows)
1½ cups Jicama-Orange Relish
(recipe follows)

In a saucepan, reduce the stock to 1 cup and set aside.

In a large mixing bowl, combine the flour, cornmeal, cumin, cayenne, and the 1 teaspoon salt. Dredge the quail in the dry ingredients. Heat the clarified butter in a large skillet until lightly smoking, and sear the quail for 4 minutes per side; the breast meat should be pink. Remove the quail from the skillet and keep warm.

In the same skillet, heat the vegetable oil or clarified butter until lightly smoking, and sauté the carrot, celery, onion, garlic, and thyme over high heat for 2 minutes. Deglaze the pan with the muscat wine and reduce the liquid by three quarters. Add the reduced stock and bring to a boil. Add the citrus juices and simmer for 1 to 2 minutes. Remove the skillet from the heat and whisk in the butter. Strain the sauce into a clean saucepan, and season with salt and pepper.

Split the quail in half and place on top of the warm pancakes. Serve with the muscat wine sauce and jicama-orange relish.

SWEET POTATO PANCAKES

8 PANCAKES

1 large sweet potato, peeled and grated
1 medium baking potato, peeled and grated
½ medium onion, grated
1 egg, lightly beaten
1 tablespoon fresh breadcrumbs
½ teaspoon salt

Freshly ground black pepper to taste
2 tablespoons pure maple syrup
Pinch of nutmeg
1½ tablespoons flour
Vegetable oil or clarified butter

Place the potatoes in a colander and drain the liquid thoroughly by pressing down on the potatoes. In a mixing bowl, combine the potatoes with all the remaining ingredients except for the oil or butter. Divide the mixture into 8 portions and pat each into a cake.

In a large skillet, heat the oil or butter to thoroughly coat the skillet. Cook the pancakes over medium heat for 3 to 4 minutes per side, until brown. Add more oil or butter as needed.

JICAMA-ORANGE RELISH

ABOUT 1½ CUPS

¾ cup jicama, cut into ¼-inch dice
3 tablespoons diced orange sections
1 tablespoon diced red bell pepper
1 tablespoon diced yellow bell pepper
1 tablespoon diced sweet onion
½ serrano chile, seeded and minced

2 tablespoons diced cucumber
3 tablespoons diced ripe mango (optional)
1 teaspoon finely chopped mint
2 tablespoons fresh lime juice
3 tablespoons fresh orange juice
Salt to taste

Combine all the ingredients in a large mixing bowl. Let marinate for 1 hour before serving.

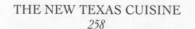

JALAPEÑO-STUFFED SMOKED DOVE WITH DRUNKEN BEANS, THREE POTATO SALAD, AND ROSY RELISH

This classic Texas recipe needs no innovation. I have eaten this dish for as long as I can remember, as dove hunting is another popular sport in the state during the fall. This particular rendition comes from my dear friend Paula Lambert.

---

4 SERVINGS

12 doves, dressed
6 jalapeño chiles, stemmed, halved, and seeded
12 slices bacon

4 cups Drunken Beans (recipe follows)
½ recipe Three Potato Salad (recipe follows)
1 cup Paula's "Rosy" Relish (see Index)

Prepare the smoker (see page 9). Remove the legs and wings from the doves, and rinse the cavities. Stuff each dove with ½ jalapeño, and wrap with a slice of bacon, secured by a toothpick. Smoke for about 1 hour, stoking the fire at least twice. Serve 3 doves per person, with beans, potato salad, and relish.

DRUNKEN BEANS

6 TO 8 SERVINGS

7 ounces bacon, diced
1 onion, diced
2 cloves garlic, minced
2 cups pinto beans, soaked overnight and drained
(page 10)

1 quart Chicken Stock (see Index) or water
2 cups beer
4 jalapeño chiles, thinly sliced, with seeds
Salt and freshly ground black pepper to taste
2 tablespoons chopped cilantro

In a large saucepan, sauté the bacon over medium heat until the fat is rendered. Remove the bacon with a slotted spoon and set aside. Pour off all but 1 tablespoon of fat and add the onion and garlic. Cook for 2 to 3 minutes, until the onion is translucent. Add the beans, stock or water, and beer. Bring to a boil, reduce the heat to a simmer, and cook for about 1 hour, checking every 30 minutes or so. Add the jalapeños after the first 30 minutes of cooking, and add more broth or water as needed to keep the beans covered. When the beans are tender, season with salt and pepper. Stir in the cilantro, and serve.

THREE POTATO SALAD
8 SERVINGS

4 oranges, juiced (about 2 cups)
6 to 8 cups water
1 pound sweet potatoes, peeled and diced
1 pound new red potatoes, diced
1 pound russet potatoes, diced
1 small red onion, minced

4 tablespoons chopped chives
1 pound bacon, diced, cooked, fat rendered,
and drained
1½ cups Mayonnaise (see Index)
4 tablespoons Dijon mustard
Salt and freshly ground black pepper to taste

In a saucepan, reduce the orange juice over high heat to 3 to 4 tablespoons, being careful not to let it burn.

In a large pot, bring the water to a boil. Add the potatoes, return to a boil, and cook until the potatoes are just fork-tender, 1 to 2 minutes. Drain the potatoes, transfer to a mixing bowl, and let cool slightly. Combine thoroughly with the reduced orange juice and all the remaining ingredients.

GRILLED SQUAB WITH CARAMELIZED BANANAS AND MANGO QUESADILLAS

We serve this dish from time to time at Star Canyon with the Tropical Black Bean Salsa (see Index), and although it's worth adding if you have the time, it's fine without it too. The combination of flavors and spices with the rich, dark squab meat is spectacular.

4 SERVINGS

½ cup Annatto Oil (see Index)
½ onion, minced
4 cloves garlic, minced
4 squab, 12 to 14 ounces each

Salt to taste
4 Mango Quesadillas (recipe follows)
Caramelized Bananas (recipe follows)

Combine the oil, onion, and garlic in a mixing bowl. Remove the backbone from each squab with a sharp knife, and marinate the squab in the mixing bowl for 1 to 2 hours. Meanwhile, prepare a wood-burning grill (see pages 4 to 6). (You can prepare the quesadillas and bananas, and keep warm.)

Remove the squab from the marinade, season with salt, and place the squab breast side down on the grill. Cook until golden, about 3 to 4 minutes. Turn over and cook for 3 to 4 minutes longer, until medium rare. Let the squab rest for a few minutes and then split each squab in half. Serve each with a quesadilla and 2 pieces of banana.

MANGO QUESADILLAS

4 SERVINGS

2 ounces fresh goat cheese, crumbled
2 ounces Monterey Jack or caciotta cheese, grated
1 teaspoon minced garlic
¼ cup chopped onion
½ poblano chile, roasted, peeled, seeded, and diced (page 6)
½ red bell pepper, roasted, peeled, seeded, and diced (page 6)

1 teaspoon minced cilantro
⅓ teaspoon salt
1 teaspoon fresh lime juice
1 ripe mango, peeled, pitted, and chopped
4 Flour Tortillas (see Index), at room temperature
2 tablespoons unsalted butter, melted

In a large mixing bowl, crumble the cheeses and stir in the garlic, onion, poblano, bell pepper, cilantro, salt, and lime juice. Carefully blend in the mango.

Spread some of the mixture over half of each tortilla and fold over. Brush each tortilla with the melted butter. Heat a large nonstick pan over medium-high heat. Cook the quesadillas for 3 to 4 minutes, until golden brown on both sides. Cut each quesadilla into 3 triangles and serve.

CARAMELIZED BANANAS

4 SERVINGS

2 large ripe bananas, peeled, halved crosswise and then lengthwise

½ cup confectioners' sugar
¼ cup clarified butter

Dredge the bananas in the sugar. In a heavy cast-iron skillet, heat the clarified butter until heavily smoking. Place the bananas cut side down in the skillet and sauté for 30 seconds, until nicely browned and caramelized. Carefully flip over and caramelize on the other side for 30 seconds.

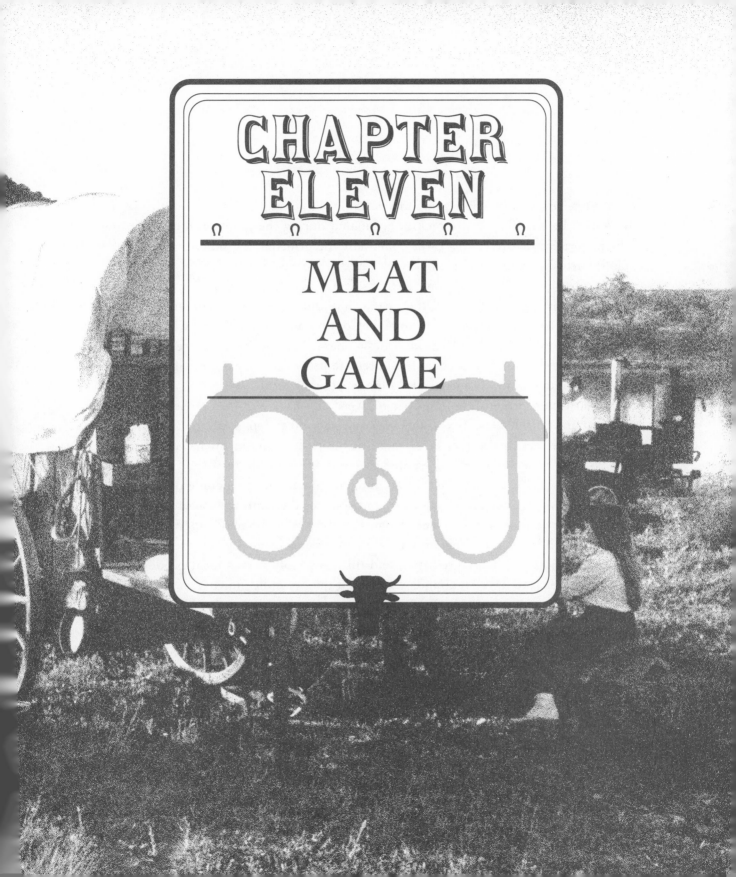

CHAPTER ELEVEN

MEAT AND GAME

Meat—beef especially—and game are certainly basic staples of Texan cuisine. In the state where beef is king, many recipes originated during the nineteenth century, the era of the historic cattle drives. Beef was commonly the principal ingredient, and dishes such as chili, barbecue, and chicken fried steak rapidly became classics.

Historically, indigenous game such as venison, wild boar, and wild sheep were widespread throughout Texas. Other game like antelope have been introduced more recently, and they have flourished in the Hill Country and South Texas, where the climate is comparable to their native Africa and India. Game has become an increasingly popular food source as the public has come to appreciate its healthful qualities; it is leaner, with a lower fat content and less cholesterol than most other meat.

When Routh Street Cafe first opened, we didn't have any beef dishes on the menu. For a restaurant in Dallas, Texas, this was quite a radical departure, but in part it was a reaction to the fact that a quarter or more of the restaurants in town were steakhouses while 95 percent served steaks. I wanted to serve different kinds of food, but over time, I realized that beef was too important an indigenous food not to include on the menu.

At Star Canyon, we use Texas beef, and some of the lamb we use during the year is also local. Our venison usually comes from the Texas Wild Game Cooperative in the Hill Country, which is the same region our wild boar comes from. I place great emphasis on using the freshest possible ingredients, and this invariably means local produce. We are fortunate in Texas to have an abundance of high-quality indigenous meat and game.

BARBECUED BRISKET OF BEEF WITH RANCH-STYLE BEANS AND ASSORTED VEGETABLE PICKLES

This recipe is as Texan as rodeos and armadillos, and can be found at a typical summer back-yard outing anywhere in the state. It is derived from the Texan cooking style that originated in the days of the cattle drives. Beef brisket is a cut that keeps its flavor and texture during lengthy cooking times over low heat, and this recipe calls for 6 to 8 hours of cooking.

Barbecue reached its zenith in the 1960s during the days of the LBJ administration, which happened to coincide with the formative years of my youth. The brisket in this recipe should marinate for about 24 hours. If you don't have the time to make the more complex barbecue sauce, substitute one of the two easier alternatives included in Chapter 2.

8 TO 10 SERVINGS

1 untrimmed beef brisket, about 4 pounds
½ cup Dry Barbecue Rub (recipe follows)
2 cups Barbecue Sauce #3 (see Index)

RANCH-STYLE BEANS:
3 cups pinto beans, soaked overnight and drained (page 10)
2 quarts Ham Hock Broth (see Index) or water
1 onion, diced
2 cloves garlic, minced

2 medium tomatoes, blanched, peeled, seeded, and diced (page 8)
3 ounces bacon, diced
2 tablespoons pure chile powder (page 4)
1 teaspoon ground cumin
1 tablespoon ancho chile puree (pages 3 to 4)
¼ cup Catsup (see Index)
Salt and freshly ground black pepper to taste

2 quarts Vegetable Pickles (see Index)

Trim all but ⅛-inch layer of fat from the brisket. Place the brisket in a large glass or ceramic dish. Sprinkle the dry barbecue rub over the meat and roll to coat completely. Marinate, covered and refrigerated, for at least 24 hours.

When the brisket has marinated, prepare the smoker (see page 9). Remove the brisket from the dish and place on the grill over a pan of water. Place a shallow pan underneath the meat to catch the drippings. Cover the smoker with a lid. Remove the meat in about 2 hours and stoke the fire, adding more soaked wood. Add more water to the water pan as needed.

Smoke brisket for 5 to 6 hours, or until fork-tender, maintaining a temperature between 190° and 225° F. When the brisket is cooked, place on a carving board and thinly slice. Slightly heat the barbecue sauce and stir in the drippings from the smoker. Serve with the brisket.

To prepare the beans, place the beans in a large pot and add the broth or water, onion, garlic, and tomatoes. Bring to a boil, reduce the heat to a simmer, and add the remaining ingredients except for the salt and pepper. Simmer for 2 to 3 hours, or until tender, checking every 30 minutes or so; add more broth or water as needed to keep the beans covered. When the beans are tender, season with salt and pepper (you should have about 2 quarts).

Serve the brisket and beans with the vegetable pickles. Use any leftover brisket for Barbecued Brisket Sandwiches (see Index).

DRY BARBECUE RUB

ABOUT ½ CUP

¼ cup salt
2 tablespoons freshly ground black pepper

2 tablespoons paprika
1 teaspoon cayenne powder

Combine all the ingredients in a mixing bowl.

BEEF FAJITAS WITH BLACK BEANS, PECANS, AND CILANTRO

Fajitas — literally "belts" — are grilled strips of meat, often marinated, traditionally served with hot tortillas, Pico de Gallo, and sour cream. In fact, this dish can be simplified by serving it with those accompaniments instead of the black bean–pecan sauce. Like nachos, fajitas are distinctly Texan in origin (rather than Mexican), although they are derived from the cuisine south of the border. Specifically, fajitas originated in the San Antonio region, and their popularity has spread far and wide.

It is important to marinate the steak, and cook it quickly over a hot fire. Turning the steak and brushing it with oil encourages a live flame, which renders the fat from the meat and gives it a good flavor.

4 TO 6 SERVINGS

1 skirt steak, 1½ to 2 pounds
2 cups dark beer
¾ cup corn oil, plus extra for brushing
2 tablespoons soy sauce
2 tablespoons plus 3 teaspoons chopped cilantro
2 jalapeño chiles, chopped (with seeds)
3 cloves garlic, chopped
1 tablespoon coarsely cracked black pepper
⅓ cup toasted pecan halves (page 9)
2 cloves roasted garlic, or 1 tablespoon roasted garlic puree (page 7)
4 serrano chiles (or 2 more jalapeños), seeded and diced

9 ounces (18 tablespoons) unsalted butter
1 tablespoon minced chives
⅓ cup Chicken Stock (see Index)
⅓ cup red wine vinegar
1 large shallot, chopped
1 teaspoon fresh lime juice
¼ cup cooked black beans (page 10), drained and rinsed
Salt and freshly ground black pepper to taste
12 to 18 warm Flour Tortillas (see Index)

Place the steak in a shallow pan. Add 1½ cups of the beer, the ¾ cup oil, soy sauce, 2 tablespoons of the cilantro, the jalapeños, chopped garlic, and the coarsely cracked black pepper. Cover and marinate in the refrigerator for at least 2 hours, and preferably overnight.

In a mortar, combine the pecans, roasted garlic, and serrano chiles. Crush with a pestle. Alternatively, you can use a spice or coffee grinder. Blend in 1 ounce (2 tablespoons) of the butter and the chives.

Prepare the grill (see pages 4 to 6) or preheat the broiler. In a medium saucepan, combine the stock, the remaining ½ cup of beer, the vinegar, shallot, and 1 teaspoon of cilantro. Bring to a boil over moderate heat and continue to boil until reduced to 2 tablespoons, 10 to 12 minutes. Reduce the heat to low and whisk in the remaining 8 ounces of butter, 1 ounce at a time. Stir in the remaining 2 teaspoons of the cilantro and the lime juice. Whisk in the pecan butter. Stir in the black beans, and season the sauce with salt and pepper; thin with a little chicken stock or water if desired. Keep the sauce warm over simmering water.

Lightly brush the steak with oil, and season with salt and pepper. Grill the steak over a medium-hot fire or broil until medium rare, about 3 minutes per side. Thinly slice the steak crosswise on the diagonal and spoon the sauce over each serving. Accompany with warm flour tortillas. If desired, you can serve the dish with Avocado-Tomatillo Salsa (see Index), or another salsa from Chapter 3.

ROAST BEEF TENDERLOIN WITH ROAST TOMATO–ANCHO CHILE SAUCE AND WILD MUSHROOM ENCHILADAS

This recipe dates back to the very beginning of Routh Street Cafe. It is a very robust dish that will appeal to beef lovers especially. The combination and layering of flavors is really striking; the spiciness of the ancho chiles and the tartness of the roasted tomatoes perfectly complement the rich earthiness of the enchiladas.

4 TO 6 SERVINGS

8 medium ripe tomatoes
2 medium onions, quartered
2 tablespoons vegetable oil or clarified butter
1 center-cut beef tenderloin, about 2 pounds when trimmed of fat
Salt and freshly ground black pepper to taste
½ cup chopped carrots
½ cup chopped celery

4 cloves garlic, diced
1 cup dry red wine
2½ cups Brown Veal Stock (see Index)
¼ cup ancho chile puree (pages 3 to 4)
½ teaspoon ground cumin
¼ cup unsalted butter, at room temperature
4 to 6 Wild Mushroom Enchiladas (see Index)

Preheat the oven to 400° F. Place the tomatoes and onions in a roasting pan, and roast in the oven until charred and blackened, about 50 minutes. Set aside to cool.

Raise the oven temperature to 450° F. Heat the oil or clarified butter in a heavy roasting pan over medium-high heat. Pat the beef dry and season with salt and pepper. Add to the pan and brown the meat on all sides, about 1 minute per side. Remove the meat and add the carrots, celery, and garlic to the pan. Cook for 2 minutes, stirring frequently. Place the beef on the vegetables in the pan, and transfer to the oven. Roast for 20 to 25 minutes for medium-rare.

When the tenderloin is cooked, remove from the pan and keep warm. Place the roasting pan over high heat, deglaze with the wine, and reduce by three quarters. Add the veal stock and stir in the ancho chile puree and the cumin. Add the charred tomatoes and onions, reduce the heat, and simmer uncovered for 20 to 25 minutes (you should have about 3 cups). Pressing hard with a wooden spoon or spatula, strain the liquid into a saucepan and press down to extract all the juice from the tomatoes. Whisk in the butter and season to taste. Slice the tenderloin and serve with the sauce and wild mushroom enchiladas.

HILL TOP CAFE CHICKEN-FRIED STEAK WITH BLACK PEPPER CREAM GRAVY AND CHILE-CORN MASHED POTATOES

Many of my multigenerational Texan friends have told me that my cookbook would be incomplete without a recipe for chicken-fried steak. The Texas Restaurant Association has estimated that a mind-boggling 800,000 chicken-fried steaks are consumed in the state daily, and that 90 percent of its members serve it. Be that as it may, there is nothing more disappointing than a poorly done chicken-fried steak, and yes, they do exist everywhere. The best chicken-fried steak I've tried in a long time provided the inspiration for this recipe, and I came across it at the Hill Top Cafe, a wonderful little place just outside Fredericksburg in the Hill Country.

The owners are Johnny and Brenda Nicholas; Johnny was formerly a member of the Texas band Asleep at the Wheel, and he has played with many of the great blues artists, including Walter Horton and Snooky Pryor. Hill Top Cafe has lots of atmosphere, and usually, after dinner, Johnny plays on his vintage upright piano in a corner of the dining room. I can really recommend the whole dining experience there.

Anyway, although this is by no means the authentic recipe for chicken-fried steak, it's one I could happily eat with great regularity. The most obvious difference from the classic version is a better cut of meat; unless the traditional round steak is tenderized completely, its texture resembles well-aged shoe leather.

---

4 SERVINGS

STEAK:
1 to 1½ pounds chuck steak
2 cups milk
1 cup flour
1 teaspoon salt
Vegetable or corn oil, for frying

BLACK PEPPER CREAM GRAVY:
5 tablespoons flour
3½ cups milk
½ teaspoon freshly ground black pepper
Salt to taste

Chile-Corn Mashed Potatoes (recipe follows)

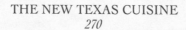

To prepare the steak, cut the meat into 4 portions and trim the fat. Pound to tenderize until as thin as possible (about ⅛ to ⅟₁₆ inch). Place the steaks in a shallow bowl or pan and cover with the milk. Let stand in the refrigerator for at least 12 hours.

In a mixing bowl, combine the flour and salt. Remove the steaks from the milk, dredge in the flour, and press firmly so a crust adheres to the steaks. In a large skillet, pour enough oil to come 1 inch up the sides, and set over medium heat until lightly smoking, about 375° F.

Cook 2 steaks at a time, for 1½ minutes per side. Remove the steaks, drain on paper towels, and keep warm while making the gravy.

To make the gravy, pour out all but 4 tablespoons of the oil from the skillet, leaving the drippings in the pan. Over medium heat, whisk in the flour and cook until golden brown, whisking continuously. Drizzle in the milk, stir in the pepper, and season with salt.

Serve the steaks and gravy with the chile-corn mashed potatoes.

CHILE-CORN MASHED POTATOES

4 SERVINGS

2 large baking potatoes, peeled and chopped
3 tablespoons unsalted butter
½ cup milk
4 cloves garlic, minced
1½ cups fresh corn kernels (2 ears)

2 teaspoons pure chile powder (page 4)
1 teaspoon chopped cilantro
1 teaspoon honey
Salt to taste

In a saucepan, place the potatoes with enough water to cover by 2 inches. Bring to a boil, reduce the heat, and simmer for about 20 minutes, until tender. Drain thoroughly.

Meanwhile, in a small skillet, melt the butter in the milk, bring to a boil, and add the garlic and corn. Reduce the heat and let simmer for 3 minutes. Sprinkle in the chile powder. Strain the mixture, reserving the corn separately from the liquid.

Place the cooked potatoes in a large mixing bowl. With an electric mixer, whip the potatoes while drizzling in the reserved liquid. When it's the right consistency, stir in the corn, cilantro, and honey, and season with salt.

VEAL CHOPS WITH BARBECUED CORN SAUCE AND BUTTERMILK-CAYENNE ONION RINGS

Barbecued corn makes a great vegetable accompaniment for almost any grilled meat. The secret to the complex flavor of the barbecue sauce is the smoking process for the chiles and vegetables. A good-quality cut of beef can be substituted for the veal, and sweet potatoes make a good alternative to the onion rings. The onion rings, by the way, go well with just about anything! Use the quicker Barbecue Sauce #1 or #2 (see Index) if you're in a hurry.

6 SERVINGS

1½ cups Barbecue Sauce #3 (see Index)
2 ears corn, shucked
3 tablespoons vegetable oil or clarified butter
6 veal chops, 8 to 10 ounces each

Salt and freshly ground black pepper to taste
Flour, for dredging veal
Buttermilk-Cayenne Onion Rings (recipe follows)
¼ cup Pico de Gallo (see Index), for garnish

Prepare the grill (see pages 4 to 6). Place ½ cup of the barbecue sauce in a small saucepan. Bring to a boil, reduce by half, and then brush onto the corn. Place the corn on the grill for about 3 minutes, turning frequently. Cut the kernels from the cobs and add to the remaining cup of barbecue sauce. Heat the sauce and keep warm while cooking the veal.

Heat the oil in a large skillet over medium heat until lightly smoking. Season the veal with salt and pepper and dredge lightly in the flour. Sauté the veal for

5 to 6 minutes per side and serve with the barbecued corn sauce and buttermilk-cayenne onion rings. Garnish with Pico de Gallo.

BUTTERMILK-CAYENNE ONION RINGS

4 TO 6 SERVINGS

1 egg yolk
1 cup flour
1 tablespoon cayenne powder
½ teaspoon baking soda

1½ teaspoons salt
2 cups buttermilk
2 large sweet yellow onions
Vegetable oil, for deep-frying

In a mixing bowl, combine the egg yolk and dry ingredients, and whisk for 1 minute. Slowly drizzle in the buttermilk while beating.

Slice the onions into rings as thin as possible, preferably using a mandolin or an electric slicer. Drop the onion rings into the batter and coat thoroughly. Pour enough of the vegetable oil to come 3 inches up the sides of a deep-fryer and heat to 375° F. Drop the onion rings into the oil and deep-fry for 4 to 5 minutes, until lightly browned. Remove with a slotted spoon and drain on paper towels.

VEAL MEDALLIONS ON WILTED GREENS WITH PINTO–WILD MUSHROOM SAUCE AND SPICY WHIPPED SWEET POTATOES

I created this dish for a dinner I prepared at the 1991 International Food Media Conference which was held in Dallas, and it has become one of my personal favorites. Although this recipe takes time to prepare, the complexity of the flavors is well worth the time invested. The sweet potatoes are absolutely delicious, and can be used as an accompaniment to almost any meat, game, or poultry.

PINTO–WILD MUSHROOM SAUCE:
½ cup pinto beans, soaked overnight and drained
(page 10)
1 quart Ham Hock Broth (see Index) or water
Salt and freshly ground black pepper to taste
1 tablespoon clarified butter or vegetable oil
2 tablespoons minced shallots
2 cloves garlic, minced
1½ cups cleaned and sliced assorted fresh wild
mushrooms, such as morels, chanterelles, oysters,
or shiitakes
½ cup fresh corn kernels (1 small ear)
½ cup dry red wine
1½ cups demiglace (see note on page 37)

1 teaspoon chipotle chile puree (pages 3 to 4)
1 teaspoon chopped sage
1 ripe medium tomato, blanched, peeled, seeded,
and diced (page 8)
1 tablespoon chopped basil
1 tablespoon unsalted butter, at room temperature

6 loin-cut veal medallions, 4 ounces each and
about 1¾ inches thick
Salt and freshly ground black pepper to taste
1 tablespoon clarified butter or vegetable oil

1 recipe Wilted Southern Greens (see Index)
Spicy Whipped Sweet Potatoes (recipe follows)

To make the sauce, place the beans in a saucepan with the broth or water. Bring to a boil, reduce the heat to a simmer, and cook for 45 minutes to 1 hour, until tender, checking every 20 minutes or so; add more broth or water as needed to keep the beans covered. When the beans are tender, season with salt and pepper, and reserve.

Heat the clarified butter or oil in a large skillet or pan over medium heat until lightly smoking. Add the shallots and garlic, and cook for 20 seconds. Add the mushrooms and corn, and cook for 1 minute longer. Deglaze the pan with the red wine and reduce the liquid by three quarters over high heat, while scraping the pan with a spatula to dissolve the solidified juices. Add the demiglace, chipotle puree, sage, reserved beans, and tomato. Reduce the liquid by one third, add the basil, whisk in the butter, and season with salt. Keep the sauce warm.

Season the veal with salt and pepper. Heat the clarified butter or oil in a large skillet over medium heat until lightly smoking. Sauté the veal until browned on one side, about 3 minutes. Turn over, lower the heat, and cook for an additional 3 to 4 minutes.

Divide the greens between the plates, place the veal on top of the greens, spoon the sauce on top of the veal, and serve with the potatoes.

SPICY WHIPPED SWEET POTATOES

6 SERVINGS

2 large sweet potatoes, peeled and diced
½ white potato, peeled and diced
6 tablespoons pure maple syrup
2 teaspoons salt

1 teaspoon cayenne powder
1 tablespoon pure chile powder (page 4)
8 tablespoons (1 stick) unsalted butter,
at room temperature

In a saucepan, bring the potatoes to a boil, reduce the heat, and simmer for 15 minutes until soft. Drain, and transfer the potatoes to a food processor. Add the maple syrup, salt, cayenne, and chile powder. Process for 1 minute while adding the butter 1 tablespoon at a time. Warm in a pan, and serve.

PORK TENDERLOIN WITH DRIED CHERRY SAUCE AND CREAMED PINE NUTS

In September 1990, I participated as a guest chef at an event at the Stein Erickson Lodge in Deer Valley, Utah, with my friend Larry Forgione. Larry prepared a main course of venison with huckleberries and creamed wild hickory nuts. That brilliant dish was the inspiration for this recipe. In this dish, the tartness of the dried cherries forms a classic marriage with the blue cheese and creamed pine nuts.

4 SERVINGS

2 pork tenderloins, 8 to 10 ounces each,
trimmed of fat
Salt and freshly ground black pepper to taste
¼ cup clarified butter or vegetable oil
2 tablespoons minced shallots
2 cloves garlic, minced
1 cup dried cherries
1 tablespoon sugar
½ cup dry red wine

½ cup port
1⅓ cups demiglace (see note on page 37)
1 teaspoon chopped basil
2 tablespoons unsalted butter,
at room temperature
½ cup toasted pine nuts (page 9)
1 cup heavy cream
2 ounces good-quality blue cheese, crumbled
1 tablespoon snipped chives, for garnish

Cut each tenderloin into 6 medallions, and season with salt and pepper. Heat the butter or oil in a large skillet over medium heat, and sauté the pork for about 3 minutes on one side; turn and cook for 2 minutes on the other. Remove from the pan and keep warm while making the sauce.

Pour all but 1 tablespoon of the butter or oil from the pan, add the shallots and garlic, and cook for 20 seconds. Add ½ cup of the dried cherries and the sugar, and cook for 1 minute longer. Deglaze with the red wine and port, and reduce by three quarters over high heat.

Transfer the ingredients from the pan to a blender and puree. Pour through a fine strainer back into a clean skillet and add the demiglace. Add the remaining ½ cup of cherries and simmer uncovered for 3 to 5 minutes. Add the basil and whisk in the butter. Set aside and keep warm.

Place the pine nuts and cream in a pan over high heat and reduce the cream by one third. Add the blue cheese and whisk until melted.

To serve, ladle the cherry sauce onto warm serving plates and place the pork on top of the sauce. Pour the creamed pine nuts on top of the medallions, and sprinkle with the chives.

PORK CHOPS STUFFED WITH ANDOUILLE, APPLES, AND CORN BREAD

Andouille is a black-skinned smoked sausage that originated in Vire, France, and which is common throughout the country as an hors d'oeuvre. Andouille also refers to Cajun smoked sausage — the style was brought to Louisiana by the Arcadians in the mid-1700s. The Cajun version is made with pork butt, shank, and a small amount of pork fat, slowly smoked over pecan and sugarcane.

Ω   Ω   Ω   Ω   Ω   Ω   Ω   Ω   Ω

8 SERVINGS

8 center-cut pork chops, 6 to 7 ounces each
1½ tablespoons olive oil
½ small onion, diced
1 stalk celery, diced
1 clove garlic, diced
½ red bell pepper, seeded and diced
1 serrano chile, seeded and minced
6 ounces andouille sausage, cut into ⅛-inch dice
2 unpeeled green apples, cored and diced

2 sage leaves, chopped
1 sprig rosemary, chopped
¼ cup crumbled Blue Corn Skillet Sticks
(see Index)
¼ cup sour cream
Salt and freshly ground black pepper to taste
2 tablespoons vegetable oil or clarified butter
½ cup port
1 cup Chicken Stock (see Index)

Preheat the oven to 160° F. Place 1 pork chop flat on a work surface, and holding it down with one hand, slice it through the middle with the point of a knife to form a pocket. Cut deeply to the bone, open the chop, and flatten each half with a meat pounder to make it a little larger for stuffing. Repeat this procedure for the remaining pork chops.

Heat the olive oil in a large skillet over medium heat until lightly smoking. Sauté the onion, celery, garlic, bell pepper, and serrano for 2 to 3 minutes. Add the sausage to the pan and cook for 1 minute longer. Add the apples, herbs, and corn-bread crumbs, and toss to heat through.

Remove the skillet from the heat, stir in the sour cream, and season with salt and pepper. When the stuffing has cooled, divide among the pork chops. Push the stuffing into the pockets and close securely. Do not overstuff, and make sure the meat is pressed together around the opening. Season the chops with salt and pepper.

Heat the vegetable oil or clarified butter in a large skillet over medium heat until lightly smoking. Add the chops and cook the first side for 3 to 4 minutes, until browned. Turn the chops over, cover the pan, and lower the heat. Cook for an additional 6 to 7 minutes. Remove the chops from the skillet and keep warm in the oven.

Deglaze the pan with the port and reduce by half while scraping the pan with a spatula to dissolve the solidified juices. Add the stock and reduce by half again. Season with salt and pour over the pork chops on a platter.

TAMARIND-GLAZED PORK CHOPS WITH GREEN CHILE SPOON BREAD AND APRICOT-ALMOND CHUTNEY

Tamarind pods are the fruit of an evergreen tree that originated in West Africa, but is now widespread throughout Southeast Asia and Mexico as well. These pods contain hard seeds and a bittersweet pulp, which is used extensively in Mexico as a flavoring (I particularly like the flavor of tamarind in Agua Fresca). The tamarind paste used in this recipe is available in Asian or Latin markets.

8 SERVINGS

1 cup red wine vinegar
1 cup dark brown sugar
1 cup Chicken Stock (see Index)
2 plum tomatoes, chopped
2 tablespoons tamarind paste

8 center-cut pork chops, about 6 to 7 ounces each
Salt to taste
Green Chile Spoon Bread (recipe follows)
2 cups Apricot-Almond Chutney (see Index)

In a medium saucepan, combine the vinegar, sugar, chicken stock, tomatoes, and tamarind paste. Cook over medium heat, stirring occasionally, until thickened, 15 to 20 minutes. Strain through a coarse strainer into a mixing bowl and allow to cool.

Preheat the broiler. Sprinkle salt on both sides of the pork chops and brush generously with the tamarind glaze. Place the chops on a broiler pan and broil for 5 to 6 minutes per side, rotating the pan as necessary, until the chops are deep brown, crusty, and just cooked through, but still moist. Alternatively, the chops can be grilled. Serve immediately with green chile spoon bread and apricot-almond chutney.

GREEN CHILE SPOON BREAD

This quintessentially Southern recipe is one of the most elegant dishes to be made from cornmeal; the chiles add a distinctive Southwestern flavor. Spoon bread is typical of the influence of Southern food in Texas. It is believed to have derived originally from the Native American porridge called suppone. This green chile spoon bread recipe has a rich, soufflélike texture and is an excellent accompaniment for any dark meat or game.

8 SERVINGS

¾ cup milk
¾ cup Chicken Stock (see Index)
½ cup yellow cornmeal
1½ teaspoons salt, or more to taste
¼ teaspoon freshly ground white pepper
2 tablespoons unsalted butter
2 teaspoons pureed roasted garlic (page 7)
¾ cup roasted corn kernels (1 large ear)
(page 7)

1 large poblano chile, roasted, peeled, seeded, and diced (page 6)
3 tablespoons diced green bell pepper
3 tablespoons diced red bell pepper
1 serrano chile, seeded and minced
½ cup heavy cream
3 eggs, separated

Preheat the oven to 325° F. Combine the milk and chicken stock in a large saucepan over high heat and bring to a boil. Let boil for 30 seconds, then reduce the heat to medium and add the cornmeal, whisking until smooth. Remove from the heat and add the salt, pepper, and butter. Mix thoroughly and transfer to a large mixing bowl. Add all the remaining ingredients, except the eggs, and combine completely. Let the mixture cool slightly.

Whisk the egg yolks into the mixture. Beat the egg whites to soft peaks and gently fold in. Pour the mixture into a lightly oiled 1 to 1½-quart baking dish or soufflé mold, and place inside a larger pan. Add enough very hot water to the larger pan to come about 1 inch up the side of the spoon-bread dish.

Place in the oven and bake for 45 minutes, or until a knife inserted in the center comes out clean. Check the spoon bread after the first half hour; if it is browning too quickly, cover with foil. Serve immediately.

LOIN OF LAMB WITH GINGERED FRUIT COUSCOUS AND TOMATO-EGGPLANT RAGOUT

This dish was inspired by a trip to Morocco. My most vivid memories are of the soukhs, or markets, of Fez and Marrakesh, which are intoxicating with their complex variety of sights, sounds, and smells. Every multicourse meal I had in Morocco ended with a big plate of couscous that was usually steamed over some kind of meat tagine (a stew usually cooked in a clay pot). In this recipe, I've brought the flavored couscous into the main course to complement the lamb. To simplify the recipe, you can forego making the serrano-cumin sauce, and simply roast the lamb in the oven or cook it on a grill.

4 SERVINGS

2 boned, trimmed lamb loins, 8 to 10 ounces each
(bones reserved for stock)
Salt to taste
2 tablespoons olive oil
½ sweet onion, such as Texas Noonday or
Vidalia
¼ carrot, chopped
½ stalk celery, chopped

SERRANO-CUMIN SAUCE:
½ cup dry red wine
¾ cup reduced lamb stock or Brown Veal Stock
(see Index)

1 teaspoon ground cumin
3 serrano chiles, halved lengthwise, with seeds
2 sprigs fresh thyme
2 sprigs fresh rosemary
2 tablespoons unsalted butter,
at room temperature
Salt to taste

Gingered Fruit Couscous (recipe follows)
Tomato-Eggplant Ragout (recipe follows)

Preheat the oven to 350° F. Season the lamb with salt. In an ovenproof pan placed over a high flame on the stove, heat the olive oil until lightly smoking, and sear the lamb on all sides. Remove the lamb from the pan and set aside.

Add the onion, carrot, and celery to the pan, and sauté for 2 minutes. Return the lamb to the pan, and place in the oven. Cook for 4 to 6 minutes for medium-rare. Remove the pan from the oven and place the lamb on a warm dish to rest.

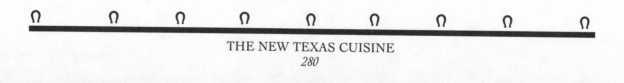

Meanwhile, to prepare the sauce, add the red wine to the oven pan and on top of the stove, reduce to a glaze over high heat. Lower the heat to medium, add the stock, cumin, serranos, thyme, and rosemary. Bring to a boil, reduce the heat, and simmer for 2 to 3 minutes. Whisk in the butter and season with salt. For a spicier sauce, let the serranos steep longer. Strain the sauce before serving. Serve the lamb and sauce with the couscous and ragout.

GINGERED FRUIT COUSCOUS
4 TO 6 SERVINGS (ABOUT 3⅓ CUPS)

1 cup Chicken Stock (see Index)
2 tablespoons peeled and roughly chopped fresh ginger
1 teaspoon salt
½ teaspoon ground cinnamon
1 cup uncooked couscous

4 tablespoons unsalted butter, at room temperature
2 tablespoons minced crystallized ginger
½ cup diced assorted dried fruit, such as apple, mango, apricot, papaya, and cherry

Bring the stock to a boil in a medium saucepan. Remove from the heat, add the fresh ginger, cover the pan, and let steep for 15 minutes. Remove the ginger and discard. Add the salt and cinnamon to the stock, and return to a boil. Add the couscous all at once, stirring until all the liquid is absorbed.

Remove from the heat and incorporate the butter with a fork. Add the crystallized ginger and diced dried fruit, and combine thoroughly. If necessary, the couscous can be reheated in a little stock and butter.

TOMATO-EGGPLANT RAGOUT

This recipe, with a Mediterranean style and flavor, is best prepared in the summer when tomatoes, eggplant, and basil are all at their peak. The recipe works well with almost any meat or fish dish, and can also be served at room temperature.

4 tablespoons olive oil	*2 tablespoons finely minced garlic*
½ cup peeled and diced eggplant	*1 tablespoon chopped thyme*
Salt to taste	*1 tablespoon chopped oregano*
½ cup diced onion	*2 tablespoons tomato paste*
½ cup diced zucchini	*2 tablespoons chopped basil*
5 medium tomatoes, blanched, peeled, seeded, and	*1 tablespoon chopped parsley*
diced (page 8)	*Freshly ground black pepper to taste*

Heat 2 tablespoons of the olive oil in a large skillet until lightly smoking. Add the eggplant, salt slightly, and sauté over medium-high heat for 5 minutes, until translucent, stirring frequently. Transfer the eggplant to a colander and weight with a plate to extract the bitter juices.

In the same skillet, heat the remaining 2 tablespoons of the olive oil until lightly smoking and add the onion and zucchini. Sauté for 2 minutes, then add the tomatoes, garlic, thyme, oregano, and tomato paste. Cook until all the liquid has evaporated, 10 to 15 minutes. Add the basil, parsley, and drained eggplant, and continue cooking for 2 minutes. Season with salt and pepper.

ROSEMARY-GRILLED LAMB CHOPS WITH CREAMED CORN PUDDING AND THREE TOMATO SALSAS

This is a dish I created for the first annual SOS (Share Our Strength) Taste of the Nation benefit, in 1988. SOS is a nonprofit organization based in Washington, D.C., whose aim is to alleviate hunger and homelessness. These are issues I feel deeply about, and it is particularly appropriate that the restaurant and hospitality industries provide leadership in dealing with these problems. Each spring, chefs from all across America hold events, sponsored by SOS, to raise money for hunger relief within their communities. These local events are a great opportunity for the public to sample the food from the best chefs in their cities, as well as to support a worthwhile cause.

8 rib lamb chops, about 1 inch thick
1 tablespoon olive oil
Salt to taste

4 to 6 large rosemary sprigs
Creamed Corn Pudding (recipe follows)
Three Tomato Salsas (see Index)

Prepare the grill (see pages 4 to 6). Brush the chops with the olive oil and season with salt. Toss the rosemary sprigs onto the coals and grill the chops for 2 minutes per side for medium-rare. Serve with the creamed corn pudding and three tomato salsas.

CREAMED CORN PUDDING

4 TO 6 SERVINGS

1 tablespoon unsalted butter
2 cups fresh corn kernels (3 large ears)
½ cup heavy cream
2 large eggs
Pinch of ground cinnamon
1 tablespoon diced red bell pepper

1 tablespoon diced yellow bell pepper
1 serrano chile, seeded and minced
1 tablespoon chopped cilantro
1 tablespoon pure maple syrup
Salt and freshly ground white pepper to taste

Preheat the oven to 375° F. Spread the butter on a small baking dish and set aside.

In a food processor, puree 1 cup of the corn kernels and set aside. In a mixing bowl, beat together the cream, eggs, cinnamon, bell peppers, serrano, cilantro, and maple syrup. Add the corn puree and the remaining cup of corn kernels, and mix together. Season with salt and pepper, and pour the mixture into the buttered baking dish. Cover the dish with foil and bake in the center of the oven for 45 to 50 minutes. The pudding is done when a skewer inserted into the center comes out clean.

CHILI AND THE TERLINGUA WORLD CHAMPIONSHIP

Chili is the official state dish of Texas, and Texans certainly take chili seriously. While it is agreed that chili originated in Texas, there are several theories regarding its exact roots. Some say it began as Chain Gang Chili, a dish served in the jails of San Antonio in the early 1800s, while others claim it was the creation of washerwomen who also cooked for the Republic of Texas Army in the 1830s: the Chili Queens of San Antonio. Another theory is that chili originated on the trail-drive chuck wagons, when the curry powder that was most commonly used as a seasoning ran out.

Chili cookoffs are a phenomenon (Texan in origin, of course!) dating back to the mid-1960s. It was in 1966 that Frank X. Tolbert, a Dallas newspaper columnist, arranged the first cookoff in Terlingua, southwest Texas, between self-proclaimed chili experts Wick Fowler, a fellow Texas newspaperman, and H. Allen Smith of New York. (Smith had challenged Fowler's claim to be chief cook of the Chili Appreciation Society.) The event, which attracted representatives from 209 chapters of the society, was proclaimed a tie, and so the Wick Fowler Memorial World Championship Chili Cookoff was born; it remains the premier event of its kind. In recent years, another chili cookoff has splintered off from the original competition; but for my money, there is still only one real world championship.

PEDERNALES RIVER CHILI

LBJ *probably did more to promote Texas cooking when he was President than anyone before or since. Just as he made barbecue a national social event, he was known for his fondness of chili; in fact, it was LBJ who suggested that chili be named the state food of Texas. This is the recipe that was always prepared at his ranch in the Hill Country. Incidentally, if you want to sound like a local, you'll need to put an extra "r" in the first syllable to pronounce "Purdn-alice" just right.*

---

8 TO 10 SERVINGS

¾ cup vegetable oil
4 pounds round steak or well-trimmed chuck, coarsely ground
1 large onion, chopped
2 large cloves garlic, minced
2 teaspoons minced oregano
1 teaspoon ground cumin

2 tablespoons pure chile powder (page 4)
6 large ripe tomatoes, blanched, peeled, seeded, and diced (page 8) 2 16 oz cans
3 tablespoons tomato paste
2 cups hot water, Brown Veal Stock, or Chicken Stock (see Index)
Salt to taste

Heat the oil in a heavy pan over medium heat and add the steak, onion, and garlic, and cook until lightly browned. Add the remaining ingredients except for the salt and bring to a boil. Lower the heat and simmer uncovered for about 1 hour. Skim occasionally, and season with salt.

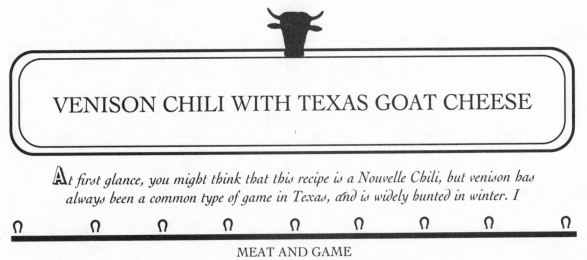

VENISON CHILI WITH TEXAS GOAT CHEESE

At *first glance, you might think that this recipe is a Nouvelle Chili, but venison has always been a common type of game in Texas, and is widely hunted in winter. I* *remember eating plenty of venison as a youngster. It's leaner than beef, so you need to cook it with a little more fat. A good chili should cook for several hours so it becomes perfectly tender. We use Texas goat cheese supplied by Paula Lambert at the Mozzarella Company here in Dallas, but any fresh goat cheese can be used. Paula has won all kinds of prizes for her cheeses, and I have enjoyed working with her to create some new varieties, such as an ancho chile–cilantro cheese and a smoked pepper cheese.*

4 TO 6 SERVINGS

½ cup vegetable oil
2 pounds venison, well trimmed of fat, finely chopped
6 cloves garlic, finely chopped
1 onion, chopped
4 tablespoons ancho chile puree (pages 3 to 4)
1 tablespoon chipotle chile puree

4 medium tomatoes, blanched, peeled, seeded, and chopped (page 8)
½ teaspoon ground toasted cuminseed (pages 8 to 9)
1 quart Brown Veal Stock (see Index) or water
Salt and freshly ground black pepper to taste
4 ounces fresh goat cheese, crumbled

Heat the oil in a heavy pan and add the venison, garlic, and onion. Cook over medium heat until the meat has browned, about 15 minutes. Add the chile purees, tomatoes, and cuminseed, and cook for 15 minutes longer. Add the stock or water and bring to a boil. Reduce the heat and simmer for 1 to 1½ hours, stirring occasionally, or until the meat is perfectly tender and the chili is quite thick. Season with salt and pepper to taste.

Ladle about 1 cup per serving into individual bowls, and garnish with the goat cheese. A good accompaniment to this dish is Blue Corn Skillet Sticks or Mexican Corn Bread (see Index).

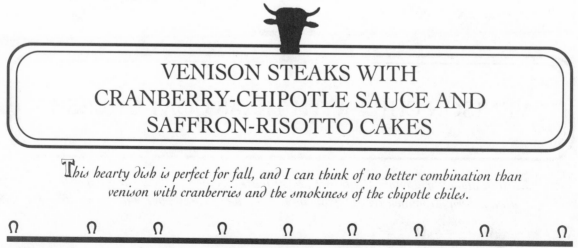

VENISON STEAKS WITH CRANBERRY-CHIPOTLE SAUCE AND SAFFRON-RISOTTO CAKES

This hearty dish is perfect for fall, and I can think of no better combination than venison with cranberries and the smokiness of the chipotle chiles.

¼ cup clarified butter or vegetable oil
8 venison loin steaks, about 4 to 6 ounces each
Salt and freshly ground black pepper to taste
2 tablespoons minced shallots
2 cloves garlic, minced
2 cups cranberries
3 tablespoons sugar
1 cup dry red wine
2½ cups reduced venison or Brown Veal Stock
(see Index)

1 tablespoon plus 1 teaspoon chipotle
chile puree (pages 3 to 4)
1 tablespoon chopped sage
3 tablespoons unsalted butter, at
room temperature
8 sage leaves, for garnish
8 Saffron-Risotto Cakes (recipe follows)

Heat the clarified butter or oil in a large skillet over medium heat until lightly smoking. Season the venison with salt and pepper, and sauté for 3 to 4 minutes per side for medium-rare. Remove from the skillet and keep warm while making the sauce.

Pour out all but 1 tablespoon of the butter from the skillet. Add the shallots and garlic, and cook for 20 seconds. Add the cranberries and sugar, and cook for 30 seconds longer.

Deglaze with the wine and reduce by three quarters over high heat (about 8 minutes). Add the stock, chipotle chile puree, and chopped sage. Reduce by one third and strain through a fine sieve. Return to a clean saucepan and heat to boiling. Whisk in the butter, remove from the heat, and season. Garnish each steak with a sage leaf, and serve with 1 saffron-risotto cake per plate.

SAFFRON-RISOTTO CAKES

The secret of making a good risotto lies in the timing, but this recipe makes things easier by having the risotto made ahead, formed into cakes, and then sautéed. This eliminates the need for perfect texture. For an interesting variation, try these cakes as an appetizer, topped with sautéed crabmeat. The rice can be cooked up to one day before forming into cakes and sautéing; a little chicken stock should be added if the risotto becomes too thick.

8 CAKES

5 cups Chicken Stock (see Index)
4 tablespoons unsalted butter
⅓ cup finely minced onion
1½ cups arborio rice
½ cup dry white wine

½ teaspoon powdered saffron
⅓ cup freshly grated Parmesan cheese
Salt to taste
¼ cup olive oil
Cornmeal, for dredging

In a medium saucepan, bring the chicken stock to a simmer. Meanwhile, heat 3 tablespoons of the butter in a heavy 4-quart casserole over medium heat. Add the onion and sauté for 1 to 2 minutes, until it begins to soften; do not brown.

Add the rice and stir for 1 minute, making sure all the grains are well coated. Add the wine and stir until it is completely absorbed. Add the saffron and the simmering chicken stock, ½ cup at a time, stirring frequently. Wait until each addition is almost completely absorbed before adding the next ½ cup. Reserve about ¼ cup to add at the end. Stir frequently to prevent sticking.

After 20 to 25 minutes, when the rice is tender but still firm, add the reserved ¼ cup of stock. Turn off the heat and immediately add the remaining tablespoon of butter and the Parmesan cheese. Stir vigorously to combine with the rice. Season with salt and allow to cool.

Form the rice by hand into large, round cakes, about 3 inches across and ½ inch thick. Heat the olive oil in a medium skillet until lightly smoking. Dredge the cakes in cornmeal and sauté over low heat for 2 minutes per side. Drain on paper towels.

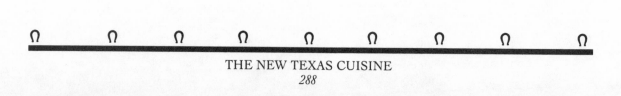

CORIANDER-CURED LOIN OF VENISON WITH SWEET ONION CONFIT AND TOMATILLO FRITTERS

This recipe comes from Jeffrey Dunham, formerly head chef at Routh Street Cafe. He developed this dish following a week he spent with my friend Madeleine Kamman at her Beringer school for professional chefs. Madeleine is not only a good friend, but an inspiration to me and a whole generation of American chefs. Barbecue sauce #3 is the perfect accompaniment to this dish, but it's also fine without it. If you are using the barbecue sauce, it should be prepared the day before.

4 SERVINGS

4 tablespoons coriander seeds	1 venison loin, about 2 pounds, cleaned
4 tablespoons black peppercorns	3 tablespoons vegetable oil
4 shallots, minced	Salt to taste
4 cloves garlic, minced	Sweet Onion Confit (recipe follows)
¾ cup kosher salt	Tomatillo Fritters (recipe follows)
6 tablespoons dark brown sugar	1 cup Barbecue Sauce #3 (optional, see Index)

In the bowl of a food processor, pulse the coriander seeds and peppercorns for about 1 minute until coarsely ground. Add the shallots, garlic, kosher salt, and sugar, and process to a thick paste. Transfer to a mixing bowl, add the venison, and let cure for at least 3 hours, turning occasionally.

Preheat the oven to 400° F. Heat the vegetable oil in the skillet over medium-high heat until lightly smoking. Remove the venison from the bowl and scrape clean. Season with salt and sear on all sides in the skillet. Transfer to an ovenproof baking dish and cook in the oven for 15 to 18 minutes for medium-rare. (Meanwhile, you can prepare the confit and fritters.)

When the venison is done, remove from the oven and let rest for 3 to 5 minutes. Slice the loin and serve with the confit, fritters, and barbecue sauce.

SWEET ONION CONFIT

4 SERVINGS

1 tablespoon unsalted butter
1 cup sliced sweet onions, such as Texas Spring
Sweet or Noonday
2 tablespoons sugar

2 tablespoons white wine vinegar
2 tablespoons balsamic or red wine vinegar
Salt to taste

Over medium heat, melt the butter in a skillet. Add the onions and sauté for 1 minute. Add the sugar and cook until it has dissolved; do not let it caramelize. Deglaze the skillet with the vinegars and cook until the liquid has evaporated, about 3 to 5 minutes. Season with salt.

TOMATILLO FRITTERS

4 SERVINGS

Vegetable or canola oil, for frying
1 cup flour
1 tablespoon baking powder
1 teaspoon baking soda
1 tablespoon paprika

Pinch of cayenne powder
Salt to taste
1 egg
1 cup beer
4 large tomatillos, husked and rinsed

Pour enough oil in a saucepan to come 1 inch up the sides, and heat to 325° F.

Meanwhile, in a mixing bowl, sift together the dry ingredients and set aside. In another mixing bowl, beat the egg and beer together. Sprinkle in the dry ingredients while whisking.

Slice the tomatillos into ¼-inch-thick slices, and cut each slice into ¼-inch strips. Dip the strips in the batter and let all but a thin film run off the strips. Fry in the hot oil until lightly browned, about 1 minute per side.

WILD BOAR, PINEAPPLE, AND TAMARIND STEW WITH CILANTRO RICE RING

This stew was inspired by the traditional Mexican dish, manchamantel, which contains pork, chiles, and fruit such as pineapple and bananas. Manchamantel literally means "tablecloth stainer," and is a deep, rich red in color. This recipe originated when I was asked by COOK'S magazine to create a Southwestern menu for their Christmas Holiday issue. This recipe was on the opening menu at Baby Routh and is an occasional feature at Tejas. You can buy the tamarind paste at Oriental or Mexican markets, and you can substitute top pork butt or pork shoulder for the boar.

---

6 TO 8 SERVINGS

*2½ pounds boneless wild boar loin, trimmed of
fat, cut into ½-inch cubes
1 large onion, chopped
2 carrots, chopped
4 large cloves garlic, chopped
½ teaspoon ground cumin
½ teaspoon cayenne powder
1 red bell pepper, seeded and chopped
1 teaspoon salt*

*1 quart stock made from boar bones and
trim, or water
5 dried ancho chiles, roasted and rehydrated
(pages 3 to 4)
1½ cups chopped fresh pineapple
¼ teaspoon ground cinnamon
1 tablespoon tamarind paste
Cilantro Rice Ring (recipe follows)*

In a large pan or stockpot, place the boar, onion, carrots, garlic, cumin, cayenne, red bell pepper, and salt. Add just enough stock or water to cover the other ingredients. Bring to a boil and skim the surface. Reduce the heat, cover, and simmer for 15 minutes. Strain the broth, reserving the meat and vegetables, and skim again.

Place the rehydrated ancho chiles and 1 cup of the broth in a blender and puree. Return the puree and remaining broth to the pan with the meat and vegetables, and add the pineapple, cinnamon, and tamarind. Bring to a simmer and continue to cook, uncovered, for 15 minutes. Season with additional salt. Serve in the center of the cilantro rice ring.

CILANTRO RICE RING

8 SERVINGS

4 tomatillos, husked, rinsed, and chopped
½ cup chopped cilantro
2 serrano chiles, seeded, deveined, and diced
3 cups water or Chicken Stock (see Index)
2 cups uncooked long-grain rice

6 scallions, diced
1 large clove garlic, minced
2 teaspoons salt
1½ ounces unsalted butter, at room temperature

In a blender, puree the tomatillos, ¼ cup of the cilantro, and the serranos in 1 cup of the water or stock. Transfer to a large saucepan and add the rice, scallions, garlic, salt, and the remaining 2 cups of water or stock. Bring to a boil and stir once with a fork. Reduce the heat to a simmer and cover. Continue to simmer for 12 to 15 minutes, or until the liquid is absorbed. Tilt the pan to make sure no liquid remains at the bottom.

Fluff the rice and fold in the butter and the remaining ¼ cup of cilantro. Cover and let sit for 5 minutes. Transfer to a well-buttered 6-cup ring mold, and press in firmly. Invert onto a hot serving platter and fill the center with stew.

BLACK BUCK ANTELOPE WITH SMOTHERED ONIONS AND SWEET POTATO TAMALES

Although antelope may seem wildly exotic, it is in fact not much different from venison in terms of preparation and flavor. Antelope, which are much smaller than the native deer, were introduced into Texas during the 1930s by Eddie Rickenbacker as hunting game, but they are now found in the wild. Sweet potatoes are the perfect accompaniment.

4 SERVINGS

¼ cup clarified butter or vegetable oil
2 sweet onions, preferably Texas Spring Sweet, Noonday, or Vidalia, thinly sliced
2 cloves garlic, minced
4 loin-cut antelope steaks, about 3 ounces each
Salt and freshly ground black pepper to taste
½ cup red wine
¾ cup Brown Veal Stock (see Index)

1 tablespoon chopped cilantro
1 teaspoon chopped thyme
1 teaspoon sugar
½ teaspoon Worcestershire sauce
1 teaspoon Catsup (see Index)
1 teaspoon cider vinegar
4 Sweet Potato Tamales (see Index)

Heat the butter or oil in a skillet over medium heat until lightly smoking. Add the onions and garlic, and sauté for 2 to 3 minutes, until translucent. Remove from the skillet with a slotted spoon and reserve.

Season the steaks with salt and pepper, and sauté in the skillet for 2 to 3 minutes per side for medium-rare. Remove and keep warm.

Deglaze the skillet with the wine and reduce the liquid to 2 tablespoons, about 5 minutes. Add the veal stock and reduce the liquid by one quarter. Add the reserved onion and garlic, and the remaining ingredients. Reduce the heat, partially cover, and simmer for 5 minutes.

Evenly divide the smothered onions and sauce among the serving plates, and place the antelope steaks on top. Serve with the tamales.

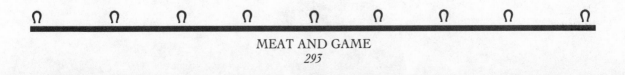

BANANA-PECAN WAFFLES WITH RUM RAISIN SYRUP AND
COUNTRY SAUSAGE   297

APPLE FRITTERS WITH CANELA   298

CHILAQUILES WITH GRIDDLED SALSA ROJA   300

GREEN CHILE SCRAMBLED EGGS WITH CHORIZO IN WARM
FLOUR TORTILLAS   301

HUEVOS RANCHEROS WITH AVOCADO-TOMATILLO SALSA   303

COUNTRY HAM WITH BUTTERMILK BISCUITS AND
RED-EYE GRAVY   304

TURKEY-YAM HASH WITH WARM
CRANBERRY-ORANGE COMPOTE   305

EGGPLANT PARMESAN TORTA WITH
BLACK OLIVE MAYONNAISE   306

SUGAR-CURED SMOKED HAM AND FRESH MOZZARELLA ON
CORNMEAL-RYE BREAD   307

SOUTHWESTERN VENISON BURGER   309

FRIED CATFISH SANDWICH WITH SMOKED TOMATO AÏOLI
AND PICKLED OKRA   310

SMOKED SHRIMP CLUB ON CHIPOTLE BRIOCHE WITH SWEET
POTATO CHIPS   311

BARBECUED BRISKET SANDWICH WITH
JICAMA COLESLAW   313

CORN GRIDDLE CAKES WITH GRILLED CHICKEN, BLACK BEAN
SAUCE, AND AVOCADO-TOMATILLO SALSA   314

CHICKEN CUSTARD STEAMED IN FRESH CORN HUSKS   316

CHAPTER TWELVE

BREAKFAST, BRUNCH, AND SANDWICHES

This was an interesting chapter to put together because there were three things we never offered at Routh Street Cafe: breakfast, brunch, and sandwiches! However, brunch and sandwiches were an important part of the menu at Baby Routh, and they have been a major source of inspiration for the recipes that follow.

A big breakfast of eggs or pancakes is a rare but welcome treat for me; there is nothing quite as satisfying as getting up late into the morning on a Sunday and having breakfast or brunch with a good Bloody Mary and plenty of strong coffee. Some of my fondest childhood memories are of weekend breakfasts when we'd stay with my grandmother, Mama Allen. She'd fix fried eggs (sunny side up) and bacon with red-eye gravy, and serve cottage fries and homemade bread to sop up the egg yolks with. We'd have coffee, which was a treat and made us kids feel like adults (actually it was four parts milk to one part coffee with two tablespoons of sugar). In the summer, she'd give us home-grown cantaloupe with cream gravy — a real delicacy to more than a few West Texans.

In the early days of Texas, breakfast was the most important meal. Wives and mothers would never send their menfolk out onto the ranch or into the fields without several helpings of fried or scrambled eggs or huevos rancheros; biscuits, grits, or tortillas; and sausage or chorizo. Brunch is believed to have originated in New Orleans in the latter part of the nineteenth century, when "second breakfasts" were served for tradespeople after the morning's shopping rush had subsided. It has developed into a distinctly civilized event, with the genteel Southern culture influencing the out-of-necessity breakfasts of former rustic times.

Sandwiches can be a great way to eat. History records that they were named after the British aristocrat the Earl of Sandwich, who sought a convenient snack while he gambled. Sandwiches are informal, quick to prepare, and need no eating utensils. There are days when nothing but a great sandwich will do.

The fun thing about sandwiches is that the only limitation in composing them is your own creativity. Use the recipes here as building blocks for new and unusual combinations. Take the breads from Chapter 13 and use filling combinations from other chapters, such

as the Smoked Pheasant Salad (Chapter 7), Seafood Cakes (Chapter 5), or even Grilled Soft-Shell Crabs (Chapter 9). Finish off the sandwiches with whichever dressings, condiments, chutneys, and pickles from Chapters 2 and 3 take your fancy.

BANANA-PECAN WAFFLES WITH RUM RAISIN SYRUP AND COUNTRY SAUSAGE

If you really want to impress your significant other, this is the perfect dish to serve for breakfast in bed. While the waffles must be made just before cooking, the sausage and syrup can be made in advance. Since this dish is not light on calories, it's best to forget about guilt and consume it with gusto.

4 TO 6 SERVINGS

SAUSAGE:
1 pound trimmed boneless pork butt,
cut into 1½-inch chunks
8 ounces fresh pork fat
½ cup finely chopped onion
3 cloves garlic, finely chopped
1 teaspoon chopped sage
½ teaspoon chopped cilantro
½ teaspoon chopped thyme
½ teaspoon pure chile powder (page 4)
¼ teaspoon cayenne powder
¼ teaspoon ground allspice
¾ teaspoon salt
½ teaspoon freshly ground black pepper

RUM RAISIN SYRUP:
½ cup raisins

½ cup Myers's dark rum
2 cups pure maple syrup

BANANA-PECAN WAFFLES:
2¼ cups flour
2 teaspoons baking powder
½ teaspoon baking soda
½ teaspoon salt
¼ cup packed brown sugar
½ cup chopped pecans
3 eggs, separated
2 to 2½ cups buttermilk
6 tablespoons unsalted butter, melted
2 very ripe bananas, peeled and pureed

To prepare the sausage, place the pork butt and fat in the freezer for 10 minutes. Remove from the freezer and push through a meat grinder, using a medium blade. Transfer to a large mixing bowl, add the remaining ingredients, and mix well with a wooden spoon until thoroughly combined. Cover and refrigerate overnight to let the flavors combine.

Form the sausage mixture into 12 patties about 3 inches wide and ½ inch thick. The sausage may be wrapped and kept for up to 6 days in the refrigerator, or frozen at this point. To cook, heat a large, heavy skillet over medium heat. When hot, cook the patties until brown on each side, about 4 minutes per side.

To prepare the syrup, plump the raisins in the rum for 30 minutes. In a small saucepan, bring the maple syrup just to a simmer, add the plumped raisins and rum, and stir to combine. Keep warm.

To prepare the waffles, sift together the dry ingredients in a large mixing bowl, and mix in the pecans. In another mixing bowl, beat the egg yolks and add the buttermilk, butter, and banana puree. Stir in the sifted dry ingredients until moistened; do not beat. Whip the egg whites into stiff peaks and fold into the batter. Pour the batter into a hot waffle iron and cook until golden brown and still moist inside, about 4 to 5 minutes. Serve with 2 to 3 sausages per plate and pour some syrup over the waffles.

APPLE FRITTERS WITH CANELA

These fritters make a great accompaniment for any breakfast or brunch. They can be served as an appetizer before an egg dish, or in a serving bowl as a buffet item. Use other fruits such as peaches or pears when they're in season; if using peaches, blanch and peel them first. Canela is a form of cinnamon grown in Sri Lanka that is not quite as strong as cinnamon, and has a subtle, pleasing mellowness. Canela sticks are a little longer than cinnamon sticks, and rather shaggy looking.

4 SERVINGS

1 cup white wine
1 cup granulated sugar
½ vanilla bean, split lengthwise
6 cloves
4 peppercorns
4 apples, peeled, cored, and quartered
2 cups flour
2 eggs, beaten
2 tablespoons unsalted butter, melted

¾ cup beer, at room temperature
½ cup sparkling water
2 tablespoons apple brandy, such as calvados
or applejack
Vegetable or canola oil, for deep-frying
2 cups cookie crumbs (gingersnaps or macaroons,
for example)
2 tablespoons ground canela or cinnamon
2 tablespoons confectioners' sugar

In a large saucepan, combine the wine, granulated sugar, vanilla, cloves, and peppercorns. Bring to a boil, reduce the heat, and boil slowly for about 8 minutes to form a syrup. Reduce the heat further to a simmer, add the apples, and cook until just tender when pierced with a fork, 6 to 8 minutes.

Meanwhile, sift the flour into a mixing bowl. In another bowl, beat the eggs with the butter, beer, sparkling water, and apple brandy until smooth. Drizzle into the flour while whisking, and continue whisking until smooth. Let the batter stand for 1 hour at room temperature before using. If the batter is too thick, thin with a little more sparkling water.

Pour enough oil in a large skillet to come 2 inches up the sides and heat to 375° F. Roll the apple quarters in the cookie crumbs, then dip into the batter and lower gently into the heated oil using tongs. Fry the apples until golden brown, about 4 minutes. Remove and drain on paper towels.

In a small mixing bowl, combine the canela or cinnamon and confectioners' sugar. Transfer to a sifter, sprinkle over the fritters, and serve.

CHILAQUILES WITH GRIDDLED SALSA ROJA

This Mexican dish was originated to use up leftovers, and it's a good way to make a tasty meal out of a number of ingredients. Chilaquiles can be made in a variety of ways: for example, with or without eggs, and with or without cheese. I prefer them with both, as well as plenty of salsa. Chilaquiles and a pitcher of Perfect 'Ritas (see Index) are an ideal way to start any Sunday.

---

8 TO 10 SERVINGS

2 small onions

1/4 cup red wine vinegar or fruit vinegar

1 1/2 cups sour cream

1/2 cup milk

Vegetable oil, for frying

12 Corn Tortillas (see Index)

1 1/2 cups Chicken Stock (see Index)

8 tomatillos, husked, rinsed, and quartered

2 jalapeño chiles, seeded and chopped

1 clove garlic, chopped

1/2 cup cilantro leaves

Salt to taste

1 tablespoon vegetable shortening or vegetable oil

1/2 cup grated Monterey Jack cheese

2 poblano chiles, roasted, peeled, seeded, and diced (page 6)

2 cups Griddled Salsa Roja (see Index)

Slice one of the onions into very thin strips, place in a bowl with the vinegar, and set aside. Chop the other onion coarsely and set aside. In a mixing bowl, whisk the sour cream and milk together and set aside.

Preheat the oven to 350° F. Pour enough vegetable oil in a large skillet to come 1/4 inch up the sides. Over medium heat, bring the oil to 350° F. or lightly smoking. Fry the tortillas, as many as will fit in the pan, just until crisp, about 1 minute. Drain on paper towels.

In a saucepan, bring the chicken stock to a boil. Add the tomatillos and cook until tender, about 10 minutes. Drain and reserve the stock.

Place the tomatillos, jalapeños, the chopped onion, garlic, and cilantro in a blender or food processor and blend until smooth. Season with salt.

Heat the shortening or oil in a large skillet over medium heat until lightly smoking. Pour in the tomatillo mixture and stir constantly for about 5 minutes, until thick and dark. Add the reserved chicken stock and bring to a boil. Reduce the heat and simmer for 8 to 10 minutes; the sauce should coat the back of a spoon.

Line an 8-inch square baking pan with 3 of the tortillas; they will overlap slightly. Pour a quarter of the tomatillo sauce over the tortillas, and pour one quarter of the sour cream–milk mixture on top of the sauce. Top with one quarter of the cheese, and place a third of the poblanos over the cheese. Repeat the process with the remaining tortillas, sauce, sour cream mixture, and cheese; the top layer will not have poblanos.

Cover the baking pan with foil and bake in the oven for 30 minutes. Remove and cover with the drained marinated onions. Serve with the griddled salsa roja.

GREEN CHILE SCRAMBLED EGGS WITH CHORIZO IN WARM FLOUR TORTILLAS

Variations of this dish are often listed on the menu as Breakfast Burritos in certain restaurants. You can substitute the spicy Country Sausage (see Index) for the chorizo, or you can leave out the meat altogether to create a vegetarian version.

4 SERVINGS

2 tablespoons olive or vegetable oil
1 small onion, diced
2 cloves garlic, minced
5 ounces Chorizo sausage meat (recipe follows)
2 poblano chiles, roasted, peeled, seeded, and chopped (page 6)
1 serrano chile, seeded and diced
1 medium tomato, diced

8 large eggs
¾ teaspoon salt
1 tablespoon chopped basil
1 teaspoon chopped cilantro
4 Flour Tortillas (see Index)
4 tablespoons sour cream
1 cup Pico de Gallo (see Index)

In a medium skillet, heat the oil over medium heat until lightly smoking. Add the onion and garlic and cook for 3 to 5 minutes, until the onion becomes translucent. Add the chorizo meat to the skillet and cook for 6 to 8 minutes while breaking up any lumps with a fork.

Add the poblanos, serrano, and tomato, and cook for 1 minute longer. Remove the skillet from the heat.

Crack the eggs into a large bowl, add the salt, and beat the eggs thoroughly. Return the skillet to the heat and pour in the eggs. Add the basil and cilantro and scramble the eggs to the desired consistency. Roll the eggs up in the warm tortillas and place 1 tablespoon of sour cream on each tortilla. Serve with Pico de Gallo.

CHORIZO

This is the ubiquitous Mexican sausage found in Latin markets everywhere. Unfortunately, the quality can be as variable as the number of markets, and sometimes the meat can be gristly and of inferior quality — I've always had better luck making my own sausage meat. Chorizo should always be highly seasoned and redolent of spices such as cinnamon.

ABOUT 2½ CUPS

8 ounces lean ground beef
8 ounces ground pork butt
2 cloves garlic, minced
½ tablespoon salt
½ teaspoon freshly ground black pepper
1 tablespoon white wine vinegar
1 tablespoon pure chile powder (page 4)

1 teaspoon paprika
½ teaspoon cayenne powder
½ teaspoon ground cinnamon
½ teaspoon ground cumin
¼ teaspoon ground cloves
½ cup boiling water
¼ cup lard or vegetable oil

Place the ground beef and pork in a mixing bowl and combine. Add all the remaining ingredients except the water and lard or oil, and combine thoroughly. Pour the water into the bowl and mix in. The chorizo may be wrapped and refrigerated or frozen at this point.

To cook, heat the lard or oil over medium heat in a large skillet until lightly smoking. Add the chorizo and cook for about 10 minutes, crumbling with a fork and stirring frequently.

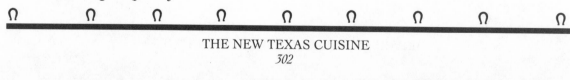

HUEVOS RANCHEROS WITH AVOCADO-TOMATILLO SALSA

The aroma of tomatoes stewing and tortillas frying was all that the ranch hands needed to know that breakfast was ready. All the cook needed to know was how they liked their eggs — fried, poached, or scrambled. There are many variations of this dish; in one that you may want to try, refried beans are spread on the tortilla before the egg goes on top. If this is your preference, use the Black Bean–Prosciutto Refrito recipe (see Index). To cut down on some of the fat used, you can poach the eggs in the salsa.

4 SERVINGS

2 cups Griddled Salsa Roja (see Index)
Vegetable oil, for softening
4 Corn Tortillas (see Index)
8 large eggs

4 tablespoons crumbled queso fresco or grated Monterey Jack cheese
1 tablespoon chopped cilantro
1 cup Avocado-Tomatillo Salsa (see Index)

Preheat the oven to 250° F. In a saucepan over medium heat, warm the salsa roja.

Pour enough oil in a large skillet to come ¼ inch up the sides. Over medium heat, bring the oil to 350° F. or lightly smoking. Submerge the tortillas in the oil one by one for 5 seconds each to soften. Place the tortillas on paper towels to drain and keep warm in the oven; do not stack the tortillas.

Reduce the heat under the skillet to medium-low and wait for 2 minutes. Crack the eggs into the skillet and cook slowly, sunny side up, until set. Remove from the skillet with a spatula and keep warm.

Set a tortilla on each plate, top with 2 fried eggs, and cover with the salsa roja, leaving the yolks exposed. Sprinkle the cheese and cilantro over the top, and serve with the avocado-tomatillo salsa.

COUNTRY HAM WITH BUTTERMILK BISCUITS AND RED-EYE GRAVY

The only thing that would make this dish more Southern is a side of piping hot grits. Although probably allegorical, there are at least a couple of theories on the origin of red-eye gravy. My favorite explanation is that Andrew Jackson and some cronies had been drinking and gambling into the wee hours of the morning. For breakfast, Jackson called for "a slice of ham with gravy as red as the eyes of that fellow yonder."

4 SERVINGS

1 recipe Mable's Buttermilk Biscuits (see Index)
4 tablespoons unsalted butter
1 pound uncooked country ham, preferably dry-cured, sliced 1/8 inch thick

1/2 cup Chicken Stock (see Index)
3 tablespoons strong brewed coffee
3/4 cup heavy cream
Salt to taste (optional)

After preparing the buttermilk biscuits, reduce the heat of the oven to 250° F.

In a large skillet, heat 3 tablespoons of the butter over medium heat. Sauté the ham slices for 2 minutes per side, until golden brown and crisp. Set aside and keep warm.

Pour off all but 1 tablespoon of the drippings. Add the stock and coffee, and bring to a boil while scraping the bottom of the skillet. Reduce to 1/4 cup, about 5 minutes. Add the cream and reduce the liquid by half. If the gravy is not as thick as you want, continue to reduce. Whisk in the remaining 1 tablespoon of butter, taste carefully, and season with salt if desired (cured ham is relatively salty and probably won't require additional salt).

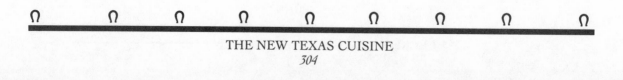

TURKEY-YAM HASH WITH WARM CRANBERRY-ORANGE COMPOTE

This is another item that was on the opening brunch menu at Baby Routh. Although it wasn't one of the most popular dishes, it was one of my favorites. It makes a full brunch meal with a poached egg on top of the hash, and it's the perfect solution for leftover turkey. Whenever I think of hash, I am always reminded of my days as chef's assistant at the Mondavi Winery Great Chefs of France Program. On one occasion, Marion Cunningham and John Carroll were preparing a Western version of red flannel hash for Michel Guerard. The winery had been transformed into a scene from the Old West, with bales of hay providing the backdrop, and waiters wearing Western garb, with hats, boots, and fringed jackets. I'm still not sure whether Michel quite "got it," but it sure was fun!

8 SERVINGS

1 medium (about 1 pound) yam or sweet potato, peeled and cut into ¼-inch dice
4 tablespoons olive oil
⅔ cup finely chopped onions
4 cloves garlic, minced
1 red bell pepper, seeded and diced
2 serrano chiles, seeded and minced
4 cups diced cooked turkey
1⅓ cups dried breadcrumbs or crumbled corn bread

1½ teaspoons salt
Freshly ground black pepper to taste
1 teaspoon chopped cilantro
½ teaspoon chopped thyme
1 cup heavy cream
1 egg, beaten
2 cups Warm Cranberry-Orange Compote (see Index)

Cook the diced yam or sweet potato in boiling salted water for 1 minute, until barely tender. Drain and place in cold water.

In a large skillet, heat 2 tablespoons of the oil over medium-high heat until lightly smoking, and sauté the onions, garlic, bell pepper, and serranos until the onion is translucent, 2 to 3 minutes. Add the turkey, breadcrumbs or corn bread, salt, pepper, herbs, cream, and cooked yam or sweet potato. Remove from the heat and stir in the egg. Transfer to a mixing bowl and let cool slightly. Form into 8 patties, 4 inches wide and 1½ inches thick.

Heat the remaining 2 tablespoons of oil in a clean skillet and cook the patties until brown on each side, about 2 minutes per side. Serve with the warm cranberry-orange compote.

EGGPLANT PARMESAN TORTA WITH BLACK OLIVE MAYONNAISE

This recipe is a good example of fusing the Mediterranean and New World cuisines together. Usually made with bolillos (hard rolls), a torta is a Spanish sandwich similar to the Mexican hoagie-type sandwich, stuffed with any number of fillings. Choose a glossy, purple-skinned eggplant that is heaviest for its size. Eggplant is actually a fruit that is very rich in potassium and calcium, and it has a natural affinity for tomatoes and olives. For a really special flavor combination, use the Smoked Tomato Aïoli (see Index) instead of the regular aïoli called for in the black olive mayonnaise.

---

4 SERVINGS

BLACK OLIVE MAYONNAISE:
4 tablespoons diced pitted black olives, preferably
Kalamata or Greek
4 tablespoons minced oven-dried tomatoes
(page 8) or sun-dried tomatoes packed in oil
4 tablespoons minced onion
4 tablespoons Aïoli (see Index)
2 teaspoons fresh lemon juice
1 teaspoon lemon zest
Salt and freshly ground black pepper to taste

TORTA:
1 medium eggplant
1 tablespoon salt
1 egg
2 tablespoons milk
1½ cups grated Parmesan cheese
Vegetable oil, for sautéing
4 Coriander Bolillos (see Index)
2 ripe medium tomatoes, cut into 4 slices each
1 cup romaine lettuce, cut into thin strips

To prepare the black olive mayonnaise, combine all the ingredients in a mixing bowl and set aside. Preheat the oven to 250° F.

To prepare the torta, cut the eggplant in half crosswise, and then cut each half lengthwise into slices ¼ inch thick. Place on a baking sheet lined with paper towels, sprinkle with salt, and let sit for 20 minutes (this process helps to eliminate any bitterness from the eggplant).

Ω   Ω   Ω   Ω   Ω   Ω   Ω   Ω   Ω

Rinse the eggplant slices with water. In a bowl, beat together the egg and milk, dip the eggplant in the egg wash, and coat with the Parmesan, patting gently to make sure the slices are completely coated.

Pour enough oil in a large skillet to come ½ inch up the sides, and heat until lightly smoking. Sauté the eggplant slices over medium-high heat in a single layer for 1 minute per side. Drain on paper towels and keep warm in the oven.

Heat the bolillos in the oven for 3 minutes to warm through. Cut in half, and spread the black olive mayonnaise on both halves. Place 2 or 3 slices of eggplant in each bolillo, top with 2 slices of tomato and some shredded lettuce. Then cut the bolillo in half crosswise, and serve with Jicama Coleslaw, Sweet Potato Chips, or Vegetable Pickles (see Index).

SUGAR-CURED SMOKED HAM AND FRESH MOZZARELLA ON CORNMEAL-RYE BREAD

I've given the recipe for smoked ham here, as it's imperative for serious cooks to know how to smoke their own ham. However, any commercial sugar-cured ham can be used, which simplifies the recipe. Of course, I use fresh mozzarella from Paula Lambert's Dallas Mozzarella Company, and if you really want the best, you can mail-order it directly (see source list). Mozzarella is very perishable, and the fresher it is, the better. While rubbery supermarket mozzarella bears only a vague resemblance to the real thing, it can be substituted if need be.

4 SERVINGS

½ cup brown sugar
1 recipe All-Purpose Brine for Smoking Meats and Poultry (see Index)
1 pork loin, about 2½ to 3 pounds, trimmed of excess fat
8 slices Cornmeal-Rye Bread (see Index)
¼ cup whole-grain or Dijon mustard

2 ripe medium tomatoes, cut into 4 slices each
1 tablespoon Routh Street Vinaigrette (see Index) or vinegar of choice (optional)
Salt (optional)
8 ounces fresh mozzarella cheese, cut into 8 slices
4 tablespoons unsalted butter

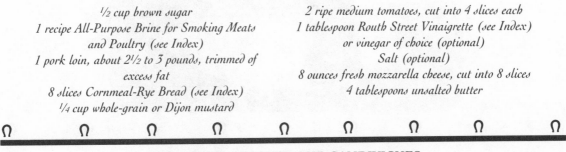

In a large bowl, add the sugar to the brine, cover the pork with it, and marinate in the refrigerator for at least 12 hours.

Prepare the smoker (see page 9). Remove the pork from the brine, pat dry, and smoke for about 3 hours.

Preheat the oven to 350° F. Place the smoked pork on a roasting pan and roast in the oven for 15 minutes. Remove and let cool. Raise the oven temperature to 400° F.

Thinly slice 12 ounces of the pork loin, and reserve the remainder for future use. Spread the slices of bread with the mustard. Place about 3 ounces of the thinly sliced pork on a slice of bread, add 2 tomato slices, brush the tomato with a little vinaigrette or vinegar with a pinch of salt, and top with 2 mozzarella slices. Repeat for the remaining sandwiches.

Place the unclosed sandwiches on a sheet pan and place in the oven for about 5 minutes, until the mozzarella begins to melt. Remove from the oven, and close the sandwiches.

Heat the butter in a large skillet and sauté the sandwiches over medium heat for 2 minutes per side, until the bread is slightly crisp and crusty. Serve immediately.

SOUTHWESTERN VENISON BURGER

Venison, like other game meat, is very lean and healthful. It is necessary to add some fat to the venison for this recipe, both for binding and moisture retention. This is a very flavorful alternative to the standard burger, and it is further spiced up and given regional flair by the addition of fresh and dried chiles.

4 SERVINGS

1 dried ancho chile, halved and seeded
1 dried chipotle chile, halved and seeded
¼ cup red wine or cold water
2 tablespoons corn oil, plus extra for patties
½ cup minced onion
2 tablespoons minced garlic
1 teaspoon ground cumin
2 teaspoons ground coriander
1 pound coarsely ground venison
4 ounces ground pork fat back

2 poblano chiles, roasted, peeled, seeded, and diced (page 6)
1 red bell pepper, roasted, peeled, seeded, and diced
1 teaspoon dried oregano
1 tablespoon chopped cilantro
½ cup breadcrumbs
1 egg
Salt and freshly ground black pepper to taste
4 All-purpose Hamburger Buns (see Index)

Prepare the grill (see pages 4 to 6). In a bowl, soak the ancho and chipotle chiles in the wine or water for 1 hour, or until rehydrated. Puree in a blender and reserve.

Heat the corn oil in a skillet and sauté the onion and garlic until translucent. Add the cumin and coriander and continue to cook for 30 seconds. Remove from the heat and let cool.

In a large mixing bowl, combine the venison, fat back, reserved chile puree, onion mixture, poblanos, bell pepper, and herbs. Add the breadcrumbs and egg, and lightly season with salt and pepper. Mix thoroughly by hand and form into 4 equal patties, about 1 inch thick.

Lightly oil the patties, and grill to desired doneness; simultaneously, grill the hamburger buns.

FRIED CATFISH SANDWICH WITH SMOKED TOMATO AÏOLI AND PICKLED OKRA

For those who have only experienced McFish and other fast-food fish sandwiches, this recipe will come as a very pleasant surprise. The combination of fried catfish, chowchow, the smoky aïoli, and the onion-dill bread is striking. You should smoke the tomatoes for the aïoli and the onion for the bread at the same time, and while preparing the whole recipe is well worth the trouble, you could save time and effort by just toasting whole-wheat bread, and substituting bottled mayonnaise and a good bottled chutney.

4 SERVINGS

1 egg
¼ cup milk
4 catfish fillets, about 4 ounces each,
halved horizontally
Salt and freshly ground black pepper to taste
Yellow cornmeal, for dredging
Vegetable oil, for frying

4 Smoked Onion-Dill Buns (see Index)
8 tablespoons (½ cup) Smoked Tomato Aïoli
(see Index)
4 tablespoons Aunt Jean's Chowchow (see Index)
4 small romaine lettuce leaves (optional)
8 spears Okra Pickles (see Index)

In a mixing bowl, beat the egg with the milk. Dip the catfish fillets in the egg wash and season with salt and pepper. Dredge in the cornmeal, patting gently to make sure the fillets are completely coated.

Pour enough oil in a large skillet to come 1 inch up the sides, and heat until lightly smoking. Place the fillets in the pan and fry for 2 minutes; turn over and cook for 3 minutes more, until the fillets are tender when pierced with a knife. Drain on paper towels.

Slice the buns in half and spread 1 tablespoon of aïoli on each bottom half. Place the fillets over the aïoli and top each with 1 tablespoon of chowchow. Add a lettuce leaf if desired. Spread the bun tops with the remaining aïoli and close the sandwiches. Serve with the pickled okra spears.

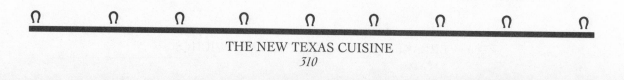

SMOKED SHRIMP CLUB ON CHIPOTLE BRIOCHE WITH SWEET POTATO CHIPS

After I've been traveling to exotic places or eating rich food for any length of time — for example, after a 3- or 4-day trip to New York — nothing can quite clean out the system like a good burger or club sandwich. No matter which hotel I'm staying in, I'm rarely disappointed in the room service club sandwich. This version is a little more decadent than the usual ham, turkey, and bacon club sandwich, but it just shows the variety of possibilities. A nice slice of white Cheddar wouldn't hurt this sandwich either.

4 SERVINGS

16 large raw shrimp (about 1 pound), peeled and deveined
½ gallon All-Purpose Brine for Smoking Meats and Poultry (see Index)
12 slices Chipotle Brioche (see Index), about ½ inch thick
½ cup Mayonnaise, Aïoli, or Cascabel Chile Aïoli (see Index)

1 head romaine or leaf lettuce, cleaned and torn
12 slices bacon, cooked until crisp
2 medium tomatoes, cut into 4 slices each about ¼ inch thick
1 sweet onion, thinly sliced (optional)
Sweet Potato Chips (recipe follows)

Preheat the oven to 350° F. Place the shrimp in the brine and let marinate for 30 minutes. Prepare the smoker (see page 9), and smoke the shrimp for 15 minutes.

Meanwhile, place the brioche slices on a sheet pan in the oven and toast for 3 minutes per side, until they're crisp but still soft. Let cool. Spread 1 side of each slice with 2 teaspoons of mayonnaise or aïoli.

For each sandwich, place 4 shrimp on a slice of brioche and top with lettuce. Layer another slice of brioche over the lettuce, then add 3 slices of bacon and 2 slices of tomato, and the onion if desired, and top with a third slice of brioche. Cut each sandwich into 4 portions and arrange on plates in the traditional manner. Serve with the sweet potato chips.

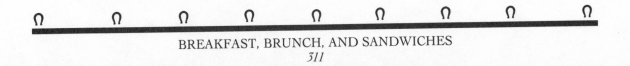

SWEET POTATO CHIPS

4 SERVINGS

Peanut oil, for deep frying
½ teaspoon sugar
¼ teaspoon salt

⅛ teaspoon cayenne powder
Dash of ground cumin
1 medium sweet potato

Heat enough oil to come 2 inches up the sides of a pan to 325° F. Combine the sugar, salt, cayenne, and cumin in a bowl and set aside. Peel the sweet potato and slice as thinly as possible, preferably with a mandolin or electric slicer. Fry in 2 batches for 4 to 5 minutes each, until crisp but not browned. Drain on paper towels. Sprinkle the reserved seasoning over the sweet potato slices.

BARBECUED BRISKET SANDWICH WITH JICAMA COLESLAW

Sometimes, there is nothing more satisfying than a barbecue sandwich, and there is nothing more Texan. This is a great way to use up leftover brisket. Coleslaw is a common accompaniment for barbecue, and I think you'll find the additional crunch and sweetness of jicama and bell peppers a real improvement on an old standard.

4 SERVINGS

JICAMA COLESLAW:
2 cups shredded radicchio or red cabbage
½ cup grated carrots
1 medium jicama, peeled and julienned
1 red bell pepper, julienned
1 yellow bell pepper, julienned
1 small onion, grated
1 jalapeño chile, seeded and minced
½ cup Mayonnaise (see Index)
1 tablespoon honey
1 tablespoon raspberry vinegar
1 tablespoon fresh lemon juice
Salt and freshly ground black pepper to taste

SANDWICHES:
½ cup Barbecue Sauce #1 or #2 (see Index)
12 to 14 ounces Barbecued Brisket of Beef (see Index), sliced as thinly as possible
4 All-Purpose Hamburger Buns (see Index)
4 teaspoons Creamy Horseradish Sauce (optional, see Index)
4 tablespoons Paula's "Rosy" Relish or diced Bread and Butter Pickles (see Index)

To prepare the coleslaw, thoroughly combine all the ingredients in a large mixing bowl. Set aside in the refrigerator.

To prepare the sandwiches, heat the barbecue sauce and brisket in a large skillet until just warmed through. Slice the buns and toast, or heat through in a warm oven, if desired. Spread the horseradish sauce on the bottom half of each bun, add the meat and sauce, and top with 1 tablespoon of relish. Close the sandwiches, and serve with the coleslaw.

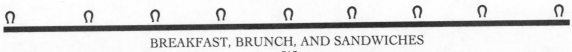

CORN GRIDDLE CAKES WITH GRILLED CHICKEN, BLACK BEAN SAUCE, AND AVOCADO-TOMATILLO SALSA

This is a dish that Marion Burros particularly liked when she ate at Routh Street Cafe years ago; so much so, that she reprinted the recipe in an article she wrote for the New York Times *Sunday magazine. It works really well as a brunch item, although it can be enjoyed for any meal. You'll find many uses for these corn cakes, and of course you can make them any size you like. Try them with sour cream and caviar, or smoked salmon with a little creamed horseradish.*

4 SERVINGS

BLACK BEAN SAUCE:
½ cup cooked black beans (page 10)
2 cloves garlic, chopped
3 serrano chiles, seeded and deveined
½ tomatillo, husked, rinsed, and chopped
1 tablespoon chopped cilantro
2 teaspoons chopped onion
2 teaspoons chopped green bell pepper
1 cup Chicken Stock (see Index)

1 teaspoon fresh lime juice
Salt to taste
4 free-range chicken breasts, about 5 ounces each
¼ cup vegetable oil or clarified butter
Salt to taste
Corn Griddle Cakes (recipe follows)
1 recipe Avocado-Tomatillo Salsa (see Index), for garnish

Prepare the grill (see pages 4 to 6).

To prepare the sauce, combine the black beans, garlic, serranos, tomatillo, cilantro, onions, bell pepper, and chicken stock in a saucepan. Bring to a boil, reduce the heat to low and simmer for about 5 minutes. Transfer to a blender and blend for 30 seconds. Add the lime juice and season with salt. Return the sauce to a clean saucepan and keep warm.

Rub the chicken breasts with the oil or butter and season with salt. Grill over medium-high heat for about 3 minutes per side. Slice the chicken and serve on top of the warmed corn griddle cakes. Spoon the warmed sauce around the corn cakes, and garnish with the avocado-tomatillo salsa.

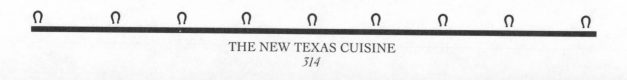

CORN GRIDDLE CAKES

1 DOZEN CAKES

½ cup cornmeal
½ cup flour
½ teaspoon baking powder
2 cups fresh corn kernels (2 large ears)
½ cup milk
2 tablespoons diced red bell pepper
2 tablespoons diced yellow bell pepper

2 teaspoons diced serrano chile
6 tablespoons unsalted butter, melted
2 eggs
4 egg yolks
⅔ teaspoon salt
Freshly ground black pepper to taste
1 cup clarified butter or vegetable oil

In a mixing bowl, combine the cornmeal, flour, and baking powder.

In a food processor or a blender, puree 1 cup of the corn kernels until smooth. Place the remaining cup of kernels and corn puree in a large mixing bowl and whisk in the milk, diced bell peppers, diced serrano, and the combined dry ingredients. Mix thoroughly.

In a separate mixing bowl, whisk together the butter, eggs, and egg yolks. Stir into the corn mixture and season with salt and pepper.

Cook the corn cakes in 2 batches. In a large skillet, heat half of the clarified butter or oil. Pour in half of the batter to make 6 cakes. Cook for about 2 minutes per side, until golden brown. Repeat for the second batch. The pancakes may be reheated for later use.

CHICKEN CUSTARD STEAMED IN FRESH CORN HUSKS

This dish was on the opening brunch menu at Baby Routh. The striking presentation of the finished product makes the effort involved well worth it. If you prefer a lighter accompaniment than the cream sauce given here, use a relish or salsa from Chapter 3.

8 SERVINGS

2 pounds chicken breast
1 quart Chicken Stock (see Index)
2 teaspoons salt, plus extra to taste
Freshly ground black pepper to taste
6 slices smoked bacon
8 medium ears of corn in husks

4 eggs, lightly beaten
1½ cups heavy cream
¼ cup finely chopped ripe black olives
½ cup Pico de Gallo (see Index)
1 tablespoon chopped basil
1 tablespoon pure maple syrup

Place the chicken breasts in a saucepan with the stock, 2 teaspoons salt, and a few grindings of pepper, and bring to a boil. Reduce the heat, cover the pan, and simmer for 15 minutes. Drain the chicken and reserve the stock for making the sauce. When cool, dice the chicken into ½-inch cubes and set aside.

Fry the bacon in a skillet until crisp, drain on paper towels, and break into small pieces.

Carefully turn back the outer husks or leaves of the corn to expose the cob. While holding the stalk and husks at the base, gently rotate the cob until it separates. Pull out the silks, and set the husks aside.

Slice the corn kernels from 4 of the cobs into a bowl and add the eggs and ½ cup of the cream. Reserve the remaining cobs for another use. Stir in the diced chicken, bacon pieces, and olives, and add salt and freshly ground black pepper to taste.

To stuff each corn husk, stand it on its base in a tall, straight glass. Separate the tops of the leaves and spread apart so that the lower half of the corn husk forms a boatlike shell. Spoon about ½ cup of the chicken mixture into the corn-husk shell. Draw the tops of the leaves together again to completely enclose the stuffing. Secure the stuffing by tying a few strips of husk or string around the ends of the corn husk.

Steam for about 20 minutes in a bamboo steamer or vegetable steamer basket in a covered pan set over simmering water.

Meanwhile, in a saucepan, reduce the reserved chicken stock by half over high heat. In a separate pan, reduce the remaining cup of cream until ¼ cup remains. Stir the reduced stock into the cream, whisk in the Pico de Gallo, basil, and maple syrup. Taste and season with salt if desired.

When the mousses have cooked, remove from the steamer, transfer to serving plates, and remove the husk ties or string. Carefully peel back 2 or 3 of the corn husks to expose the chicken mousse, while still keeping the appearance of a corn cob. Serve with a spoonful of sauce over the top of the mousse.

CHAPTER THIRTEEN

BREADS AND TORTILLAS

The bread recipes in this chapter encompass the essence of Texas: its history and heritage, its wide variety of cultural and ethnic groups, and its geographical diversity. From Mexican tortillas to Native American fry bread, Southern corn bread, Western range skillet sticks, and European brioche and kolaches, these breads reflect the many influences that have shaped the Lone Star State.

Having worked closely with French chefs and traveled often to France, it has been ingrained (no pun intended) in me that bread is an important element of any meal. In fact, sometimes an entire meal might consist of cheese, fruit, pâté, and a good, crusty baguette. It's hard to imagine a good meal in Italy, especially in my favorite region, Tuscany, without a big crusty loaf of bread.

Unfortunately, growing up in Texas (and America in general) in the '50s and '60s, the bread we usually had with meals was an unpalatable, presliced white bread. We always looked forward, however, to those evenings when we did have homemade buttermilk biscuits, Mexican corn bread, or real yeast rolls. That was an era of convenient, fast food, but the subsequent food revolution and renaissance in American cuisine has resulted today in the availability of a wide range of interesting flavored breads. Their popularity reflects a substantial and appreciative audience for such innovative creations as Nancy Silverton's chocolate-dried cherry bread, which is always sold out by noon at her La Brea bakery in Los Angeles.

Many of these bread recipes are "in the same mold" (pun intended) as flavored breads, and contain a variety of strong and intense flavors. The ingredients are mostly indigenous, and the breads match other dishes in the book well. In general, I prefer more neutral breads for serious meals, as highly flavored breads can obscure some of the more subtle ingredients of a dish; flavored breads go best of all with sandwiches, simple soups, and salads.

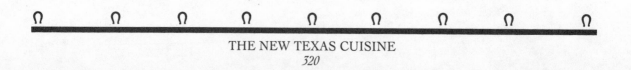

FLOUR TORTILLAS

Tortillas are a mainstay and building block of Texas cooking, both traditional and modern. It is impossible to imagine this style of cuisine without enchiladas, burritos, or fajitas, all of which begin with the ubiquitous flour tortilla. The tortillas at Routh Street Cafe were made by Timo, a Mexican fellow who had been with me for years, and he had the process down to an exact art. He kept two cast-iron skillets on the stove, and while he rolled out one tortilla, a second had just gone into one of the skillets and another tortilla was ready to come out—it was a very efficient assembly line. A rolling pin the size of a broom handle is best, and it's important to roll out the dough as thinly as possible.

ABOUT 20 TORTILLAS

2 cups flour, plus extra for coating
1½ teaspoons salt
1½ teaspoons baking powder

4 to 5 tablespoons vegetable shortening
¾ cup warm water

Sift the dry ingredients together into a mixing bowl. Using a fork or your fingers, cut in the shortening and mix until it is evenly distributed and the mixture has the texture of coarse cornmeal.

Stir about half of the water into the dry ingredients, or enough to form a soft dough. Knead the dough for 15 to 20 seconds and form into a ball.

Gradually add all but 2 tablespoons of the remaining water, all the while working the dough with your hands. Periodically dip your fingers into the remaining water and continue to knead the dough for 3 to 5 minutes longer. The texture of the dough should be soft and wet, but not sticky.

Divide the dough into 20 equal 1-ounce pieces. Stretch each piece out and fold the sides inward to adhere and form a round ball, about 1 inch in diameter. Place the balls of dough on a sheet pan and cover with plastic wrap. Let rest for 5 to 10 minutes.

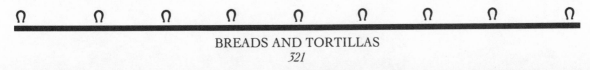

Heat a cast-iron skillet over medium-high heat to about 425° F. (a drop of water should sizzle on the skillet). Dip each ball in flour to lightly coat it. Using your thumbs, gently stretch each ball into a 2-inch circle. On a clean work surface, roll each piece of dough into as thin a circle as possible.

Carefully lift each circle and place in the skillet. Cook for 35 to 40 seconds, until bubbles appear on the tortilla surface. Flip the tortillas with a spatula and cook for an additional 5 to 10 seconds on the other side. Stack the tortillas and wrap in a towel or foil.

WHOLE-WHEAT TORTILLAS

The addition of whole wheat to tortillas puts a new spin on an old tradition. These tortillas make a great alternative to pita bread, and can be used as a substitute for buckwheat blinis; cut into quarters and serve with sour cream and caviar.

ABOUT 20 TORTILLAS

1 cup stone-ground whole-wheat flour	1½ teaspoons baking powder
1 cup all-purpose flour	4 to 5 tablespoons vegetable shortening
1½ teaspoons salt	¾ cup warm water

Sift the dry ingredients together into a mixing bowl. Using a fork or your fingers, cut in the shortening and mix until it is evenly distributed and the mixture has the texture of coarse cornmeal.

Stir about half of the water into the dry ingredients, or enough to form a soft dough. Knead the dough for 15 to 20 seconds and form into a ball.

Gradually add all but 2 tablespoons of the remaining water while working the dough with your hands. Periodically dip your fingers into the remaining water

and continue to knead the dough for 3 to 5 minutes longer. The texture of the dough should be soft and wet, but not sticky.

Divide the dough into 20 equal 1-ounce pieces. Stretch each piece out and fold the sides inward to adhere and form a round ball, about 1 inch in diameter. Place the balls of dough on a sheet pan and cover with plastic wrap. Let rest for 5 to 10 minutes.

Heat a cast-iron skillet over medium-high heat to about 425° F. (a drop of water should sizzle on the skillet). Dip each ball in flour to lightly coat it. Using your thumbs, gently stretch each ball into a 2-inch circle. On a clean work surface, roll each piece of dough into as thin a circle as possible.

Carefully lift each circle and place in the skillet. Cook for 35 to 40 seconds, until bubbles appear on the tortilla surface. Flip the tortillas with a spatula and cook for an additional 5 to 10 seconds on the other side. Stack the tortillas and wrap in a towel or foil.

CORN TORTILLAS

If you're lucky enough to live in a large city with Hispanic markets where prepared masa is available, don't hesitate to use it. I've rarely found any prepared masa dough in Dallas that is not of high quality. There is a definite skill involved in making corn and flour tortillas, but corn tortillas are definitely the harder of the two. You could try to pat the tortillas into the right size and shape before cooking them on a griddle, but a tortilla press makes the whole process a lot easier. Besides, patting corn tortillas is best left to the expert women of Mexico, who have perfected the skill over the centuries. Corn tortillas can be cooked in advance, stacked in a towel or plastic wrap, and then refrigerated. To reheat them, wrap the tortillas in foil and place in a 350° F. oven for 5 minutes, or heat on a griddle or in a greased skillet.

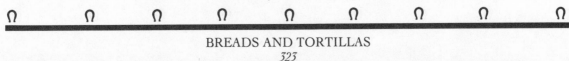

ABOUT 20 TORTILLAS

4 cups masa harina
1¼ teaspoons salt

2½ cups warm water (105° to 110° F.)

In a large mixing bowl, thoroughly mix the masa harina, salt, and water together with your hands until the dough comes together in a soft ball. Divide the dough into 20 pieces, roll into small balls, and cover with plastic wrap.

Heat a cast-iron skillet over medium-high heat to about 425° F. (a drop of water should sizzle on the skillet).

Meanwhile, open the tortilla press and lay a sheet of plastic wrap just large enough to cover the base. Place a ball of dough in the center of the plastic wrap, and cover with a second piece of plastic wrap. Close the press and squeeze down hard on the handle. Open the press and peel off the top piece of plastic wrap, starting with the side opposite the handle. Pick up the plastic wrap underneath the dough and invert so that the dough is lying on the palm of your hand. Carefully peel away the plastic wrap. Repeat for the remaining balls of dough.

Gently place the tortillas in the skillet. After a few seconds, the dough will begin to dry out at the edges. After 25 to 30 seconds, flip the tortilla and let it cook for another 45 seconds. Turn again, and cook for another 30 seconds, until the tortilla is slightly puffed but still pliable.

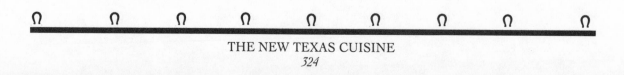

BLUE CORN SKILLET STICKS

These versatile corn sticks are the only item to be served on a daily basis at all four of our restaurants. While yellow cornmeal can be substituted, the blue cornmeal makes a more attractive presentation and adds a distinctively Southwestern element. Corn of various colors was cultivated by the Native Americans of the Southwest for centuries, and used for ceremonial as well as culinary purposes. These skillet sticks are incredibly moist, and if you are not serving them straight away, don't be tempted to blot off the excess oil, as it's reabsorbed. They are best served hot, or at least warm; they can be reheated in a 350° F. oven for 5 minutes.

ABOUT 18 TO 20 CORN STICKS, OR 8 TO 10 MUFFINS

8 tablespoons unsalted butter
8 tablespoons shortening
4 serrano chiles, seeded and minced
3 garlic cloves, minced
1 cup flour
1¼ cups blue cornmeal or yellow cornmeal
2 tablespoons sugar

1 teaspoon baking powder
1½ teaspoons salt
3 eggs
1¼ cups milk, at room temperature
3 tablespoons chopped cilantro
Olive oil, for brushing

Preheat the oven to 400° F.

In a small saucepan, gently melt the butter and shortening over low heat. Add the serranos and garlic, and sauté for 10 minutes. Set aside.

Place cast-iron nonstick corn-bread molds in the oven to warm for at least 5 minutes.

In a large mixing bowl, sift together the flour, cornmeal, sugar, baking powder, and salt, and set aside. In a medium bowl, beat the eggs lightly, and then add the melted butter, shortening, serranos, and garlic. Stir in the milk. Pour the liquid ingredients into the dry ingredients and beat just until smooth; do not overmix. Add the cilantro.

Remove the cast-iron corn-bread molds from the oven and brush generously with the oil. Reheat the molds for about 2 minutes, and then pour the batter into the molds. (Alternatively, use a cast-iron corn-stick pan or a muffin pan.) Bake in the center of the oven for 20 to 25 minutes, until the corn bread is golden brown and springy to the touch.

JALAPEÑO–BLUE CORN HUSH PUPPIES

These hush puppies accompanied the whole fried catfish that was on the original menu at Baby Routh, and they make a perfect addition to any fish fry. They are much lighter than the traditional Southern hush puppies and have an appealing color because of the blue cornmeal. There are many theories about the derivation of the name: one of the most popular is that in former times, these crisp, crunchy balls of corn bread were thrown by camp cooks to howling, hungry puppies to quiet them.

2 DOZEN HUSH PUPPIES

Vegetable oil, for deep frying
1½ cups blue cornmeal
1½ cups flour
1 tablespoon baking powder
1 tablespoon salt
1¼ cups milk

¼ cup diced onion
1 tablespoon diced yellow bell pepper
1 tablespoon diced red bell pepper
1 tablespoon diced green bell pepper
2 jalapeño chiles, seeded and minced
3 egg whites

In a deep fryer, heat the oil to 350° F.

In a large mixing bowl, combine the dry ingredients. Stir in the milk, onion, bell peppers, and jalapeños. In another bowl, whisk the egg whites to stiff peaks and then fold into the cornmeal-milk mixture.

Spoon the mixture, about 3 tablespoons per hush puppy, into the hot oil and deep-fry for 3 to 4 minutes. Remove with a slotted spoon and drain on paper towels.

MEXICAN CORN BREAD

When I was growing up, I looked forward with anticipation to those evenings when my mother would cook up a pot of pinto beans, a mess of greens, and corn bread. She made her Mexican corn bread with canned cream-style corn, but for obvious reasons, this recipe uses fresh corn. I've tried different versions of Mexican corn bread throughout Texas, and all seem to include Cheddar cheese, whole corn kernels, and roasted chiles. It's a great example of the way in which Texas cuisine incorporates diverse styles, in this case, both the Southern and Mexican influences.

8 TO 10 SERVINGS

1 cup yellow cornmeal
½ teaspoon salt
½ teaspoon baking soda
2 eggs
⅔ cup buttermilk
⅓ cup shortening, melted and cooled

¾ cup fresh corn kernels (1 ear)
½ cup heavy cream
2 jalapeño chiles, seeded and minced
1 small poblano or anaheim chile, roasted, peeled, seeded, and diced (page 6)
1 cup grated sharp Cheddar cheese

Preheat the oven to 375° F. In a mixing bowl, combine the cornmeal, salt, and baking soda, and set aside. In another bowl, lightly whisk the eggs, add the buttermilk and shortening, and combine thoroughly. Add the liquid ingredients to the dry ingredients, and fold in the corn, cream, and chiles.

Place a large cast-iron skillet in the oven for 5 minutes to heat through. Remove the skillet and pour in half of the mixture. Sprinkle in the cheese, and then pour in the remaining mixture. Return the skillet to the oven and bake for 30 to 35 minutes, until golden brown.

MABLE'S BUTTERMILK BISCUITS

Mable Stanley is the mother of my dear friend Sharron Smith. Mable is a Southern classic with deep roots in Mississippi, and people are drawn to her as if she were a magnet. She possesses many talents, not the least of which is the way she makes her buttermilk biscuits. I thought my great grandmother or mother's were the best until I tried Mable's. The only other person in America who makes such delicious biscuits is another good friend, Edna Lewis. If you really love biscuits, you probably already have Edna's recipe; if you don't, you need her books anyway, such as The Taste of Country Cooking *and* In Pursuit of Flavor. *One ingredient you'll only find in this recipe is self-rising flour. Mable swears by it, and it makes the recipe much simpler as it already contains baking soda and salt. To my surprise, self-rising flour has been around longer than I expected: Mable says her grandmother used to bake with it. While I've never used it before, the proof is in the pudding — or in this case, the biscuits.*

---

8 TO 10 BISCUITS

4 teaspoons unsalted butter
5 tablespoons vegetable shortening

1½ cups self-rising flour
⅔ cup plus 1 tablespoon buttermilk

Preheat the oven to 400° F. Place the butter in a 9½-inch skillet. Place the skillet in the oven for 5 minutes to heat through and to melt the butter.

In a mixing bowl, crumble the shortening with the flour, using your fingertips, until the mixture is crumbly and the size of small peas. Add the buttermilk in 3 or 4 additions, while stirring with a wooden spoon or spatula, and mix until the buttermilk is thoroughly incorporated. Do not overbeat. The dough should be quite sticky and hold together.

Turn out onto a floured surface and lightly flour the top of the dough. Using a rolling pin, roll out the dough into a circle about ½ inch thick. Cut the biscuits into 2½-inch circles (or 2- or 3-inch circles if you prefer). Dip each biscuit on both sides into the melted butter in the heated skillet, and arrange them in the skillet.

Bake in the oven on the middle rack for 8 to 10 minutes, or until the biscuits have risen and are lightly browned on the bottom. Turn on the broiler, transfer the skillet to the upper rack of the oven, and bake for 4 to 5 minutes more, or until the biscuit tops are browned. Turn out onto a rack to cool.

ALL-PURPOSE HAMBURGER AND SANDWICH BUNS

This is a straightforward recipe for basic burger or sandwich buns that's a good starting point if you've never made bread before. These buns have a spongy texture, which is important for burgers, and they freeze well. It's definitely worth the effort to make these, as they're so much better than store-bought buns.

1 DOZEN BUNS

1 tablespoon dry yeast	*3 eggs*
1 cup warm water (105° to 110° F.)	*2 teaspoons salt*
6 cups bread flour	*½ teaspoon freshly ground black pepper*
½ cup sour cream	*1 tablespoon milk*
Pinch of baking soda	*1 teaspoon sesame seeds*

Using a mixing bowl or the bowl of an electric mixer, combine with a wooden spoon or a paddle attachment half of the flour, the sour cream, baking soda, 2 eggs, and the yeast mixture, and mix for 3 to 4 minutes, or until thoroughly incorporated. Place the remaining 3 cups of flour, the salt, and pepper in a separate bowl.

If using a mixer, replace the paddle attachment with a dough hook. Add the seasoned flour mixture to the dough in ½ cup increments until the dough moves freely and feels elastic. Alternatively, turn the dough out onto a lightly floured surface and knead for 3 to 5 minutes. Transfer the dough to a greased bowl, cover with a damp towel or plastic wrap, and let the dough rise in a warm place until it doubles in volume, 1½ to 2 hours.

Gently deflate the dough and turn out onto a floured surface. Cut off 12 equal portions and form into balls. Place the balls on a sheet pan lined with parchment paper, pressing on top of the balls to flatten slightly. Cover loosely with a damp towel or plastic wrap and let rise until doubled in volume again, 45 minutes to 1 hour.

Meanwhile, preheat the oven to 375° F. Beat the remaining egg with the milk, and when the dough has risen, gently brush with the egg wash. Sprinkle the buns with sesame seeds.

Bake in the oven for 15 to 18 minutes, until golden brown. Turn out onto a rack to cool.

CHIPOTLE BRIOCHE

I originally created this bread for the Smoked Duck Salad (see Index) that I served as an hors d'oeuvre at the fiftieth anniversary gala for the March of Dimes, held in Washington, D.C., in 1988. I remember that Elaine Whitelaw, one of the true grandes dames of the American restaurant scene and a driving force behind the March of Dimes, was particularly impressed by this bread. The chipotle puree adds an earthy, bricklike color, as well as a little punch at the back of the palate when the other flavors have subsided. This bread makes a great accompaniment to any meal, especially sliced and toasted. It's also ideal for making club sandwiches (see Index).

1 LOAF

12 tablespoons (6 ounces) unsalted butter
1 tablespoon dry yeast
2 tablespoons lukewarm water (about 85° F.)
1 tablespoon sugar
3½ cups flour

6 eggs
1½ teaspoons salt
5 tablespoons chipotle chile puree (pages 3 to 4)
1 tablespoon milk
Olive oil, for brushing

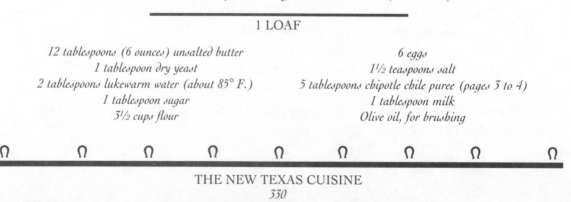

Remove the butter from the refrigerator 1 hour before preparing the dough; it should be pliable but not too soft.

In the bowl of an electric mixer fitted with a paddle attachment, combine the yeast, water, and sugar. Stir to dissolve and let stand for about 5 minutes. Gradually mix in 2 cups of the flour. Add 3 of the eggs and continue beating until smooth.

Combine the salt and the remaining 1½ cups of flour in a separate bowl and gradually add to the dough while beating. Add 2 eggs and the chipotle puree, and beat for about 2 minutes, until combined.

Replace the paddle attachment with a dough hook. With the machine running, incorporate the softened butter in tablespoon increments. Beat for 5 to 7 minutes, until smooth and silky and the dough pulls away from the sides of the bowl.

Place the dough in a greased bowl, cover with a damp towel or plastic wrap, and let it rise in a warm place until it doubles in volume, 45 minutes to 1 hour. Punch the dough down and let it rest, covered, in the refrigerator overnight.

The next day, remove the dough from the refrigerator and shape it to fit a 5-x-9-x-3-inch baking pan. Let the dough rise, loosely covered with a damp towel or plastic wrap, until it has doubled in volume again, about 45 minutes. Meanwhile, preheat the oven to 425° F.

Beat the remaining egg with the milk, and when the dough has risen, gently brush with the egg wash. Bake in the oven for 15 minutes at 425° F. Lower the heat to 375° F. and bake for about 25 minutes longer, or until brown. The bread should sound hollow when tapped. Turn out onto a rack to cool.

Meanwhile, turn the oven down to 350° F. When the bread has cooled, slice the brioche and brush lightly with olive oil. On a sheet pan, toast in the oven for 2 to 3 minutes.

SPICY TOMATILLO LOAF

The tartness of the tomatillos and the spiciness of the black pepper and cayenne make for a very intriguing combination that will zip up plain sandwiches and soups. For an interesting snack, try spreading this bread with Jalapeño Jelly (see Index) blended with a little cream cheese.

---

2 LOAVES

1 pound (about 10) tomatillos, husked and rinsed	*2 teaspoons ground cumin*
2 cups water	*1½ teaspoons cayenne powder*
1½ tablespoons dry yeast	*2 teaspoons salt*
4 cups bread flour	*1½ teaspoons freshly ground black pepper*
3 eggs	*2 tablespoons sugar*
3 tablespoons chopped cilantro	*1 tablespoon milk*

Place the tomatillos in a heavy saucepan, cover with the water, and bring to a boil. Reduce the heat and simmer until the tomatillos are soft, about 5 minutes. Remove the tomatillos and reduce the water to ½ cup; set aside in a bowl. Puree the tomatillos in a blender, return them to the saucepan, and cook over medium-high heat for 4 to 5 minutes, until the liquid has evaporated; reserve.

When the reserved water has cooled to 105° to 110° F. (or just warm to the touch), sprinkle the yeast over and let dissolve for 5 to 8 minutes, or until the yeast is foamy.

Place 1½ cups of the flour in the bowl of an electric mixer fitted with a paddle attachment and add the yeast mixture, 2 of the eggs, and the tomatillos. Mix until incorporated, add the cilantro, and then mix with a dough hook.

In a mixing bowl, combine the remaining 2½ cups of flour with the cumin, cayenne, salt, pepper, and sugar, and add to the mixer ½ cup at a time until the dough moves freely in the bowl. Transfer the dough to a greased bowl, cover

Ω   Ω   Ω   Ω   Ω   Ω   Ω   Ω   Ω

with a damp towel or plastic wrap, and let the dough rise in a warm place until it doubles in volume, about 1½ to 2 hours.

Gently deflate the dough and turn out onto a floured surface. Divide the dough into 2 pieces, form into loaves, and place into two greased 9-x-5-inch loaf pans. Cover loosely with a damp towel or plastic wrap, and let the dough rise until it has doubled in volume again, 30 to 45 minutes.

Meanwhile, preheat the oven to 375° F. Beat the remaining egg with the milk, and when the loaves have risen, gently brush with the egg wash. Bake in the oven for 18 to 22 minutes, or until golden brown. Turn out onto a rack to cool.

BEER BATTER BREAD

This recipe was developed by Mark Murphy, who worked with me for many years at Routh Street Cafe and Baby Routh. It became a staple for staff lunches when he was in charge of the kitchen. It's a simple recipe, and best served warm straight from the oven.

1 LOAF

3 cups flour	1 teaspoon salt
1 tablespoon baking powder	1 bottle (12 ounces) beer, at room temperature
3 tablespoons sugar	¼ cup unsalted butter, melted

Preheat the oven to 375° F. In a mixing bowl, combine all the dry ingredients. Add the beer all at once, mixing as little as possible; the batter should be lumpy.

Pour the batter into a 9-x-5-x-3-inch loaf pan and brush with the melted butter. Bake in the oven for 35 to 40 minutes, or until an inserted skewer comes out clean. Turn out onto a rack to cool.

CORNMEAL–RYE BREAD

Rye is a hardy cereal grass that is the only other grain, apart from wheat, from which leavened bread can be made. Rye is low in gluten or protein, and unless wheat flour is added, all-rye loaves are dense and heavy. I have made this sour rye bread recipe more Texan by adding cornmeal. I think rye breads have a natural affinity for Dijon or whole-grain mustards, as well as pork or ham; we use this one for the Sugar-Cured Smoked Ham and Fresh Mozzarella Sandwich (see Index).

2 LOAVES

1½ tablespoons dry yeast	2 cups bread flour
1 cup warm water (105° to 110° F.)	1 tablespoon salt
4 cups (1 quart) black coffee	1 tablespoon caraway seeds
¾ cup yellow cornmeal	2 tablespoons sugar
1 cup rye flour	3 tablespoons balsamic vinegar
½ cup whole-wheat flour	2 eggs
½ cup durum wheat flour	3 tablespoons unsalted butter

In a mixing bowl, sprinkle the yeast over the water and let dissolve for 5 to 8 minutes, or until the yeast is foamy. Meanwhile, place the coffee in a saucepan and reduce to ½ cup.

Combine the cornmeal, flours, salt, and caraway seeds in another mixing bowl.

Add the sugar and vinegar to the yeast mixture. In the bowl of an electric mixer fitted with a paddle attachment, combine 2 cups of the flour mixture, the yeast mixture, reduced coffee, and eggs. Mix until thoroughly incorporated.

Replace the paddle attachment with a dough hook. Add the remaining flour mixture in ½ cup increments and continue to mix until the dough moves freely in the bowl. Add the butter and mix until just incorporated. Transfer the dough to a floured surface and knead for 3 to 4 minutes, until it feels elastic but is still a little sticky. Place the dough in a greased bowl, cover with a damp towel or plastic wrap, and let it rise in a warm place until it doubles in volume, 1 to 1½ hours.

Gently deflate the dough and turn out onto a floured surface. Cut the dough in half and form into 2 round loaves. Place on a greased baking sheet, cover loosely with a damp towel or plastic wrap, and let the loaves rise until they have doubled in volume again, 30 to 45 minutes.

Meanwhile, preheat the oven to 375° F. Bake the loaves for 30 to 35 minutes, until golden brown. The bread should sound hollow when tapped. Turn out onto a rack to cool completely.

SMOKED ONION–DILL BREAD

This is a bread that we often used for lunchtime sandwiches at Baby Routh. Kirk Parks, our baker, had the idea of smoking the onions one day when the smoker happened to be in use. While this step is not necessary, it gives a similar depth of flavor as grilling a slice of brioche or yeast bread over a fire.

2 LOAVES, OR 12 TO 14 BUNS

1 tablespoon dry yeast	3 eggs
2 tablespoons sugar	4¼ cups high-gluten or bread flour
6 tablespoons warm water (105° to 110° F.)	1½ teaspoons salt
1 small sweet onion, smoked and chopped (page 9)	1 teaspoon freshly ground black pepper
1 cup plus 2 tablespoons cottage cheese	1 tablespoon dried dill
Pinch of baking soda	1 tablespoon milk

In the bowl of a mixer fitted with a dough hook, combine the yeast, sugar, and water, and let dissolve for 5 to 8 minutes, or until the yeast is foamy. Meanwhile, place the onion, cottage cheese, and baking soda in the blender and puree until smooth. Transfer the puree to the mixer bowl, add 2 of the eggs, and beat together with the dough hook.

In a mixing bowl, combine the flour, salt, pepper, and dill, and gradually add to the mixer, beating into the liquid ingredients. Continue to beat until the dough moves away from the edges of the bowl but is still somewhat sticky.

Transfer the dough to a greased bowl, cover with a damp towel or plastic wrap, and let rise in a warm place until it doubles in volume, 1½ to 2 hours.

Gently deflate the dough and turn out onto a floured surface. Stretch the dough and form into 2 loaves, or cut off 12 to 14 equal portions and form into buns. Place the loaves into two 9-x-5-inch loaf pans or place the buns on a sheet pan, pressing on top of the buns to flatten slightly. Cover loosely with a damp towel or plastic wrap and let rise until doubled in volume again, 45 minutes to 1 hour.

Meanwhile, preheat the oven to 375° F. Beat the remaining egg with the milk, and when the dough has risen, gently brush with the egg wash. Bake the loaves in the oven for 22 to 25 minutes, or until golden brown (buns will take 15 to 20 minutes). Cool for 8 to 10 minutes, and turn out onto a rack to cool completely.

CORIANDER BOLILLOS

Bolillos are those crusty little rolls so common in Mexican bakeries. In small towns and villages in Mexico, bolillos are still cooked in wood-fired brick or adobe ovens, which give the bread its crust. Julia Child once showed me an alternative technique for steaming French bread in an oven that works equally well here for an attractive, crispy exterior: take a small firebrick and place on a stove burner until it becomes red hot. Fill a roasting pan with 1 inch of water. Place the pan on the bottom rack of an electric oven or on the floor of a gas oven. Just before putting the rolls in, add the firebrick to the pan of water with tongs and close the oven door immediately. The oven will then fill with steam. This bread goes with almost any dinner, and it also makes a terrific sandwich loaf, especially for the Eggplant Parmesan Torta (see Index).

1 DOZEN ROLLS

1 tablespoon dry yeast
4½ cups flour
2 tablespoons sugar
1 teaspoon salt
9 tablespoons (4½ ounces) shortening

1½ cups water
1½ teaspoons ground coriander
1 egg
2 tablespoons milk

In the bowl of a mixer fitted with a dough hook, combine the yeast, 2 cups of flour, sugar, and salt. In a saucepan, gently melt the shortening in the water over low heat. Cool to 105° to 110° F. (or just warm to the touch), add to the dry ingredients, and combine.

Add the coriander and the remaining 2½ cups of flour, ½ cup at a time, until a soft dough forms and moves freely in the bowl. The dough should be soft and elastic, but not sticky. Place the dough in a greased bowl and cover with a damp towel or plastic wrap. Let the dough rise in a warm place until it doubles in volume, 1½ to 2 hours.

Gently deflate the dough and turn out onto a floured surface. Divide the dough into 12 equal pieces (about 3 ounces each) and roll each into an elongated (hoagielike) shape, pinching each into a point, and place on a baking sheet lined with parchment paper. Press on the top of each roll to flatten slightly, and make 2 parallel slash marks with a knife or razor blade. Cover loosely with a damp towel or plastic wrap and let the dough rise again until it has doubled in volume, 45 minutes to 1 hour.

Meanwhile, preheat the oven to 375° F. Beat the egg with the milk, and when the rolls have risen, gently brush with the egg wash.

Bake in the oven for 15 to 18 minutes, or until the rolls are golden brown. Turn out onto a rack to cool.

ALMOND-ROSEMARY OAT BUNS

These unusual, flavorful buns are very versatile and can be used in a number of ways. They can be served as rolls for dinner, they are great for sandwiches — especially Barbecued Brisket Sandwiches (see Index) — or they can be used as burger buns.

---

6 BUNS

1 tablespoon dry yeast
¼ cup warm water (105° to 110° F.)
½ teaspoon sugar
¼ cup warm milk (105° to 110° F.)
2 tablespoons honey
1 tablespoon unsalted butter
1½ to 2 cups flour

1 teaspoon salt
½ teaspoon freshly ground black pepper
2 teaspoons chopped rosemary
½ cup oatmeal
¼ cup pureed almonds
1 egg
1 tablespoon milk

In a mixing bowl, sprinkle the yeast over the water and let dissolve for 5 to 8 minutes, or until the yeast is foamy. In another bowl, combine the sugar, milk, honey, and butter. In the bowl of an electric mixer fitted with a dough hook, combine ½ cup of the flour with the salt, pepper, rosemary, and oatmeal. Add the yeast and milk mixtures into the dry ingredients and mix until any lumps disappear. Add the almonds and then the remaining 1 to 1½ cups flour, ¼ cup at a time, mixing until a soft dough forms.

Transfer the dough to a greased bowl, cover with a damp towel or plastic wrap, and let the dough rise in a warm place until it doubles in volume, 1½ to 2 hours.

Gently deflate the dough and turn out onto a floured surface. Divide the dough into 6 pieces, form into balls, and place on a parchment-lined sheet. Press on the top of the buns to flatten slightly. Cover loosely with a damp towel or plastic wrap and let the dough rise until it has doubled in volume again, 45 minutes to 1 hour.

Meanwhile, preheat the oven to 375° F. Beat the egg with the milk, and when the buns have risen, slash the tops once with a knife or razor blade and gently brush with the egg wash.

Bake in the oven for 12 to 15 minutes, or until the buns are golden brown. Turn out onto a rack to cool completely. Slice and toast before using.

POTATO–MEXICAN OREGANO ROLLS

These rolls are another invention of Kirk Parks, former baker for Routh Street Cafe and Baby Routh. They can also be baked as a loaf, but either way, they make a good change of pace as the combination of the batter and potatoes is a little unusual. They go particularly well with lamb or dark meat, and you can substitute cilantro, Italian parsley, or regular oregano for the intensely flavored Mexican oregano.

18 ROLLS OR 2 LOAVES

1 large potato, peeled and cut into large dice
2 tablespoons dry yeast
2 tablespoons sugar
1 cup buttermilk
2 tablespoons unsalted butter
6½ to 7 cups flour

1 tablespoon salt
1 teaspoon freshly ground black pepper
2 shallots, minced
2 tablespoons chopped Mexican oregano
1 egg
1 tablespoon milk

Place the potato in a saucepan, cover with water, and cook until soft. Drain the potato and reserve 1 cup of the liquid. Mash the potato and set aside.

Transfer the potato liquid to a mixing bowl and cool to 105° to 110° F. (or just warm to the touch). Sprinkle the yeast over and let dissolve for 5 to 8 minutes, or until the yeast is foamy. In another mixing bowl, beat together the sugar, buttermilk, and butter until incorporated, and add the mashed potato. Then add the yeast mixture and mix until thoroughly combined.

In the bowl of an electric mixer fitted with a dough hook, place 2 cups of flour with the salt and pepper, add the buttermilk-yeast mixture, and mix until all the lumps are gone. Add the shallots and oregano, and then the remaining 4½ to 5 cups of flour, 1 cup at a time, until a soft dough forms; it should be soft and springy.

Place the dough in a greased bowl and cover with a damp towel or plastic wrap. Let the dough rise in a warm place until it doubles in volume, 1½ to 2 hours.

Gently deflate the dough and turn out onto a clean, floured surface. Divide into 18 equal pieces (about 2 ounces each), roll into balls, and place in a greased muffin pan. (Alternatively, form into 2 loaves and place into two 9-x-5-inch loaf pans). Cover loosely with a damp towel or plastic wrap and let the dough rise again until it has doubled in volume, about 45 minutes to 1 hour.

Meanwhile, preheat the oven to 375° F. Beat the egg with the milk, and when the dough has risen, slash the top of the rolls with a knife or razor blade and gently brush with the egg wash.

Bake in the oven for 12 to 15 minutes, or until the rolls or loaves are golden brown. Let cool for 5 minutes; remove from the pan, and serve warm.

HONEY-INDIAN FRY BREAD

Fry bread is a traditional specialty of Southwestern Native Americans such as the Navajo, Hopi, Zuni, and Pueblo Indians of the Rio Grande Valley; it remains an important feature of feast day and family meals. The bread can be used to accompany savory dishes, stuffed with meat, bean, or cheese fillings, or served with cinnamon sugar or honey and eaten as a snack or dessert, rather like a buñuelo (fritter) or sopaipilla.

Ω   Ω   Ω   Ω   Ω   Ω   Ω   Ω   Ω

4 cups flour
1 teaspoon salt
2 tablespoons baking powder

1½ cups warm water (105° to 110° F.)
½ cup honey
Vegetable oil, for frying

In a mixing bowl, combine the flour, salt, and baking powder. In a separate bowl, combine the water and honey and stir until dissolved. Add the liquid to the dry ingredients and mix until soft and pliable.

Transfer to a floured surface and knead the dough for 5 minutes, stretching out and folding inwards. Place the dough in a greased bowl, cover with a damp towel or plastic wrap, and let it rise in a warm place for about 45 minutes.

Turn the dough out onto a floured surface and divide it into 12 egg-sized balls. Roll out into 5-inch circles and poke a small hole in the center of the dough, to prevent splattering while frying.

Put enough oil in a pan to come 1 inch up the sides then heat over medium heat until hot but not smoking. Gently place a circle of dough into the oil. Cook for 1½ minutes on each side until golden brown and puffy. Drain on paper towels, repeat for the remaining dough, and serve immediately.

PUMPKIN GINGERBREAD

This bread is the very essence of ginger, and contains both powdered and candied forms. I have always particularly enjoyed the flavor of ginger combined with pumpkin. If you're making this bread outside the holiday season when fresh pumpkin is difficult to obtain, you can substitute an equal amount of cooked and pureed sweet potatoes. This bread will last for weeks in the refrigerator, and it's wonderful served warm with coffee for breakfast. It even makes a great dessert, served with a scoop of Hazelnut or Almond Ice Cream (see Index).

¼ cup unsalted butter
½ cup vegetable oil
1 cup brown sugar
2 eggs
Juice of ½ orange
1¾ cups pumpkin puree
2 tablespoons diced candied ginger
3 cups flour

5 teaspoons ground ginger
2 teaspoons ground cinnamon
2 teaspoons baking powder
¼ cup dark corn syrup
½ cup molasses
1 teaspoon baking soda
¾ cup boiling water

Preheat the oven to 350° F. In a mixing bowl, cream the butter, oil, and brown sugar together until smooth. Add the eggs, 1 at a time, and incorporate. Fold in the orange juice, pumpkin puree, and candied ginger.

Sift together the flour, ginger, cinnamon, salt, and baking powder in a mixing bowl and reserve. In another mixing bowl, combine the corn syrup, molasses, baking soda, and boiling water.

Alternately add the dry and wet ingredients to the pumpkin mixture, and blend until just incorporated. Pour the mixture into a 9-x-5-inch loaf pan and bake in the oven for 1 hour, or until an inserted knife comes out clean. Turn out onto a rack to cool.

DRIED CRANBERRY-COCONUT-BANANA BREAD

Every January, I teach a series of cooking classes at Cuisine Concepts in Fort Worth, which is run by my good friend Renie Steves. Five years after my first class, three quarters of my students are still the same, and I always find it a very challenging, thought-provoking experience. My classes are always thematic, and recently one of them focused on Sunday brunch. This is the recipe that I came up with. If dried cranberries are unavailable, use dried cherries or even dried apricots.

Ω   Ω   Ω   Ω   Ω   Ω   Ω   Ω   Ω

1½ cups flour	*¼ cup walnut oil*
½ cup sugar	*1 cup very ripe mashed bananas*
2 teaspoons baking powder	*½ cup dried cranberries*
½ teaspoon baking soda	*½ cup lightly toasted shredded coconut*
½ teaspoon salt	*½ cup chopped walnuts*
2 eggs	

Preheat the oven to 350° F. Butter and flour a 9-x-5-x-3-inch baking pan.

In a large mixing bowl, combine the dry ingredients. In another bowl, lightly beat the eggs, and add the remaining ingredients. Add the moist ingredients to the dry ingredients, stirring just until the flour is moistened. Pour the batter into the prepared baking pan.

Bake in the oven for 50 to 55 minutes, or until an inserted knife comes out clean. Let the pan cool on a rack for 10 minutes before turning out the bread. Let the bread cool completely on the rack.

RHUBARB-MAPLE MUFFINS

When Routh Street Cafe first opened, we served different muffins every evening, but within a year, the Blue Corn Skillet Sticks (see Index) permanently replaced the muffins. This recipe is still well worth sharing, and seems particularly appropriate as my former partner John Dayton is from Minnesota where rhubarb grows in abundance.

ABOUT 18 MUFFINS

1 cup chopped rhubarb	*¼ teaspoon ground allspice*
⅓ cup sugar	*6 tablespoons unsalted butter, softened*
2½ cups flour	*½ cup pure maple syrup*
1 tablespoon baking powder	*1 egg*
1 teaspoon salt	*½ cup milk, at room temperature*

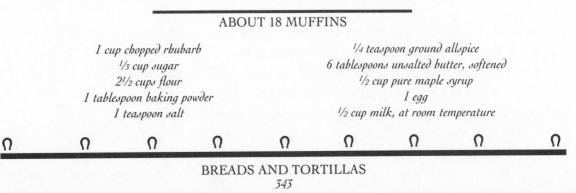

Preheat the oven to 400° F. Place the rhubarb in a mixing bowl, sprinkle the sugar over, and let macerate for 1 hour, stirring occasionally. In a separate mixing bowl, sift the dry ingredients together and reserve.

In another mixing bowl, beat the moist ingredients together until smooth. Add the macerated rhubarb. Quickly fold the dry ingredients into the rhubarb mixture until just incorporated. Pour into muffin tins and bake for 15 to 20 minutes, or until the muffins are golden brown. Turn out onto a rack to cool.

KOLACHES

Each spring, my friend Paula Lambert and I make our annual trek to Austin for the Texas Hill Country Food and Wine Festival, produced by Susan and Ed Auler of Fall Creek Vineyards. We've always faithfully made a stop in West, about 70 miles south of Dallas, which has one of the largest Czech populations in Texas. There, we head straight for one of the many bakeries that serve kolaches. The Czechs first arrived in Texas around 1852, bringing with them their folk customs, music, and food. With their fruit and cheese fillings, kolaches are a little like Danishes, and they make a wonderful addition to a Sunday brunch.

18 KOLACHES

2 cups warm milk (105° to 110° F.)
2 tablespoons sugar
1½ tablespoons dry yeast
2 eggs, lightly beaten

8 tablespoons (1 stick) unsalted butter, melted
1½ teaspoons salt
6½ cups flour

In a mixing bowl, combine the milk and sugar, sprinkle the yeast over, and let stand for 5 to 8 minutes, or until the yeast is foamy. Whisk in the eggs, butter, and salt, and gradually add the flour. Knead until a very soft dough forms. Cover the bowl with a damp towel or plastic wrap, and let the dough rise in a warm place until it doubles in volume, about 1 hour.

Lightly oil a baking sheet. Gently deflate the dough and shape into 18 equal balls about 2½ ounces each. Press the balls into flat disks about 3 inches across. Place on the baking sheet and cover loosely with a damp towel or plastic wrap. Let the dough rise again until it has doubled in volume, 30 to 45 minutes.

Meanwhile, preheat the oven to 350° F. When the balls of dough have risen, make an indentation in the center of each and add the desired filling (see below).

Bake in the oven for 20 to 25 minutes, until the kolaches are golden brown.

DRIED FRUIT FILLING

FOR 18 KOLACHES

8 ounces dried fruit, such as apricots, cherries, or cranberries
⅓ cup sugar

Juice and zest of ½ lemon
2 tablespoons unsalted butter

Place the dried fruit in a large pan, cover with water, and bring to a boil. Reduce the heat and simmer until the fruit becomes soft, 20 to 25 minutes. Strain the fruit, reserving the liquid.

Place the fruit in a blender with the sugar, lemon juice and zest, and the butter, adding just enough reserved cooking liquid to make pureeing possible. Let cool thoroughly before adding to the dough.

RICOTTA CHEESE FILLING

FOR 18 KOLACHES

1½ cups fresh ricotta cheese
½ cup sugar
1 egg
1 teaspoon vanilla extract

1 teaspoon lemon zest
1 tablespoon orange zest
¼ teaspoon ground cinnamon
2 tablespoons unsalted butter, melted

Place the cheese on some cheesecloth in a strainer until the ricotta is completely drained. Transfer to a large mixing bowl and combine with the remaining ingredients until thoroughly blended. Add to the dough.

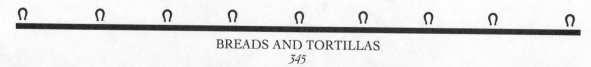

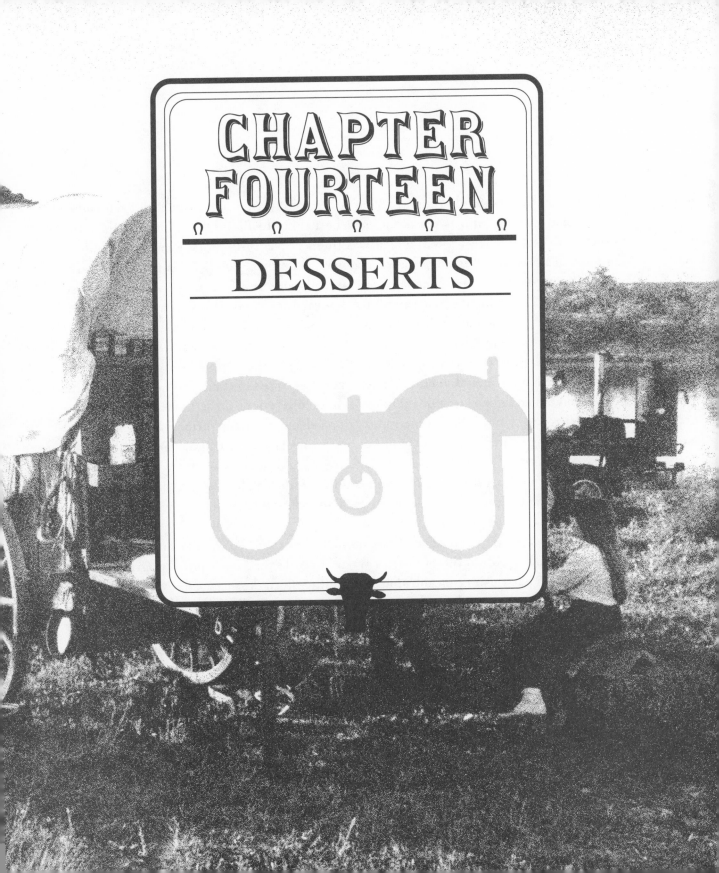

CHAPTER FOURTEEN

DESSERTS

Desserts were the first food group to seriously attract my attention as a child. I remember thinking that making piecrusts was the next best thing to Play-Doh. Not only that, but desserts satisfied my sweet tooth, which was the best part. My mother made all kinds of Southern desserts in my family's cafés: cobblers, fruit pies, devil's food chocolate cake, buttermilk custard pies, and banana-pecan layered cake were the ones I recall the most. It is this Southern influence that I particularly draw on for the desserts at Star Canyon; in fact, desserts are the most obviously Southern element of the whole menu.

The other main influence has stemmed from my visits to France over the years. On my first trip nearly twenty years ago, it was the beauty of the sculpted desserts, with their elaborate decoration and almond-paste features that impressed me the most along with the rich flavors and gooey textures that were quite different to those I was used to. When I returned to the United States after this trip, I decided to get serious about food and take up cooking professionally. One of my first projects was to make every single recipe in Gaston Lenôtre's *Desserts and Pastries*. Lenôtre is the best-known pastry chef in France, as well as the largest caterer. Later on, I studied with him for two weeks at his pastry school in Plaisir-Grignon, just outside Paris. This training provided me with the foundations.

Although I used to make a classic strawberry cake — bagatelle aux fraises — for special occasions at Routh Street Cafe, it wasn't very Texan, and I have progressed from making French pastries to concentrating on Southwestern desserts. Central to my philosophy is that desserts must be satisfying. My favorites are still the home-style pastries of the type my mother used to make: apple spice cake, cobblers, cream pies. I can think of nothing better than a hot peach cobbler with ice cream, served in the middle of July!

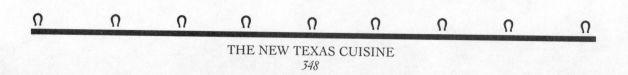

SUMMER BERRY BUCKLE WITH PECAN ICE CREAM

While buckles are similar in make-up to cobblers or crisps, they are different in that they have a layer of pastry underneath the fruit. I enjoy the texture of a buckle for a change, with the fruit sandwiched between the cakelike layer on the bottom and a crunchy topping usually containing nuts.

8 TO 10 SERVINGS

FILLING:
1 cup (2 sticks) unsalted butter
½ cup granulated sugar
1 egg, beaten
1½ cups flour
2 teaspoons baking soda
1 cup buttermilk
6 cups assorted berries (such as blueberries, raspberries, blackberries, and strawberries)

TOPPING:
½ cup granulated sugar
½ cup dark brown sugar
1 cup flour
¼ teaspoon grated nutmeg
½ cup (1 stick) unsalted butter
⅓ cup chopped toasted pecans (page 9)

1 pint Pecan Ice Cream (see Index)

Preheat the oven to 350° F. Butter and flour a 9 x 12-inch baking dish.

To make the filling, in a bowl beat the butter and sugar together until they're light and fluffy. Add the egg and mix in. Sift the flour and baking soda together and add to the butter mixture alternately with the buttermilk. When combined, spread the crust in the prepared dish and cover with berries.

To make the topping, place all the ingredients for the topping in a mixing bowl and combine until crumbly. Sprinkle the topping mixture over the berries in the baking dish.

Bake the buckle in the oven for 45 minutes, until nicely browned. Serve with a scoop of pecan ice cream for each person.

CRANBERRY-MANGO COBBLER WITH CINNAMON-PECAN CREAM

I vividly recall that my great-grandmother made blackberry cobblers with garden berries that she picked every July, while my mother's favorite was a peach cobbler that she always served piping hot with plenty of ice cream on top. Neither one of them ever made a cranberry-mango cobbler, but that's only because the combination probably never occurred to them; I'm sure they'd have liked it! This cobbler is a celebration of fall, when mangoes are still available and cranberries are just coming into season; in fact, the cranberries make this an obvious holiday dish. You can substitute papaya for the mango, and I've also substituted pumpkin with terrific results: use 2 cups diced raw pumpkin cooked at a boil for 1 minute with ½ cup sugar in 3 cups water.

---

8 TO 10 SERVINGS

4 cups (1 quart) fresh cranberries	1½ cups flour
1 cup plus ⅓ cup sugar	1 tablespoon baking powder
2 tablespoons orange zest	½ cup heavy cream
6 tablespoons unsalted butter	3 ripe mangoes, peeled, pitted, and cubed
1 egg, lightly beaten	Cinnamon-Pecan Cream (recipe follows)

Preheat the oven to 350° F. Lightly butter and flour a 9-x-12-inch baking dish. Roughly chop the cranberries and place in a large mixing bowl with the 1 cup sugar and orange zest. Let macerate for 15 minutes, stirring occasionally.

To make the dough, beat together the butter and ⅓ cup sugar until light and fluffy. Add the egg, and mix well. Sift the flour and baking powder together and add to the butter mixture alternately with the cream. Spread the mangoes and cranberries evenly over the bottom of the pan. Spoon the cobbler dough over the fruit, covering it completely.

Bake in the oven until browned, about 1 hour. Remove from oven and let stand for 5 to 10 minutes. Spoon the cobbler on serving plates and drizzle with the cinnamon-pecan cream.

CINNAMON-PECAN CREAM

ABOUT 2⅓ CUPS

1 cup milk
½ cup chopped toasted pecans (page 9)
½ vanilla bean, split in half lengthwise
1 cinnamon stick, crumbled

3 egg yolks
⅓ cup sugar
⅓ cup heavy cream or Crème Fraîche
(see Index)

Combine the milk, pecans, vanilla bean, and cinnamon in a large saucepan and bring to a boil. Remove from the heat and let infuse.

Whisk the yolks and sugar together in a large mixing bowl until the yolks are thick and pale. Bring the milk back to a boil. Strain the milk into the yolks and sugar, stirring constantly. Return the milk mixture to the saucepan. Cook over low heat until the custard thickens and a candy thermometer registers 180° F. Scrape down the sides and bottom of the pan constantly with a wooden spatula while cooking.

Set the saucepan over ice and stir in the heavy cream or crème fraîche. Refrigerate until the cobbler is ready.

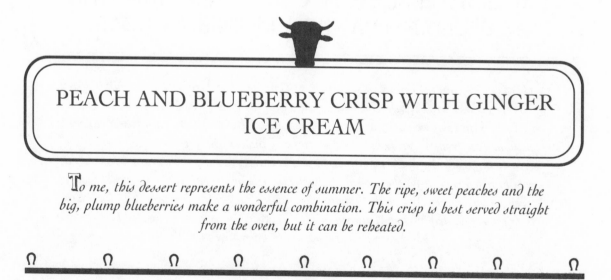

PEACH AND BLUEBERRY CRISP WITH GINGER ICE CREAM

To me, this dessert represents the essence of summer. The ripe, sweet peaches and the big, plump blueberries make a wonderful combination. This crisp is best served straight from the oven, but it can be reheated.

FILLING:	TOPPING:

FILLING:
5 medium-sized ripe peaches, peeled
and thinly sliced
2 cups washed blueberries
2 teaspoons fresh lemon juice
3 tablespoons granulated sugar
½ teaspoon ground ginger

TOPPING:
¼ cup unsalted butter
½ cup flour
¾ cup brown sugar
½ cup chopped pecans
1 teaspoon ground cinnamon
½ teaspoon grated nutmeg
1 pint Ginger Ice Cream (see Index)

Preheat the oven to 375° F.

To prepare the fruit filling, toss the peaches and blueberries in a large bowl with the lemon juice, sugar, and ginger. Lay the fruit in a buttered 9- or 10-inch baking dish and set aside.

To prepare the topping, place all the ingredients in a mixing bowl. Mix with your fingertips until crumbly and thoroughly incorporated. Cover the fruit filling with the topping. Bake in the oven for 30 to 35 minutes, or until the topping is browned. Serve with ginger ice cream.

WARM APPLE SPICE CAKE WITH CARAMEL SAUCE AND VANILLA BEAN ICE CREAM

This is one of my trademark dishes at Star Canyon. Together with our Double Dark Chocolate Cake with White Chocolate Sauce and the Lace Cookie Dessert Tacos (see Index), it's an item we dare not take off the menu. This recipe is similar to a cake my grandmother from West Texas used to make; I improvised until it tasted right. It's dense and moist, and holds for at least a week, covered, in the refrigerator. In fact, it seems to reach a peak on the second or third day. It's great with coffee for breakfast, or dressed up for dessert. When the famous wine writer Anthony Dias Blue held his fiftieth birthday party hosted by Tor Kenwood at the Beringer Winery, he requested this cake for his dessert; Grandma would have been proud!

1 cup cake flour
2 cups all-purpose flour
1½ teaspoons baking soda
½ teaspoon grated nutmeg
½ teaspoon ground cinnamon
¼ teaspoon ground mace
¼ teaspoon ground ginger
½ teaspoon salt
1½ cups vegetable oil

2 cups sugar
3 eggs
3½ cups chopped raw unpeeled green apples, such as Granny Smith or pippin (about 5 apples)
¾ cup chopped toasted pecans (page 9)
1 cup raisins, plumped in bourbon
Caramel Sauce (recipe follows)
1 quart Vanilla Bean Ice Cream (see Index)

Preheat the oven to 325° F. Butter and flour an 8-inch springform pan.

In a mixing bowl, sift all the dry ingredients together and set aside.

Blend the oil and sugar in an electric mixer at medium speed for 5 minutes. Add the eggs, one at a time, and beat well. Gradually fold the dry ingredients into the oil mixture and combine thoroughly. Add the apples, pecans, and raisins, and blend well with a spatula.

Pour the batter into the prepared pan. Bake in the oven for 1 to 1½ hours, or until a knife inserted comes out dry. Drizzle some caramel sauce over slices of the cake and serve with a scoop of vanilla bean ice cream for each person.

CARAMEL SAUCE

ABOUT 2¾ CUPS

⅓ cup granulated sugar
1 cup light brown sugar
¼ cup pure maple syrup

¼ cup dark corn syrup
1 cup heavy cream

Mix all the ingredients in a heavy-bottomed saucepan. Cook over high heat until the mixture reaches 200° F. on a candy thermometer. Let cool for 20 minutes, and skim the surface if necessary.

WARM MINTED SWEET BISCUITS WITH STRAWBERRIES AND WHITE CHOCOLATE ICE CREAM

When Mikhail Gorbachev visited Minneapolis in June 1990, and Goodfellow's was asked to prepare a luncheon in his honor at the Governor's Mansion, we served this dish for dessert. Mr. Gorbachev cleaned his plate, so there were no food shortages that day! This dessert is good all summer long using whichever fresh fruit is available; you can just as easily use peaches, plums, blueberries, or raspberries. The shortcake has an interesting texture that lies somewhere between a biscuit and a cake.

6 TO 8 SERVINGS

3 cups cake flour
2¼ cups granulated sugar
1½ tablespoons baking powder
1 teaspoon salt
¾ cup vegetable shortening
2 eggs
½ cup milk
2 tablespoons chopped mint

1 teaspoon vanilla extract
7 cups strawberries
2 tablespoons Grand Marnier
2 cups heavy cream
Confectioners' sugar
6 to 8 mint sprigs, for garnish
1 pint White Chocolate Ice Cream (see Index)

In a mixing bowl, combine the flour, 1 cup of the granulated sugar, the baking powder, and salt. Cut the shortening into the mixed dry ingredients with a fork or an electric mixer. Whip together the eggs and milk in a separate bowl, blending them until smooth. Add with the chopped mint to the dry ingredients, and incorporate thoroughly. The dough should be thinner and more sticky than regular shortcake or biscuit dough. Refrigerate for at least 30 minutes.

Meanwhile, clean and slice 5 cups of strawberries. Puree the remaining 2 cups of strawberries with 1 cup of granulated sugar and the Grand Marnier. Pour over the sliced berries and fold together. Whip the cream with the remaining ¼ cup of sugar. Set aside. Preheat the oven to 325° F.

When the shortcake dough has chilled, remove from the refrigerator and place on a well-floured surface. Roll or pat it by hand to a ¾-inch thickness. Cut the dough with a biscuit cutter into 6 to 8 shortcakes. Place on a greased baking sheet and return to the refrigerator to chill for 30 minutes.

Bake the shortcakes in the oven for 20 to 22 minutes, until golden brown. Slice the shortcakes in half while they're still hot. Spoon the strawberry filling on the bottom half of the shortcakes, and top with the whipped cream. Dust the top crust with confectioners' sugar, garnish with a mint sprig, and serve with a scoop of white chocolate ice cream.

SWEET POTATO POUND CAKE WITH PRALINE ICE CREAM

This is a simple, homey dessert that could not be more satisfying. It's good to snack on any time of day, and it's especially good for breakfast.

8 TO 10 SERVINGS

1½ cups cake flour
½ teaspoon salt
½ teaspoon baking soda
½ teaspoon ground cinnamon
½ teaspoon grated nutmeg
8 tablespoons (1 stick) unsalted butter, at room temperature

½ cup sour cream
1⅜ cups sugar
4 ounces baked sweet potatoes, flesh scooped out and pureed
3 eggs, lightly beaten
1 teaspoon vanilla extract
1 pint Praline Ice Cream (see Index)

Preheat the oven to 300° F. Lightly oil a 9-inch loaf pan. In a mixing bowl, sift together the dry ingredients and set aside.

In a separate bowl, mix together the butter, sour cream, and sugar until smooth. Add the sweet potato puree and eggs, and mix until incorporated. Add the vanilla, then fold in the combined dry ingredients.

Pour the mixture into a loaf pan and bake in the oven for 40 to 50 minutes, or until a toothpick or skewer inserted comes out clean. Remove from the oven and allow to cool. Serve with praline ice cream.

BLACK BOTTOM–PECAN PIE WITH WHISKEY SAUCE

*P*ecan pie is a traditional Southern dessert that is prepared for special occasions such as Thanksgiving and over the holiday season. The addition of chocolate to form the black bottom layer of the pie creates an irresistible touch to an already appealing dessert.

8 TO 10 SERVINGS

1 ounce bittersweet chocolate
5 teaspoons heavy cream
1 teaspoon granulated sugar
One 9-inch Unbaked Piecrust, chilled
(recipe follows)
9 tablespoons unsalted butter
1 cup plus 2 tablespoons light brown sugar

1 cup light corn syrup
2 teaspoons vanilla extract
5 teaspoons bourbon
5 eggs
1 cup pecan halves
Whiskey Sauce (recipe follows)

Preheat the oven to 350° F. Melt the chocolate in a double boiler set over simmering water. Heat the cream and granulated sugar in a saucepan and stir until the sugar is dissolved. Whisk in the melted chocolate and continue whisking until thoroughly blended.

Pour the chocolate mixture over the bottom of the chilled piecrust, and spread evenly. Place the piecrust in the freezer for 5 minutes to set the chocolate.

Melt the butter and set aside. In a large mixing bowl, place the brown sugar, corn syrup, vanilla, and bourbon. Beat with an electric mixer until smooth. Add the eggs, one at a time, blending thoroughly after each addition. Add the melted butter and beat until smooth.

Remove the pie shell from the freezer. Spread the pecan halves evenly over the bottom of the pie shell. Pour the filling over the pecans. Bake in the oven for about 30 minutes. Turn the heat down to 300° F and continue baking for 15 to 20 minutes, until the center of the pie is set. Serve chilled with the whiskey sauce.

UNBAKED PIECRUST

This recipe is also ideal for apple pie.

ONE 9-INCH PIECRUST

1½ cups flour
¼ teaspoon salt

½ cup vegetable shortening
3 to 4 tablespoons cold water

In a mixing bowl, combine the flour and salt. Add the shortening and incorporate with your fingertips until the mixture resembles very coarse cornmeal. Sprinkle the water over the flour mixture in tablespoon increments while stirring with a fork. Form the dough into a ball and let rest in the refrigerator for 1 hour.

On a lightly floured surface, roll out the dough in a circle to ⅛-inch thickness. Place the dough in a pie pan; trim and crimp the edges. Fill the crust with the filling and bake according to the recipe.

WHISKEY SAUCE

1 TO 1¼ CUPS

4 tablespoons (¼ cup) unsalted butter
⅓ cup sugar
1 egg

½ tablespoon very hot water
¼ cup heavy cream
¼ cup rye whiskey

Melt the butter in a double boiler and set over gently simmering water.

In a small bowl, beat the sugar and egg until blended. Stir the mixture into the butter. Add the tablespoon of hot water and stir until the mixture coats the back of a spoon, about 7 minutes. Remove from the double boiler and let cool to room temperature. Stir the cream and whiskey into the sauce.

PEANUT BUTTER–BANANA CREAM PIE

This dessert is a lot lighter than it might sound. It's a regular item on the menu at Star Canyon, and I often teach how to make it in my cooking classes. Banana cream pie is a true Southern dessert, akin to banana pudding, and I've taken it a step further in that direction by adding peanut butter on top of the pastry shell. Bananas and peanut butter make a great combination, which gets even better with the addition of chocolate; a little Hot Fudge Sauce (see Index) sends this recipe into the realm of decadence!

---

8 TO 10 SERVINGS

¼ cup banana liqueur
½ teaspoon unflavored powdered gelatin
2¾ cups milk
½ vanilla bean, halved lengthwise and scraped
4 eggs, separated (whites reserved at room temperature)
1½ cups sugar
3 tablespoons cornstarch

2 ripe bananas
Juice of ½ lemon
¼ cup smooth peanut butter, at room temperature
One 9-inch Baked Piecrust (recipe follows)
¾ cup chopped roasted peanuts (page 9)
Pinch of salt
Pinch of cream of tartar

Place the banana liqueur in a small mixing bowl, sprinkle the gelatin on top, and allow to soften for 5 minutes. Place the bowl over simmering water until the gelatin is completely clear. Set aside.

In a saucepan, combine the milk and vanilla bean. Bring to a boil, remove from the heat, cover, and allow to steep while preparing the yolk mixture.

In a mixing bowl, whisk the egg yolks while gradually adding ¾ cup of sugar. When the yolks have lightened, whisk in the cornstarch. Strain the milk and gradually pour into the yolk mixture while stirring. Return to a clean saucepan set over medium heat, and stir constantly until the mixture begins to boil. Reduce the heat and continue to stir for 2 to 3 minutes. Remove from the heat, whisk in the gelatin mixture, and incorporate thoroughly. Allow the pastry cream to cool completely.

Slice the bananas on the bias and brush with lemon juice. Whip the peanut butter to make it easier to spread, then spread on the top side of the piecrust. Sprinkle half of the peanuts on top of the peanut butter. Arrange half of the banana slices on top of the peanuts and spread the pastry cream over the bananas. Arrange the remaining banana slices over the pastry cream, and then sprinkle the remaining peanuts on top of the bananas. Refrigerate while making the meringue.

Preheat the oven to 400° F. Place the egg whites in a mixing bowl with the salt and cream of tartar. Beat with an electric mixer until soft peaks form. Gradually add the remaining ¾ cup of sugar while beating, until stiff peaks form and the meringue becomes glossy. Spread the meringue on top of the pie, or place in a pastry bag and pipe on decoratively. Make sure the meringue touches the pie shell all over.

Place the pie in the oven for no more than 1 minute. Watch constantly, and remove when the meringue is lightly browned. Refrigerate for at least 30 minutes before cutting.

BAKED PIECRUST
ONE 9-INCH PIECRUST

1½ cups flour
¼ teaspoon salt
½ cup vegetable shortening

4 to 5 tablespoons cold water
Rice or dried beans, for weighting
1 egg white

In a mixing bowl, combine the flour and salt. Add the shortening and incorporate with your fingertips until the mixture resembles very coarse cornmeal. Sprinkle 3 to 4 tablespoons of the water over the flour mixture in tablespoon increments while stirring with a fork. Form the dough into a ball and let rest in the refrigerator for 1 hour.

On a lightly floured surface, roll out the dough into a circle to ⅛-inch thickness. Place the dough in a pie pan; trim and crimp the edges. Place the shell in the freezer for 20 minutes. Preheat the oven to 425° F.

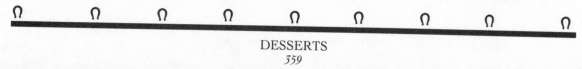

Remove the shell and prick the bottom and sides with a fork. Press foil snuggly over the bottom and sides of the crust. Pour rice or dried beans over the foil and bake in the oven for about 6 minutes. Whisk together the egg white and remaining tablespoon of water in a bowl. Remove the foil from the pan and brush the sides and bottom of the crust with the egg wash. Return to the oven and bake for an additional 8 to 10 minutes. Let cool before adding the pie filling.

WALNUT BREAD PUDDING

This Creole-inspired dessert was introduced to the Baby Routh menu by Rex Hale, who came to us from Brennan's in Houston. A traditional Whiskey Sauce (see Index) or a whiskey or bourbon butter would be a good accompaniment to this pudding; alternatively, simply top with some whipped cream. Note that the bread should be soaked overnight in the refrigerator.

8 SERVINGS

5 eggs
1½ cups brown sugar
1 teaspoon ground cinnamon
2 tablespoons vanilla extract
5 tablespoons bourbon

3 cups milk
6 ounces French bread, cut into 2-inch cubes
3 tablespoons unsalted butter, cut into pieces
¼ cup raisins
1 cup chopped walnuts

In a large bowl, whip the eggs and brown sugar together until smooth. Add the cinnamon, vanilla, and bourbon, and whisk in the milk. Place the bread cubes in the egg-bourbon mixture and soak overnight in the refrigerator.

Preheat the oven to 350° F. Lightly butter the bottom and sides of a 10-inch round cake pan. Place the raisins in the bottom of the pan and pour the bread pudding mixture over. Dot the top with the butter, and sprinkle with the chopped walnuts.

Bake the pudding in the oven for approximately 50 minutes, or until a toothpick or skewer inserted comes out clean. Remove from the oven and allow to cool slightly. Serve the pudding warm.

CARAMELIZED PEAR TART WITH MACADAMIA NUT ICE CREAM

This dessert is a variation on the classic tarte Tatin, but uses pears instead of apples. The addition of the buttery macadamia nuts provides a perfect foil for the fruit. I can't think of a better way to end a meal in the fall than with this dessert.

10 TO 12 SERVINGS

6 ounces puff pastry (recipe follows)
2½ pounds pears, such as Anjou or Bartlett
8 tablespoons (1 stick) unsalted butter
1¼ cups sugar
¼ teaspoon ground cinnamon
⅛ teaspoon grated nutmeg

1 tablespoon flour
½ cup coarsely ground toasted macadamia nuts (page 9)
Pinch of salt
1 quart Macadamia Nut Ice Cream (see Index)

Preheat the oven to 400° F. On a floured surface, roll out the puff pastry in a circle about ⅛ inch thick. Place the puff pastry on a sheet pan and let it rest in the refrigerator while preparing the pears.

Peel, core, and cut the pears into eighths. In a large ovenproof skillet, melt the butter and sugar over medium heat, stirring occasionally. Arrange the pears evenly on the butter mixture. Continue to cook over medium heat for 15 to 20 minutes, shaking the skillet occasionally; the juice from the pears will bubble up and finally form a thick, light brown syrup. Transfer the skillet to the oven for 5 minutes.

In a mixing bowl, combine the cinnamon, nutmeg, flour, macadamia nuts, and salt. Remove the skillet from the oven and sprinkle the nut mixture over the

pears. Top with the puff pastry, gently pressing onto the sides of the skillet. Pierce 3 holes in the pastry with a knife to allow air to escape.

Return the skillet to the oven and bake for 15 minutes more, or until the pastry has browned nicely. Remove from the oven and let rest for a few minutes. Invert the tart on a platter and unmold. Serve with the macadamia nut ice cream.

PUFF PASTRY

This "quick" method owes its inspiration to Julia Child, who has influenced cooks in America for generations. This recipe literally saves hours from the classic French method, and is well worth the effort involved. The pastry is best made in a 5-quart KitchenAid electric mixer.

ABOUT 2½ POUNDS

*1¼ pounds (5 sticks) unsalted butter, cut into
½-inch dice
3 cups unbleached flour*

*1 teaspoon salt
¾ cup ice water*

Place the butter in the freezer to chill. Sift the flour and salt together in the bowl of a mixer with a flat paddle attachment, and stir to combine. After the butter has thoroughly chilled, add to the mixer and combine on low speed until the mixture is the size of lima beans. If mixing by hand, blend the flour and butter together rapidly to form large (¾-inch) flakes. Add the ice water all at once and continue to mix, just until the mixture has incorporated and the dough has bound together.

Remove the dough from the mixer and place on a floured surface (the mixture should be very sticky and may seem difficult to work with). Lightly flour your hands and pat the dough out into a rectangle about ½ inch thick; the short side should be facing you. Using a metal scraper, fold the top one third of the dough over the middle third, and fold the bottom third over the other 2 layers, making a total of 3 layers. You have now completed the first "turn." Lift the dough off the work surface, scrape the surface clean, and re-flour it. Return the dough, and lightly flour the top.

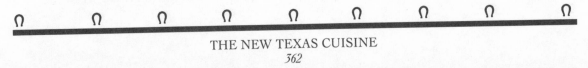

Using a rolling pin, roll the pastry out to a ½-inch thickness, flouring and scraping the rolling pin as necessary. Fold the dough into thirds as before and repeat the process to complete the second turn. You need to complete 4 turns before refrigerating the dough. It is important to work as quickly as possible to prevent the butter from melting.

After completing the fourth turn, cover the dough in plastic wrap and place in the refrigerator for at least 1 hour, and up to 1 day. After the dough has completely chilled, remove and complete 2 more turns, this time rolling the dough to a ¼-inch thickness. After the final turn, wrap the dough and chill in the refrigerator for 1 hour before use.

Cut off the amount of puff pastry required. Keep the rest covered tightly in several layers of plastic wrap in the freezer; it will keep for up to 1 month.

CAJETA FLAN WITH CINNAMON CACTUS COOKIES

Cajeta is the goat's milk caramel from Mexico with a distinctive, earthy flavor. Once you become acquainted with cajeta, you may never go back to using regular caramel. Goat's milk is available at specialty and natural food stores.

8 SERVINGS

2 cups Cajeta (recipe follows)
½ cup sugar
1½ tablespoons water
1½ cups milk

½ cup heavy cream
3 whole eggs, plus 2 egg yolks
2 dozen Cinnamon Cactus Cookies (see Index)

Preheat the oven to 325° F. Let the cajeta rest while preparing the caramel glaze for the flans.

Heat the sugar in a saucepan over low heat. When it begins to melt around the edges, stir slowly but continuously. When fully melted, add the water all at once and stir. Divide the caramel among the ramekins or custard cups.

Combine the milk and cream in a mixing bowl and add 1 cup of the cajeta, dissolving it into the mixture. Lightly beat the eggs and yolks, and whisk into the cajeta-cream mixture. Pour into the ramekins and place them in a large baking dish. Pour enough boiling water into the baking dish to come halfway up the sides of the ramekins.

Bake the flans in the oven for 30 minutes, or until set, so that a toothpick or skewer inserted comes out clean. Refrigerate for at least 3 hours before unmolding. When ready to serve, unmold the flans and top each with some of the remaining 1 cup of cajeta. Serve with the cinnamon cactus cookies.

CAJETA

Cow's milk can be substituted for the goat's milk, but the flavor will be different.

---

2 CUPS

1½ cups sugar
2 cups goat's milk
2 cups cow's milk

1 teaspoon cornstarch
Pinch of baking soda

Place ¾ cup of the sugar in a small skillet and melt over medium heat for about 7 minutes, stirring continuously, until golden brown and free of lumps. Remove from the heat.

Combine the 2 milks and pour about one quarter of the mixture (or about 1 cup) into a bowl. Add the cornstarch and baking soda, and set aside.

Add the remaining ¾ cup of sugar to the 3 cups of milk and heat in a saucepan over medium heat. Stir occasionally, bring just to the boiling point, and add the caramelized sugar all at once while stirring vigorously. Add the reserved milk-cornstarch, and stir well.

Reduce the heat to low and simmer for 50 to 60 minutes, stirring occasionally. Cajeta will begin to thicken during the last 15 minutes of cooking; stir more frequently to prevent sticking.

WHITE CHOCOLATE BROWNIES WITH HAZELNUT ICE CREAM

These rich, chewy brownies are a chocolate-lover's delight. The crunchy hazelnuts add to the richness as well as the texture. As an alternative to the ice cream, you can serve this dessert with Hot Fudge Sauce (see Index), which satisfies even the most ardent chocoholic!

ABOUT 20 BROWNIES

1 cup unbleached flour
¼ teaspoon salt
2 large eggs
½ cup sugar
12 ounces white chocolate, coarsely chopped

8 tablespoons (1 stick) unsalted butter, melted
1 teaspoon vanilla extract
1 cup toasted, unsalted hazelnuts, chopped (page 9)
1 quart Hazelnut Ice Cream (see Index)

Preheat the oven to 350° F. Butter and flour a 9-x-9-inch baking pan. Sift together the flour and salt, and set aside.

In a mixing bowl, beat the eggs at high speed until frothy. Gradually add the sugar, and beat for about 3 minutes, until thick and pale. In a double boiler, melt 7 ounces of the chocolate and gently fold into the egg mixture. Add the melted butter and vanilla, and stir well; the mixture may appear curdled. Add the flour and salt, and mix thoroughly. Fold in the remaining 5 ounces of chocolate and the hazelnuts. Pour the batter into the prepared pan and bake for about 20 minutes, until a toothpick or skewer inserted comes out not-quite clean. Let cool in the pan, and cut into squares.

Serve the brownies with the hazelnut ice cream.

CHOCOLATE PUDDING CAKE WITH MOCHA SAUCE

Pudding cakes seem to go in and out of fashion with some regularity. This chocolate pudding cake is one of the best I've tasted yet; of course, you can't go far wrong with chocolate and coffee.

8 TO 10 SERVINGS

CHOCOLATE CAKE:
½ cup cake flour
½ cup unsweetened cocoa powder
¾ teaspoon baking powder
6 eggs
¾ cup granulated sugar
¼ cup melted unsalted butter, cooled to room temperature
Pinch of salt
¼ teaspoon cream of tartar

CHOCOLATE-PECAN PUDDING:
5 ounces bittersweet chocolate, chopped

6 egg yolks
2½ cups heavy cream
5 tablespoons granulated sugar
½ cup chopped toasted pecans (page 9)

Mocha Sauce (recipe follows)

GARNISHES (OPTIONAL):
Strawberries
Chocolate shavings
Confectioners' sugar

To prepare the chocolate cake, lightly oil a 9-inch springform cake pan and set aside. Preheat the oven to 350° F.

Sift together the flour, cocoa, and baking powder until combined. In a mixing bowl, place 3 whole eggs and 3 of the yolks, reserving the 3 egg whites for later. Beat the eggs and yolks with ½ cup of the sugar until the mixture is very thick and light in color. Fold in the butter. Add the dry ingredients and thoroughly incorporate.

In another mixing bowl, beat the egg whites with the salt and cream of tartar to form soft peaks. Add the remaining ¼ cup of sugar and beat to form stiff peaks. Fold the meringue into the cake batter and combine thoroughly but quickly. Transfer the batter to the prepared cake pan, and bake in the oven for 30 minutes, or until a skewer inserted in the center comes out clean. While the cake is cooling, prepare the chocolate pudding.

To prepare the pudding, melt the chocolate in a double boiler. Remove from the heat and whisk in the egg yolks one at a time. In a small saucepan, bring the cream and sugar to a boil. Pour slowly into the chocolate mixture, whisking until incorporated. Fold in the pecans and keep at room temperature.

When the chocolate cake has cooled, remove the sides of the cake pan. Make 2 horizontal slices to create 3 equal layers and leave the bottom layer in the cake pan. Reattach the sides of the pan.

Pour one-third of the chocolate pudding on the bottom layer of the cake and place another layer of the cake on top of the pudding. Continue to layer the pudding and cake until they're finished. Let sit at room temperature for 2 to 3 hours to allow the cake to absorb the pudding filling. Refrigerate until chilled, and slice. Let sit at room temperature for 1 hour before serving.

Ladle some of the mocha sauce on serving plates and place a slice of the cake on top. Garnish with strawberries, chocolate shavings, and confectioners' sugar.

MOCHA SAUCE
ABOUT 2½ CUPS

2 cups heavy cream
2 tablespoons Tia Maria
½ vanilla bean, split lengthwise and scraped
2 egg yolks

½ cup sugar
1 teaspoon coffee extract, or 2 tablespoons very strong coffee

In a saucepan, bring the cream and Tia Maria to a boil with the vanilla bean. Cover the pan, remove from the heat, and set aside to infuse for about 15 minutes.

In a mixing bowl, whisk the egg yolks while gradually adding the sugar. Pour the hot cream into the egg mixture while whisking. Pour back into the saucepan and cook over medium heat until the mixture smoothly coats the back of a spoon. Strain and cool. Whisk in the coffee.

DOUBLE DARK CHOCOLATE CAKE WITH WHITE CHOCOLATE SAUCE

This is another of my trademark dishes. The chocolate cake was inspired by a recipe of Julia Child's that I first made for her when I was working as a chef's assistant for the Great Chefs Program at the Mondavi Winery in Napa in 1981. This version is a little more sinful! It's a good dessert to serve at the end of a meal if you're trying to impress — it's really rich, and a chocoholic's delight. It should be served at room temperature.

For a simplified version, you can serve this cake with a little whipped cream instead of the chocolate mousse and white chocolate sauce. In this case, it can be reheated in a low oven for 5 minutes and served warm. This cake is nothing if not versatile!

8 TO 10 SERVINGS

CHOCOLATE MOUSSE:
4 ounces semisweet chocolate, chopped
5 tablespoons unsalted butter, softened
1 tablespoon bourbon whiskey
2 eggs, separated
1½ tablespoons sugar

CHOCOLATE CAKE:
1 cup heavy cream

10½ ounces semisweet baking chocolate, chopped
2 ounces unsweetened chocolate, chopped
5 eggs
⅓ cup sugar
1 teaspoon vanilla extract
White Chocolate Sauce (recipe follows)

To prepare the mousse, melt the chocolate and butter in a double boiler set over simmering water, stirring occasionally. When the chocolate has melted, remove from the heat and allow to cool slightly. Add the bourbon and stir. Add the egg yolks, one at a time, whisking after each addition. Set aside.

Beat the egg whites to soft peaks, then gradually add the sugar. Beat for 2 minutes longer until stiff peaks form. Fold one quarter of the egg whites into the chocolate mixture, and then gently fold in the rest. Fold only until the meringues are incorporated. Chill the mixture for 2 hours.

Meanwhile, to make the cake place a round of parchment (or wax) paper in the bottom of a 9-inch cake pan. Butter and flour the pan and paper. Preheat the oven to 350° F.

In a medium saucepan, bring the cream to a boil, and then remove from the heat. Add both chopped chocolates and stir to blend. Cover the pan and allow the chocolate to melt, about 5 minutes. When melted, stir to blend completely, and set aside.

Place the eggs, sugar, and vanilla in a mixing bowl, and set over simmering water. Whip the mixture until warm to the touch, about 1 minute, and then remove from the heat. Beat the mixture with an electric mixer at high speed until tripled in volume, about 7 to 10 minutes.

Gently whisk one quarter of the egg mixture into the chocolate and incorporate completely; then gently fold in the rest, taking care to deflate the egg mixture as little as possible. Pour the chocolate mixture into the prepared cake pan and place inside a slightly larger pan. Pour boiling water into the larger pan until it comes halfway up the side of the 9-inch cake pan.

Bake in the oven for 50 minutes, or until an inserted toothpick or skewer comes out clean. Remove from the oven and let the pan sit in the water for 30 minutes more. When cool, invert on a platter and remove the parchment paper.

Remove the chocolate mousse from the refrigerator and scrape into a pastry bag with a star tip. Pipe the mousse onto the cake in a circular motion. Slice the cake with a knife dipped in hot water, as this cake can be crumbly and difficult to cut. Ladle some of the white chocolate sauce on serving plates and place a slice of the cake on top.

WHITE CHOCOLATE SAUCE

ABOUT 1½ CUPS

5 ounces white chocolate   1 cup heavy cream

In a double boiler set over simmering water, melt the white chocolate. While still over the heat, gradually whisk in the cream. Remove from the heat and let cool to room temperature.

CHOCOLATE DIABLO WITH CHERIMOYA CUSTARD SAUCE

Mark Haugen and I developed this recipe in 1987 for our new restaurant in Minneapolis, Tejas — Mark is still the chef there. The combination of chiles and chocolate may sound a little odd at first, but one only has to consider the ingredients of the classic mole sauce to realize that it is in fact centuries old. Ancho chiles do have chocolatey tones, so the combination makes perfect sense to me. This dessert quickly became one of the most popular items on the menu at Tejas, and it continues to fascinate diners still.

10 TO 12 SERVINGS

4 ounces unsweetened chocolate, chopped   3 tablespoons ancho chile puree (pages 3 to 4)
4 ounces semisweet chocolate, chopped   1 tablespoon vanilla extract
8 ounces (2 sticks) unsalted butter, softened   ½ cup finely chopped roasted hazelnuts
4 eggs   (page 9)
1½ cups sugar   Cherimoya Custard Sauce (recipe follows)

Preheat the oven to 350° F. Place a round of parchment (or wax) paper on the bottom of a 9-inch cake pan or a loaf pan. Butter and flour the pan and paper.

In a double boiler set over simmering water, melt both chocolates. Add the butter and remove from the heat. Stir often until the butter has melted.

Using an electric mixer, whip the eggs and sugar together in a bowl until a ribbon forms. Slowly stir in the chocolate mixture and then add the ancho puree and vanilla extract. Stir in the hazelnuts.

Spread evenly in the prepared pan and loosely cover the top with some parchment paper so that a hard crust will not form. Set the pan in a larger baking pan filled with hot water, and bake in the oven for 1½ hours, or until a toothpick or skewer inserted comes out clean.

Remove the pan from the oven and the water bath and let cool on a rack for 15 minutes. When cool, invert the cake on a serving platter, remove the parchment paper, and cut into slices. Ladle some of the cherimoya custard sauce on serving plates and place a slice of the cake on top. Serve warm or at room temperature.

CHERIMOYA CUSTARD SAUCE

Cherimoyas are a combination of exotic flavors including mango, coconut, pineapple, and vanilla, and are a perfect pairing for chocolate and chiles.

ABOUT 2½ CUPS

*3 very ripe cherimoyas (custard apples),
peeled and seeded
1 cup milk
½ vanilla bean, or 1 teaspoon vanilla extract*

*⅓ cup sugar
3 egg yolks
⅓ cup heavy cream or Crème Fraîche
(see Index)*

Press the cherimoyas through a Mouli grater or strainer. Transfer to a food processor and process for 1 minute. Pass through a fine strainer and reserve.

In a saucepan, bring the milk and vanilla bean or extract to a boil. Cover the pan, remove from the heat, and set aside to infuse for about 5 minutes. Meanwhile, whisk the sugar with the egg yolks until a ribbon forms.

Strain the infused milk into the yolk mixture and return to a clean saucepan. Cook gently over medium heat until thickened and the mixture registers 185° F. on a candy thermometer, about 5 to 10 minutes. Immediately add the cream or crème fraîche. Chill for at least 1 hour in the refrigerator. When chilled, whisk in the cherimoya puree.

LACE COOKIE DESSERT TACOS WITH RASPBERRIES AND CARAMEL

These tacos can be formed into many different shapes, and we use the same recipe for our lace cookie cups at Star Canyon. We have some regular customers who would never come back if we took this dish off the menu! It really makes an impressive, elegant dessert; however, they keep for only a day or so at most, and they should be stored in an airtight plastic container. These tacos are most successfully made when the weather is not too humid. Raspberries make a wonderful filling, but as with other recipes in this chapter, use your discretion and choose whatever fruit is in season and looks freshest.

12 SERVINGS

1 cup finely ground whole almonds
¾ cup granulated sugar
8 tablespoons (1 stick) unsalted butter,
at room temperature
4 teaspoons flour
2 tablespoons milk

1 cup heavy cream
2 tablespoons confectioners' sugar
1 tablespoon vanilla extract
4 cups fresh raspberries
Caramel Sauce (page 353)

Preheat the oven to 350° F. Combine the almonds, granulated sugar, butter, flour, and milk in a mixing bowl, and form into a smooth dough.

Cut wax paper or parchment paper into four 6-inch squares and place on a large cookie sheet. Place 1 tablespoon of the cookie dough in the center of each square. Wet your fingers thoroughly with cold milk or water and flatten the dough. Continue wetting fingers and patting dough until it is so thin that it becomes transparent; the dough should be in rounds about 3 inches across.

Bake in the oven for 12 minutes, until the cookies are golden brown and have spread to about 5 inches in diameter. Remove from the oven and let set for about 45 seconds. Remove the paper from the cookies and mold each one on

a rolling pin to resemble a fried taco shell. When hardened and cooled, remove from the rolling pin. Repeat the procedure until 12 cookies have been molded.

In a medium mixing bowl set over a larger bowl of ice and water, whip the cream with an electric mixer. Sprinkle in the confectioners' sugar and continue to whip until the mixture resembles thin sour cream. Add the vanilla and whip until soft peaks form; do not overwhip.

Fill each taco with 2 tablespoons of the whipped cream and some berries. Serve each portion on top of some of the caramel sauce.

FROZEN MACADAMIA NUT BOMBE WITH VANILLA CUSTARD SAUCE

This dessert was inspired by a recipe of Michael James, who invited me to participate as a chef's assistant in the Great Chefs of France cooking school at the Mondavi Winery in 1980. Michael, who with Billy Cross was co-director of the program, has a special touch with desserts; he is equally adept at working magic with elegant French creations, or turning the humblest of desserts into something special. Only Michael could have had an American pie shop on Rodeo Drive in Beverly Hills!

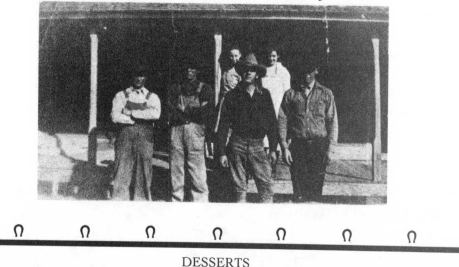

1 pint raspberries, blackberries, or strawberries
1 tablespoon plus ¾ cup sugar
2 cups heavy cream, chilled
½ teaspoon vanilla extract
3 egg whites, at room temperature

Pinch of cream of tartar
Pinch of salt
¼ cup water
Macadamia Nut Brittle (recipe follows), chopped
Vanilla Custard Sauce (recipe follows)

Place the berries in a mixing bowl and sprinkle with the 1 tablespoon of sugar. Crush the berries with a fork and let macerate while completing the recipe. Adjust the amount of sugar, depending on the sweetness or tartness of the berries.

Pour the cream and vanilla into a chilled mixing bowl and whip until the cream is almost firm. In another bowl, beat the egg whites with the cream of tartar and salt with an electric mixer until stiff but not dry.

Place the ¾ cup sugar and water in a saucepan, bring to a boil, and cook over high heat until a candy thermometer registers about 210° F. and the mixture forms a thick syrup, about 5 to 7 minutes. Pour the syrup, a little at a time, into the egg whites, beating constantly. When the syrup is thoroughly incorporated, beat continuously until smooth. Set the bowl over a bowl of ice and continue to beat until the mixture is thick and cool. Fold the meringue into the whipped cream.

Spoon the mixture into a 2-quart mold or bowl and freeze for about 2 hours. Set an empty bowl in the freezer to be used later.

When the meringue mixture has set around the edges, take the mold and the empty bowl from the freezer. Scoop out the center of the frozen mixture, leaving about 1 inch on the sides and bottom. Place the scooped mixture into the chilled bowl and add the chopped macadamia nut brittle and 1 cup of the vanilla custard sauce. Mix well.

Pour the mixture back into the mold and spread to level it off. Return to the freezer for 2 or 3 hours. The center should not be as hard as the edges and should remain a little creamy.

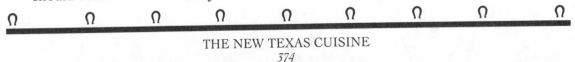

Invert the frozen bowl onto a large plate and place a hot, wet towel around the bowl for 1 minute to release the bombe. Slice into 10 portions and serve each over the remaining vanilla custard sauce. Garnish with the macerated fruit.

MACADAMIA NUT BRITTLE
ABOUT 1 CUP

½ cup macadamia nuts
½ cup sugar

3 tablespoons water

Preheat the oven to 350° F. Place the macadamia nuts on a baking sheet and brown slightly in the oven, about 3 minutes. Place the sugar and water in a saucepan, bring to a boil, and cook over high heat until a candy thermometer registers about 350° F. and the mixture is a mahogany brown, about 8 minutes.

Immediately add the warmed macadamia nuts to the caramel and stir over the heat for a few seconds to distribute the nuts evenly. Pour the caramel onto a lightly oiled pan, spreading the caramel with a spatula. Set aside to cool and harden. Chop finely, or break up and place in a food processor and grind for 5 to 10 seconds.

VANILLA CUSTARD SAUCE
ABOUT 4 CUPS

2 cups milk
1 vanilla bean, split in half lengthwise
⅔ cup sugar

6 egg yolks
¾ cup heavy cream or Crème Fraîche
(see Index), chilled

In a saucepan, bring the milk to a boil with the vanilla bean. Remove from the heat, cover, and let infuse for 15 minutes.

In a mixing bowl, add the sugar to the yolks while whisking. Continue to whisk until the yolks have lightened in color. Bring the milk back to a boil. While

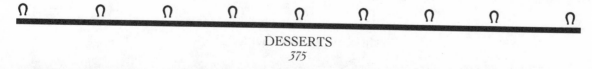

stirring, pour the milk slowly through a strainer into the yolks. Discard the vanilla bean.

Pour the strained mixture back into the saucepan and cook over low heat, while stirring constantly with a wooden spatula. Scrape down the sides and bottom of the pan, and continue to cook until the mixture registers 185° F. on a candy thermometer and has thickened considerably, about 5 to 10 minutes. Immediately remove from the heat and place over ice. Stir in the chilled cream or crème fraîche and let chill thoroughly in the refrigerator.

PECAN SOUFFLÉ WITH BOURBON BUTTER

Although soufflés seem to have gone out of style and lost favor on American dessert menus, I believe there are times when nothing makes a meal more special than a soufflé, if only because of the time and effort involved. This recipe is very Southern, and the pecans and whiskey make a terrific pairing.

4 SERVINGS

1 cup milk
½ vanilla bean, split lengthwise
3 egg yolks
⅓ cup plus 2 tablespoons granulated sugar
1 tablespoon flour
1½ tablespoons cornstarch

5 ounces pecans, toasted and finely chopped (page 9)
4 egg whites, at room temperature
Confectioners' sugar
Bourbon Butter (recipe follows)

Preheat the oven to 375° F. Butter and lightly sugar a deep soufflé mold 8 inches wide and 2½ inches deep, or four ½-cup individual molds.

Pour the milk into a small saucepan and bring to a boil with the vanilla. Remove from the heat and set aside. With an electric mixer, or by hand, beat the yolks in a mixing bowl while gradually adding ⅓ cup granulated sugar. Continue beating until the yolks have lightened in color. Sift together the flour and cornstarch, and fold into the yolk mixture.

Slowly pour the scalded milk into the yolk mixture and stir to blend. Pour the mixture back into the saucepan and return to medium heat. With a flat-bottomed wooden spoon, stir the mixture until it reaches a boil. Cook for 1 minute, scraping down the sides and bottom of the pan constantly. When the mixture thickens, remove from the heat and add the pecans.

Beat the egg whites to form soft peaks. Gradually add the 2 tablespoons sugar, and continue beating for 1 minute. Fold one quarter of the egg whites into the pecan pastry cream and incorporate completely. Gently fold in the remaining egg whites just until blended.

Pour the mixture into the prepared soufflé mold and bake for 20 minutes, or 15 minutes if using individual molds. (Note: the soufflé mixture may be kept in molds for up to 1 hour before baking). Sprinkle the confectioners' sugar on top of the soufflé, cut the top of the soufflé with a spoon, and pour the bourbon butter over.

BOURBON BUTTER
ABOUT 1 CUP

4 tablespoons unsalted butter, diced
⅓ cup sugar
1 small egg

¼ cup bourbon whiskey
¼ cup heavy cream

Melt the butter in a double boiler set over simmering water. Beat the sugar and egg together for 1 minute and add to the butter. Stir the mixture until the sugar dissolves completely (½ tablespoon of very hot water may be added to hasten the dissolving process).

Remove the top part of the double boiler and let cool to room temperature. Stir in the whiskey and cream, and mix thoroughly.

WHITE CHOCOLATE–RICE PUDDING TAMALES WITH RUM CREAM

When I was invited to prepare dinners in Tokyo at the Palace Hotel in 1991, this dish seemed to baffle the cooks there more than any other. Perhaps this was because no sooner had I got them used to the concept of using corn husks in savory dishes than I introduced them to this unusual dessert!

6 SERVINGS

½ cup uncooked Arborio rice
1 cup water
3 tablespoons sugar
2 eggs, lightly beaten
1 cup heavy cream
¼ cup milk
½ teaspoon vanilla extract
½ teaspoon ground cinnamon

¼ teaspoon grated nutmeg
¼ cup golden raisins, soaked in rum
¼ cup dried cherries, soaked in kirsch
¾ cup grated white chocolate
13 corn husks, soaked in water for at least 30 minutes
Rum Cream (recipe follows)

Preheat the oven to 300° F. In a saucepan, cook the rice in the water with 2 tablespoons of the sugar. When the rice is cooked, spoon it into a mixing bowl, add the eggs, cream, milk, vanilla, cinnamon, nutmeg, the remaining tablespoon of sugar, raisins, and dried cherries, and mix thoroughly.

Pour the mixture into a small baking pan and cover with foil. Bake in the oven for 20 minutes. Remove from the oven, stir thoroughly, and let cool. Mix in the grated white chocolate.

Drain the corn husks and pat dry. Tear six ¼-inch strips from one of the husks; these strips will be used to tie the tamales. Place 2 husks together with large ends overlapping by about 2 inches. Spread about 6 tablespoons of the rice pudding mixture down the middle of the corn husks, leaving 1 inch at each end uncovered.

Roll the corn husks so that the filling is completely enclosed (as for a crêpe). Twist and tie each end of the tamale with the strips from the corn husks. Repeat the procedure for the remaining tamales.

Place the tamales in a steamer set over gently boiling water and steam for 5 to 7 minutes. Remove the tamales; slice them from end to end with a knife. Push the ends together, as for a baked potato. Pour some of the rum cream into each tamale.

RUM CREAM

ABOUT 1 CUP

1 egg yolk	*1 cup heavy cream*
¼ cup sugar	*1 tablespoon dark rum*

In a mixing bowl, beat the egg yolk and sugar together and set aside. In a saucepan, bring the cream and rum to a boil and pour half of the mixture into the yolk mixture. Beating vigorously, put the remaining cream mixture in the pan back over the heat. Slowly pour the egg mixture in the mixing bowl into the saucepan, whisking vigorously until incorporated. Cook until the mixture smoothly coats the back of a spoon, about 5 minutes. Strain and cool.

CINNAMON COUSCOUS CRÈME BRÛLÉE
WITH CANDIED GINGER

I recently took a culinary tour of Morocco. Wherever I traveled, after every meal and before dessert, I would be served a large mound of couscous with steamed vegetables. I was left wondering why couscous was not incorporated into other dishes or different parts of the meal. On returning to this country, I decided to experiment with couscous as a dessert. The addition of couscous to crème brûlée results in an interesting texture akin to rice pudding, and an excellent medium for other flavors.

8 SERVINGS

CINNAMON COUSCOUS:
6 tablespoons milk
1 cinnamon stick
Pinch of salt
½ cup uncooked couscous
1 tablespoon unsalted butter
½ teaspoon ground cinnamon

BRÛLÉE:
8 ounces fresh ginger, peeled and thinly sliced
8 egg yolks
14 tablespoons (7 ounces) sugar
3 cups heavy cream
½ vanilla bean, split in half lengthwise

8 teaspoons candied ginger, for garnish

To prepare the couscous, bring the milk to a boil in a saucepan and add the cinnamon stick. Remove from the heat, cover, and infuse for 15 minutes. Remove the cinnamon stick and discard. Add the salt and return to a boil. Remove the pan from the heat again and add the couscous all at once, stirring until all the liquid is absorbed. Incorporate the butter with a fork, breaking up any lumps, and add the ground cinnamon. Combine thoroughly.

To prepare the brûlée, place the ginger in a saucepan and cover with water. Bring to a boil, boil for 30 seconds, and drain, reserving the blanched ginger.

In a large heatproof bowl set over gently simmering water, whisk the egg yolks and 6 tablespoons of the sugar vigorously until the mixture thickens, forms a ribbon, and resembles a thick hollandaise sauce. Take the bowl off the heat briefly if the mixture gets too hot and starts to cook too quickly around the edges; however, it is essential that the yolks be warmed through.

In a saucepan, bring the cream to a boil with the vanilla bean and blanched ginger. Slowly strain into the yolks while stirring. Cook over barely simmering water for 40 to 45 minutes, stirring occasionally, until the custard is slightly thickened. The heat should be very low and the custard should never be too hot to the touch. The mixture is cooked when it heavily coats the back of a spoon. Strain through a fine-mesh strainer into a bowl set over ice. Fold in the couscous.

Chill the crème brûlée, stirring occasionally. When chilled, spoon the brûlée into ½-cup ramekins and refrigerate for at least 2 hours.

Sprinkle the remaining 8 tablespoons of sugar evenly over each brûlèe (1 tablespoon per brûlée). Caramelize with a propane torch or under a broiler until the sugar browns. Return to the refrigerator for 20 to 30 minutes to allow the brûlées to reset. Garnish each portion with a teaspoon of candied ginger.

MARGARITA MOUSSE WITH CANDIED LIME SLICES

Try this wonderful dessert after eating fajitas or other Southwestern dishes that might be accompanied by margaritas. For a little added texture, serve with one or more of the cookies, such as Cinnamon Cactus Cookies (page 385).

8 SERVINGS

¼ cup cold water
1 teaspoon unflavored powered gelatin
¼ teaspoon salt
½ cup fresh lime juice
1½ teaspoons minced lime zest, blanched in boiling water for 30 seconds

3 tablespoons Triple Sec
¼ cup tequila
4 eggs, separated
⅔ cup sugar, plus extra for glasses
Candied Lime Slices (recipe follows), for garnish

Pour the water into a metal measuring cup and sprinkle the gelatin over it. Let the liquid stand for 4 to 5 minutes, until spongy. Stand the cup in a water bath with simmering water until the gelatin becomes clear and dissolves, about 2 minutes.

In a mixing bowl placed over iced water, combine the gelatin liquid, salt, lime juice, blanched lime zest, Triple Sec, and tequila. Stir until the mixture is the consistency of unbeaten egg whites, about 10 minutes.

In another bowl, beat the egg yolks with ⅓ cup of sugar for 4 to 5 minutes, or until they're thickened and a ribbon forms. Stir thoroughly into the gelatin mixture.

In a separate bowl, beat the egg whites until they form stiff peaks. Slowly add the remaining ⅓ cup of sugar. Beat until the whites are firm and shiny, and fold into the egg yolk mixture. Turn into margarita glasses with sugar on the rim. Garnish the rims with candied lime slices cut to fit. Alternatively, turn the mousse into a well-oiled 6-cup mold or decorative glass bowl. Chill for at least 2 hours, until firm.

CANDIED LIME SLICES

2 limes
1 cup water

⅔ cup sugar

Cut the limes into very thin slices. In a saucepan, bring the water and sugar to a boil. Add the lime slices, reduce the heat, and simmer uncovered very slowly, for 2 hours. Remove from the heat, pour the syrup and limes into a bowl, and refrigerate overnight. Remove the slices from the bowl and serve.

BABY ROUTH BANANA SPLIT
WITH "THE WORKS"

Friends joke that the real reason I opened Baby Routh was that I could enjoy a banana split! It's been on the menu since the day we opened, and I can guarantee it will remain there in perpetuity. This banana split makes the perfect entrée for a child's birthday party, or a perfect ending to a meal for adult children.

8 SERVINGS

2 cups heavy cream
4 tablespoons confectioners' sugar
2 tablespoons vanilla extract
8 bananas
1 pint Vanilla Bean Ice Cream (see Index)
1 pint Strawberry Ice Cream (see Index)
1 pint Dried Cherry–Chocolate Chip Ice Cream (see Index)
½ cup warm Butterscotch Sauce (recipe follows)
½ cup warm Strawberry Sauce (recipe follows)

1 cup Hot Fudge Sauce (recipe follows)

GARNISHES:
1 cup finely chopped mixed nuts, such as macadamias, pecans, hazelnuts, walnuts, and peanuts
2 cups seasonal berries
8 cookies, such as Cinnamon Cactus, Chocolate Chip, or Maple Pecan (see Index)
8 mint sprigs

In a medium mixing bowl set over a larger bowl of ice and water, whip the cream with an electric mixer. Sprinkle in the sugar and continue to whip until the mixture resembles thin sour cream. Add the vanilla and whip until soft peaks form; do not overwhip. Keep refrigerated.

Peel the bananas and slice in half lengthwise; place each in an "au gratin" dish. Using a 1½-ounce ice cream scoop, place 1 scoop of each flavor of ice cream in the center of each dish, between the banana halves. Drizzle each split with 1 tablespoon butterscotch sauce, 1 tablespoon strawberry sauce, and 2 tablespoons hot fudge sauce.

Using a pastry bag, pipe the whipped cream around the sides of the dish. Garnish each dish with mixed nuts, berries, a cookie, and a sprig of mint.

BUTTERSCOTCH SAUCE

ABOUT 1¾ CUPS

½ cup heavy cream
½ cup light brown sugar
½ cup granulated sugar

¼ cup unsalted butter
1 teaspoon vanilla extract

In a saucepan, heat the cream and both sugars over low heat. Allow to melt slowly, and when melted, add the butter, whisking in to incorporate thoroughly. Remove from the heat and add the vanilla. Strain the sauce through a fine-mesh sieve. Keep warm.

STRAWBERRY SAUCE

ABOUT 2 CUPS

2 cups strawberries, washed and quartered
1 cup sugar

2 tablespoons Grand Marnier

Place 1 cup of the strawberries in a blender together with the sugar and Grand Marnier. Puree and transfer to a saucepan with the remaining cup of strawberries. Bring to a boil and simmer for 30 seconds while stirring. Keep warm.

HOT FUDGE SAUCE

ABOUT 1 CUP

⅓ cup light corn syrup
¼ cup water
¾ cup sugar
¼ cup unsweetened cocoa powder

1 tablespoon chopped unsweetened chocolate
2 tablespoons unsalted butter
⅓ cup heavy cream

In a small saucepan, boil the corn syrup for 1 minute. Stir in the water; be careful, as the mixture may spatter.

In a mixing bowl, sift together the sugar and cocoa. Stir into the corn syrup mixture. Bring to a boil, stirring until the sugar is dissolved. Add the chocolate and butter, and whisk until melted. Add the cream and return to a boil. Remove from the heat.

The sauce can be prepared a day ahead; reheat gently.

ASSORTED COOKIE PLATE

This book would not be complete without at least a few cookie recipes, as I confess to a particular weakness for cookies. Just as when I was eight years old, there's still no better cure for being down than a plate of warm cookies and a glass of milk. Perhaps it was no coincidence that our offices adjoined the bakery for Routh Street Cafe and Baby Routh. First thing in the morning, and last thing at night, I had to pass through the bakery, which was a good excuse for a little hands-on cookie quality control! Some mornings Kirk, our Pastry Chef, left a plate of cookies on my desk . . . now that's what I call an occupational hazard!

CINNAMON CACTUS COOKIES

Cactus-shaped cookie cutters can be obtained from Williams-Sonoma or other specialty stores.

ABOUT 2 DOZEN COOKIES

8 tablespoons (1 stick) unsalted butter,
at room temperature
1 cup sugar
1 egg plus 1 egg yolk
1 teaspoon vanilla extract
1²/₃ cup flour

¹/₂ teaspoon baking soda
¹/₂ teaspoon salt
¹/₄ teaspoon ground cloves
¹/₄ teaspoon grated nutmeg
1 tablespoon ground cinnamon

In a mixing bowl, combine the butter and ¾ cup of the sugar and beat until blended. Add the egg, yolk, and vanilla, and beat until light and fluffy.

Sift together the remaining dry ingredients except cinnamon. Add to the butter and egg mixture, and mix until the dough is thoroughly blended. Cover the dough with plastic wrap and chill for 30 minutes.

Preheat the oven to 375° F. Lightly oil a cookie sheet. Combine the remaining ¼ cup of sugar and the cinnamon. Roll out the cookie dough on a lightly floured surface to a ½-inch thickness. Cut out the cookies with a 3-inch-long cactus-shaped cookie cutter. Sprinkle with the cinnamon-sugar mixture and place on the prepared cookie sheet. Bake for 5 to 7 minutes, until lightly browned.

CHOCOLATE CHIP COOKIES

ABOUT 20 COOKIES

1 cup plus 2 tablespoons flour　　*⅓ cup light brown sugar*
½ teaspoon baking soda　　*⅓ cup granulated sugar*
Pinch of salt　　*1 egg*
8 tablespoons (1 stick) unsalted butter　　*1 cup chocolate chips*

Preheat the oven to 325° F. Butter and lightly flour a cookie sheet.

In a mixing bowl, sift together the flour, baking soda, and salt. In an electric mixer (or by hand in a separate bowl), cream the butter and both sugars together. Add the egg and thoroughly incorporate. With the mixer running at low speed, gradually add the sifted dry ingredients and mix until incorporated. Fold in the chocolate chips.

Spoon the mixture onto the prepared cookie sheet in 2-tablespoon portions. Bake in the oven for 20 minutes, until golden brown.

MAPLE PECAN COOKIES

ABOUT 30 COOKIES

1 cup (2 sticks) unsalted butter, at
room temperature
½ cup sugar
1 egg yolk

3 tablespoons pure maple syrup
1 teaspoon vanilla extract
1¾ cups flour
1¼ cups toasted pecans (page 9)

Preheat the oven to 325° F. Butter and lightly flour a cookie sheet.

In an electric mixer (or in a mixing bowl, by hand), cream the butter and sugar together. Add the egg yolk and beat in, and then mix in the syrup and vanilla. With the mixer running at low speed, gradually add the flour and mix until incorporated. Sprinkle in the pecans and combine thoroughly.

Spoon the mixture onto the prepared cookie sheet in 2-tablespoon portions. Bake in the oven for 20 minutes, until golden brown.

CHAPTER FIFTEEN

ICE CREAM AND ICES

It's hard to imagine making it through a hot Texas summer without frozen desserts. Ice creams and ices are by no means seasonal, but the heat of summer and the availability and quality of fresh fruit of all kinds make it the most obvious time of year to indulge in these desserts. In the South in general, and Texas in particular, finishing a meal or picnic with home-churned ice cream is an important tradition. And wherever you are, after a rich meal, there is nothing more satisfying than a simple sorbet or ice.

When I was growing up in West Texas, all my relatives claimed to have the best recipe for homemade ice cream. While this friendly competition was mainly limited to the women in the family, some of the men fiercely defended their skill (the culinary expertise of the males in my extended family seemed limited somehow to barbecue, chili, grilling, and ice cream). My family's ice cream recipes were not, for the most part, as rich as those included here, which is partly because mine have been influenced by French techniques and ingredients.

The ice creams of my childhood usually were not cooked. I have added a recipe for uncooked cream, but my preference is for recipes that involve cooking since this enhances the consistency and flavor of the finished product. You'll notice in many of the recipes I've added sour cream or crème fraîche at the end after cooking the custard. This introduces a pleasant acidity that balances the rich sweetness of the ice cream. I love to combine flavors that shock the taste buds; for example, by using chiles or spices such as clove.

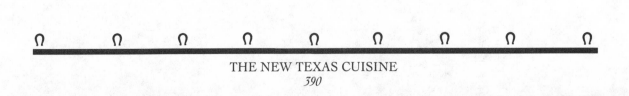

VANILLA BEAN ICE CREAM

Sometimes you crave nothing more complicated than plain vanilla ice cream. The best vanilla beans should be supple, moist, and plump; my favorite type are the Tahitian beans. Try to avoid bottled vanilla beans if at all possible. If vanilla beans are unavailable, you can use vanilla extract in this recipe; however, the appearance and texture will be different, as the tiny black seeds will be absent.

Use this recipe as the base for any fruit-flavored ice cream; simply puree and strain the fruit of choice into the ice cream before adding to the ice cream maker.

ABOUT 1 QUART

2 cups milk
1 vanilla bean, split in half lengthwise and scraped, or 2 teaspoons vanilla extract
⅔ cup sugar

6 egg yolks
¾ sour cream or Crème Fraîche (see Index), chilled

Have ready 1 large bowl filled with ice, and a smaller clean bowl.

In a medium saucepan, bring the milk to a boil with the vanilla bean or extract. Remove from the heat, cover, and let infuse for 15 minutes.

Meanwhile, in a mixing bowl, add the sugar to the yolks while whisking. Continue to whisk until the yolks lighten in color and form a ribbon. Bring the milk mixture back to a boil and gradually pour through a strainer into the yolks, stirring with a spatula. Discard the vanilla bean.

Pour the mixture into a clean saucepan and cook over low heat, continuing to stir. Scrape the sides and bottom of the pan, and continue cooking until the custard thickens and reaches 185° F. on a candy thermometer, and coats the back of a spoon, about 5 to 10 minutes. Do not let the mixture boil.

Immediately remove the pan from heat, strain mixture into the clean bowl, and set over the bowl of ice. Stir in the cream or Crème Fraîche and let chill thoroughly in the refrigerator. Place into an ice cream machine and freeze according to the manufacturer's directions.

GINGER ICE CREAM

ABOUT 1 QUART

12 ounces fresh ginger, peeled and minced
1 cup milk
1 cup heavy cream
½ vanilla bean, split in half lengthwise and scraped, or 1 teaspoon vanilla extract

⅓ cup sugar
4 egg yolks
½ cup sour cream or Crème Fraîche (see Index)

Have ready 1 large bowl filled with ice, and a smaller clean bowl.

Blanch the ginger in boiling water for 30 seconds, and drain well. In a medium saucepan, bring the milk and cream to a boil with the blanched ginger and vanilla bean or extract. Remove from the heat, cover, and let infuse for 30 minutes.

Meanwhile, in a mixing bowl, add the sugar to the yolks while whisking. Continue to whisk until the yolks lighten in color and form a ribbon. Bring the milk mixture back to a boil and gradually pour it through a strainer into the yolks, stirring with a spatula. Discard the ginger and vanilla bean.

Pour the mixture into a clean saucepan and cook over low heat, continuing to stir. Scrape the sides and bottom of the pan, and continue cooking until the custard thickens and reaches 185° F. on a candy thermometer, and coats the back of a spoon, about 5 to 10 minutes. Do not let the mixture boil.

Immediately remove the pan from the heat, strain mixture into the clean bowl, and set over the bowl of ice. Stir in the sour cream or Crème Fraîche and let chill thoroughly in the refrigerator. Place into an ice cream machine and freeze according to the manufacturer's directions.

PECAN ICE CREAM

ABOUT 1 QUART

2 cups milk
1 cup chopped roasted pecans (page 9)
1 vanilla bean, split in half lengthwise and scraped, or 2 teaspoons vanilla extract

⅔ cup sugar
6 egg yolks
¾ cup sour cream or Crème Fraîche (see Index), chilled

Have ready 1 large bowl filled with ice, and a smaller clean bowl.

In a medium saucepan, bring the milk to a boil with the pecans and vanilla bean or extract. Remove from the heat, cover, and let infuse for 15 minutes.

Meanwhile, in a mixing bowl, add the sugar to the yolks while whisking. Continue to whisk until the yolks lighten in color and form a ribbon. Bring the milk mixture back to a boil and gradually pour through a strainer into the yolks, stirring with a spatula. Discard the pecans and vanilla bean.

Pour the mixture into a clean saucepan and cook over low heat, continuing to stir. Scrape the sides and bottom of the pan, and continue cooking until the custard thickens and reaches 185° F. on a candy thermometer, and coats the back of a spoon, about 5 to 10 minutes. Do not let the mixture boil.

Immediately remove the pan from the heat, strain mixture into the clean bowl, and set over the bowl of ice. Stir in the sour cream or Crème Fraîche and let chill thoroughly in the refrigerator. Place into an ice cream machine and freeze according to the manufacturer's directions.

PRALINE ICE CREAM

ABOUT 1 QUART

3 cups heavy cream
1 cup milk
¾ cup sugar
½ vanilla bean, split lengthwise and scraped,
or 1 teaspoon vanilla extract

4 egg yolks
1 cup chopped Pecan Pralines (recipe follows)

Have ready 1 large bowl filled with ice, and a smaller clean bowl.

In a medium saucepan, heat the cream, milk, sugar, and vanilla bean or extract, stirring occasionally, until the sugar is dissolved and the mixture is hot. Remove from the heat, cover, and let infuse for 15 minutes, if using the vanilla bean. If using vanilla extract, proceed with the recipe.

Meanwhile, in a mixing bowl, whisk the egg yolks for about 30 seconds. Gradually pour about 1 cup of the cream mixture through a strainer into the yolks, stirring with a spatula.

Pour the mixture into a clean saucepan together with the remaining cream mixture, and cook over low heat, continuing to stir. Scrape the sides and bottom of the pan, and continue cooking until the custard thickens and reaches 185° F. on a candy thermometer, and coats the back of a spoon, about 5 to 10 minutes. Do not let the mixture boil.

Immediately remove the pan from the heat, strain mixture into the clean bowl, and set over the bowl of ice, stirring the mixture occasionally. Place into an ice cream machine and freeze according to the manufacturer's directions. When almost frozen, fold in the chopped pralines and continue to churn for 3 to 5 minutes.

PECAN PRALINES

16–18 PRALINES

6 tablespoons butter
½ cup sugar
½ cup light brown sugar, packed
2 tablespoons corn syrup

¾ cup cream
1½ cups pecan pieces
1 teaspoon vanilla extract
1 teaspoon orange zest

In a large, heavy saucepan, melt the butter over high heat. As soon as it has melted, add the sugars, corn syrup, and cream. Cook, 1 minute, whisking constantly. Add the pecan pieces and cook 4 minutes more, whisking constantly. Reduce heat to medium and continue cooking and whisking 5 minutes longer. Add the vanilla and orange zest and continue whisking and cooking until done, about 15 to 20 minutes longer. If using a candy thermometer, it should read about 240° F.

Remove pan from heat. Quickly and carefully drop the batter onto a cookie sheet by heaping spoonfuls, using the second spoon to scoop the batter off the first. The pralines should be about 2 inches wide and ½ inch thick. Cool, then store in an airtight container.

CARAMEL ICE CREAM

ABOUT 1 QUART

¾ cup sugar
½ cup boiling water
1 cup heavy cream
1 cup milk

1 teaspoon vanilla extract
4 egg yolks
¾ cup sour cream or Crème Fraîche
(see Index), chilled

Have ready 1 large bowl filled with ice, and a smaller clean bowl.

In a medium saucepan, stir the sugar over medium heat until dissolved, smooth, and golden brown. Remove the pan from the heat and pour in the boiling water. Stir over medium heat until smooth. Continue to cook for 8 to 10 minutes, until the caramel is the texture of corn syrup. Stir in the heavy cream, the milk, and vanilla extract. Bring to a boil, remove from the heat, and cover.

In a mixing bowl, whisk the egg yolks for 2 minutes. Gradually pour the caramel cream through a strainer into the yolks, stirring with a spatula.

Pour the mixture into a clean saucepan and cook over low heat, continuing to stir. Scrape the sides and bottom of the pan, and continue cooking until the custard thickens and reaches 185° F. on a candy thermometer, and coats the back of a spoon, about 5 to 10 minutes.

Immediately remove the pan from the heat, strain mixture into the clean bowl, and set over the bowl of ice. Stir in the sour cream or Crème Fraîche and let chill thoroughly in the refrigerator. Place into an ice cream machine and freeze according to the manufacturer's directions.

Texas State Fair

Left: Seafood harvest in South Padre Island restaurant

Right: Shrimping boats in Corpus Christi

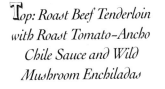

Top: *Roast Beef Tenderloin with Roast Tomato–Ancho Chile Sauce and Wild Mushroom Enchiladas*

Bottom: *Pork Tenderloin with Dried Cherry Sauce and Creamed Pine Nuts*

Scenes from Fiesta in San Antonio

Barbecue pit at The Salt Lick near Dripping Springs

*Top: Corn and Red Pepper
Soups with Southern Creams*

*Bottom: Smoked Duck Salad
with Chayote, Mango, and
Fried Cayenne Pasta*

MACADAMIA NUT ICE CREAM

ABOUT 1 QUART

1½ cups roasted macadamia nuts (page 9)
2¼ cups milk
½ vanilla bean, split lengthwise and scraped,
or 1 teaspoon vanilla extract

1 cup sugar
6 egg yolks
¾ cup sour cream or Crème Fraîche (see Index),
chilled

Have ready 1 large bowl filled with ice, and a smaller clean bowl.

In a food processor, puree the macadamia nuts with ¼ cup of the milk to make a paste. Set aside.

In a saucepan, bring the remaining 2 cups milk and the vanilla bean or extract to a boil. Stir in the nut paste, remove from the heat, and cover. Let infuse for 15 minutes.

Meanwhile, in a mixing bowl, add the sugar to the yolks while whisking. Continue to whisk until the yolks lighten in color and form a ribbon. Bring the milk mixture back to a boil and gradually pour through a strainer into the yolks, stirring with a spatula.

Pour the mixture into a clean saucepan and cook over low heat, continuing to stir. Scrape the sides and bottom of the pan, and continue cooking until the custard thickens and reaches 185° F. on a candy thermometer and coats the back of a spoon, about 5 to 10 minutes. Do not let the mixture boil.

Immediately remove the pan from the heat, strain mixture into the clean bowl, and set over the bowl of ice. Stir in the sour cream or Crème Fraîche and let chill thoroughly in the refrigerator. Place into an ice cream machine and freeze according to the manufacturer's directions.

HAZELNUT ICE CREAM

ABOUT 1 QUART

1½ cups roasted hazelnuts (page 9)
1 cup milk
1 cup heavy cream
½ vanilla bean, split lengthwise and scraped,
or 1 teaspoon vanilla extract

⅔ cup sugar
3 egg yolks
¾ cup sour cream or Crème Fraîche
(see Index), chilled

Have ready 1 large bowl filled with ice, and a smaller clean bowl.

Rub the roasted hazelnuts by handfuls in a rough towel to remove the loose skins. Transfer to a food processor and grind the nuts almost to a paste.

In a saucepan, bring the milk, heavy cream, vanilla bean or extract, and the hazelnuts to a boil. Remove from the heat and cover. Let infuse for 15 minutes.

Meanwhile, in a mixing bowl, add the sugar to the yolks while whisking. Continue to whisk until the yolks lighten in color and a form a ribbon. Bring the milk mixture back to a boil and gradually pour through a strainer into the yolks, stirring with a spatula.

Pour the mixture into a clean saucepan and cook over low heat, continuing to stir. Scrape the sides and bottom of the pan, and continue cooking until the custard thickens and reaches 185° F. on a candy thermometer, and coats the back of a spoon, about 5 to 10 minutes. Do not let the mixture boil.

Immediately remove the pan from the heat, strain mixture into the clean bowl, and set over the bowl of ice. Stir in the sour cream or Crème Fraîche and let chill thoroughly in the refrigerator. Place into an ice cream machine and freeze according to the manufacturer's directions.

ALMOND ICE CREAM

ABOUT 1 QUART

2 cups milk
1 cup chopped roasted almonds (page 9)
1 vanilla bean, split in half lengthwise and
scraped, or 2 teaspoons vanilla extract

⅔ cup sugar
6 egg yolks
¾ cup sour cream or Crème Fraîche (see Index),
chilled

Have ready 1 large bowl filled with ice, and a smaller clean bowl.

In a medium saucepan, bring the milk to a boil with the almonds and vanilla bean or extract. Remove from the heat, cover, and let infuse for 15 minutes.

Meanwhile, in a mixing bowl, add the sugar to the yolks while whisking. Continue to whisk until the yolks lighten in color and form a ribbon. Bring the milk mixture back to a boil and gradually pour through a strainer into the yolks, stirring with a spatula. Discard the almonds and vanilla bean.

Pour the mixture into a clean saucepan and cook over low heat, continuing to stir. Scrape the sides and bottom of the pan, and continue cooking until the custard thickens and reaches 185° F. on a candy thermometer, and coats the back of a spoon, about 5 to 10 minutes. Do not let the mixture boil.

Immediately remove the pan from the heat, strain mixture into the clean bowl, and set over the bowl of ice. Stir in the sour cream or Crème Fraîche and let chill thoroughly in the refrigerator. Place into an ice cream machine and freeze according to the manufacturer's directions.

BUTTERMILK-CINNAMON ICE CREAM

ABOUT 1¾ QUARTS

2 cups heavy cream
4 cinnamon sticks
⅔ cup sugar

2 eggs, plus 4 egg yolks
1 quart goat or cow buttermilk

Have ready 1 large bowl filled with ice, and a smaller clean bowl.

In a medium saucepan, bring the cream to a boil with the cinnamon sticks. Remove from the heat, cover, and let infuse for 30 minutes.

Meanwhile, in a mixing bowl, add the sugar to the eggs and yolks while whisking. Continue to whisk until the eggs lighten in color and form a ribbon. Bring the milk mixture back to a boil and gradually pour through a strainer into the yolks, stirring with a spatula. Discard the cinnamon sticks.

Pour the mixture into a clean saucepan and cook over low heat, continuing to stir. Scrape the sides and bottom of the pan, and continue cooking until the custard thickens and reaches 185° F. on a candy thermometer, and coats the back of a spoon, about 5 to 10 minutes. Do not let the mixture boil.

Immediately remove the pan from the heat, strain mixture into the clean bowl, and set over the bowl of ice. Stir in the buttermilk and let chill thoroughly in the refrigerator. Place into an ice cream machine and freeze according to the manufacturer's directions.

BANANA, RUM, AND BLACK WALNUT
ICE CREAM

ABOUT 1 QUART

1½ cups milk
½ cup heavy cream
½ vanilla bean, split lengthwise and scraped, or
1 teaspoon vanilla extract
⅔ cup sugar

4 egg yolks
5 medium very ripe bananas
2 tablespoons dark rum
¾ cup finely chopped black walnuts

Have ready 1 large bowl filled with ice, and a smaller clean bowl.

In a medium saucepan, bring the milk and cream to a boil with the vanilla bean or extract. Remove from the heat, cover, and let infuse for 15 minutes if using the vanilla bean. If using vanilla extract, proceed with the recipe.

Meanwhile, in a mixing bowl, add the sugar to the yolks while whisking. Continue to whisk until the yolks lighten in color and form a ribbon. Bring the milk mixture back to a boil and gradually pour through a strainer into the yolks, stirring with a spatula. Discard the vanilla bean.

Pour the mixture into a clean saucepan and cook over low heat, continuing to stir. Scrape the sides and bottom of the pan, and continue cooking until the custard thickens and reaches 185° F. on a candy thermometer, and coats the back of a spoon, about 5 to 10 minutes. Do not let the mixture boil.

Immediately remove the pan from the heat, strain mixture into the clean bowl, and set over the bowl of ice. While the custard is cooling, peel and puree the bananas in a food processor. Whisk into the custard and let chill thoroughly in the refrigerator. Place into an ice cream machine and freeze according to the manufacturer's directions. After about 15 minutes, fold in the rum and walnuts, and continue to churn until frozen.

STRAWBERRY ICE CREAM

ABOUT 1 QUART

2½ pints strawberries, stemmed, cleaned, and sliced
½ cup sugar
2 cups milk
1 teaspoon orange zest

½ vanilla bean, split lengthwise and scraped, or
1 teaspoon vanilla extract
6 egg yolks
¼ cup sour cream or Crème Fraîche (see Index)

Have ready 1 large bowl filled with ice, and a smaller clean bowl.

In a medium saucepan, cook the strawberries and ¼ cup of the sugar over medium heat for 15 to 20 minutes, to a jamlike consistency. Transfer to a blender, puree, and set aside.

In another saucepan, bring the milk to a boil with the orange zest and vanilla bean. Remove from the heat, cover, and let infuse for 15 minutes.

Meanwhile, in a mixing bowl, add the remaining ¼ cup of sugar to the yolks while whisking. Continue to whisk until the yolks lighten in color and form a ribbon. Bring the milk mixture back to a boil and gradually pour through a strainer into the yolks, stirring with a spatula. Discard the orange zest and vanilla bean or extract.

Pour the mixture into a clean saucepan and cook over low heat, continuing to stir. Scrape the sides and bottom of the pan, and continue cooking until the custard thickens and reaches 185° F. on a candy thermometer, and coats the back of a spoon, about 5 to 10 minutes. Do not let the mixture boil.

Immediately remove the pan from the heat, strain mixture into the clean bowl, and set over the bowl of ice. Stir in the sour cream or Crème Fraîche and let chill thoroughly in the refrigerator. When chilled, fold in the strawberry puree. Place into an ice cream machine and freeze according to the manufacturer's directions.

DRIED CHERRY–CHOCOLATE CHIP
ICE CREAM

ABOUT 1 QUART

2 cups milk
1 vanilla bean, split in half lengthwise and
scraped, or 2 teaspoons vanilla extract
⅔ cup sugar
6 egg yolks
¾ cup sour cream or Crème Fraîche (see Index),
chilled

1½ cups dried tart cherries, soaked in port for
2 hours and drained
6 ounces bittersweet chocolate, chopped into chips
(about 1½ cups)

Have ready 1 large bowl filled with ice, and a smaller clean bowl.

In a medium saucepan, bring the milk to a boil with the vanilla bean or extract. Remove from the heat, cover, and let infuse for 15 minutes if using the vanilla bean. If using vanilla extract, proceed with the recipe.

Meanwhile, in a mixing bowl, add the sugar to the yolks while whisking. Continue to whisk until the yolks lighten in color and form a ribbon. Bring the milk mixture back to a boil and gradually pour through a strainer into the yolks, stirring with a spatula. Discard the vanilla bean.

Pour the mixture into a clean saucepan and cook over low heat, continuing to stir. Scrape the sides and bottom of the pan, and continue cooking until the custard thickens and reaches 185° F. on a candy thermometer, and coats the back of a spoon, about 5 to 10 minutes. Do not let the mixture boil.

Immediately remove the pan from the heat, strain mixture into the clean bowl, and set over the bowl of ice. Stir in the sour cream or Crème Fraîche and let chill thoroughly in the refrigerator. Place into an ice cream machine and freeze according to the manufacturer's directions. After about 15 minutes, fold in the soaked cherries and chocolate chips, and continue to churn until frozen.

WHITE CHOCOLATE ICE CREAM

ABOUT 1 QUART

³/4 cup milk
10 ounces white chocolate, finely chopped

½ teaspoon vanilla extract
2 cups heavy cream, at room temperature

Place the milk and chocolate in a mixing bowl and set over a saucepan of barely simmering water. Stir occasionally until the chocolate has melted. Set aside and cool to room temperature.

Stir in the vanilla and cream while whisking; if mixture is not perfectly smooth, pass through a fine strainer. Place into an ice cream machine. Freeze according to the manufacturer's directions.

TEQUILA-GRAPEFRUIT ICE

ABOUT 1 QUART

1 cup premium silver tequila such as Hornitos,
El Tesoro, or Herradura
Juice of 4 large grapefruits, preferably ruby
(about 2½ cups)

Juice of 2 limes (about 3 tablespoons)
1³/4 cups Simple Syrup (recipe follows)

In a small saucepan, bring the tequila to a boil, and continue to boil until it is reduced to ½ cup. Set aside to cool.

Strain the grapefruit and lime juices through a fine strainer into a large mixing bowl. Stir in the tequila and simple syrup. Place the mixture into an ice cream machine and freeze according to the manufacturer's directions. If chilled overnight, transfer the ice from the freezer to the refrigerator for 30 minutes before serving.

SIMPLE SYRUP

This mixture is a foundation for making all types of ices; it keeps indefinitely in the refrigerator.

ABOUT 1 QUART

3 cups sugar   *2½ cups water*

In a large saucepan, combine the sugar and water. Cook over high heat, stirring with a wooden spoon, until the sugar dissolves, about 3 to 4 minutes. Continue cooking until the syrup comes to a full boil. Immediately remove from the heat and set the pan aside to cool completely. Keep refrigerated in an airtight container.

PASSION FRUIT–SERRANO CHILE ICE

This is my version of fire and ice. It's especially fun to serve without revealing its identity. First you taste the rich ripeness of the passion fruit, and then the kick in the back of the mouth and in the throat. It's a unique sensation!

ABOUT 2½ CUPS

8 ripe passion fruit, halved and pulp scooped out   *Juice of ½ lime (about 2 teaspoons)*
(about ½ cup pulp)   *½ serrano chile, seeded and finely diced*
Juice of 2 oranges (about ¾ cup)   *1 cup Simple Syrup (see Index)*

In a medium saucepan, bring the passion fruit pulp, orange and lime juices, and serrano to a boil. Reduce the heat and simmer for 10 minutes. Remove the pan from the heat and let cool.

Place the simple syrup in a mixing bowl. Pour the cooled passion fruit mixture through a strainer into the mixing bowl and stir to thoroughly combine with the syrup. Place into an ice cream machine and freeze according to the manufacturer's directions.

PINEAPPLE-CLOVE ICE

ABOUT 1 QUART

¹⁄₃ cup cloves
1¹⁄₂ cups dry white wine
1 medium very ripe pineapple, peeled, cored, and chopped

Juice of 1 lemon (about 2 tablespoons)
1 cup Simple Syrup (see Index)

In a medium saucepan, bring the cloves and wine to a boil. Reduce the heat and simmer for 5 minutes. Remove from the heat and let infuse for at least 4 hours. Strain into a mixing bowl and discard the cloves.

Puree the pineapple in a blender or food processor, and press through a fine strainer into the mixing bowl with the strained wine mixture. Add the lemon juice and simple syrup to the mixing bowl and thoroughly incorporate.

Place into an ice cream machine and freeze according to the manufacturer's directions.

CACTUS FRUIT–ZINFANDEL ICE

The fruit from the prickly pear cactus is possibly one of the most underutilized sources of vitamin C. You can buy the cactus pears, which are actually berries, at Hispanic, Latin, or ethnic markets. It provides an earthy fruit flavor that matches Zinfandel wine perfectly.

2½ TO 3 CUPS

2 cups fruity Zinfandel wine
8 to 10 (about 2 pounds) very ripe cactus pears
Juice of ½ lime (about 2 teaspoons)

½ cup Simple Syrup (see Index)
1 egg white

In a saucepan, reduce the Zinfandel to ½ cup. Remove from the heat and let cool.

Wearing thick gloves (to avoid the fine thorns), slice the cactus pears in half lengthwise. Scoop out the red pulp and place in a food processor. Whirl for 1 minute, then press the pulp and liquid through a food mill to remove the seeds. You should have about 1½ cups of puree.

In a mixing bowl, combine the fruit puree with the reduced Zinfandel, lime juice, and simple syrup. In another mixing bowl, whisk the egg white until very frothy, and slowly add the fruit mixture while still whisking. Place into an ice cream machine and freeze according to the manufacturer's directions.

PAPAYA-MANGO ICE

ABOUT 1 QUART

2 very ripe mangoes, peeled
2 very ripe papayas, peeled, seeded, and chopped

Juice of 1 lime (about 4 teaspoons)
1⅓ cups Simple Syrup (see Index)

Cut the mango flesh from the pit, place the flesh in a blender with the chopped papaya, and puree. Transfer to a mixing bowl and thoroughly combine with the lime juice and simple syrup.

Place into an ice cream machine and freeze according to the manufacturer's directions.

APPENDIX: TEXAS WINES
A Brief Survey from Pre-Prohibition to the Post-Oil Boom
by Rebecca Murphy

In the last twenty years, the Texas wine industry has developed from virtually nothing into a burgeoning, healthy enterprise of twenty-six wineries and has helped stimulate and support the development of a dynamic regional cuisine. Furthermore, several Texas wines have won awards on the national and international level, a remarkable achievement in a relatively short period of time.

In the early 1970s, curiosity and old-fashioned determination were planting the seeds for the rebirth of a wine industry among different people from diverse backgrounds. In places as disparate geographically and climatically as the Texas High Plains, the Hill Country, the Big Sky country of West Texas, north-central Texas, and the humid south-central part of the state, doctors, lawyers, college professors, and a number of others were planting grapevines. If they had listened to the "experts," they would have never allowed those tender grape cuttings to stretch their roots into the earth. Some of them speculate that if they had known then what they know now, they might have been more receptive to the skeptics. Then with a slow smile, they admit they'd have changed a few things, but basically they would do it all over again. These early growers are the true pioneers of Texas wine, and although they were probably not aware of it at the time, they were an integral part of the culinary transformation that was to follow.

In fact, winemaking is not new to Texas—wine was produced in the state about a hundred years before the first grapes were cultivated in California. The winemakers were Franciscan monks who founded the Ysleta mission in the El Paso Valley in 1622 and planted vineyards so they could make sacramental wines. And, significantly, one Texan stands tall in the annals of international wine history. Texas lays claim to botanist and horticulturist Thomas Volney Munson, a native of Illinois, who moved to Texas in 1876, and settled in the Denison area because of the large number and assortment of grapevines growing wild. He traveled throughout the United States and into Mexico gathering grape specimens and, through hybridization, developed more than three hundred new grape varieties.

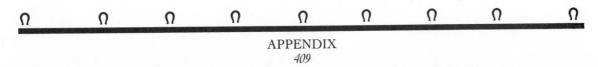

However, Munson's contribution to the vineyards of Europe is what made him a legend. Because of the practice of exchanging grapevines and cuttings between the United States and Europe, a plant louse native to American vines infected the vineyards of France, Germany, and Italy. This louse, called phylloxera — to which native vines are resistant — attacked the roots of the *Vitis vinifera* vines growing in Europe, and by the 1880s had very nearly destroyed them all.

France asked Munson for help. Because native American rootstock is resistant to phylloxera, Munson and Hermann Jaeger, a horticultural colleague from Missouri, sent shipments of this stock to Europe. There, the vinifera vines were grafted onto American rootstock, resulting in a plant resistant to the louse and able to produce fine wine grapes. In 1888, Munson and Jaeger — who are still considered the saviors of France's wine industry — received membership in the Legion of Honor, Croix de Merite Agricole, from the French government. They are the only Americans who have ever been given this award.

Largely due to Munson's studies and encouragement, nearly thirty wineries were in production in Texas when Prohibition began in 1920. Prohibition killed all but one — the Val Verde Winery in Del Rio — which survived by making sacramental wines and selling grapes to home winemakers. Similar activities helped a handful of wineries survive the Prohibition era in other parts of the country as well.

Prohibition was repealed in 1933, but no new winery was bonded in Texas until 1975, when the Schlaraffenland Winery (now the Guadalupe Valley Winery) was opened near Gruene in the Hill Country. A year later, two professors from Texas Tech University began Llano Estacado Winery near Lubbock and the new Texas wine industry was on its way.

One of these founding academics was a chemistry professor at Texas Tech — Clint McPherson, affectionately known as "Doc." He recalls that in the early 1970s, the university plowed up an experimental vineyard and Dr. Bob Reed, professor of horticulture at Texas Tech, managed to save a vine or two. Transplanted to Reed's patio, the vines bore fruit which McPherson made into wine in his basement cellar. In 1973, Texas Tech opened a new chemistry building that had more space than they needed at the time. Doc convinced the administration to let him operate an experimental winery in the extra space. A visitor to the experimental winery, San Antonio businesswoman Jean Dorn, was impressed enough with the operation to offer $50,000 to start a commercial winery. Thus, in 1976, Llano Estacado was born.

Doc strongly encouraged his son, Kim McPherson, to study winemaking at the

University of California at Davis after he graduated from Texas Tech with a degree in food science. It was Kim's 1984 Chardonnay that won a double-gold award in 1985 at the San Francisco Fair National Wine Competition, an award that captured national media attention and made the wine world sit up and take notice of Llano Estacado in particular and Texas wines in general.

Since 1985, when Don Brady became the winemaker at Llano Estacado, production has increased from 14,000 cases per year to 63,000 cases, making it the second largest winery in Texas, behind St. Genevieve. His outstanding achievement over an extended period of time is borne out by the fact that every wine Don has released has won an award or medal in national, international, or regional competition. Among the most prestigious of the more than 350 awards that Llano Estacado has won since 1985 are the gold medal for the 1985 Cellars Select Cabernet Sauvignon at the London International Wine Festival, and the 1989 Chardonnay which won six gold medals in various competitions.

Another nationally acclaimed Texas winery is Pheasant Ridge, also near Lubbock. Bobby and Jennifer Cox, owners of Pheasant Ridge Winery with Bobby's parents, came to wine by way of their interest in food. In 1972, the couple visited the Copper Kettle in Aspen, Colorado, a renowned restaurant at that time. The visit inspired the Coxes to take home the restaurant's cookbook and try out the recipes. They had never heard of some of the wines suggested as accompaniments to the recipes, nor were these wines easily available in Lubbock.

Bobby started working with Doc McPherson and Bob Reed in their experimental vineyards and winery. In 1975, he and Jennifer tagged along on an equipment-buying trip to California. Bobby came back very discouraged about his ambition of owning a winery after seeing the sophisticated equipment and technology that was standard in so many California wineries. A trip to France in 1977, however, showed him that a simpler approach to winemaking was feasible. He started planting his vineyard in 1977 and bottled his first wine in 1982. At the same San Francisco competition in 1985 that the Llano Estacado Chardonnay won a double-gold, Bobby's 1983 Cabernet Sauvignon also won a gold. Lubbock wines were well and truly on the map.

Teysha Cellars opened in 1988 amid great glitter and fanfare as the first publicly held winery in Texas. Its 1988 Gewürztraminer won gold medals in two major national wine competitions and according to wine guru Robert Parker, won more awards than any other American Gewürztraminer produced that year. Teysha Cellars also easily lays claim to the most spectacular winery building in Texas; it would be right at home in a

glitzier landscape like Napa Valley. Unfortunately, Teysha was forced to shut down for financial reasons just before its second harvest. In 1990, the Plains National Bank acquired the winery through a bankruptcy sale. Kim McPherson was hired as the winemaker and Teysha was renamed Cap Rock Winery.

Texas Hill Country is also home to several wineries, one of which got its start in Lubbock. For several years the vineyards of Slaughter-Leftwich, planted near Lubbock in 1979, provided the fruit for many a prizewinning Texas wine. In 1986, the first wines (made at Llano Estacado under the Slaughter-Leftwich label) were released, and in October of 1988, the winery was officially opened. It is located near Lake Travis, outside the state capital of Austin, and the winery is well situated to welcome the thousands of tourists and travelers to the Texas capitol.

Nestled on sixty-five acres of picturesque vineyards next to Buchanan Lake in the Hill Country is the Fall Creek winery. Owners Ed and Susan Auler became so fascinated with the world of wine while on a tour of French vineyards in 1973 that they decided to plant their own vines on the family ranch in 1975. Since then, they have not only become full-time vintners, but tireless preachers throughout the country (and the world) of the virtues of Hill Country wines.

Ed Auler also volunteers a great deal of his time to act as watchdog for the industry's interests in the Texas state legislature. Susan masterminds the annual Hill Country Wine and Food Festival—an outstanding three-day event which brings together both professional and amateur wine and food lovers from Texas and the Southwest to share in gastronomic pleasures.

In another part of the state—Springtown, in north-central Texas just west of Fort Worth—Dr. Bobby Smith, the son of a northern Alabama grape farmer, started planting his vineyard in 1972 and made his first wine in 1978 under the name of La Buena Vida Vineyards. He had twelve acres of commercial vineyards under cultivation before he realized that it would not be legal for him to make wine, as his vines were planted in a dry precinct. This "dry" condition did not refer to rainfall patterns; the citizens of the area had voted to prohibit local sales of alcoholic beverages. The law also meant that Dr. Smith could not make wine from his grapes. Working with advice from Leon Adams, America's wine historian, and in conjunction with several other Texas growers and potential vintners, Dr. Smith assisted in getting the Farm Winery Act passed in the Texas legislature in 1977. He still could not sell his wine on the premises of the winery, but at least he could now make it.

In 1982, Ron Wetherington, professor of anthropology at Southern Methodist University, made his dream of owning a winery come true when he purchased Sanchez Creek Vineyards. Also located to the west of Fort Worth, Sanchez Creek is named for a creek that runs through the property. About eight acres were in grapes when Wetherington purchased the winery with the help of his father-in-law, Joseph Swift; Wetherington personally tends the vines.

Almost to the Oklahoma border to the north, the old Texas Vineyards–Ivanhoe Winery was reborn as Schoppaul Hill Winery. The original corporation declared bankruptcy in 1988 and the vineyard was purchased from the bank by Denton orthopedic surgeon, John Anderson. Schoppaul Hill's consulting enologist is Kim McPherson, formerly of Llano Estacado.

The University of Texas owns thousands of acres of land in West Texas, and in addition to income from mineral rights, the university decided in the early 1980s that other income could be generated from the land by planting and leasing vineyards. The original group to undertake this challenge and to build the state's largest winery — Ste. Genevieve, in Pecos County — was a partnership of two Texans, Tony Sanchez and Richarson Gill, and two French companies, Richter and Cordier. Because of various differences, the partnership wound up in courts in a debacle of suits and countersuits. Subsequently, one of the two French partners involved, Henri Bernabé, who represented Richter's interest, dug his heels into the Hill Country and bought the Moyer Champagne Cellars. The sparkling wine facility is located in New Braunfels and plays host to visitors with tastings on weekdays and full winery tours on Saturdays.

Cordier, the other French partner in Ste. Genevieve, is now the owner of the winery. Cordier owns prestigious French estates such as Château Talbot and Gruaud-Larose in Bordeaux, and the company has embarked upon a program of upgrading the vineyards and planting new vines. The Domaine Cordier label was introduced in Texas in the spring of 1989.

Another of the pioneers of Texas wines is Dr. Paul Bonarrigo, whose physical therapy practice brought him to Bryan, which is located between Houston and Austin, and is the home of Texas A & M (Agriculture and Mechanical) University. Bonarrigo's family were originally winemakers from Messina, Italy, and this tradition gave him an obvious interest in wine. By getting Bonarrigo involved in grape growing, another Texas university — Texas A & M — was instrumental in putting a vineyard on the map.

How this happened was, in the early 1970s Ron Perry, an A & M Ph.D. candidate working under the direction of Texas A & M professor and grape expert, George Ray McEachern, had planted an experimental vineyard in order to try and determine the

feasibility of growing grapes commercially in Texas. At the time, the common wisdom was that vinifera vines such as Chardonnay and Cabernet Sauvignon would not grow in the Texas climate. However, it is very difficult, if not impossible, to have a thriving wine industry without vinifera wines. Initially, Bonarrigo was put off by the perceived problems in growing vinifera vines, as well as the Texas laws that neither understood nor encouraged winemaking. Nevertheless, family tradition and Texan enthusiasm prevailed; Bonarrigo with his wife, Merrill, established Messina Hof Wine Cellars by planting a vineyard in 1977 and starting the winery in 1983.

This brief conspectus of the history of Texas wines underscores the fact that the industry is in its infancy. The prospects for the future are bright and the potential is very exciting. Texas wines are limited in total volume of output and national distribution, so they are still relatively unknown and underestimated, especially outside the state. This is a pity for non-Texans, but after all, someone has to do the job of drinking all that excellent wine, and it may as well be us natives! The impact of the developing wine industry on the restaurant business in Texas (as well as the choice of wines now available to the home cook) is highly significant. It strengthens the credentials of Texas cuisine as a legitimate regional cuisine with depth and breadth, just as Californian cuisine was given momentum in the 1970s by the symbiotic relationship with the state's developing wine industry. The parallel to French cuisine, with all of that country's viticultural resources, hardly needs stating.

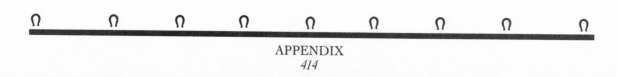

SOURCE LIST

This list gives mail-order sources for ingredients that are harder to find or unavailable locally.

AMERICAN SPOON FOODS
411 E. Lake St.
Petoskey, MI 49770
(800) 327–7984
Dried fruit, nuts, preserves, and condiments.

BLUE CORN CONNECTION
3825 Academy Parkway N.W.
Albuquerque, NM 87109
(505) 344–9768
Blue cornmeal.

ELIZABETH BERRY
144 Camino Escondido
Santa Fe, NM 87501
(505) 982–4149
Specialty beans, corn, herbs, and produce.

GOLDEN CIRCLE FARMS
PO Box 2235
Corsicana, TX 75151
(214) 225–0500
Epazote, hoja santa, marigold mint, lemon verbena, squash blossoms, and other fresh herbs and produce.

LOS CHILEROS
PO Box 6215
Santa Fe, NM 87501
(505) 471–6967
Chiles and Southwestern ingredients.

LUCINDA HUTSON
4612 Rosedale
Austin, TX 78756
(512) 454–8905
Limited supplies of Southwestern herbs such as hoja santa, marigold mint, and epazote. Consulting expert on Southwestern herbs and author of The Herb Garden Cookbook.

LUNA'S TORTILLA FACTORY
1615 McKinney Ave.
Dallas, TX 75202
(214) 747–2661
Masa dough, tortillas.

MOZZARELLA COMPANY
2944 Elm St.
Dallas, TX 75266
(214) 741–4072
Mozzarella, goat cheeses, crème fraîche, mascarpone, and flavored caciottas such as ancho, smoked pepper, and marigold mint.

PREFERRED MEATS
PO Box 565854
Dallas, TX 75207
(214) 565–0243
Meats, game, and poultry.

TAXCO PRODUCE CO.
1801 S. Good Latimer
Dallas, TX 75226
(214) 421–7191
Chiles, Southwestern produce and ingredients.

INDEX

Ω   Ω   Ω   Ω   Ω   Ω   Ω   Ω   Ω

Ω　　Ω　　Ω　　Ω　　Ω　　Ω　　Ω　　Ω　　Ω

Ω   Ω   Ω   Ω   Ω   Ω   Ω   Ω   Ω

Ω   Ω   Ω   Ω   Ω   Ω   Ω   Ω   Ω